Souls
Looking
Back

Souls Looking Back

LIFE STORIES
of
GROWING UP BLACK

edited by

ANDREW GARROD

JANIE VICTORIA WARD

TRACY L. ROBINSON

ROBERT KILKENNY

foreword by

JAMES P. COMER

ROUTLEDGE
New York and London

*In recognition of their perseverance, insight, and honesty,
this book is dedicated to the 16 student autobiographers
whose essays are presented here.*

Published in 1999 by
Routledge
29 West 35th Street
New York, NY 10001

Published in Great Britain by
Routledge
11 New Fetter Lane
London EC4P 4EE

Copyright ©1999 by Routledge

Printed in the United States of America on acid-free paper.

Library of Congress Cataloging-in-Publication Data

Souls looking back: life stories of growing up Black / Andrew Garrod . . . [et al.], eds.
    p. cm.
   Includes bibliographical references and index.
   ISBN 0-415-92061-2 (hc.). — ISBN 0-415-92062-0 (pbk.)
   1. Afro-American youth—Race identity—Case studies. 2. Afro-American youth—Biography. 3. Afro-American youth—Social conditions—Case studies. 4. Racially mixed children—Race identity—Case studies. 5. Racially mixed children—Biography. 6. Racially mixed children—Social conditions—Case studies. 7. United States—Race relations—Case studies. 8. Canada—Race relations—Case studies. 9. West Indies—Race relations—Case studies. I. Garrod, Andrew, 1937–
E185.625.S675 1999
305.235—dc21
                                                 98-42839
                                                   CIP

Contents

Foreword

JAMES P. COMER

At the outset of a new millennium, race promises to be the most challenging issue facing the United States. Yet many Americans don't want to talk about the topic. A recent report on the seriousness of race by President Clinton's Commission on Race barely made a ripple. The highly acclaimed film *Amistad* played to small audiences. Too many parents don't discuss race with their children, leaving them vulnerable to negative and limiting experiences in society. And many blacks and whites born after the visible period of Civil Rights activism in the 1950s and 1960s ask, "What's the problem?" Most people want to "move on" to the bright new America without undoing the ill effects of the past. The reasons for this are understandable, but it can't be done.

While there has been much progress in American race relations, similar and new problems remain. In a recent issue of the Indiana University College of Arts and Sciences magazine, an article entitled "A Sense of Belonging, A Spirit of Hope" by Lisa Sorg described the racial challenges confronting today's black students. Sorg compared some of my experiences at the university almost 50 years ago (drawn from my book *Maggie's American Dream*) with those of today's students. I was struck by the multiple similarities and one key difference: only slightly increased black student and faculty numbers; persistent isolation; strained black-white interactions in- and outside of classrooms; and subtle and occasional overtly racist acts that challenge the sense of belonging and, I am sure, impair the performance of too many black students. The difference is that such an article would not have appeared 50 years ago. Today, university officials are aware, concerned, and trying to create better conditions.

In a nation caught in a historical contradiction—slavery and oppression in the midst of a commitment to freedom and opportunity—denial is deep and well protected. Fear of both confronting the "big lie" of white superiority and losing the short-term benefits of racial scapegoating underlines the nation's inability to listen and talk about race. Getting past the myths and blinders that protect denial is a significant challenge. For this reason almost all of my work during the past 30 years flows from an initial discussion of my own life experiences. My personal story allows the reader to see, hear, and, most importantly, feel as I do to a greater extent than does the "cold" analysis of the social scientist. And because of the process of identification with the author, self-disclosure provokes less guilt and obstructive defensiveness.

Souls Looking Back presents the emotionally honest reflection of 16 young people still very close to the challenging experience of establishing a positive sense of self, as either black people or, in some cases, as black and white people, in an often antagonistic and sometimes facilitating environment. The honesty and freshness of their feelings, thoughts, development, and behavior create a special kind of power. Their stories deepen our understanding of how damage is done and how development and educational institutions might work to enhance individual resistance and resilience. They provide the kind of understanding of the challenges facing black children and families that people trying to create social justice and opportunity need. They touch the reader at the feeling level, not only the cognitive, thereby making denial less possible.

Deep levels of exploration of the kind presented here can weaken some of today's myths and help us grapple honestly with some of the still-to-be-explained mysteries of racism. We see and hear in these stories the overwhelming power of the social environment, or more precisely, the power of experiences, and how the individual and meaningful others manage them. New brain research tells us that the social environment both limits and facilitates full expression of genetic potential, that mastery can be enhanced by facilitating environments. While the strong evidence to date has to do with early childhood, it supports the speculation that negative social environments interfere with performance throughout life.

Why is it that black students scoring at the same level as white students on the Scholastic Aptitude Test achieve grades significantly below their white counterparts? Why was Claude Steele, a Stanford University psychologist, able to close the achievement gap in an experiment at the University of Michigan with a modest effort that included a rigorous math course and an opportunity to raise questions of all kinds in a comfortable, racially mixed, interactive setting? Why is it that the African American students at some of the most selective schools are disproportionately West Indian or African, or one generation removed, or mixed race? And when high-achieving students have no recent foreign-born history, why are they so often from the leadership group of a black church culture? And why are black college students disproportionately women?

The ability to close the achievement gap, the intragroup differences, and racial-group achievement differences despite similar aptitude strongly suggests a noxious racial environment, not genetically determined intelligence limits. Also, the immigrant selection explanation does not hold here. What are the crucial protective and promotive factors operating for successful black groups, and how can they be extended to all? These are sensitive and divisive questions and issues; thus, they don't receive the attention they deserve. In fact, they hold the key to understanding the kind of interventions that need to be made. The students presented here, who shared their struggles and triumphs so openly with all of us, have provided powerful windows for understanding and, in turn, for better intervention.

The issues raised here are multiple and complex, and the power of the personal is commanding. It would be possible to get caught up in the rich and moving discussions to the point of losing important insights. The wise use of theoretical frameworks help to keep the reader focused on the underlying processes.

Honest self-reflection improves thinking and promotes psychological and emotional growth. I am sure that the students realized personal gains from their efforts. In the course of my work with precollegiate young people, I have long believed that the kind of reflection carried out here would protect and promote the achievement of elementary and secondary students, if carefully done. I am persuaded by this collection to try similar efforts with younger students.

This project was thoughtfully carried out during a 5-year period. The final product, *Souls Looking Back,* is a giant contribution to literature. I am sure it was well worth the effort for all of those who participated. Moreover, I am hopeful that it will spark self-reflection, analysis, and writing among many more students. I believe that learning about the self and the way we manage is one of the best ways to learn about others and how to manage the world we live in.

Preface

S *ouls Looking Back: Life Stories of Growing up Black* contains the personal narratives of black and biracial students who have studied at Dartmouth College in New Hampshire, Simmons College in Boston, and McGill University in Montreal. During the past 5 years, the editors approached approximately 50 students (men and women in equal numbers), and invited them to write about the experience of growing up as a person of color in the United States, Canada, or the West Indies.

In gathering the contributions, the editors (Janie Victoria Ward and Tracy L. Robinson are black; Andrew Garrod and Robert Kilkenny are white) encouraged participants to work from broad outlines, reflecting on how the formative influences of home, school, church, and neighborhood had shaped their life courses. We asked them to discuss relationships within the family and parental attitudes toward education; we invited them to explore their first awareness of racial differences and to examine friendships that crossed the lines of race, class, and sex.

While the editors worked on a weekly basis with writers—the writing was often done as part of an independent study—we made an effort to keep assumptions about where the individual stories might go in our view but out of the way of the participants. Because the emphasis was on process—helping the contributors to undertake that most complex of all writerly tasks, the location of voice—we made no editorial interventions during the generative stage. Although the parameters were necessarily established by the editors, we encouraged the writers to develop their own themes and make analytical sense of their experience in ways that helped them find significant meaning in their own lives. All we requested was that their thinking, feeling, and writing be as honest as possible. There was no assumption on either part that the story was "there," waiting to come out already formed; rather, we shared the belief that the story had to be "found"—built little by little as patterns emerged and themes revealed themselves.

The writers themselves decided when their first draft was complete, at which time the discretionary work of revision began in earnest. Some writers went through three drafts, while others did as many as eight or nine rewrites. Some took 2 academic terms to complete their essays, others reached a publishable stage in 10 weeks. It was a labor-intensive job that surprised and challenged many contributors and required editorial choices that were, in some cases, agonizing. Indeed, the relationships formed between the editors and contributors felt deeply privileged, which added to the always demanding task of selection.

How did we choose? Of the approximately 45 essays completed or almost completed, we selected 16—8 by women and 8 by men, 15 by undergraduates and 1 by a graduate student. We took into account the significance of the issues tackled, emotional and intellectual honesty, self-awareness, linguistic vividness, coherence, and the degree to which personal experience spoke to larger societal values and problems. Though all students wrote anonymously, some students withdrew permission for their essay to be considered for publication. It is likely that among these students the opportunity for writing and self-reflection through the independent study was always more important than the possibility of a later publication. Once the "therapeutic" purpose had been served within the confines of the academic term requirements, there was no further incentive for revision. Some others withdrew prior to completion, perhaps because they had reached the limits of their self-understanding. The editors are deeply grateful to these students, who also gave so generously of themselves.

Informing the revision process at all times was the belief that student writers can best build confidence in their approaches to personal prose incrementally, gradually finding the detail that resonates with their own memories and perceptions. Because of the nature of these essays and the purpose of the book, the variations in tone, facility with the English language, degree of self-analysis, and style of expression that were deliberately cultivated did not get flattened into one editorial mould. Manuscripts originally ranged in length from 30 to 90 pages. The process of trimming narratives down to a publishable length means inevitably that critical experiences and reflections were eliminated. Any writer's narrative here is just one of all the possible stories he or she did or could tell, as much has been omitted. With regard to stories not told, the editors observe—in parenthesis—that some of our contributors seemed unable to assess the extraordinary role that their mothers, for example, had played in their success, perhaps because the writers were so close to them and, as late adolescents, had insufficient "objectivity" to celebrate or analyze their influence. A problematic relationship with an often distant father appears, for a few, to become a more accessible focus.

We consider that the process of generation and revision was deeply collaborative and reflects the editors' teaching emphasis on reflective learning. Indeed, the editors firmly believe in the educational value of personal memoir, both for the writer and the reader. We found students overwhelmingly open to the invitation to make sense of childhood and adolescent experiences that up to then had been inchoate, unintegrated, and insufficiently reflected upon. Seldom at college does academic coursework surrender authority to the student or confirm for the student the validity of his or her most personal experiences and analyses. Generating personal narrative is not only a process that is essentially writerly—requiring precision, nuance, and a suppleness of syntax—but also one that offers both a therapeutic and hermeneutic opportunity. For some students the text that is developed can act as a template in later stages of development, when increased sophistication will allow the material to be recast fruitfully.

It is incumbent on the supervising teacher, then, to be sensitive to the therapeutic, cathartic, interpretive, and compositional dimension of the task. In our editorials roles, we have felt deeply privileged in aiding the student writers to greater levels of self-understanding and into gaining purchase of the world through reflection and articulation. Most importantly, at the end there is the artifact of the essay—often compelling, brave, vivid—to show for the labors, one that could enlighten and embolden student readers for generations to come.

As Carol Witherell and Nel Noddings (1991) point out in *Stories Lives Tell: Narrative and Dialogue in Education*, narrative has the power not just to change the teller-writer but to affect the listener-reader as well. While exploring the authentic related experiences of others, we enrich our understanding of our own experience and of the worldviews that this experience helps to construct. This book tells the stories of unique African American, Afro-Caribbean, and biracial individuals from a broad diversity of backgrounds who have tackled significant obstacles to achieve degrees of self-understanding and success.

This volume is divided into three thematic sections: (1) class and race in negotiating identity; (2) identity and intersections of identity; and (3) resilience and resistance. Each section opens with a theoretical overview by an African American scholar in which the author outlines his or her particular focus, followed by four to six personal narratives.

In the introduction to the first section, Peter C. Murrell Jr. writes on class and race in negotiating identity. He interrogates the narratives "to explore the development of both the personal and the political in the lives of black youths, tracing the complex dynamics of race and social class as they interact with the processes of identity." Murrell introduces the notion of political stance, a unique spiritual and ethical perspective, as it is revealed in the black adolescents' struggle to negotiate the duality of experience related to race and social-class status. These narratives shed light on the formation of race and class self-definition from different perspectives with respect to social class, allowing us to understand what Murrell suggests is the black adolescents' search for "a credible reference group to provide them adult role models that fit their sensibilities as to whom they should be."

The section on identity opens with two theoretical overviews. In the first, Jewelle Taylor Gibbs offers a brief historical account of the social construction of race within the United States. Given the state of race relations today, she integrates international perspectives, devoting considerable attention to bicultural and biracial populations, whose numbers are increasing nationwide and whose members have contributed significantly to this work. Gibbs also focuses on the psychological adaptations many of the biracial narrators had to make in order to create self-definitions and establish themselves socially.

In the intersections of identity overview, Tracy L. Robinson uses several theories of identity development to explore the narrators' behavioral and emotional states and their parents' racial socialization behavior. Robinson also shows how some black youths and the adults in their lives successfully integrate and negotiate their multiple and textured identities. Some experience identity confusion and ambivalence, particularly regarding their racial identity, and face difficulties that impinge on their abilities to meet corresponding developmental tasks and, in time, life responsibilities. Robinson identifies factors that delay positive racial identity. These are continuous isolation from racial and cultural community, parental silence about race, and facets of the self that can overshadow components of identity and significantly influence overall development.

Janie Victoria Ward, in opening the section on resistance and resilience, investigates the literature on coping and psychosocial resilience. She situates resilience for black children and youths within specific characteristics of the racial socialization process. Ward names resistance as a developmental process, one that facilitates being able to stand up to and oppose environmental forces that impede positive psychological and social development. Ward uses the narratives in her section to provide evidence of how black parents and other adults help children psychologically to resist racism, gender, and class oppression, the "quick fixes" of substance abuse, delinquency, unplanned sexual activity, and school failure, and, at the intrapsychic level, the internalization of self-hatred, low self-esteem, racial alienation, and disconnection.

This project has been 5 years in the making, and the editors are deeply grateful to friends and student assistants for enlightenment, moral support, and practical assistance during this period. Karen Maloney, Dody Riggs, Gail Taylor, and Kari McCadam were especially helpful with their insightful readings of texts and editorial suggestions. Joy Harding of Simmons College and Dorothy Smith of Harvard Graduate School of Education offered vital help with pertinent references and readings and in subtle analysis of the narratives' themes. Marie HcHugh provided invaluable administrative aid. To two Dartmouth College students we are enormously indebted—Matthew K. Nelson and Megan Cummins. Their commitment to the book, eye for detail, computer dexterity, friendliness, and reliability made the task of preparing the manuscript for publication immeasurably lighter. They were ably assisted by Julia Webb, Kimberly Williams, Pete Fritz, and Jason Alphonse. Finally, we gratefully acknowledge the enthusiastic reception our project received from the outset by Professor Jewelle Taylor Gibbs of the University of California at Berkeley, Professor Charles Willie of Harvard Graduate School of Education, Professor Theresa Perry of Wheelock College, and Heidi Freund of Routledge and her assistant Shea Settimi.

Introduction

Black Children and Youths in Context

There is a transformative power in both the hearing and telling of people's stories. Standing in the presence of others' lived experiences, the reader is allowed access to the writer's world and, inevitably, to his or her own. Because struggle without community can lead to despair, it is essential to create spaces where people can share their stories and, in the process of telling and hearing, be transformed. As with the oral tradition, the written word stimulates reflection, dialogue, and action that lead to greater awareness. While stories are created in the everyday process of being and doing, in telling our stories each of us is essentially re-created. The 16 narrators featured in this work invite us to hear their stories and, in so doing, to be transformed. We recognize that the writers themselves are also different after looking at their own lives so closely. The writing process was liberating for these students as they took the time to reflect on their own personal journeys. Learning to honor choices that were made to survive the growing-up years is a sacred lesson that, hopefully, many of them internalized or are in the process of learning. In addition to exploring their own personal growth and emergence, most of these students felt a personal responsibility to tell their stories, perhaps as a way to extend arms of support to other young people experiencing similar challenges. Although all of the contributors to this volume (except one) were enrolled in undergraduate academic programs when they were first invited to participate, the stories they share cross boundaries of family structure, social class, geographic region, sexual orientation, ethnicity, and national origin. Thus they represent the wide variety of circumstances in which black people live their lives. Such intraracial diversity makes it difficult to categorize, and especially to stereotype, black adolescents and their families. The erroneous supposition that the 30 million people of African descent now residing in the United States are a monolithic group should be put to rest.

The African American autobiographical tradition is a unique genre that has its genesis in the oral tradition that distinguishes African culture. However, when we began this project, there was a conspicuous absence of African American voices in adolescent psychology textbooks. *Adolescent Portraits* (1995), which included two narratives by black youths, was one of the first contemporary collections of life stories written by adolescent men and women since George Goethal and Dennis Klos's *Experiencing Youth*, originally published in

1970. The response to *Adolescent Portraits*, with its focus on minority youth, was one of the inspirations for the formulation of this book.

Within the social sciences, historically, the powerful have been allowed to study and define the powerless (Nobles, 1980). Western philosophers and psychological theorists assume a universal Eurocentrically defined standard of development. The study of ego as well as cognitive and moral development in adolescence has largely been a study of white, middle-class, male children and youths. In uncovering the sequence of stages during which developmental issues such as identity, autonomy, attachment, and separation are addressed, key theorists (e.g., Erikson, 1968; Kohlberg & Gilligan, 1972; Piaget, 1972) have paid scant attention to the ways in which the socially constructed categories of race, class, and gender interact with processes of individual development (Garrod, Smulyan, Powers, & Kilkenny, 1995). Subsequently, differences within and between groups have been ignored and misunderstood. Within the research literature, African American children and adolescents are, relative to other minority groups, more frequently researched (Spencer, Dornbusch, & Mont-Reynaud, 1990). Despite their inclusion in psychological studies and theory construction, methodological problems tend to plague the research on black youths. Problems with assessment tools, sampling designs, data collection procedures, and data analysis (The Consortium for Research on Black Adolescence, 1990; Murray, Smith, & West, 1989) have been documented. Variables of social class and gender are repeatedly confounded and entangled with minority status (Spencer et al., 1990) in research studies, and non-American-born black children and their families are seldom investigated. Variables such as racism, prejudice, discrimination, oppression, and the visibility of racial characteristics that have implications for understanding the developmental trajectory of black youths continue to be peripheralized (Garcia-Coll et al., 1996). More studies of black youth are needed that are historically, culturally, and socially grounded and that consider the ecological context within which development takes place.

This collection of autobiographical portraits written by 16 adolescents of African descent describes their childhood memories of growing up in nations that depict black boys as violent predators and black girls as sexually irresponsible, future welfare recipients. Most of the contributors are native to the United States and some, while born and raised in the States, are children of the 1.3 million immigrants (currently about 4 percent of the total U.S. black population) from the Caribbean and West Indian islands, Latin America, Canada, and Africa (R. Taylor, 1998). The significant immigration of Afro-Caribbean groups to black neighborhoods in U.S. cities countrywide has enlarged and enriched the African American population. In so doing, it has revealed the traditions, values, and mores that emanate from our shared African cultural roots and provided evidence of the variations in experience of black family dynamics and child socialization (see Millett, 1998).

Honoring this diversity, we've included in this text a number of autobiographical portraits from adolescents who define themselves as biracial or of mixed race, an ethnologically complex group whose increasing numbers in the United States add further diversity to the nation's population in general. Mixed race or biracial children have always been present in this nation and have, by convention, had to choose their racial membership or have it chosen for them. The United States maintains a binary classification system based primarily on white purity—one is either white or nonwhite. The "one drop of black blood" rule, coupled with the visibility of "Negroid" characteristics, not only marks the mixed race offspring of people of African descent as "black" but also necessarily cancels out their whiteness.

The mixed race youths who contributed their stories (all of whom have black fathers) grew up in a historical moment in which biracial individuals have begun collectively to question the veracity of racial classification, demanding an end to our reliance upon archaic, mutually exclusive racial categories. In this book we record the inner frustrations and private musings of a number of mixed race youth. In their recollections of childhood and adolescence, these biracial children describe how they have come to terms with, integrated, and eventually reconciled their racial and cultural identities, thus contributing to a deeper understanding of the processes of identity development and self-definition. In the process, as Robinson (this volume) shows, these young people illuminate important experiential differences that don't always fit traditional theoretical racial identity constructs.

BLACK CHILDREN AND YOUTHS IN CONTEXT: THEORETICAL CONSIDERATIONS

Developmental theorist Erik Erikson (1968) determined in his now-classic study that behavior makes sense when it is understood as part of a whole culture. Erikson, best known for his ideas about identity formation in youth, addressed the importance of group identity when he wrote, "only an identity safely anchored in the patrimony of cultural identity can produce a workable psychosocial equilibrium" (1950, p. 412). Identity ("knowing who you are") and ideology ("knowing what you believe") are necessary conditions for individual maturation, and their synthesis leads to what Erikson considered a higher, more inclusive definition of identity, one that connotes (a) a conscious sense of individual identity, (b) continuity of personal character (ego synthesis), and (c) the maintenance of inner solidarity with group ideals and identity (1956, p. 56). In his explicit appreciation of the role of a people's values and cultural history in the making of identity, Erikson was one of the first developmental psychologists to focus attention on sociocultural influences on processes of development. Nevertheless, it was many years before scholars would truly move beyond equating cultural difference with cultural deficiency.

Negative identity, low self-esteem, "a tangled web of pathology"—these and many other pejorative conceptualizations of black families grew out of thematic preoccupation with deficiency. The structure, norms, values, expectations, and behaviors of white individuals and families have been seen as normative, whereas black families were, by comparison, considered inadequate. Because blacks often score at lower levels on psychology tests, from intelligence testing to social development scales to stages of moral reasoning, black children's experiences are presumed to be disordered inherently, unhealthy, and inferior across the physical, cultural, and intellectual domains (Gibbs, 1988).

Fortunately, the past 30 years have seen an explosion of research findings that effectively challenge the pejorative view of black families as dysfunctional, pathogenic units that are responsible for barriers to both individual and group mobility (e.g., Moynihan, 1965). Instead, such research illuminates the effects of social positionality on black family life (Willie, 1985) and explores how family organization and processes reflect differential access to the economic resources, benefits, and rewards of American society (Scanzoni, 1971; R. Taylor, 1998). Further, they identify the adaptive strengths of black families, such as the orientation toward a strong work ethic, religion, educational achievement, strong kinship bonds, and flexibility and complementarity in family roles that have traditionally served to mitigate racial discrimination and economic oppression (Hill, 1972). Still others (Nobles, 1980; Sudakarsa, 1988) assert that specific values, like interconnectedness, collective responsibility, and cooperation, are recognizable in contemporary black families and continue to inform and influence the behavior of individuals and families of African descent. They cite, for example, the fact that many blacks in the United States continue to live within and rely heavily upon the extended family network, blood and fictive kin, often residing in households inhabited by several generations. We learn from these studies that African American adolescents within extended families absorb and are influenced by the cross-generational perspectives, learning to depend on a variety of family members to meet their needs.

There is a great deal of solid, informative research currently being conducted on black children and families. Much of it serves to dispel the many enduring myths about black youths. Rather than ignoring the psychosocial experiences of African Americans or forcing them to fit into existing white cultural frameworks, they are, in the aggregate, presenting a more inclusive and balanced view of African Americans across socioeconomic groups. They identify a number of risk factors in the social environment—namely the home and community—such as family poverty (McLloyd, 1990), crime, drugs, and neighborhood violence, and in the larger society, where the effects of racism and other forms of individual and systemic discrimination are impediments to healthy development (Spencer, 1987). They are also uncovering important strengths in family relationships (Giordavo, Cernkovich, & DeMaris, 1993) and in the ability of many black youths (particularly girls) to attain and sustain high levels of self-esteem over time (Ward, 1995). While some researchers focus on inappropriate child-rearing practices in low-functioning black families that can lead to difficulties in educational socialization (Ogbu, 1986), sex-role socialization (Oliver, 1989), and the establishment of a positive racial identity (Comer, 1995), still others raise important questions about the relevance of applying traditional indicators of successful developmental outcomes to inner-city, low-income African American youths. For example, Burton, Obeidallah, and Allison (1996) ask if adolescents whose access to mainstream opportunities are constrained or restricted end up developing their own alternative perspectives about what constitutes "social adulthood"? Finally, information like the stories in this volume that is gleaned from blacks in America who are reflecting upon their lived experiences of struggle help us to understand how and why the majority of black adolescents growing up in the United States today successfully manage to avoid and even transcend the environmental risks factors related to their devalued racial status.

EDUCATION AND FAMILY LIFE

Our contributors arrived at their respective colleges by very different paths. The settings from which these young adults have written their stories represent a wide range of educational institutions, from large state universities to small, prestigious Ivy League colleges. Some of the authors were educationally privileged before college, having attended elite, independent schools, while others were highly successful at public and parochial institutions. For several of these narrators, and many other black students, traveling the road to higher education required them to overcome tremendous obstacles, such as intermittent or persistent poverty, chronic illness, the premature death of a parent, and other instances of familial disruption and instability. Scholars of black family life have determined that the role of the family in fostering academic achievement is key to the individual and collective success of African Americans (Bowman & Howard, 1985; R. Clark, 1983; Billingsley, 1968). Certainly the influence of the family, for good or ill, resonates across these narratives. Regardless of the family constellation, these stories strongly suggest that messages promoting educational achievement and productivity were stressed by parents or significant adults in each child's life. The educational achievement described in this work exemplifies the successful internalization of strong values, combined with a quality education, supportive teachers and parents, personal responsibility, hard work, and grace.

During the past decade, school dropout rates have declined and the percentage of black youths completing high school has increased (R. Taylor, 1995). In fact, recent indicators suggest that "when blacks and whites with similar test scores and high school grades are compared, blacks are actually somewhat more likely than whites to finish high school, go to college, and complete a college degree" (Entwisle, 1990, p. 201). Despite these encouraging trends, academic underachievement and school failure still most accurately describe the educational experience of a disproportionate number of African American youths, particularly those from disadvantaged economic backgrounds. Black children continue to lag behind their white counterparts in standardized tests (Children's Defense Fund [CDF], 1994), racial gaps in academic achievement increase among older students and at higher grade levels (Holmes, 1983), and black youths continue to be overrepresented among high school dropouts, particularly in central city school systems, where students often attend resource-poor schools segregated by income and race (CDF, 1994). Meanwhile, economists have long warned that the solid job opportunities of the future will require increasingly higher skill levels; for those who lack the necessary education and training, employment prospects look bleak. The rate of college participation is considerably lower for African American high school graduates than their white counterparts. Currently, about one-third of black youths age 18 to 24 are enrolled in college, compared to more than 40 percent of white youths (U.S. Department of Education, 1997). Rising tuition costs, cutbacks in government support, the elimination of equal opportunity programs in higher education, and recent challenges to affirmative action have precipitated a steady decline in college participation rates for black youths.

Many of the contributors to this volume, although educationally successful themselves, were, at some time in their lives, the friends, neighbors, and classmates of black students who either dropped out, were pushed out, or flunked out of the public school system. Determining why some students succeed while others fail is a complex and multifaceted task, beyond the scope of this work. Included here, however, are personal narratives of students who have met with some success, and their stories, beyond providing inspiration and instruction, suggest certain connections that less qualitative or more objective studies cannot capture. Despite their personal struggles against environmental obstacles, our contributors have proven to be psychologically resilient, as well as intellectually capable of personal development and advanced educational pursuits.

The life experiences of these black youths have been significantly influenced by a host of social, economic, and political developments. Directly or indirectly, either they or their families have been touched by an increasingly materialistic society, the forces of economic downsizing, hip-hop culture, widespread political conservatism, and the beating of Rodney King. The developmental history of each author is linked to the historical period of which they are a product (Erikson, 1950, Gibbs & Huang, 1989). These writers came of age in the decades following the 1960s, a period of heightened social consciousness that gave rise to the struggle for civil rights, political power, and systemic change. These teens are members of the first generation of African Americans who have come of age in the post-civil rights society. Born in an era marked by the promise of racial equality, they nonetheless grew up witnessing a steady erosion of the gains their parents had made. Greater numbers of black children growing up in the United States in the 1970s and 1980s were more advantaged than previous generations of African Americans; they and their families were better educated, earned higher incomes, and found employment in more stable and prestigious jobs (Jaynes & Williams, 1989). Nevertheless, although social and economic conditions in the United States generally improved overall during these decades, progress was significantly uneven within the African American community. By the end of the 1980s increasing numbers of better educated African Americans had joined an expanding and affluent middle class, while significant numbers of struggling working-class and low-income black families fell further behind, many of them trapped in poverty, either intermittently employed or dependent on welfare (R. Taylor, 1998; Wilson, 1987). During a 20-year period, as the economic gap grew between the black "haves" and "have nots," black communities across this nation were radically transformed. The black middle class followed their jobs and their dreams out to the more integrated suburbs, leaving behind them communities beset by chronic financial instability, family disintegration, the influx of illicit drugs, and a rising rate of violent crime (Wilson, 1987). National statistics indicate that the crime victimization rates are generally greater for blacks than whites at all income levels (Gibbs, 1989b), that inner-city residents are most vulnerable, and that violent crime is often perpetrated by young people, usually preying on one another. By the late 1980s, homicide became the leading cause of death among black youths in the 15 to 24 age group (National Center for Health Statistics, 1994). So many black children had been murdered or maimed that social scientists declared black youth violence a public health epidemic, and black males, who were often both the perpetrator and the victim of violence, were described as "an endangered species" (Gibbs, 1988). Staggering numbers of black children in the 1980s grew up in homes and neighborhoods wracked with fear, instability, and hopelessness. Feeling no sense of future, these teens expected their lives to be cruel, unfair, and short.

The stories in this collection reveal the myriad conditions that shape the lives of black children and their families and, in so doing, expose how children's lives are arranged and how meaning is made of those arrangements. Black families vary in their knowledge of and degree of access to the existing socioeconomic opportunity structure. Along the class spectrum from the comfort of affluence to the chaos and desperation of poverty, black parents struggle to find their balance in a world tipped in favor of Eurocentric domination. We expected to find significant differences in the perceptions and experiences of racial discrimination faced by the black children and their families in this volume. There are, however, striking similarities across the narratives concerning the pervasive effects on their lives of systemic racial oppression and in their interpretations and explanations of prejudice and discrimination. This volume captures the theme of racism, subtle and overt, as a persistent, unrelenting presence in the lives of all people of African descent, independent of other valued identities, such as being financially and professionally successful. Moreover, in regard to child-rearing practices, our writers provide dramatic evidence of the ways in which racism's omnipresence shapes the socialization agenda of black families. While preparation for and protection against the bitter reality of racism is a cultural imperative that is not always espoused, black parents and other adults meet this need by inculcating in their children specific protective interventions, attitudinal and behavioral, to mitigate racism's destructive effects. These writers shed light on the "kitchen table wisdom" transmitted from parent to child that serve to counter racial rejection by helping to develop ego strength and adaptability bent on personal and collective survival.

Theorists have long argued that African Americans have the special and complex task of socializing their children to a bicultural existence, teaching them to negotiate both social worlds, black and white (DuBois, 1961). Psychologists Wade Boykin and F. D. Toms (1985) postulate that African American children are actually socialized to three realms of experience: (a) the mainstream culture; (b) their minority status; and (c) the black culture, each of which requires developmental and historical analysis (p. 39). Given that the diversity found in black families and the differential effects of the social and economic determinants of African American life (such as income, education, family, and community social structure) are mediated through the social stratification mechanisms of race, gender, and class positionality, we can presume experiential variability in black family members' tricultural negotiation. For example, non-American-born blacks may find their relationship to the American mainstream culture mediated by processes of acculturation and assimilation and influenced by the length of exposure to and degree of contact with American culture, as well as by the strength with which they retain the values and mores of their culture of origin. Blacks who have been socialized outside of the United States, particularly within predominantly black nations, often do not share the psychological and sociopolitical baggage accompanying the "minority status" experienced by blacks in white America. Moreover, there is a great deal of variation in the group's orientation to and creation of "black cultures," given the dispersion of African people throughout the world and the multiple black ethnic and national identities that now exist. Cultural and racial socialization for black children, particularly those of biracial heritage, is complicated by such factors as their phenotypical characteristics (e.g., skin color, hair, and facial features), and the levels of parents' racial identity development. As we had assumed, the representative diversity of the life stories in this book shed light on previously obscured complexities in social and political interpretations and assumptions derived from actual life experiences. Not only do the stories in this volume contribute to our knowledge of how race, ethnicity, and family structure affect the transition into adolescence but they also illuminate the uniqueness of the individual in the context of the black group experience.

This is a critical time for presenting and understanding the life stories and developmental trajectories of African American children and youths. First, the number of blacks in U.S. society, particularly young African Americans, is increasing; more than one-third of the black population is under 18 years of age (U.S. Bureau of the Census, 1994). The youthfulness of the black population has important implications for educators, mental health specialists, counselors, and youth workers fostering the healthy development of black children and families.

Poverty places millions of children at risk for negative developmental outcomes and for black children economic disadvantage is the rule. The psychosocial implications of the frighteningly high rate of poverty for African American children, more than double the rate for all American children (CDF, 1994), cannot be dismissed or ignored. More than half of all African American children under 18 years of age live with one parent, usually the mother, and more than half of single-parent African American families headed by women live at or below the poverty line (Randolph, 1995). According to Ronald L. Taylor, "the average black child can expect to experience poverty lasting almost two decades. Thus, a considerable number of black youths can expect to face their first years of adult life in poverty" (R. Taylor, 1998, p. 33). The feminization of poverty is all too real, and "fertility as destiny" is a truism whose consequences severely restrict the life options of far too many black mothers and their offspring. Poverty is known to be associated with a number of adverse factors, ranging from inadequate educational attainment (Feldman & Elliot, 1990), to poor health outcomes (CDF, 1994), to inadequate preparation for consistent and family-sustainable adult employment, to involvement in delinquency and crime (Freeman & Holzer, 1985). For a significant percentage of black youths, particularly those reared in poverty-stricken homes and in communities in which poor schools, drugs, high crime rates, and the fear of violence prevail, the invidiousness of economic deprivation exacts a high cost. Until we as a nation make the decision to address seriously the complex moral crisis of children living in poverty amidst affluence, this group of black youths, relative to many of their white counterparts, will continue to suffer disproportionate losses in school achievement as well as increased unemployment, delinquency, substance abuse, adolescent pregnancy, AIDS infection, and suicide rates (Gibbs, 1989b).

The stories presented in this volume shed light on these issues in both direct and indirect ways. They also uncover unique personal and cultural strengths that inform our understanding of psychological resistance and resilience, social support, positive racial identity, and academic success. Since educational achievement continues to be an important marker in U.S. society, these students can be deemed successes. Their stories, however, are not predictable, nor has their success been easily won. What can we learn from their journeys? What individual assets or family or community characteristics have strengthened their resolve and contributed to their success? As we uncover the sources and mechanisms underlying their positive psychological and social functioning, we can derive greater understanding of both the losses and gains associated with growing up black. Moreover, their stories shed light on the developmental questions across the junctures of childhood, adolescence, and adulthood. What specific developmental outcomes are predictable from conditions and behaviors existing earlier in life? What specific vulnerabilities and strengths get carried over into adulthood, enhancing or impeding healthy psychosocial development in the adult years?

This collection of personal narratives allows readers a rare and intimate look into the minds and hearts of black adolescents, who tell their stories with purpose and conviction. In tracing the contours of the life events that shaped who they would become and what they would believe, these young men and women offer us a privileged view of human struggle and of the richly diverse and complex social contexts within which black and biracial adolescents develop a sense of self in the post-civil rights decades.

PART I

Social Class and Race

Class and Race
in Negotiating Identity

PETER C. MURRELL JR.

For me becoming an adult has meant primarily thinking of myself as a black woman. In some ways, in order to become me I had to find a definition or version of blackness that I could feel comfortable with and seemed to belong to me.

—Maria

[A]n oppressed people cannot understand the nature of their oppression before they are inspired with hope and a vision of freedom that they desire. *To understand the nature of their oppression, a people must first know who they are.*

—Reverend Effie Clark
Outstanding Black Sermons

Institutionalized rejection of difference is an absolute necessity in a profit economy which needs outsiders as surplus people. As members of such an economy, we have *all* been programmed to respond to the human differences between us with fear and loathing and to handle that difference in one of three ways: ignore it, and if that is not possible, copy it if we think it is dominant, or destroy it if we think it is subordinate. But we have no patterns for relating across our human differences as equals. As a result, those differences have been misnamed and misused in the service of separation and confusion.

—Audre Lorde

In the contemporary literature on human development, adolescence is characterized as a transitional period between the more family-oriented world of the young person and the more socially diffuse adult world. According to this literature, the central developmental task of this transitional period is a process of psychological and social differentiation from the family, experienced as a period of confusion and instability as the young person strives to achieve an integrated sense of self (Erikson, 1968; Marcia, 1980). These changes do not take place in a vacuum, but in a context of social worlds constituted by school, peer reference groups, and communal culture. Among these social worlds inconsistencies in the codes, values, roles, or expectations add to the difficulty of identity development.

Theories of identity development and self-definition generally account for the reciprocity between the self-concept of the developing adolescent on the one hand, and the social context of his or her communal culture on the other. Adolescents constantly reinvent and rediscover themselves through interaction with social structures—particularly peer reference groups and institutionally circumscribed roles, values, and ideologies. But, as the editors point out in their introduction to this volume, the complexity of identity development in African American adolescents is not successfully accounted for in contemporary theory on racial identity and adolescent development.

The case autobiographies in this section dramatically illustrate the condition of an increasing number of young people of color struggling for an integrated racial identity and sense of personal agency (see Darder, 1992; Tatum, 1997). Each of the young autobiographers—Prince, Maria, Rob, and Alessandro—are black adolescents who chronicle their experiences in early life, through elementary and high school and, finally, college. Each developed a strong identity as a "good student" and experienced academic success in schools in privileged settings. Finally, each had to negotiate being the "exceptional minority" among privileged white people throughout most of their schooling and socialization.

Most important in the presentation of these case autobiographies is what they reveal about the complex dynamic of class and race. The nexus of these two dimensions is political stance, and more will be said about that presently. Suffice to say at this point that the dimension of social class introduces an interesting point of divergence for these stories of emerging selfhood. The narrators are coming to terms with their social class conversion at the same time they are confronting issues of racial identity. But they do so from different subject positions with respect to social class.

Alessandro is from a working-class background and is the son of émigrés to the United States from the Dominican Republic via Puerto Rico. He labors under the feeling of inadequacy for not being smart enough or able to speak English well enough. On his first day of prep school, Alessandro writes:

> I had no idea what to say and could only repeat to myself over and over, "I don't belong in this place. Everyone here is smarter than I am. They'll just laugh at me if I speak in my Spanish accent."

Alessandro's experience is unlike educational career paths of most working-class and poor youngsters whose prerogatives and educational opportunities are foreclosed because they lack the cultural capital (see Bourdieu & Passeron, 1977; McLeod, 1985; Willis, 1977). Alessandro perseveres and becomes academically successful despite his sense of being out of place—of being "out-classed" in educational settings.

Rob is an academically successful black man of privileged background. He suggests that the sense he has of himself as a member of a black elite was inherited from his grandfather:

> My grandfather would always make a distinction between other blacks and himself. As far as he was concerned, his education and profession put him in a separate class.

Rob grew up in a predominantly white suburban community with few contacts with black people. His mother was a doctor, his grandfather a dentist, and his parents' friends were "all college-educated blacks who seemed to be still celebrating the gains of the 1960s."

Maria's background is similar to Rob's—both grew up and were socialized in all-white, suburban contexts. Maria writes:

> Growing up in suburbia, I was just another happy, self-confident, smart kid, who happened to be black. I remember applying to college as a pivotal moment that forced me to think about my status as a black person in a white world.

That Maria and Rob seem raceless (see Fordham, 1988) is a function of their social class privilege. Their white, suburban social contexts afforded them few opportunities for encountering blackness as a cultural form. From the perspective of their social class privilege, racial pride is based on hard-earned "dues paying" by family members, and the payoffs are the distinctions of being "Negro firsts" who are seen to have paved the way for the next generation of African Americans.

Prince's background is similar to Alessandro's—both come from working-class or "underclass" (see Wilson, 1987) backgrounds; both express a diminished self-esteem through striving to compete academically in school contexts. Prince's experience is one of accessing educational opportunity from a self-described "ghetto life." In 7th grade he "flunked out of the gifted program and lost my transfer to the 'rich white' school." He then attended the local high school and went on to college.

All of the narrators in this section provide insights that will inform new theory for addressing how race, class, and gender interact with the processes of identity development for young people of color. Although there is much in contemporary literature on adolescent development that attempts to link bicultural identity formation to social contexts—such as affluent suburban community and urban inner-city community contexts—there is little to address the cross-context experiences of a growing number of young people. What happens to adolescents of color who stand with a foot in each of these two worlds?

Contemporary theory sidesteps what may be the most important feature of the embedded identities of African American students and other students of color—a political consciousness. Even though current ecological perspectives (e.g., Bronfenbrenner, 1986) rightly view the family, community, school, and peer groups as multiconstitutive factors in adolescent identity development, the theory is not specific enough to account for the role political and social awareness plays. That is, there is still too little account of how choices made by the bicultural adolescent shape the patterns of his or her social relationships and determine the directions of his or her development.

The community, neighborhood, familial, and civic settings furnish adolescents with a variety of signs and supports for the construction of their social identity and credible adult roles. Some of these signals and foundations of assistance may be inconsistent or contradictory because they emanate from different environments of concern—such as the local political economy, the church, community-youth organizations, the family, and the school. McLaughlin (1993) terms these "embedded contexts" and argues that young people construct their identities within these embedded, diverse, and complex environments. It is in these overlapping social-cultural spaces that the bicultural adolescent may be, quite literally, a different person in each of the different contexts. The organizing principle for a consistency of identity is decision making—how the individual makes choices in these different embedded contexts as unified sets of political sensibilities.

From this standpoint, there is a wisdom among the narrators in the recognition of the polarities in their lives. The emotional landscape of each of the young autobiographers reveals ways in which bicultural adolescents negotiate these tensions. We can see developmental destinations for these journeys. We can see desirable directions for the next generation of bicultural adolescents in reference to questions such as: How do young people in these circumstances struggle through the conflicts of belonging and identity when the values, ideologies, and perspectives of their communal culture are inconsistent with culturally mainstream settings? How do black adolescents work through the dual consciousness resulting from negotiating contradicting social worlds en route to academic achievement and opportunity?

Race and class are conflated in the narratives of these young people. They have not been unpacked, a fact that reveals the difficulty of the developmental tasks facing them. The narratives point to a synthesis of contradicting embedded identities. What are the possibilities of elements of racial identity development that would complete the synthesis? One is a political perspective. Another is a spiritual and ethical perspective. Both perspectives are ways of taking a deeper look at social context and the choices bicultural adolescents make in that social context. We get from the narratives a glimpse of what it means to synthesize a sense of self based on dimensions beyond coexisting and successfully competing among whites in an educational or social setting.

POLITICAL PERSPECTIVE—DUAL CONSCIOUSNESS

Adolescents need intellectual tools for developing critical consciousness—a robust racial identity as well as a sense of self-agency and self-determination. These tools are necessary to counter the manner in which racism works to decompose the cultural integrity of blackness. Racism is a system of privilege based upon race and upon the maintenance of white supremacy. As such, racism is a sociopolitical phenomenon that inscribes itself in social practices (e.g., acts of violence, marginalization, exclusion, contempt, and exploitation), as well as in the discourses and popular representations (e.g., demonized and buffoonlike representations of blackness in popular media) in America.

As Hilliard notes (1996), the unpreparedness of black people to repel successfully expressions and institutions of white supremacy is exemplified in tomes such as Close's *Rage of a Privileged Class*. This work documents the laments of the "black middle class" at feeling betrayed by the continued experience of overt and covert white supremacy, despite having "played the game" and done everything they were supposed to do (like the narrators). The developmental task is made complex by the fact that the schools the narrators attend not only fortify white supremacist logic but also they serve to reproduce class privilege (Bourdeiu & Passerson, 1977; Bowles & Gintis, 1976; Harris, 1982).

For integrated and robust cultural and racial identity development to happen, the peer reference group must include a politics of identity that resists the mainstream cultural optics ("I don't think of you as black," "You're not really black"). As bell hooks points out, the identity themes inscribed from culturally mainstream optics are not the only ones important to the reconstruction of black subjectivity. She writes:

Assimilation, imitation, or assuming the role of rebellious exotic other are not the only available options and never have been. This is why it is crucial to radically revise the notions of identity politics, to explore marginal locations as spaces where we can best become whatever we want to be while remaining committed to liberatory Black liberation struggle. (1994, p. 24)

Support structures for investing African American adolescents with subjective agency must provide a credible reference group through which they can "explore marginal locations as spaces where they can best become whatever they want to be" and still be fully empowered participants in society. The narrators describe their experience in finding and relating to such a reference group that permitted them to dynamically engage what DuBois (1961) called "dual consciousness"—the intrapersonal conflict of identity and belongingness facing black people in America. It is an intrapersonal conflict never fully resolved but that nonetheless is significant in the developing identity of every young person of color. From Prince we get a clear statement of the polarities of his existence and the sense of self he is formulating for himself:

The identity I have become comfortable with proves the truth of the "two souls warring"—I am *not* a middle-class "African American" wishing he had experienced the gritty poverty and violence of his underclass brother so that he could feel connected to blackness, nor am I simply a poor black who vainly wishes, Bigger Thomas-like, for the freedom and affluence of the whites.

DuBois's dual consciousness is a dialectical lens providing the "double vision" through which adolescents of color attempt to resolve "dilemmas of belonging and being" in the developmental task of identity formation.

Each of the narrators struggles to find a credible reference group to provide them with adult roles that fit their sensibilities as to whom they should be. For most adolescents, the communal culture provides believable roles for young people that allow for growth and eventual identity achievement. But for adolescents of color whose relationship to their communal culture is problematized by having to negotiate a duality of experience, the developmental task is much more complicated. In each case there is an issue regarding their alienation and disaffection from a reference group. For example, Prince writes:

While in high school I experienced patronizing white attitudes toward the "only black student in class" and "that talented young black man," but that was really nothing compared to the isolation forced on me by my former black peers. I never did figure out how to regain their acceptance, which at the time I felt I had to have.

These are stories of critical reconciliation of two social worlds circumscribed by the tapestry of white supremacy in America. The narrators describe their struggles to become whole by integrating two polarities—one being their "otherness" as members of a historically oppressed group and the other being what Audre Lorde (1988) termed the "mythical norm,"[1] or the standard of American, white, mainstream acceptability. For example, Prince states:

> I had to speak two languages—one of poverty and tired resignation, and one of hope and bright futures. I had to be aware of one group while in the midst of another, and succeed in both!

Each of the narrators tells the story of how they moved from a place of defining themselves in relation to the mythical norm, toward a destination not yet reached—critical consciousness regarding their own racial identity. Alessandro writes:

> As a poor Latino student, I never felt comfortable in the predominantly white, wealthy environment of Lewisburg. The reason was not just the color of my skin but also the difference in culture. Although I felt isolated from the mainstream community, I never felt a need to look for the support of the school's Latino and African-American community. In the cafeteria, most of the black and Latino students sat together in one corner of the dining hall. Although I knew some of the minority students, I never separated myself from the larger community. . . . I think I also distinguished myself as an individual who did not belong to one particular group.

The narrators are also explicit in their awareness of their struggle with the dualities. Prince, for example, seems to feel somewhere in between:

> From what my experience shows, I should be thoroughly fucked up in one way or another. If I am not a token-for-life-selling-out-dollar-chasing-white-man-in-black-skin because of the inferiority complex I got by encountering extreme affluence at school and desperate poverty at home, I should be a forty-ounce-drinking-blunt-smoking-rap-listening-bitch-slapping-ho-chasing-crack-slinging-street-nigger acting out hostility, violence, and self-destruction that I witnessed at an early age and throughout my life.

Prince says, "I am amazed that I do not have a more intense conflict about race," suggesting a movement through a possible bifocal foreclosure—where the perception is that there are basically only two modalities and that the dual consciousness is a permanent schism one merely comes to accept. Foreclosure would mean that the adolescent ceased contesting the mythical norm and ceased trying to synthesize a new identity between what one isn't and what one currently is.

PERSPECTIVE ON SPIRITUALITY—REDEMPTION

Concomitant with the process of struggling with self-definition is that of determining "what's the right thing to do." In that sense, the four narratives are conversion narratives, not unlike that of *The Autobiography of Malcolm X.* The challenge that each of these narrators faces on this account is the critical contemplation on their notion of one's own people—and defining self in relationship to black people. For example, Alessandro, after significant self-discovery through the reference group of the Latino drama group wrote:

> As I look back, I now know that I stood in between the black fraternity and the Latino community. My worst fear came true: I was not part of any one group and never will be.

What is the way to redemption for Alessandro? What is the way to redemption for Prince? Is there really a middle ground between Bigger Thomas and Clarence Thomas where the narrators can embrace a unified sense of self, given conflicts inscribed by race and class? For Prince and Alessandro, the question becomes one of redeeming their sense of self in light of the elevated social class status that comes with successfully completing college. The collection of narratives brings forth critical issues of political consciousness in relation to racial identity and integrated selfhood. The stories address the question of how African American adolescents develop subjectivity and critical agency in light of the contradictory roles that the social milieu of college inevitably poses for them.

The narratives are both compelling and instructive in relation to the task of determining self in a racist society. By the same turn, we can see they are journeys that are not yet complete. In a sense, these narrators are successfully contesting the duality of their existence on two planes. The first is psychological—that of the individuation adolescents experience as they differentiate themselves from parental figures in family contexts. The second is political, and by far more significant for biracial or bicultural identity development. It is differentiation from the mythical norm that the narrators experience as they begin to question and contest the normative whiteness and class privilege that suffuse their immediate social environments.

This critical consciousness involves actively confronting the contradictions imposed by the white supremacist logics of contemporary society. These are tricky and treacherous journeys because the contesting of "whiteness" cannot overwhelm the undeniable personal history. The tentativeness is expressed by Maria, who writes:

> Without being at all critical of what some would call my "whitewashing," I unconsciously learned and mastered the unwritten rules of social success in a small, white, suburban environment. I wore the right clothes, listened to the right music and had easy friendships with girls and boys: All of these things seemed to mean more than being of the "right" race.

Maria is expressing an awareness of the mythical norm she terms as her "whitewashing" and is also interrogating "whiteness" as the "correct" or "desirable" way of being. Her encounter experiences included the reflections on her identity in relation to applying to college (and the questioning of the role race played in her high rate of acceptance), her relationship with her white boyfriend, and her dis-ease in the relationship with her black roommate in college. But she is also tentative in derogating her "white" experience. Similarly, Rob interrogates his role among his peer reference group while participating in an all-white fraternity:

> This causes me to wonder whether I am giving these people a false sense of security about their dealings with black people, and whether I should be more persistent in voicing black concerns in dealings with my fraternity brothers. However, I believe that I should not seek to place a special burden upon myself to "educate" my white friends. To do so would reduce my ability to function, and hence, succeed.

Both Maria and Rob move from the privileged end of the polarity of dual consciousness to what Cross (1991) calls the Encounter stage in his theoretical framework of racial identity development. For Maria, the journey is from racelessness to the beginnings of a critical race consciousness. Up until the point of her encounter late in her high school career, her race identity was abstract and located in categorically inscribed notions of "black as achiever"—the emissary for the race, the exceptional black. The "black as achiever" category, inscribed by wider society in a white supremacist tone, was a phase for both Prince and Maria. Maria states, "From early on in my schooling, my categorization as 'smart' seemed to supersede and erase any other label, of race or class that I could personify."

The autobiographies of Prince and of Alessandro provide narratives of the starkest contrasts between two social worlds. For Prince, the polarities of experience were between "ghetto life" on the one hand, and a very privileged, preppy life on the other. Prince attended a culturally white and mainstream elementary school in the San Fernando Valley on the basis of his label as a "gifted and talented" black boy. The construction of a personal identity as a gifted and talented student is significant for each of the individuals in this section.

For Alessandro and Prince, the redemption is of a different sort—as in the comparison to El Malik Hajj El Shabazz's (Malcolm X's) conversion narrative, particularly the themes of redeemability from a successful ghetto life. An unmistakable analogy to *The Autobiography of Malcolm X* as a conversion narrative is Prince's experience in Oakland that was marked by loneliness and unhappiness—reading anything and everything in the isolation of the Oakland environment:

> I read whatever I could get my hands on: old Richie Rich comic books, science fiction of all kinds, Disney books, Aesop's fables, Black and African history, and so on. I was lucky that my mother always bought me books. She ensured that I had something to do when I was sent to my room for stealing!

The maintenance of the academic achiever certainly is an important theme for all of the young autobiographers in this section. Prince states: "If my mother taught me about anything besides God, she taught me to excel at school. . . . From a very early age I learned that education was the way out."

Similarly, Alessandro wrote of his mother:

> In school, her children were expected to be the best in their class; no report card could be brought home unless it was straight As. We knew that receiving anything less than an A meant a whipping with the thick leather belt.

There is much to be unpacked here for each of the autobiographers. What is meant by a formal education? Is it the experience and credentials? Or is it experience, credentials, and something else (an integrated identity?) that the young person finds in himself or herself vis à vis the struggle?

> Some people like my father and every drug dealer/gangbanger/hustler in America learn that school is not the only option before they figure out what other options are viable.

What are the alternative options? What would it mean to realize them? The illegitimate economy? The obverse of the legitimate market economy? Is it the notion of redemption Louis Farrahkan presented in an address suggested by the conversion of Malcolm X in prison? Mr. Farrakahn indicated that in some sense the "best and brightest" of African American males are those who fill the prisons or are dead, because they are the ones who meet the oppressive system head on, rather than submit to it as the cost of being "successful." This puts a new light on "unredeemability."

CONCLUSION

I proposed two elements of identity development heretofore overlooked by contemporary theory—a political stance and a spiritual and ethical stance. I do not mean to suggest here that the project of critical consciousness for African American adolescents is merely political action or a judgment about "what's the right thing to do." The essence of a liberatory identity development is the cultivation of a critical race consciousness in conjunction with the development of academic proficiency and social competence.

We see in the following narratives the development of both the personal and the political—and the critical role that a credible reference group and relationships play in this development. The title of Beverly Tatum's most recent book asks, "Why are all the Black kids sitting together in the cafeteria?" (1997). We find in the following narratives an explanation of why Prince, Maria, Rob, and Alessandro *never* sat with that group, and *why they would now*. These four autobiographies pose and address three essential questions regarding racial identity development of adolescent people of color:

1. How do relationships established across divides of racial, economic, and cultural difference function in the development of a stable and robust racial identity?
2. How do young people of color successfully negotiate the polarities of belonging—the dual consciousness resultant from negotiating two social worlds—en route to academic achievement and opportunity?
3. What kinds of social supports and educational experiences must young people of color have to steward them successfully into empowered adulthood in America?

NOTE
1. Audre Lorde says that the mythical norm resides on the edge of consciousness and is what each one of us designates as "not me." She states that in America, "this norm is usually defined as white, thin, male, young, heterosexual, Christian, and financially secure. . . . It is with this mythical norm that the trap-

pings of power reside within this society. Those of us who stand outside that power often identify one way in which we are different, and we assume that to be the primary cause of all oppression, forgetting other distortions around difference." (1988, p. 353)

1

Born with a Veil

PRINCE

Prince shows amazing strength and resiliency despite a childhood of extreme instability, poverty, and frequent upheavals, against a backdrop of crime, prisons, drugs, and violence. He eventually escaped the hardships of his youth, by way of "rich white" schools, which his mother always sought out for him, and through emulating positive role models as opposed to the omnipresent negative forces in his life. He excelled in school, being the only black kid in advanced classes. With the strong influence of teachers and a highly successful black Big Brother, Prince rose above his situation—to attend a prestigious college—while still feeling connected to his past and his "people."

Prince epitomizes the transformative power of the psyche, as he looks back on all the people who "hurt" him in life and reframes situations, viewing them as ultimately "helpful" in arriving at his present identity. This essay was written in his sophomore year.

My father received a phone call from some of his friends. They were going out and wanted him to come along. He said, "Hell, yeah. You know I'm down for some action. When y'all coming by here?" As he got ready to go out, my mother grew worried. She had asked him to stop hanging around this set of friends, but he had told her to shut up and leave her alone.

"You trying to run my life again? I'm a man! Damn, I can make my own motherfucking decisions!"

He pushed her aside gently and she jumped right back in his face and told him, "I am telling you not to go out tonight! I have a bad feeling." He looked at her funny. She said, "I had a dream this morning that you would go out and not come back for seven years. Don't leave! *Please* stay with me tonight!" He said, "Awww, fuck that old voodoo shit. I'm going out, woman." That was the end of their discussion until his friends came by. She protested again for him not to leave, but he was even more adamant because his friends were there waiting. He did not want to look pussy-whipped and he wasn't about to go out like some kind of sucker. He pushed her away from the door and left. He pulled his coat around him as he climbed into the back seat. She watched from the balcony as the mist swallowed the car.

That night, my father and his friends robbed a convenience store. During the crime they shot and killed a bystander, the son of a wealthy local car dealer. Newly identified as one of the area's most wanted criminals, my father went into hiding for more than a year. The police continued to search for him and ultimately followed my mother on one of her regular visits to his secret apartment. The police arrested both my parents and took them to jail, where I was born a few days later.

While my mother was in custody for aiding and abetting a fugitive, she went into labor. She was taken to the hospital where, after my birth, they took me away from her and sent her back to her cell. My grandmother picked me up from the hospital. At the time, my mother had been going to school and working. She was released from jail a week after my birth and turned to my father's mother, Jenelle, for support. We moved to an apartment in South Central L.A. I would frequently spend the night at my Uncle William's house. Though William is my father's younger brother, he is only four years older than I am. We had lots of experiences together—good and bad. When we were older, we grew close through fending off gang assaults and finding our way across South Central L.A. William is more like a brother to me than an uncle. These days, though, because he did not get out of that environment, he is hard to talk to. He still lives with my grandmother and is struggling to support her, his daughter, and himself.

Some weekends, my mother would pack up our old Mercury Comet (complete with tail fins and rust spots) with cold fried chicken and lemonade and take William and me to visit my father in Soledad State Prison, some 250 miles north of Los Angeles. We always ate at Denny's on the way up because the drive took so long. On the visits we met my father in a common room with other prisoners, where he would show us off to the other inmates and then proceed to argue with my mother about the course of his life and whether they could be back together after he was released. William and I would escape this situation as fast as we could. We usually asked my mom for the car keys so that we could go and get some lemonade out of the back of the car. When my mother returned from the meeting room, she would have tears in her eyes. She would tell me, because there was no one else to tell, how my father was trying to change her into something she was not. I still do not know what she meant, but I do know that it greatly troubled her. I could never watch my mother cry without crying myself.

My first experiences with my father in prison struck me then as merely inconvenient and a little troubling because of the fighting and tears. I did not feel that something was strange or missing in my life. My mother took very good care of me on her own, so I managed to ignore the gentle voice in my mind that told me something was seriously wrong with my father's situation and his relationship with my mother.

My mother and I soon moved from South Central L.A. to a suburb in the San Fernando Valley, known as the home of the "valley girls." By that time my father had been in prison for 5 years, and my mother and I were living with a man named Lewis who owned a new Cutlass Supreme. I'm not sure who he was or why we lived with him; I guess he was my mother's boyfriend. It is an indication of the relationship I have with my mother that I don't particularly resent her or look down on her for living with another man while her husband, my father, was in jail; for the first 8 years of my life my mother and I struggled by ourselves, relying heavily on each other. We were always very close; I got to know her as a human being—sometimes more than I wish I had. If I didn't know so much about how she struggled to raise me, I could be more selfish and just blame her for all of our problems, like most children do. Instead I find myself blaming others!

When we were living in Canoga Park [San Fernando Valley], I had my first experience with racism. William came over and we decided to go to the park. We dug in the sand, played with the sand hornets, and made mud pies to throw at each other. Then, as we were about to get on the merry-go-round, a mother ran up and yanked her child off of it. On the way home William told me she had muttered to her child about us "nigger children," and I was incredulous. I did not yet have the slightest idea of what it meant to be black, much less black and living in a valley suburb. That lady helped me to begin to understand.

My early school experience in the valley was the first indication of what would become a trend in my life. I attended a preschool best characterized as a white hippie experimental school. The school was built out of dark wooden logs to give it a natural look, like a logger's cabin, out there in the tree-covered valleys of Southern California. I guess I must have excelled at this school because I was labeled "gifted" and received lots of compliments. Teachers always liked me, because I was eager to learn and intelligent to boot.

My own school experience makes me thoroughly aware of the identity problem that faces young black students who have a drive or natural tendency to excel. If my mother taught me about anything besides God, she taught me to excel at school. From a very early age I learned that "education was the way out." I no longer believe this is the only way—it is possible for a man like me to excel in the world without formal education—but this valuable lesson helped me through the first 18 years of my life. It kept me focused, out of trouble, and on a generally good track, so now my options are open. Some people, like my father and every drug dealer/gangbanger/hustler in America, learn that school is not the only option before they figure out what other options are viable. They often make the wrong choices and ruin their futures. Some good and valuable lessons have to be taught early, before other lessons of life poison the mind.

That is why my teachers always singled me out. Not only was I intelligent but also I was already psychologically primed to learn and endure ridiculously long-suffering classroom "education." I am happy to say that since then I have thoroughly rid myself of this patient Protestant work ethic! I now work only for who and what I love and want, unless I am coerced by the trusty "low grades versus future options" temptation.

Just as I had lessons in "academic achievement," I also got instruction in irresponsibility, mainly from my father, but sometimes even from my mother. I remember one night we went in Lewis's Cutlass to pick up my mother's younger brother Jeffrey. I recall the group Frankie Beverly and Maze on the radio singing a bluesy, slow, soul song called "Happy Feelings." I seem to remember that while we were driving around, we continued to collect passengers, people I thought I knew. Marijuana smoke filled the car, which is probably why I don't remember any of them. I was laughing along with the adults. My Uncle Jeffrey was sitting in the front seat and he turned around to me in the back, where I sat between two other people. He told me to come a little closer to him and close my eyes, which I did. He put his hand over my mouth and his mouth over my nose and told me to inhale. My lungs were quickly filled with the heavy, fragrant, painful smoke that burning marijuana leaves produce. I got so high that night!

My mother mildly protested my corruption, but then took the joint from her brother. She was driving and damned if she wasn't going to have any. She finished the joint and drove on. A while later my mother and uncle started arguing about something. The other people in the car went silent, and the music stopped. My mother was yelling at the top of her lungs at her brother. He was cursing her and yelling too. I was upset because I had seen what happens when men start to yell at women. They continued yelling and my mother, cursing, pulled over to the shoulder of the freeway and told my uncle, "Get the fuck out of my car!" He said, "Bitch! You get out of the car! Fuck you!" She was furious, her eyes were red from the smoke and the anger, her arms had stiffened and her fists were clenched tighter than her teeth. My uncle's bottom lip was hanging and his brow was frowned. My mother opened up her door and told him again to "get the fuck out" before she had to make him. He now had an excuse to get really mad, so he said, "Fuck you bitch! Come take me out!" My mother wasn't playing that night. She got out, and I gasped when a car sped right past her as she walked around the front of the Cutlass. My mother threw open his car door and pulled him out. They continued to yell and then my uncle hit her across the face and kicked her so that she fell into his seat. He pulled her out of the car again and hit her some more. I screamed at him at the top of my lungs, telling him to stop and leave her alone. I had a feeling in the back of my head from the weed and a burning sensation under the skin. He stopped hitting her but continued his yelling. The other people got out of the car, and one man held him back even though he had stopped. He was still mad and wanted the other man to let him go, but the man didn't, so they started fighting. My mother got in the car and left them. The car aired out as we drove back home. That was my first exposure to drugs and the whole party scene.

In the years since, I have gotten to see firsthand what that lifestyle did to my Uncle Jeffrey. He never developed the maturity to take responsibility for himself. He now has several terminal, malignant brain tumors from 20-odd years of chronic drug use. He has come back to my mother time and time again for a place to stay now that he has cancer, because he cannot cope in the world by himself. The unfortunate part is that even before he had cancer, he was incompetent. Seeing his sad state helped me decide against drugs and irresponsibility as a way of life. Those who hurt you can actually help you.

Speaking of hurt, my mother and I had to move suddenly from our nice two-story home in the San Fernando Valley. I don't know why, but one day all of our furniture was gone, her boyfriend Lewis was gone, and we were in dire straits. The last afternoon we were in that house, with the sun shining through the bay windows upstairs, across the desolate, dust-covered floor, I asked my mother for a spoonful of peanut butter, my favorite snack. She cried the bitterest tears because she could not give it to me. We had nowhere to go, so we spent that first night in a park restroom. I was sensitive about sleeping on the floor of the women's restroom in a municipal park. After I awoke (my mother didn't sleep) and washed up as best as I could in the sinks there, we bought some cherries from a Mexican street vendor with the little bit of money mom had. We did not live on the street for long, though. We moved in with our lesbian cousin Esther and her son, Samuel, but soon found a place around the corner from Esther's. At first we had no furniture or food—only some books. Even though we were right around the corner from an elementary school, I was "bussed" to integrate a white school because of the "gifted" status I had acquired at my preschool. I was stamped legitimate: "Class A1 Negro—Handle Carefully," or, in the words of Ralph Ellison, "Keep this nigger running!" In any case, it helped me more than it hurt.

My father finally got out of prison after 6 years. He was 6 feet 3 inches tall and weighed a lot. He had very crude but handsome features. I look just like him, except that my features were mellowed by my mother's. I have good memories of him holding my mother and smoking weed, talking to me as a father should talk to his son. He always offered me some of his weed. I accepted once, much to my mother's chagrin. She had become a little less tolerant of my corruption. I didn't appreciate her concern then—in fact, like most children I knew, I loved my "nice" father more than my "mean" mother. I often told him he was nicer than her, especially after he let me do something I wanted to do.

He was a brilliant man, but his brilliance had been corrupted by the way he grew up. As a child he faced a bleak future and he was not capable of hoping to create more for himself. Like most poor blacks, he was a victim of the hopelessness and despair that permeates the ghettos. His environment never even hinted to him that he could possibly succeed. His mother (my grandmother and William's mother) lived fast when he was growing up. She never told him that he could succeed and never gave him a reason to hope. He needed attention; she needed gin. She got her gin; he went to juvenile hall. He was classified as "incorrigible" by the age of 13. He was in and out of the juvenile system regularly until the year he turned 18 and went to the state penitentiary. He never got the help I did, and by the time my grandmother calmed down, it was too late for my father.

I remember one time he took me to the movies. We had to ride the bus to get to the double feature, and on the way we stopped at an apartment complex where my father met briefly with some of his associates. He was wearing a black jacket, a burgundy braided tie, and some slacks. He looked very sharp. He shook hands with some laughing, jive-talking men and we then got on the bus again. He began to explain to me some of his religious beliefs: that man created himself, that God had never done anything for him, and that each man needed to do for himself. I asked him, in my misunderstanding of atheism, if he meant that God would only help those who helped themselves. He said, "NO! I mean there is no God." I still did not understand how God could not exist, so I just left that topic alone.

We got off the bus for a second time, but we still weren't at the movie theater. We went into a cheap motel, he rented a room for a couple of dollars, and we proceeded to the room. Once we were in the room, the conversation died down. I watched curiously as he produced a vial, a small mirror, and a rolled up hundred dollar bill from his stylish black jacket. He poured some powder, cut it into lines, rolled his hundred tighter than it had been, and took a snort. Several snorts and high sighs later, he told me, "Don't you ever let me catch you doing this stuff." I said, "Okay." I didn't know what the fuss was about. I did not know what he had done nor had I seen anyone else do it, so I did not understand his warning or his newly excited, happy conversation.

We soon had to change houses again because my father double-crossed some "business partners," who came one night and shot up our house with automatic rifles, hoping to kill him and not caring if they killed us, his family. My mother had a premonition and woke us up before they came. We drove out of the apartment complex with my father in the trunk of the car, just in case they drove by. My parents moved to Oakland to start a carpet-cleaning company. They bought the equipment with money from some of my father's illegal exploits. I was to stay with my grandmother and William. I ended up having to move to Oakland, though, because my uncle went into the hospital. My grandmother had been leaving me at home alone a lot to look after him before he went to the hospital.

Oakland, for me, was a place of loneliness and unhappiness. I stayed in the house for the most part, where I read and read and read. I read whatever I could get my hands on: old Richie Rich comic books, science fiction of all kinds, Disney books, Aesop's fables, black and African history, and so on. I was lucky that my mother always bought me books. She ensured that I had something to do when I was sent to my room for stealing! I had no friends in Oakland. My mother and father were always fighting. He would beat her up and bruise her face, she would throw things, and then they would make up. My father had friends in Oakland, so he left us. The rent ran out, and one cold rainy night we had to get our bags and move back to Los Angeles. My mother and I left on a bus for L.A. in the middle of the night. I don't know where my father was.

In L.A. we had to live with my father's mother, Jenelle, for a while. When my mother and father got back together, we moved again. In L.A. I was still able to attend the same rich white integrated school. My mother was now pregnant. My father owned a dry-cleaning store, and things were going well financially, so we moved into a duplex on a relatively nice street. The nice times did not last. My father continued to beat my mother. She was getting more and more pregnant and they continued to fight about the type of food she was eating: She was a vegetarian, but my father wanted her to eat meat for the baby's sake. My father was an atheist and my mother was a born-again Christian, which produced more conflict. I could never help my mother. When, late at night, the screams or thuds or bumps would interrupt my descent into sleep, I could not help her. Several times I tried, but I was always told, "Go back to your room, Prince! This doesn't concern you!", or "Prince, leave us alone right now." I shuffled quietly back to my room and slept fitfully on my box mattress with layers of old blankets and quilts to offer a little padding.

My mother finally could not take it anymore. I was 7 going on 8 at this time, and one day right after school let out for summer vacation she approached me saying, "We are going to stay with your grandmother Jenelle." I was happy that I would get to hang out with William, but I sensed that something was wrong. We moved in with Jenelle for the second time in a year, and things were rough. When my mother was 8-months pregnant, she went into labor in the kitchen, and my grandmother had to whisk her off to the hospital.

My mother returned from the hospital, and as she walked in the door I caught a glimpse of the baby in her arms. It was white as chalk—I could see the veins in its head and the light brown downy hair. "It's a boy," she said, noting my wonder. "It's your little brother." She cooed gently to him. He gurgled. She walked over to the liquor cabinet and put the hand-held cradle on top of it. William and I gathered around the cradle to examine my baby brother. His eyes were closed, and he looked nothing like a regular person. He was so yellow! "What is his name?" I asked. "His name is Raphael," said my mother. I thought he looked like a Raphael, such a gentle sounding name, and this baby was so harmless and unprotected. What better name could there be for such a creature? I liked him.

The next day my mother and my grandmother had a fight.

"I'm sorry," my grandmother said, "but I will not have you in my house one more day! You have got to go!"

"What do you mean?" my mother protested. "You're going to throw us out in the street? You know we don't have anyplace else to go!"

"I'm sorry, but I can't help you," my grandmother replied. "You have *got* to go."

So we left. My grandmother cursed at us on the way down the stairs and on our way out the driveway. The whole apartment complex was aware of our departure.

We went back to our old street, but this time we did not go back to my father. My mother had gotten to be close friends with our landlady, who lived next door. She was a middle-aged white woman with a very nicely furnished apartment. I was amazed that this comfortable home was right next door to us the whole time.

My mother cradled Raphael in her lap while she went through the agonizing humility of explaining her situation to this woman. Thank God that the woman was kind-hearted and a friend to my mother in her time of need. I was happy to be there. I slept comfortably in a fully mattressed bed with new, clean-smelling comforters. But I awoke the next morning to the sound of anxious knocking at the front door.

"Open the door! Is my wife in there?

"No, she is not here."

"You're lying! Open the damn door! I need to talk to her!" He knocked at the door with his foot.

"I told you. She is not here." This old white lady was very cool about it. She did not start to panic, though she did get nervous. Finally she convinced him to go away, although she was aware that my father knew my mother and I were there. Later she told my mother, "I have got to ask you to leave. I cannot have all of this destruction and confusion coming to my house. I'm old, and I need my peace." My mother replied, "I don't want to burden you, so I'll go."

My mom decided it was time to move to Atlanta. She started to pack up the mufflerless Volvo we bought from a friend for $200. It had rust spots like our old Comet, but it ran. My mother still had her key to our duplex next door, so we went in, hoping that my father was not there. He wasn't. We packed our clothes swiftly and made many trips back and forth to the car, which was parked behind the apartment. Our Volvo was blocking the driveway, the nose was facing the street so that when we finished we could leave. The phone rang. My mom looked at it the first time it rang and then proceeded to pick up another bag. It rang three more times. Exasperated, she picked up the phone and dropped the duffel bag to the floor. "Hello?" A look of terror came over her. "Is that you? What are you talking about?" She hung up the phone, looking pale. My mother began talking to herself in a low, angry, growling voice. I couldn't help but hear what she was saying. "Do you know what your father just said? That motherfucker says he is going to come over here and kill me if we try to leave. Bastard! Hurry up and pack, God damn it."

We packed fast and furious, gathering what we could fit in the trunk and backseat. My mother handed me the last bag to put in the car and she got in to open the door for me. Just then a car pulled up in the driveway blocking us and my father leapt out, shining black metal in his left hand. He stomped up to my mother who had gotten out of the car and said, "You ain't taking my son nowhere!" She yelled back, "We are leaving! You wanna kill me, go right ahead! But motherfucker, I'm leaving!" She got in the car and told me to do the same. I was standing there on the passenger side looking at them argue, and my dad came around the back of the car to tell me to come with him. "Come on with me, son," my dad said calmly, putting his gun back in his pants. "Prince, get your ass in this car!" my mom screamed at me. "Son!" my father pleaded. My mother was screaming for me to get in the car, or "I will leave your ass here!" I was in a tug of war, and only I could sway the balance. I decided to get in the car with my mother, and she proceeded to push the other car out of the way. Once we were on the street, she headed west into the sunset and never looked back. But I looked back and I saw my father standing there alone. Sunlight shined in the sweat that rolled down his face, making it glisten. He stood in that sharp black jacket with his hands on his hips. That was the last time I saw my father.

Leaving my father and other family in California was a turning point in my life. My quest for identity was made more difficult, but at least I knew I was capable of making decisions. I can all too easily imagine what might have happened to me had I stayed in Los Angeles with my father. I would have grown up even more quickly than I did with my mother. I would have been forced to assume responsibility for myself that I was simply not capable of handling.

After I grew frustrated with the institutional academic route to success, I would probably have joined a gang to fulfill my inner drive and motivation. Even considering all the poverty, crime, delinquency, drugs, violence, and abuse that surrounded me in the South, I am still glad I made the choice to go with my mother and brother.

My father left Los Angeles for the South himself, back to Mississippi where he was born. He tried to rob a bank there but was hit by a bus while fleeing, fell into a coma, and went to prison for 4 years. The same year he got out he went back for armed robbery and is still there today. It seems like I might have ended up with my mother either way!

Three days after we left Los Angeles, we arrived in Houston, Texas. My mother's father lived there, and it was supposed to be just a "rest stop" on the way to Atlanta, but it turned into our home. We stayed with my mother's father while my mother drove a paper route. She eventually found a better job at a day-care center and we were able to get our own place.

As we had done in L.A., my mother and I sought out the best school to enroll me in. The morning we found it, we stepped off the city bus into a new world filled with elegance and style. Southern plantation-style affluence had a different look than big city affluence, which was gaudy and glittery, like neon lights. Southern affluence was understated and elegant: wide streets lined with oak trees, Porsches, and Rolls Royces. That was the street that led to Tall Oaks Elementary. Even the hot-lunch trucks had style.

While a day at school was a welcome escape from the troubles of home, school was still hard emotionally. The wealth of the other students made me very self-conscious. I was very aware of my poverty each time I had to borrow money from my teacher or the cashier in the cafeteria line to pay for lunch. Sometimes I just couldn't bring myself to ask them for help again, so I would fast. My self-esteem plummeted even though I was doing well in my classes.

I often got into trouble and was sent to the principal's office more than once. I took many notes home to my mother. My teachers made contracts with my mother: If I did my homework for the week, I would get a star sent home on Friday; if I didn't do it, I would get a sad face. Even when I wasn't doing my work, I always hoped for the star. When I didn't get it, my mother would fuss at me or whip my ass, depending on her mood. I would come from the bus every Friday and walk into the day-care center where my mother worked. My mother would take me to the back so that she could examine my grades for that week. "Why the hell aren't you doing your homework?" I would make up an excuse or just say, "I'm bored." That was one that always seemed to work for us "gifted" children.

My family and I made seven moves in our first 2 years in Houston. We moved from my grandfather's house through a series of crime-infested neighborhoods, even to the day-care center where my mother worked. We would sleep in the back and wake before the kids started to arrive. Finally, we settled in a subsidized apartment in the same complex where one of my cousins lived. At last I was able to grow a little when we settled in this apartment. I would walk with my brother Raphael down to the library and look across the street at the city's university looming large upon the hill. I thought occasionally that I might go to college someday. In the meantime, while my classmates were enjoying chauffeured rides home in Rolls Royces and Aston Martins, I was enduring city bus rides (our Volvo broke down) to the health and human services department to cheat the government into giving us food stamps. Although my mother was employed and not "technically" eligible for public assistance, we managed to persuade them to our cause. It was a great assistance indeed— we ate well and did not have to worry about food for about 2 years. But my mother's "persuasive" tactics eventually got her into trouble. She was almost sentenced to prison for food stamp fraud, but because she had children they let her off with 10 years' probation. In order to feed us and to make sure she had enough income to pay our rent and keep our lights on, she had risked her freedom. This is but one of the sacrifices my mother had to make to raise me and my brother over the years. Regardless of what popular opinion has to say about "welfare queens," I know for a fact that my mother had to do what she did to pave the way for me and my brother.

At school I was the "special black student," a role that I quickly grew tired of. Once, when I cursed out a teacher who had been picking on me, I walked down to Mrs. Briggs office to talk to her about it. Mrs. Briggs was an understanding old white lady who seemed to look right inside of me. When I talked with her, I did not have to say much because she knew me so well. She had seen it coming and she helped me out a lot. "I understand that a lot of people are always pressuring you. Sometimes it doesn't feel so good, but you really do have to do your homework. And your teacher is just trying to push you because she cares about your education." I knew that already, but I still didn't like it. She gave me some advice that I will never forget. She told me that when I got home and went outside to play, if I heard a voice inside my head that told me to do my homework, that is what I should do. I should not ignore that little voice, because it was only looking out for me. The more I ignored it, the worse my grades and the pressure would be. I loved Mrs. Briggs for teaching me to listen to my conscience.

Another lesson I learned is that the best schools were rich and white. Being young, I did not know cause from effect, so I assumed that they were good because they were white. I had no idea that money and resources played a role in the matter. This lesson was reinforced by the simple fact that Tall Oaks was in a neighborhood as unlike mine as possible. Having said that, I have to say that the years from 2nd grade to 6th grade were the most joyful of my life! I was able for the first time to act like the child I was. I still had some adult responsibility, but more and more the freedom of childhood was within my grasp. In our apartment complex, I was able to make friends and play and fight and throw eggs at buses and do all the things that poor black boys do. I was comfortable because I was doing "normal things." I had not yet become frustrated and jaded by the poverty that confined us to the ghetto, nor had I become sensitive to the forces working to keep us there. I thank God that my mother was.

When I was 12, my mother put me in a program called Big Brothers and Sisters. Although the program is advertised for everyone, it is generally focused toward poor black and Mexican kids, who usually end up matched with upper-middle-class whites. I was lucky because my big brother, Leon, was black and upwardly mobile. My involvement in the program opened up many opportunities for me, the value of which I was not aware at the time. Leon was one of the most positive elements in my life. I have not had many influential black role models in my life, and those that have been close enough to influence me have not been good influences. My Uncle Jeffrey and my father taught me how to use drugs and beat women! The lack of role models for black youth is a reality that I lived with for a long time, but I was rescued from my ignorance before it was too late.

Leon had had a relatively happy, working-class, two-parent upbringing. He went to a state college and a historically black law school, so he could offer me plenty of advice on school and on making plans for the future. I loved his rationality. I was a close-mouthed, shy, silent kid when I met him, but over the years, he helped me out of my shell, taught me things I knew nothing about, showed me parts of town I had never seen, and allowed me to witness his success. Last year he became a partner in his law firm and got married.

I got together with Leon in the middle of 6th grade. Under his tutelage and my mother's nourishment, my confidence grew and I was better prepared for school that next fall. However, 6th grade was the first and the last year (even in college!) that I went through exactly the same process as all the other students in preparation for school. I went school shopping for clothes and filler paper, I went to register on time, I went to orientation on time and with everyone else. It was a great experience. I felt really good about myself for the first time since we had moved to Houston. That confidence did not last past that year. In 7th grade, economic problems and the upheaval of more moving caused my grades to drop. I flunked out of the gifted program and lost my transfer to the "rich white" school, which meant that I had to attend my home school.

I have still not figured out exactly why I gave up on my schoolwork. I felt I really didn't belong at my home school, even though I had friends there. My home school reflected the poverty and anomie that marks inner cities across

America. My brief stay there forced me to make more conscious decisions about the course of my life because I knew that I didn't want to fit in with these students, even though I felt attached to them. I would have to work to make it out of there and into a better life for myself, and whether or not I succeeded was entirely up to me. Not even my mother or Leon could help me. Leon and my mother were disappointed in my poor school performance, but what could they do? I did make it out of there and back to the better junior high school the next year, from which I eventually graduated with average grades and low self-esteem. My experience of flunking and being transferred to a poor school was another milestone in my search for identity; I learned that I am human and that even the most driven, talented, ambitious youngsters can fail. I was not as exceptional as others said I was. I was a human being, and human beings sometimes make the wrong choices, or just mess up. A wise man once said, "Even men of steel rust."

My family moved again during my freshman year, and I enrolled in the regular curriculum at the local high school because I was not willing to try to challenge myself by taking the advanced classes. I did well in school without even trying and kept a low profile. I made two friends and mainly hung out with them. I made enough As that by the fall semester of 10th grade my guidance counselor and science teacher (both black women) noticed that I was doing too well to be in regular classes.

My guidance counselor said, "I think you need to think about getting into more challenging classes."

"Naw, I don't think I should do that," I replied. I was still discouraged from middle school. She insisted that I undertake the challenge and recommended an advanced English class. "No, I really don't think I could handle the reading." The class required students to read five books during the whole term. I was lazy when it came to reading books for school. I had the most ravenous appetite for them if they were not assigned, but the stigma of schoolwork killed (and still kills!) my desire. So I went home to enjoy my Christmas vacation and to eat turkey.

My jaw dropped when I got back to school and saw my schedule: advanced English *and* advanced math. What was my guidance counselor trying to do? The thought of refusing her intimidated me, so I decided to just take it as it came. I thought I could at least keep up if I kept doing what I was doing in the regular classes. I was right. The advanced classes were not that much harder than the regular classes. In fact, they were easier because the teachers expected you to do well and provided encouragement. Although I had to read a book a week for my English class, I also got to do creative things with my work. Oral presentations, which came to be my favorite thing to do, were required of me for the first time in my life.

My isolation began that term. Though my two friends, Avery and Dwayne, were smart and capable of making it in the accelerated track, I was the only black student in the whole school in any advanced classes. Slowly, other friends and acquaintances began to fall away, so that when I graduated from 10th grade, the only two friends I had left were Avery and Dwayne. The isolation hurt, but I see now that it was a long time coming. All my schooling in Houston, except for my brief stint at the local junior high school, had set me up for it.

On the other hand, I had learned to use words to cope with every type of social situation. All the talking I had done to get out of fights, to repel potential offenses, and to persuade teachers that my work really was good, had prepared me for my next adventure in high school—debate. When I decided to take debate, I had expected to go into class, glibly discuss an arbitrary topic, and, as usual, win the argument. My debate coach, Mrs. Kendall, a short, round, motherly yet sardonic, chain-smoking white lady, quickly dispelled those ideas. Extensive amounts of research and preparation goes into debate, not only presentation and persuasiveness. I cannot say that I have mastered the activity yet, but I continue to learn in college as a member of one of the top collegiate debate teams.

Like Leon, Mrs. Kendall introduced me to many subjects that I had never been exposed to before. She introduced me to extracurricular activities that helped pave my way into college and prepare my mind for the tasks before me, and I love her for that. I learned more than I did in all of my other classes. Debate was the only forum in high school where I learned anything of intellectual value. Debate was the most satisfying thing I ever did with my time; it was the only activity that gave gratification in return for hard work. My teammates and I also learned about life as we traveled across Texas with Mrs. Kendall. She loved us all, and I love her for that too.

Debate made me feel that I was on my way. But to where? To college and my destiny, I suppose. I chose my college based on the strength of its debate team. My time at college has allowed me to put the past and the present in perspective. I have come to believe that I am either great, lucky, or blessed. I don't believe in luck so I must have some greatness in me and I must have a mission in life. From what my experience shows, I should be thoroughly fucked up in one way or another. If I am not a token-for-life-selling-out-dollar-chasing-white-man-in-black-skin because of the inferiority complex I got by encountering extreme affluence at school and desperate poverty at home, I should be a forty-ounce-drinking-blunt-smoking-rap-listening-bitch-slapping-ho-chasing-crack-slinging-street-nigger acting out the hostility, violence, and self-destruction that I witnessed at an early age and throughout my life. Having learned to snort cocaine and smoke marijuana at such a young age, I should be involved more deeply in the drug subculture than I am. I did become involved with drugs briefly in high school. A lot of the debaters (all white kids and advanced-class students) drank, smoked weed, and did acid, so I did too. I quickly learned that I was *not* drug-user material.

I am amazed that I do not have a more intense conflict about race. Incredibly, even my experience in high school reinforced the lesson that white is right when it comes to education. As I grew more sophisticated, I did escape the post-hoc fallacy I had fallen into earlier; I realized that it is money, not race, that is the defining factor in school quality. Tracking can segregate even the blackest neighborhood school systems! While in high school, I experienced patronizing white attitudes toward the "only black student in class" and "that talented young black man," but that was really nothing compared to the isolation forced on me by my former black peers. I never did figure out how to regain their acceptance, which at that time I felt I needed. So, out of frustration and pain, I just figured, hell, they might be right about the value of education and other ideas about what constitutes success. There was nothing I could rely upon to strengthen me because my role models were few and like most kids, my identity was strongly influenced by the acceptance of my peers. I know now how foolish we all were.

I learned from my high school experience just how correct W. E. B. DuBois was when he wrote in *The Souls of Black Folk*:

> After the Egyptian and Indian, the Greek and the Roman, the Teuton and Mongolian, the Negro is sort of a seventh son, born with a veil, and gifted with second sight in this American world,—a world which yields him no true self-consciousness, but only lets him see himself through the revelation of the other world. It is a peculiar sensation, this double-consciousness, this sense of always looking at oneself through the eyes of others, of measuring one's soul by the tape of a world that looks on in amused contempt and pity. One ever feels this twoness—an American, a Negro; two souls, two thoughts, two unreconciled strivings; two warring ideals in one dark body, whose dogged strength alone keeps it from being torn asunder.

My perception of myself in early life reveals the truth of "the veil." It was only rarely and in the midst of a crisis that I was able to come to a conclusion about myself, by myself! In fact, this is a common dilemma of poverty and blackness in America, and perhaps of humanity. You find yourself constantly fighting everyone else around you to get what you need, so that you never have time to figure out what you want.

My entire school experience shows the truth of the "double-consciousness." I had to speak two languages—one of poverty and tired resignation, and one of hope and bright futures. I had to be aware of one group while in the midst of another and succeed in both! School also showed me how resentful blacks and patronizing whites looked upon my experience with "either contempt or pity," respectively.

The identity I have become comfortable with proves the truth of the "two souls warring"—I am *not* a middle-class "African American" wishing he had experienced the gritty poverty and violence of his underclass brother so that he could feel connected to blackness, nor am I simply a poor black who vainly wishes, Bigger Thomas-like, for the freedom and affluence of the whites. I have experienced the violence and desperate poverty of the ghetto and continue to live too close to it for comfort, but I have always seen a way out. The value my mother placed on education, the keystone of middle-class values, allowed me to learn the language and ways of middle-class America, but the center of my being still lies with my people. It has made for an interesting life.

The college experience has allowed me a chance to put my relationship with my mother into perspective. Recently she was diagnosed with breast cancer, and although she has undergone an operation, there is no telling whether the cancer may come back to kill her. When she was in the hospital she missed some probation hearings (from the food stamp fraud), and her probation officer decided to crack down on her and become a hard-ass. This put my mother on the spot again, and for what? For trying to take care of me and my little brother. The criminal process against my mother has begun again. The real crime is what they do to her, but I now can understand that all the persecution she has endured is simply the price she paid to ensure my brother's and my future. But having said that, I still feel hatred for those who have unjustly imposed such burdens on us throughout our lives. The forces which created the situation that produced my father are the same ones which continue to persecute my mother.

My personal growth has naturally included forays into the realm of the romantic. I am in a relationship with a young woman on campus, and she loves me, but we have been having problems recently. My early experience with my mother and father has kept me from making some of the same mistakes my father made, like hitting her or otherwise abusing her, but other problems fill the gaps. All the time I spent as a child struggling to maintain my sanity and be cool about things when hell was all around me, makes me a little difficult to communicate with. I also have a hard time listening and understanding other people's needs. It is the same callousness that allows desperate people to deal drugs to their neighbors and greedy people to colonize and enslave others. My obsession with my own well-being makes me stubborn, and once I make up my mind about how I feel, it is damn near impossible for me to understand how I can be wrong. It causes problems, but I want to change and experience the joy that comes from true intimacy and communication. I love my woman friend, but it is sometimes hard for me to express it. Same goes for her. But after all the fighting and all the crying, we still talk heart to heart. Although we do not "go out" anymore, we are starting again as friends. I guess friendship is what marriages or any other long-term relationships are built on. The best lesson to be learned from love can be found in Christ or Buddha; give without expecting something in return. Give something freely without tying your heartstrings around it. I have learned that lesson.

After all is said and done, I think it all comes down to faith. Faith is not required of most Americans, I think, and it is withheld by circumstance from those of us who need it most. Most of us cannot see beyond the four dim candle-lit walls that surround us when the light bill has not been paid. The darkness dims the spirit, and the pain of deprivation makes us callous and unfeeling.

I am currently studying in one of the most selective colleges in the country. I stand on the cusp of personal and financial success. My situation, however, is nothing I alone can be credited with, nor is it merely luck. It is just a blessing. I am grateful because I must be. I thank all the people who tried to hurt me but actually helped me: to the lady in the park who didn't want her daughter playing with "nigger" children, to all the gang members that sweated me over the years, to the racist teachers, to the folks who introduced me to drugs, to my father, to my drunken grandmother—and to all the "help" along the way. I thank all the people who wished me well: Mrs. Kendall, Mrs. Briggs, my high school guidance counselor, and science teacher. Finally, I thank my mother for all the sacrifices she made and continues to make for me and my brother Raphael. I also thank God for my destiny.

2

What Is Black Enough?

MARIA

Having grown up in a largely white suburb as a child of middle-class privilege, Maria explores issues of identity in the face of racial isolation and affirmative action's corrosive effect on pride in achievement. With few opportunities for friendships with other blacks, finding a place in the black social world at college proved difficult. Now from her perspective as a graduate student, Maria raises questions about her own and others' motivations for interracial friendships and dating as sometimes being based in interracial "thrill seeking" or other complicated needs. The opportunity in college to take courses on African literature and joining a mentored support group for future black academics has proved to be an entry point into a new and positive identity as a black intellectual.

When did I know that I was black? You might think that someone like me, one of the few black kids in my neighborhood and frequently the only black student in my classes at school, would be extremely conscious of the obvious difference between myself and my white peers. You would think that even if I was not aware of the contrast, someone must have certainly pointed it out to me. Not that I walked around completely oblivious to my racial identity, but I had little anxiety about my light brown skin and head full of curly hair. Growing up in suburbia, I was just another happy, self-confident, smart kid, who happened to be black.

I remember applying to college as a pivotal moment that forced me to think about my status as a black person in a white world. The application process was as confusing as it was empowering and self-defining. On the encouragement of my high school teachers and like most of my friends, I had chosen to apply to a good portion of the Ivy League, a few women's colleges, and the state university. Like everyone else, I listed my extracurriculars, collected the required number of recommendations, neatly typed out the informational part of the application, checked all the appropriate boxes, including that marked "Race or national origin." I sent them off on January 1. Notification came early from the state university—I had been named one of the top 15 black applicants in the state, given a full scholarship and entrance into their high honors program. On a single day in early April, I pulled six other acceptance letters out of my mailbox. The rumor of my success spread quickly to my classmates and teachers—I was congratulated by everybody the next day at school. Not used to such attention, I allowed myself an uncharacteristic feeling of pride—until, I heard a classmate say, "She only got in because she's black."

Ironically, the essay that I had written to gain entrance to all of these prestigious places had been my first written attempt at working out my feelings about being a successful black student, who had enjoyed all the advantages of an upbringing in a middle-class, suburban, mostly white community. Just as I was ready and willing to think about these very personal issues, I was shocked and threatened by my (former) friend's use of my racial status as an excuse for my success. Having checked the African American box on all of my applications and realizing that doing so meant putting myself in a different and "special" category in the eyes of admissions officers, I had done some very speculative thinking in my essay about how weird and complicated this distinction seemed to me. Having not had any personal experiences that I thought merited special consideration or treatment by an admissions committee, I tried to write something provocative about how I saw myself as a person with a particular perspective, one somehow conversant between black and white. But, while the essay showed promise as the beginning of a theoretical understanding of my somewhat unusual situation, it was of no real use in this emotionally fraught circumstance. Called upon to answer such a charge, I had to not only defend my intellect, rehearse my accomplishments, and point to demographics but also work through a sudden surge of self-doubt that I had never experienced before.

Soul-piercing questions confronted me for the first time as a result of this snide remark: Was my success only a result of some kind of quota or affirmative action? Is this what being smart, black, and a woman was going to mean? Did my peers, application committees, the world at large, really see me as black first and intelligent, ambitious and compelling second? Was my classmate, in what I will assume was a jealous reaction, actually voicing a latent fear of my own? Time has shown that these questions, though surfacing here for the first time, will be with me forever. While at the time I did not think of extending gratitude to this classmate for voicing her opinion (within my earshot), I am now oddly grateful that she provided me with an experience that forced me to undertake more seriously a critical investigation of myself—past and present.

This incident—because of its marked difference from other more typical moments of a kind of "racial awareness"—oddly characterizes my pre-high school racial experiences. Although I'm making a broad generalization, I would say that most minorities have had to negotiate situations in which race was called upon not as a justification for success, but rather as a reason or cause of failure. While even then I was not naive enough to believe that my small northeastern hometown was an oasis free from prejudice and racism, as far as I knew, I had not been singled out racially for good or ill. From early on in my schooling, my categorization as "smart" seemed to supersede and almost erase any other label, of race or class, that I could personify. As a young girl, I was able to take advantage of the economic and educational gains that my parents and their generation of my extended family had made. Their hard work, coupled with opportunities I now know were gained through affirmative action, had elevated them into the middle class; economic well-being allowed them a good deal of social mobility. I had not yet experienced the potential negative side of this— the suspicion such mobility could engender. Up until that point, I had understood my own and my family's success as something overwhelmingly good, purely a result of hard work and ambition. It hadn't ever crossed my mind that other people could think otherwise and complicate or compromise my perception of myself or my family.

My childhood was surrounded by family members who worked extremely hard to rise above prejudicial laws and customs. Expressing "racial pride" through their values and standard of behavior as good, ambitious people, they benefited and contributed to the growing concern for black civil rights on a personal and local level. My parents and aunts and uncles were responsible for continually breaking down stereotypes as they became the first members of our family to graduate from college and among the first blacks to have prominent positions in our community and state. As I grew up, I followed their example, without really understanding how hard they had fought for their own accomplishments in the hope of providing opportunities for others.

"We were poor, but we didn't know it": This is how my mother describes her own childhood in what is known as the "West Side" of our hometown. A neighborhood of immigrants in the 1940s to 1960s, the West Side at that time was probably the most "multicultural" neighborhood our town has known—residents included Polish, Irish, Italian, and Portuguese immigrants. My mother and her three brothers grew up in a neighborhood full of other people who were just as "ethnic" as they were; the fact that they were black seemed to mean more to those outside of the neighborhood than within it. My mother's family had a reputation of being hard-working and ambitious; only outside of the community (during the racially volatile 1950s and 1960s) were my uncles harassed and wrongly accused of juvenile delinquency (this is ironic because one later became a high-ranking official in the state's division of criminal justice).

Although my grandfather died before I was born, I remember my grandmother as an extremely kind woman who was very interested in teaching me the proper way to behave and conduct myself. She and my grandfather clearly emphasized the same with my mother and her siblings; proper behavior, a sense of responsibility to self and society, and education were the keys to success in their eyes.

Despite what my mother was taught at home, she, like many others, was judged not on her own merits but according to the standards of the contemporary racial climate. Even though she was clearly an above-average student, active in the high school marching band and school government, her guidance counselor told her that she "wasn't college material." While the logic behind this perverse advice was never elaborated, my mother attributes it to prejudice; she always invokes this incident as ironic inspiration when she speaks about her many subsequent professional accomplishments. Also, despite her counselor's misguided advice, my mother went to nursing school and worked as a psychiatric nurse until she married my father. Her only stint as a housewife was during the Vietnam War when she and my father (who had enlisted in the Air Force) were posted to England. After my parents returned from England and had me, my mother made a major career change and went to the state police academy to become the second black state policewoman in my state. The risks she took to achieve all that she has were both professional and personal. When I was in 1st and 2nd grade, my mother was working undercover in the narcotics and organized crime divisions of the state police. Needless to say, I wasn't really aware of what she was doing, although I knew that she was a "cop" from her car and our frequent visits to the state police barracks. Although she left the state police in the late 1970s, she went on to make two other career changes: She became the first woman and first black detective for the state's division of criminal justice and, after early retirement, is now my state's only black woman licensed private detective.

More impressive than the actual accomplishments on her resume is the way in which my mother taught me the positive value of risk. While she was making all of these career changes, redefining herself and the institutions which she integrated as a woman or a black, she seemed unflappable. Obviously, my mom was very busy when I was small, but I have absolutely no memories of an "absent" mom—she seemed to balance her professional and personal life with ease. As I've matured, I've come to realize that each step was much more of a trial than she let on, especially from the humorous yet horrific tales she tells of sexism in the state police. Because I am now aware of her experiences, I admire her resolve and self-confidence all the more. She showed me by example that I could aspire to anything—that she expected me to work hard and fully commit myself to whatever it was that I decided to do was obvious.

"By example" is perhaps an even better way to describe how I have learned from my father, as he is a man of few words. Never didactic, exceedingly humble, my father taught me lessons of pride and generosity by example. My father came from an educational and economic background similar to that of my mother, but went about his education and career advancement differently. In contrast to my mother's family, my father's family of five (my grandmother was a single, working mother after my grandfather died when my dad was a teenager), knew that they were poor. Growing up in a predominantly black neighborhood, my father was much more aware of his family's and community's economic want—he went to work immediately after graduating from high school. Though obviously important, education beyond high school was more of a luxury for my father. My uncle, my father's younger brother by 10 years, was the first four-year college graduate in the family; ironically, he and my father were in college at the same time—my uncle going straight from high school and my father in night school after serving in the Air Force. Starting first in community college and then enrolling in four-year university, my father worked and went to school for 12 years before he was awarded his bachelor's degree in the early 1980s.

One of my earliest memories, probably from when I was about 6 or so, is of him teaching me by example his unbelievable perseverance in securing an education. Waking up to get a drink of water in the middle of the night, I followed the shadows cast by a light in the kitchen down the hallway and remember seeing him, bleary-eyed, sitting at the head of the table surrounded by books and papers. I got my drink and then climbed into his lap and asked him what he was doing. He told me that he was going to college. At the time I didn't understand the kind of discipline and tenacity that years of late nights like this demanded. Now, as I will effectively be getting paid to go to graduate school and pursue my studies in relative comfort and ease, I can grasp the true nature of his accomplishment. My father's late nights helped him to earn associate's and bachelor's degrees, enabling him to advance from labor to midmanagement within the pharmaceutical company where he's worked for the last 30 years. He never told me outright the importance of education, never was explicit about the economic opportunity to be gained, but he has always communicated to me the pride it has instilled in him.

Since I'm an only child, my parents and I are very close. They are role models for me not only in terms of their accomplishments but mostly because of their attitudes toward life and who they are as people. My mother has an amazing sense of humor—she loves making people smile and laughing herself. At this point in my life, when graduate school and pursuit of my own professional accomplishments seem at times overwhelming, she is a much needed outside advisor, always ready to put my anxieties in perspective. She is one of the few people who is nearly always successful at getting me to lighten up, as I have a tendency toward being stern and serious, probably as a result of too much time spent with books. She and my father are my constant cheerleaders and even though they do not know much about the literature that I plan to study or the demands of an academic profession, I know I can always count on them to tell me that I am smart and that they are proud of me.

My mom is very invested in our family, not just the three of us, but our extended family also. She is very close to all of her brothers and spends a great deal of time encouraging and supporting everyone in their pursuits. She has recently taken an interest in a part of our family heritage that we have not really explored, our Native American ancestors. Through her work and research, we have recovered a part of the family lost years ago through a family feud and (unrelated) death of a grandparent. She is now active with the Tribal Council and in local Native American politics generally. My mom is a generous spirit, selfish only in that she has difficulty in allowing others to be concerned about and care for her.

My father's quietness contrasts with my mother's boisterousness. My mother describes him as a man of few words—even though she and I tease him about having absolutely no common sense and being in a kind of world of his own, he often surprises both of us with the accuracy of his observations of people and situations. He often pretends not to hear everything, but we suspect that he watches and analyzes constantly. Wise even when being silly, he teaches me things that are difficult to articulate, from pride of self to pride of education. Even though he says little about himself directly, his funny stories from his childhood, which he calls "Little Butchie Stories," dramatize his uncanny ability to get out of any compromising situation at school or at home. These often "tall" tales taught me about his true resourcefulness and practical intelligence and, most of all, about appreciating what you have, even when you don't have much. These days, even though my parents are busy—mom spends a lot of time running around to various meetings for reunion committees, tribal business, or business of her own and my father spends a lot of time at the golf course—I really enjoy the time I spend with them as we get to know each other as adults.

For me, becoming an adult has meant, primarily, thinking very seriously about myself as a black woman. In some ways, in order to become "me," I had to find a definition or version of "blackness" that I felt comfortable with and that seemed to belong to me. During my childhood, blackness was not something that I thought about with any rigor. My family moved from the West Side, where my mother had grown up, to a middle-class, nearly all-white neighborhood when I was in kindergarten. Not consciously trying to remove me from what little "black culture" our town had to offer, they nevertheless wholly changed the environment in which I would grow up. I was one of a handful of minority kids in my school and one of four black kids in my neighborhood.

From kindergarten onward, and especially once schools began tracking students according to ability, I was the only black and frequently the only minority in all of my classes.

My peers and I noticed that we were of different races during my early school years; but, for whatever reason, the difference really became an issue only twice a year—Martin Luther King Jr.'s birthday and the month of February—Black History Month. Each year, I approached the observance of this holiday and month-long celebration of black achievement with a curious mixture of pride and anxiety. Black History Month, by its very nature as a 28-day opportunity to think about racial issues, caused me less stress than Martin Luther King Jr.'s birthday. A single day during which I felt a pressure to summon up racial pride and present it to my class like "show and tell," the King holiday was the one day when I both shrunk from and gladly absorbed the stares of my classmates as the teacher gave her Civil Rights Movement lesson. My parents had given me the information I needed to do justice to any inquiry a grammar school mind might have concerning Martin Luther King Jr., but the pressure of having to emphasize my blackness every January 15th caused me some distress. Every day except January 15th, I was a smart kid, just me. On the 15th, I was black and expected to exhibit or add the "multi" to any classroom discussion of other cultures. Depending on the year, I felt pride or irritation at the task. Apart from this phenomenon, probably experienced by a host of other minority kids, I spent my early school years more concerned about being overweight than black. It was during this time that I first heard my white friends say things like, "You're not really black . . . , " or "I know you are black but. . . ."—statements or "compliments" that, despite the type of anxiety I experienced in the face of events like Martin Luther King Jr.'s birthday, I had a hard time saying "thank you" to.

In junior high, academic "tracking" predictably (with a few exceptions) translated into social tracking. As it would also happen in high school, the sons and daughters of my hometown's middle and upper-middle class were my classmates and friends. For me, academic prowess provided access into a group that considered itself "cool" and manifested this attitude by being on the tip of 1980s teen culture—we all wore neon clothes, listened to punk and New Wave, skateboarded and religiously watched MTV's precursor, *Friday Night Videos*. Without being at all critical of what some would call my "whitewashing," I unconsciously learned and mastered the unwritten rules of social success in a small, white, suburban environment. I wore the right clothes, listened to the right music, and had easy friendships with girls and boys. All of these things seemed to mean more than being of the "right" race. My racial difference seemed to disappear perhaps too easily until it became an issue with my first boyfriend, Eric.

Though brief in terms of its 4-month duration, my relationship with Eric has taken on a sort of iconic role in my life, not only because he was my first real boyfriend but also because—as I figured out—his attraction for me was partially fueled by our racial difference and the idea that he was transgressing. We were introduced by mutual friends at a skateboard exhibition and dated for about 2 months before we had a conversation whose full implications I only understood years later. One afternoon, as he was giving me a skateboard lesson in a parking lot, he invited me to dinner at a nice restaurant. Up until that point, we had been seeing each other mostly during the day, somewhat on the sly from my parents, who would have disapproved of him not because he was white but older (I was 16; he was in college). Interpreting this invitation to dinner as a step forward in our relationship, I suggested that he pick me up at my house and meet my parents, a gesture that would simultaneously allow me to fulfill an odd 1950s notion of propriety, as well as eliminate the need for some of the creative half-truths I had been telling to explain my whereabouts.

My proposition—a meeting which I anticipated would be a 5-minute hand-shaking exercise and visual check—caused him to snap his head back as he traveled ahead of me down an incline, to bring himself to a full stop and say, "Are you serious?" Of course I was serious and completely confused by his reaction. By way of explanation, he then offered this shocking statement: "If my parents ever met you, they'd completely disown me." Describing his raving racist Italian grandfather who was known to shout at "niggers" when black people drove down his street, Eric explained that his family, especially his mother, would first disbelieve and then firmly denounce a relationship like ours. That I took his family's racism as a personal affront, that I was unable to think (even theoretically) of myself as an anathema, quickly manifested itself on my face. Although I was unable to say anything, my face gave away the fact that I was hurt and shocked. In a consolatory and conciliatory display, he then bravely announced that given the choice between me and his racist family, I would win out—a heart-swelling, gallant gesture that overwhelmed my 16 year-old psyche. Pacified, I continued to skate. In retrospect, it seems preposterous that he was willing to lose his family over a weeks-old love of a 16 year-old girl. But, I was naive at the time and more than happy to have someone make such a grand gesture for me. I think that both he and I were completely unaware of the seriousness of the issue that was confronting us both. He was able to be gallant and I was able to be pacified because both of us were unrealistic.

When the dinner date came a week or so later, Eric gained my parents' approval despite the ubiquitous but fashionable rips in his jeans and his avant-garde footwear. My parents' assent at that point proved somewhat unnecessary; by then, he had decided to move back to his hometown and in with his parents, more than 600 miles away, for financial reasons. We were forced to keep the flame alive through letters—he repeated his pledge to choose me over his family so often that it became a kind of mantra. The almost incessant repetition of this supposed symbol of his devotion and commitment caused me to suspect that for him, dating me was exciting not only because of who I was but also for what I was—a black girl sure to make his entire family nervous and angry. I was very happy with myself when I figured this out and vowed to be on the lookout for seemingly well-intentioned white boys in the future. This was my first indication that, given my circumstances as a black girl in a white environment, dating was going to be difficult. Interracial relationships seemed to be all that was available to me and, as such, would always have to be subject to many levels of approval. I was confronted with the task of finding a nice guy who liked me for who I was more than what I was and whose family was, at the very least, tolerant.

In spite of the vehemence of his theoretical position, Eric's conviction was never tested; the distance, coupled with my adolescent attention span, caused our relationship to end. We have kept in touch since then and recently were in the same city for two years. Soon after I arrived, he came over to inspect my new apartment and, after not seeing me for 4 years, stared at me and said, "I don't know how to say this, but I didn't think that you were so dark." Having spent the summer after college employed at nothing other than sitting by my parents' pool, I had a tan and replied, saucily, "Remember? I'm black." Soon after that, I ran into him on the street and was greeted with, "Hey! It's my Negro friend!" Shocked, dismayed, angry, and finally catching on, I kept walking. He ran after me and nervously apologized. About a year later, we discovered during a phone conversation that we had applied for the same job, which I had gotten. Congratulating me with an audibly trembling voice, he launched into an anti-affirmative action talk that I listened to with too much patience. When he finished, I suggested that a defeatist, self-victimizing attitude like his was a more likely factor in his long and fruitless job search. I defended my credentials for the job, which were more than adequate as it was an entry-level administrative position. I tried very hard to make him understand that affirmative action, if it was a factor here, was not an antiwhite, antimale conspiracy designed to effect a gradual takeover by minorities and women nationwide. I reasoned that certainly I might be benefiting from the policy, but he should understand that its principal benefits weren't designed to serve people like me—a culturally, if not financially, privileged girl from the suburbs. Then I hung up on him.

Before these incidents, I attributed Eric's early actions simply to ignorance. I had recognized that our relationship was the first time that he had personally confronted the racism within his own family. Not that I had wanted to be his or anyone else's test case or interracial-dating experiment; I had nevertheless withheld judging him, allowing a certain slack for inexperience. While I had decided not to take his inexperience personally, he had let his naiveté infect our relationship on a personal level. Now more mature myself and disappointed by Eric's lack of progress, I weighed the cumulative effect of these more recent incidents and decided that I had neither the time nor patience to continue our friendship. Since I have moved far away from the city where he now lives, the tapering off of our friendship has been easy and has probably gone unnoticed by him. We do not communicate anymore, with the exception of a seasonal Christmas card exchange. Of course I cannot say that my initial interest in him was free of racial curiosity; however, because of the environment in which I had grown up and my interaction with relatives and friends of my parents who had married interracially, the novelty of the situation played itself out quickly. Even though our long friendship indicates that we had more in common than mutual objectification, my memories of him and us unfortunately have been forever altered.

The frenzied social atmosphere of high school helped me to get over Eric. Our relationship—partially because it had taken place during summer vacation—was a hot topic for the high school rumor mill. My peers gossiped about the difference in our ages and his status as an "outsider" instead of our racial difference, emphasizing the sexual innuendo that dating an older guy automatically engenders. Looking back, I think that I was the only one even to point out to my peers that our relationship was interracial. I don't know whether they did not think about it, talked about it when I was not around, thought that it truly did not matter, or if they simply expected me to date a white man (given the prospective pool from which we all dated). In any case, the rumors disappeared as soon as they appeared. This particular relationship, coming as it did when I was just 16, has made me cautious about dating men who do not, in some way, signal to me that they are interested in me and not what they think I represent. In the years since, I have dated men from many different backgrounds and have found that as my own sense of self emerged, I have had less and less trouble discerning the well-intentioned from those looking for a "racial thrill."

Despite the hardship of dealing with comments like, "She only got in because she's black," or "She's not really black," by the time I was in high school, I had frankly gotten used to being one of the few minorities in my social and educational group. Although I was aware of and concerned about the identity questions that this situation raised, nevertheless I had grown comfortable. Socializing outside of my white suburb meant renegotiating questions that my previous environment had effectively shelved. A series of incidents during my college years caused me to question the "comfort" and familiarity of my social world and academic pursuits. I have my college's housing policy of random placement to thank for installing me in a freshman-year rooming situation which would bring all of those issues to the fore.

I was assigned to share a triple with Angela, a black woman from Detroit, and Fay, a white woman from the northeast. I was the first to arrive in our room; Fay came next. She was from a small, middle-class town like myself—we quickly became good friends. My relationship with Angela proceeded much differently. Although I attributed the incredible tension between myself and Angela to the insularity of *her* upbringing, I see now that *my own* insularity was equally at fault. From an urban environment, educated in single-sex Catholic schools her whole life, Angela was different from any of the black people I knew (most of whom were my relatives). I had almost no contact with blacks from big cities (or all-black neighborhoods), honestly did not know that there were many black Catholics, and had no idea what a shock living on a coed dormitory floor would be to someone who had gone to an all-girls school, graduating with a class of less than 20. I'm sure that Angela found me as much of a curiosity. Instead of learning from each other, we clashed almost immediately.

Throughout my freshman fall, the African American society duly extended information and invitations to all incoming black students. Even before I arrived on campus, I had been invited to barbecues, study groups, mixers, dances, offered a "Big Sister," and information on the procedure for moving into the all-black affinity house (after my first year). Believing that my experiences were vastly different from "theirs" and that "they" could easily look at me and ask that haunting question, "Is she black enough?" I ignored nearly all of their copious mailings. Given the somewhat limited number of social alternatives and options on the campus, during the first term I found myself, like most of my peers, hanging out in the fraternity basements every Wednesday, Friday, and Saturday. Angela, gladly accepting the support I disdained, became a regular member of the African American society and attended all of their mostly all-black social events. While the difference in our choices does not sum up the whole spectrum of our conflict, it does provide a useful symbol. We had all of the normal disagreements roommates have over levels of cleanliness and noise, but our complaints eventually became more personal.

In my eyes, Angela's mere existence in the bunk below me heightened my anxiety and feelings of inadequacy because she did all of the "black things" on campus and had her identity continually reinforced by the Afro-Am society. I reacted to her threat by treating her badly: Mean and inconsiderate, I flaunted all of my middle-class, suburban pretensions and privileges. I think that Angela was both disdainful and jealous of me; she perceived me as an assimilationist "wannabe" (the actual words she used in a conversation I overheard) as well as someone who was familiar with the strategies that black students must learn in order to negotiate educational and social environments like that of our college. The resident advisor for our floor in the dorm tried to counsel each of us after we went to him individually with vague complaints about "not liking each other" and "simply not being able to get along," charges that were just symptoms of the larger problem. After this talk with the advisor, Angela and I managed the rest of the year with an awkward politeness that was at times no better or different than the earlier stress. We never really resolved or even verbally recognized the true source of the tension between us. Needless to say, we did not room together again and saw each other only sporadically for the next few years. During our senior year, Angela and I did socialize, as we had mutual friends (my frat-girl stint lasting only that first term). It was only then that we were really able to talk to each other and be considerate of each other, a sign of respect for our differences and our sameness.

A further source of tension between myself and Angela, or between myself and other blacks, has been the lightness of my skin. A product of black, Native American, and Portuguese (via Cape Verde) ancestry, my family and I have fair skin and, often, hazel or light brown eyes and wavy black or brown hair. It has taken a long time for me to be comfortable with a question I receive constantly—"Where are you from?" It is usually obvious that the person asking the question is not interested in the northeastern inflection in my accent, but in my racial makeup. Sometimes, if I were feeling saucy, I'd confront the questioner, saying, "What do you mean?" Recently someone was very straightforward and simply asked, "Which of your parents is white?" I realize now that my annoyance stems partially from my discomfort at not being easily recognizable, of being thought not black enough both internally and externally. Sometimes I ask people to guess what they think I am—I've had responses from Turkish to Swedish (this was obviously a joke!). Being a kind of racial chameleon has some anxieties and advantages; I used to think that I could be inside or outside of a group (of blacks, Native Americans, etc.) almost at will. As I get older, I realize the psychological as well as political danger of such thinking. Such notions left me more often feeling outside of these groups than inside them and merely heightened my anxiety about belonging.

College and university divestment from South Africa was a burning topic on many campuses when I started college. Filled with the stereotypical yet heartfelt fervor of political protest that often infects college students, I soon found myself occupying administration buildings, storming trustee meetings, and organizing a protest against a visiting South African government official. During this time, I also took an African and African American studies class, embarrassingly called "Introduction to Africa," in which the professor taught West African and South African literature alongside more historical, political, and sociological readings. Totally captivated by the South African literature section of the class, I asked my South African friends to recommend other books which I then read voraciously. Though I did not recognize it until a few years later, my interest in South African literature and Apartheid politics in some ways helped me to work through some of the racial anxiety I felt. Of course, I was not consciously involved in anti-Apartheid protest as a form of personal therapy, but the ability to be vociferous about injustice, to educate myself about a society in which there were few racial arbiters, was a way for me to approach and evaluate racial issues from a distance that I needed at the time. The idea of linking my academic work to contemporary issues, infusing a political focus in my work, not only appealed to me but also soon became the obvious and only direction in which I wanted my studies to go.

I received a fellowship in my sophomore year that enabled me to pursue this new interest in African literature. Offered to five minority students a year who were interested in graduate school and academic careers, the fellowship was designed to foster a close mentoring relationship between each student and a faculty member of his or her choosing. The research we did was to serve as an example of the type of independent work that would be required for a senior thesis and graduate school. Apart from the administrative advantages it provided (financial aid, help in finding mentors), the program gave us a forum in which to explore any issues relevant to us as future minority academics or to us individually.

The support of the program administrators and the group of students with whom I went through the program was absolutely essential to my academic success and personal growth at college. Each week we gleefully retreated to a conference room in the library to swap stories, to gripe, to celebrate someone's success—we consciously set out to create an environment in which we all felt comfortable and able to discuss anything no matter how controversial. For the first time, I had found a group of other minority students who shared many of my personal and academic concerns and anxieties. Because we came from different disciplines (all within the humanities) but were interested in many of the same issues (for example, revisionist readings of literature, history, anthropology with a race, class and/or gender focus), we had a common personal and academic vocabulary. As my academic focus narrowed in on issues that were not being addressed by any classes in the somewhat traditional English department in which I was a major, the encouragement I received from my mentors was a critical factor in getting me through a long project whose issues I'm still exploring today. A center of emotional support and academic encouragement, the program helped me to find a way to begin reconciling identity issues with my academic and professional aspirations.

The freedom and support that I experienced in this program eased the shift in my academic focus, from classics (I had studied Latin in high school) to English literature. I immersed myself in literature while in London on the English department's foreign study program during my junior year. London not only gave me a respite from Latin but also opened my eyes to the experiences and resistance projects of the huge number of people from former British colonies living in London. While in London, I decided to spend my senior year writing a thesis on black South African women's writing. Although my classics professors realized that this choice was analogous to cutting the cord, they were supportive of me anyway and encouraged me to pursue an advanced degree, regardless of the discipline. Graduate school seemed like my obvious next step. In spite of my excitement and ultimate commitment to academia as a career, I decided to take some time off and work for a few years.

I spent two intense and rewarding years working in museum education in San Francisco. After spending the majority of my formative years in suburbia and my college years in mostly rural surroundings, complaining frequently about isolation, political conservatism, and racial polarization, I felt great relief upon arrival there. While it seems such a cliché to describe the city as multicultural, I cannot emphasize how much joy that term connotes. I felt in San Francisco the same way I had felt in London—free from the onus of "representing" minority concerns of any kind, unless I chose to. Because San Francisco is a city that has three minority cultures that together make up a majority, I found my friends and co-workers there to be aware of and well versed in even the subtleties of racial and cultural issues.

As impressive as my resume was, I knew from the beginning that I had been hired at the museum in part because I could serve as a minority "role model" for the students participating in our education programs. As a person of color who had gone to a good college and used my education to do museum work, I was to serve as an example. In years past, I would have been very uncomfortable serving as an "example," as I did not feel my person or my experience to be "representative." However, having learned so much about myself by working with other minority scholars in college and students in museums, I felt comfortable representing my own experience as *an* example, not *the* example. For the first time, this expectation did not make me uncomfortable; my experiences in college and the comfort I felt in San Francisco had given me a useful combination of self-confidence and self-awareness that I was happy to share.

Even though I was learning a lot about American and Mexican art, teaching techniques, counseling, and administrative skills at my museum jobs, I missed the sort of passion that I had invested in my academic work. After a year of working, I decided to apply to Ph.D. programs in English, hoping to continue the work that I had done as an undergraduate concerning black women writers and their negotiation of politics, gender, and postcoloniality. This time, I had no trepidation about checking various boxes on the application. Anxieties about belonging or being black enough to represent "blackness" do not plague me anymore, now that I understand that "black" is not a monolithic, essentialized category of people with exactly the same, "right" experiences. Worries that I will always be *only* an affirmative action "hire" or "pick," have lessened also, now that I understand how much my family and I have benefited from such programs, whether they concern job opportunities or entrance into the academy. I know that these programs are about opportunity for those with ability, they are not about making race or gender an "excuse."

Fortunately, the transition from the working world to the academy was eased at a conference that I attended this summer. More like a reunion than a conference, the meeting brought together minority students from all over the country who were awarded the fellowship I received as an undergraduate (the program is administered at 20 or so colleges and universities nationwide). For three days, I listened intently as my peers discussed everything from the work they were doing to how frustrating it was (once again) to be asked to deliver the black, Latino, or Native American perspective in a seminar. Talking with this group of students, hearing the seriousness with which they take their work and the critical perspectives they bring to an analysis of their place and race within the academy was intimidating, yet unbelievably empowering for me. I left the conference hoping that I am prepared mentally, if not academically, to continue the process of thinking about race and representation, both personally and professionally.

3

Living between the Lines

ALESSANDRO

Having come to the United States from Puerto Rico at age 11, Alessandro describes the struggle to find an identity that is true to his social, cultural, and racial background as the child of Dominican parents. His mother insisted that he maintain a strong Latino identity while also succeeding in the English-speaking world. As a top student in junior high school, he was selected to attend an elite prep school where he felt out of place and intimidated by the easy privilege of his classmates. He survived with the help of a best friend, another scholarship student from his hometown. At college he realized for the first time that he had only perceived himself as Latino, but that in America he was perceived as black first—even by other Latinos. Exploring his dark-skinned identity, he joined a black fraternity and began to come to terms with the ambiguity of being a black Latino in the world he was determined to succeed in. This essay was written in Alessandro's sophomore year.

My story begins in the rural towns of the Dominican Republic, where both my parents were born. Raised in households of land-owning farmers, my mom and dad learned at an early age that their manual labor was of greater value to their parents than their brain power. With the little money they earned they bought their own clothes and the books they needed to finish the 8th grade. As my parents grew older and stronger, their parents increased their responsibilities both at home and in the fields. The first priority was to keep the family well fed and cared for financially; any profits made from selling the bananas and pla-tanos went to buy other necessary food and supplies. With the help of their children's free labor, my grandparents were able to increase their yield enough to break even or even to make a profit each month. Knowing how important their labor was to their family's economic survival and that they would need their own money to build futures for themselves, my mom and dad decided to end their schooling and take jobs during the school day, while still working for their parents. My mom sewed dresses to earn enough money for a plane ticket so she could move to Puerto Rico. My dad worked as a field hand for another farmer when he wasn't helping his father, thereby saving enough money to buy a plane ticket so he, too, could settle in an apartment in Puerto Rico.

Not until both were settled in their new jobs did my mom and dad have the chance to meet and marry. With the help of a cousin who lived on the island, my mom had found a job as a personal nurse to an old woman. Living in the woman's home, my mom was provided for and was able to send half of her paycheck to her parents. As a mechanic's apprentice, my dad learned his way in and out of an airplane's engine. Using his new vocation, he earned enough money to settle in a small apartment and send a quarter of his paycheck to his parents. My parents were not young and innocent when they met; my mom was almost 30 and my dad was in his late 30s. My parents had learned the meaning of working for what little they owned. When they married, my parents knew they would have to stop sending money back home in order to create their own home in Puerto Rico. Both my mom and dad worked long hours before they had enough to pay for the down payment on a newly built house, where they would raise four children.

My pleasant experiences of a happy childhood in Puerto Rico were interrupted when my father lost his job and had to move to the States. At the age of 18, my oldest brother, Ricardo, left to go away to school. Finally, my mom, my sister Juanita, my brother Jose, and I emigrated from Puerto Rico to New Haven, Connecticut, in order to keep the family together. At 11 years of age, I was excited to see a brand new place, but I never realized then that I would not be able to return to my homeland.

As the oldest child, Ricardo had the responsibility of opening up the roads of opportunity for his three siblings, especially for my sister. Ricardo was only a year older than Juanita, 5 years older than Jose, and 7 years older than I. He entered an enormous state university without even knowing how to communicate in English. Living in New Haven was a tough transition for all of us. Although we had a couple of family members in New Haven, we were largely on our own trying to settle in the unknown, unfriendly environment of a small city in a foreign culture.

Ricardo enrolled in the army reserve and worked at a fast food restaurant to pay for his college tuition. At 19, he tackled the English language, the first year of college, a job, and the army. After 5 years, he was the first in our family not only to graduate from college but also to graduate with honors. From Ricardo, I learned that I had a long and arduous road ahead in school, but that I could make it as long as I put all my efforts into what I wanted to accomplish.

Juanita graduated from her high school in the top of the class, as everyone in my family must do, and entered college. When Juanita began to attend college, my mom placed her in Ricardo's hands, expecting him to protect and take care of her. I still remember attending their college graduation where my mom's tears showed how proud she was of her children. In school, her children were expected to be the best in their class; no report card could be brought home unless it was straight As. We knew that receiving anything less than an A meant a whipping with the thick leather belt. When my mom punished me, the red imprints of the belt flared on my legs for hours. In my entire elementary school career, I received only one B on a math test in 2nd grade and one C on a science test in 5th grade. I knew what I had coming to me if I came home with a C on my test, but I never received a whipping for being lazy and not doing my work in school. I graduated at the top of my class every year.

The one rule we always were punished for was disobeying our parents. The only reasons my brothers and I could leave the house were to attend Catholic school, go to church, play baseball, or deliver newspapers. My mother's strict rules extended to our social lives, or what little social activity we were allowed to have. My brothers and I had friends in school and on the baseball teams, but interactions with the opposite sex were essentially forbidden. My brothers delivered newspapers around town and they were able to talk to girls then. As for me, I didn't have a relationship with a woman until my sophomore year in college. Although my mom's guidelines for our social development were rather strict, I believe she gave us a strong basis for our own personal moral standards. Therefore, the only relationships we have with members of the opposite sex tend to be extremely personal and serious.

As for my dad, he always provided for our well-being and established a secure place for us to accomplish what we could accomplish, both in Puerto Rico and the United States. Although he never received his high school diploma, my dad has put four children through college. I truly admire him, and although we have never discussed our problems with each other, he has always been a pillar of strength I could hold onto. When I needed courage and confidence, he stood by me and helped me in every way he could, especially when the opportunity to attend prep school came along.

As my father and I drove into the town of Lewisburg, I stared at the picture-perfect snow sparkling in the bright winter sun. The application I had received a month before showed a great lawn on which a group of students from different ethnic and racial backgrounds sat in a circle, books open, and a teacher sitting in the middle of the circle reading to them. This was the picture I had in my mind the day I visited Lewisburg Academy for my final interview. (Lewisburg is not the school's real name; suffice it to say that the school is among the top five prep schools in the nation.) In the brochure, the students were dressed in casual clothes to attend classes, so I thought that I should try to fit into this image.

As my father parked the red '77 Pontiac in the visitors parking spot, I did not even feel a nervous twitch as I slammed the rust-ridden car door. I felt confident in the brand new high tops, blue jeans, and gray sweatshirt I had worn that day to public school. My father wore something similar, except that his jeans where quite faded and worn in places where patches were needed. The receptionist showed us to the waiting room, which looked like the living room of a rather expensive house. Gazing around the room, I marveled at the antique sofas and chairs, the fragile coffee tables, and the gray stone fireplace. I carefully sat down on one of the sofas, afraid that it might break under my weight. As my father and I read the brochures about the prep school, another prospective student walked into the waiting room. He, however, wore a blue coat and tie, khaki pants, and brown leather shoes. I first thought, "Hmm . . . He's overdressed!" But remembering the receptionist's comment, "Hey, your sneakers match my red dress. I should be wearing those," I looked down at my discount sneakers realizing that I was the one wearing the inappropriate clothes. The interview itself seemed short and pointless, as I answered with the same responses I had written on my application. As we drove away from the campus, my father told me that he had answered the questions he understood with the little English he could fragment together. I knew he had tried his best, that he cared so much about my opportunity to get admitted that he would have done everything he could to present me in the best light. After describing his interview, he asked me, "Do you think they will accept you?" Looking at my father's concerned expression, I knew he wanted me to reassure him that he had done his best. I responded solemnly, "I don't know, dad. I don't think I did very well in the interview. But we'll see what kind of letter they send with their decision." I didn't want to disappoint my dad, but I also didn't want to raise his hopes without knowing for certain I had a chance to attend prep school.

When I received the letter of acceptance from Lewisburg, my excitement was overwhelming. Since my parents were not fluent in English, I knew I would be the one handling all the financial, academic, and commuting arrangements. It would be my responsibility to read and translate all the application forms my parents had to sign. I realized that if I decided to go to public school, my parents and I would have had an easier time. Not only was the high school within walking distance from home but also the community and the school were both tightly intertwined with the Latino culture and the Spanish language. I knew that I would definitely have an easier transition going to the public high school. However, I couldn't turn down this opportunity, which had been offered to only one member of my junior high school graduating class. I knew the choice had been made even before I made up my own mind. Such an opportunity for a prep school education was hard to turn down.

Although the prep school owned acres of green land on which stood buildings for every academic subject imaginable, I never felt as safe and as wanted there as I had in the long, three-story public school building that held my classes for inner-city students. As soon as I was accepted to prep school, my junior high teachers and guidance counselor warned me that it would be a tough and challenging environment for me. However, they also encouraged me saying, "Don't worry! If anyone deserves to go to Lewisburg Academy, it's definitely you. Good luck next year!" I arrived on campus as the smartest student from my junior high school, which really did not amount to much in a class full of smart students from all over the country and the world.

The only person who introduced himself to me at the day-student orientation seemed like a good-natured guy. I had no idea then that he would turn out to be my best friend and crucial to my personal growth and success. Looking at the tall, blond, blue-eyed boy who stood before me, I remembered meeting him the day we took the national test required to apply to prep schools. With a warm, welcoming smile he said, "Hey, how are you? Remember me? I'm Ben and this is my grandmother." I smiled back and introduced my parents, quickly explaining that my mom couldn't understand English very well. My dad ventured into a small conversation with Ben's grandmother, who seemed rather patient trying to understand him. Saying good-bye we got into our cars, and I felt relieved; I had survived the first experience with my parents at prep school without any major embarrassments. I promised myself, however, that I would keep social engagements involving the presence of my parents to a minimum.

As I think back, I realize that my family and I lived in two distinctly separate worlds. My city flourished with the Latino culture, Spanish language, and the bonds of community. Over the hill, the town of Lewisburg operated under the guidelines of the American culture, the English language, and a sense of individual success. Remembering my mom's fearful eyes masked under her smiling face, I now understand her feeling helpless in a world she could not comprehend. She did not possess enough English language to express her feelings or concerns. As for my father, he always made a brave attempt at making people understand him. Although he has a thick Spanish accent, I have always been proud of how my dad has been able to take care of his own affairs with little or no help from me or my brothers.

My parents always taught me the importance of speaking in my native tongue. My mom made it clear that we were only to speak Spanish at home. She thought that the only reason we kids spoke English at home was because we spoke of things we didn't want her to understand. I must admit that my brother and I usually did talk explicitly about girls in English, which always kept my mom in the dark. However, she encouraged us to speak Spanish in order to help us retain our culture and heritage. She reminded us every day, "I know you have to learn how to speak English, but don't forget your own language. Remember that you're my sons and that you are Latino. You will be able get more in your life if you are bilingual." Speaking Spanish at home reinforced my Latino identity. Although I spent most of my day in the English-speaking world, when I came home from school at the end of my day to tell my mom about what I had done, I felt reassured to know that I would always be able to return to my own world, no matter what happened in the English-speaking world.

The town of Lewisburg was very different from the city I lived in. In Lewisburg, the streets gleamed with the beauty of spring. The sun barely shone through the trees whose branches spread over the streets, providing a cool shade to those walking on the sidewalk. Green grass covered the front and backyards of the single-family homes. The houses were painted in bright, vivid colors that contrasted with the dull red bricks of the chimneys. The prep school proudly boasted about its Great Lawn and its beautiful fall and spring seasons, which could only be fully appreciated in the New England setting. On the other hand, in the city where I lived, the streets were too dangerous to walk at night. Covered with trash, they wore the nocturnal skid marks from the tires of yet another stolen car. Trees were only seen in the common park across the street from the junior high school. Only narrow driveways divided the houses that still stood on the street; most of the houses on the block had either been boarded up or demolished. The three-family homes that were in good condition were painted in dark, dead colors. But no matter how awful the city was, it was the place I called home, where I yearned to return every night after the school day ended.

From the first day I arrived at Lewisburg, I felt intimidated by the enormous campus, the classes, and even the students. Like every freshman, I was lost in an unknown place in which we were told we either had to swim like the rest of the fish or drown. Prep school was a whole new world for me. The system I had learned in junior high school was simple: To get good grades you behaved in class by not talking to other students and you did your homework. Everything you needed to know to get a good grade would be on the blackboard, and our chairs were all set in rows with the teacher's desk placed at the front so that we could only make eye contact with her. The public school assumption evident in the seating arrangement was that all we needed to know would come from the teacher, so that was the only person we needed to see and the only person we should speak to. In the prep school system, the chairs were set in a semicircle around the room, with the teacher's desk placed at the opening of the semicircle so that everyone could see each other equally. The prep school assumed that we would learn from each others' ideas, so we needed to be able to see and speak to one another.

Waiting for the teacher to come in that first day of prep school, I sat silently, not saying a word to any of my classmates. I had no idea what to say and could only repeat to myself over and over, "I don't belong in this place. Everyone here is smarter than I am. They'll just laugh at me if I speak in my Spanish accent." I was completely intimidated and petrified to know whether my fears would all come true in front of me that morning. As the bell rang, the teacher walked into the room with nothing in her hands but her purse and house keys which she dropped on the desk. I must admit that I was not expecting an African American teacher for English class. She introduced herself as Mrs. Brown and gave us the list of books we would be reading for the term. Then she sighed and said, "Now that I've covered the course, do you think it would be all right if I spent the rest of the period getting to know you?" No one disagreed, and I felt some of the tension diminish. Mrs. Brown was the first teacher I had ever met who wanted to get to know her class. After writing journal entries for her for a year, I knew that she knew me better than any other teacher on campus. After four years, Mrs. Brown knew me well enough to recognize that Lewisburg had been a different experience for me as a Latino day student in a predominantly white prep school than it had been for most students. It was Mrs. Brown who asked me to write about my experience at Lewisburg, which I was happy to do.

During my first year at Lewisburg, I didn't risk taking any high-level courses. Every course on my schedule was carefully picked as the lowest level course I could possibly take. My first term at Lewisburg was the toughest academic transition I had ever experienced. Even when I arrived in the United States and entered the 6th grade, I at least had the confidence that I could do well if I applied myself. At Lewisburg, I saw that hard work did not always pay off. I convinced myself that I obviously had not worked hard enough. In order to do well, I promised myself that academics would be my only priority and everything else, including sports and social life, would have to be accommodated within my academic work schedule. Although my mom didn't approve of me leaving at dawn and returning home well after dusk, she eventually understood that I was trying to work hard and stopped nagging me about not spending enough time at home. I eventually compromised with my mom and decided to stay at home on the weekends when I didn't have any athletic events.

As a sophomore, I thought I finally had a handle on what I needed to do in order to earn good grades. I had never counted on staying up all night writing papers for my English class, but regardless of the length of the paper I would be up all night trying to figure out how to write down what I was thinking about. I became critical of the way I wrote every single sentence. I convinced myself that I couldn't merely write down what came to my head, that I had to make it sound more intelligent or sophisticated by using big words and long sentences in order to sound as intelligent as my classmates. I never thought that my original ideas or word choices were appropriate for any part of my papers. Aware that the teacher might read the paper to the class, I wanted to make sure that I would present the best image of myself in my writing. I was willing to spend an enormous amount of time if it meant handing in a paper that read like the others. Therefore, I literally blocked off the nights of the week I would be writing. But though I had as long as I needed to work on papers, I couldn't avoid the time limits of in-class essays. Every time we were given 45 minutes to write an essay in class, I ended up writing half of what I wanted to say and handing in a fraction of the writing my classmates did. You can't disguise yourself as a smart student when you pass in a paragraph and everyone else in the class has two pages.

Although I was still earning honors in my classes, I never felt that I was doing well enough. There was always someone I knew who was doing better and, in such a competitive environment, I learned to accept not being the best. Since kindergarten, my parents had pushed me to be the very best and stand out from the rest of my classmates. Once I arrived at Lewisburg, I warned my mom, "I don't know how well I'm going to be able to do in prep school." Seeing my worried expression and fearful eyes, my mom hugged me and said, "I know it's a hard school. I just want you to work hard and do well for yourself, not for me."

Once I finally realized that I would push myself just as hard even if another activity took up some of my time, I decided to try out for the baseball team in my junior year. Making the final cut for the junior varsity team turned out to be my first accomplishment outside of the classroom. I felt so proud to have made the team that I didn't even care if I played in the games at all. All I ever wanted was to be part of the team, as being an athlete in prep school meant an increase in popularity and face recognition.

By senior year, I finally knew how to play the academic game and spent more time on campus participating in the activities I wanted to do. I realized that the key to classes included two things: taking classes taught by the teachers with whom you had done well, and simply doing a good job on the first exam or paper. As a senior, I took complete advantage of the system that I knew worked. I had my academics under control, I knew exactly what I had to do in order to get a good grade from each teacher. Even in my senior year, I still had few friends and not many people on campus knew who I was.

As senior spring finally rolled in, I became actively involved with the community service program led by the school's priest. Father P is the most generous man I have ever met. In addition to teaching classes and providing the Catholic services, he cooked and invited people over to eat dinner at his house practically every night. I became involved with his project of prep school students tutoring public junior high school students. The kid I tutored, Mike, had the potential to become a great student, but he found he could have more fun leading his friends into trouble. I still remember the day I met him at the public school gym with all the other junior high kids. Mike called Father P over and pointed at me, saying, "I want him to be my tutor." Mike was an African American kid in the same school system I had come out of 4 years earlier. He had the initiative and drive of a leader, but I wish he would have used that energy and leadership to get his work done and finish his application for admission to Lewisburg. For the first time I had the chance to give back to the community that had helped me survive the Lewisburg experience.

My best friend Ben was at my side throughout prep school. He gave me the courage to meet new people and participate in social events. I always felt awkward around people when he was not with me. Although we were completely different, Ben and I complemented each other. While Ben helped me develop my social skills, I helped him develop his academic skills. We relied on each other to survive throughout the 4 years of academic and social torture we faced at Lewisburg. Ben was the exact opposite of me; he was the all-American boy, 6 feet 2 inches tall, blond hair, blue eyes, and a laid-back attitude about everything. I, on the other hand, was a Latino immigrant with dark skin, black hair, brown eyes, and a serious attitude toward my academic work. Ben had the confidence and charm, and I had the knowledge to back up his smart talk.

No matter how different we seemed together, we had one thing in common: Both day students from the same city, we came from similar economic circumstances. We were definitely not part of the crowd whose parents were doctors or lawyers and Lewisburg alumni. As financial aid students, Ben and I shared a completely different experience from all the boarding students and the other wealthy day students. Although I never fit into the social environment at Lewisburg, I never felt isolated because I had Ben as a friend. Every morning, I woke up at dawn to walk downtown to the bus stop where Ben would be waiting for me. I still remember the early mornings when we stood waiting underneath the small sheltered bus stop as the sun rose over the river. From the time we got on the bus until we left for our first morning class, Ben and I would just talk about everything. Ben told me about his problems living at home with his grandmother, his job at the ice cream parlor, and his social life.

I think I learned everything I knew about girls in high school from Ben. I remember confessing once, "I really like Alicia but I don't even know how to let her know I'm interested." Ben gave me his usual wide smile because he knew how seriously I considered a crush on a new girl. He would always come up with advice. "Why don't you spend some time with her helping her with Spanish class? We can come to the next dance and invite her." I always asked him any questions I had about girls, dating, and sex. I began to develop an interest in girls after Ben began dating. When he told me his stories of taking a girl out to eat, I began to feel jealous because he was experiencing the feelings I only talked about. Everything I thought and talked about regarding dating and women, Ben had the courage to go out and do, even if the girl rejected him. I never had the guts to flirt with a girl I liked, but Ben was comfortable and confident about himself and had the type of personality that made girls laugh and talk with him.

As a poor Latino student, I never felt comfortable in the predominantly white, wealthy environment of Lewisburg. The reason was not only the color of my skin but also the difference in culture. Although I felt isolated from the mainstream community, I never felt a need to look for the support of the school's small Latino and African American community. In the cafeteria, most of the black and Latino students always sat together in one corner of the dining hall. Although I knew some of the minority students, I never separated myself from the larger community. In turn, I think I also distinguished myself as an individual who did not belong to one particular group. The few friends I had were day students who attended the same classes with me. I didn't really trust them enough to tell them everything I was thinking about. Most of the day students knew me because I was the only dark-skinned Latino among them. I felt that Ben was truly the only person who saw past the color of my skin and stopped asking me about how tough it must be for me in a place like Lewisburg. From the first day we took the bus together, Ben wanted to get to know me as the person I had grown to be, not as an immigrant in the United States.

The day students often asked me, "Why are you friends with Ben?" They labeled him as a loser or stupid because he didn't conform to their group standards. Ben never cared about how he dressed, mainly because he had no money to spend on the clothes that were in style. He never seemed to get his academic work done between working nights and weekends and taking care of his grandmother. We were best friends simply because we understood and lived in each other's situations. Knowing that he faced the same problems and hassles made me feel like I was not the only one struggling through my adolescent years. He was the one person I placed my complete trust in. Even if he didn't have all the answers, at least I knew that we would be lost together in the trials of adolescent relationships.

During my 4 years at Lewisburg, I only faced a single blatantly racist episode which pulled my feelings of isolation and intimidation together. I played on the junior varsity football team as a senior and I was one of two dark-skinned linemen. As we lined up two by two, I faced Tony, the only other black lineman. We set up in our three-point stance in front of the tackling sled and waited for the coach's whistle to signal us to push the sled. Before the whistle blew, I heard someone yell, "Here come the *brothers*." At the whistle, I slammed all my anger into the sled as if I was pushing the words back into the guy's mouth. Although I was furious, I went straight to the back of the line. A teammate came up to me after practice and said, "I told him that you weren't black but that you were Hispanic. And he said, 'I guess I should have called him a spic, huh!'" Although I had been called "nigger" on two occasions by strangers, I had never experienced racism from people I felt I was a part of, such as my teammates. I never told anyone except Ben about the incident and I never faced the teammate who made the comment. After that, I saw the campus with a new perspective; I knew I couldn't trust everyone in the so-called "multicultural community" of the prep school.

During the winter break of my sophomore year, my older brother Jose and I shared our experiences in prep school with each other. Jose and I shared a bedroom when he was home from school, and as we lay in our beds, I innocently asked him, "How is school going?" We had never really talked to each other about the one thing we shared in common, prep school. As we began to talk, I felt a sense of relief as he began opening up to me. With tears in my eyes, I told him how hard it was for me to do well in school, how I had no idea how to get a girl to like me, and how lonely I felt with all my siblings away at school. He never saw the tears roll out of my eyes in the darkness, but he knew how I felt. We shared all of our experiences, fears, and expectations, as if trying to get everything we had been holding back off our chests. He told me about his first girlfriend, how lonely he felt in school without me and our family, and how he never knew how to really talk to me when I was young. Throughout the winter break, my brother and I spoke late into the night, trying to catch up with each other's lives. We had missed out on too much in a year and a half away from each other. During that winter break, I shared and learned more from my brother than ever before with any other member of my family.

Therefore, when the time came to choose what college I would attend, I decided I would not let the opportunity to be with my brother pass me by. I had the chance to get a good education anywhere, but I only had one brother from whom I could learn about myself and spend time together for what could be the last carefree years of our lives. Although it took me some time to adjust to the college environment, I finally got my goals straight with my brother at my side.

At the start of my freshman fall, I found it hard to make friends, so I immersed myself in the college's Latino community in order to meet people. I ended up learning more about myself than about other people and to proudly define who I am. During the first term, I joined the Latino Theater Group organized and run by other Latino students. After the first meeting of the group, I was cast in the role of a street-wise, right-hand man to the main character, Ernesto, for whom the play was named. A week before opening night, April, the student who founded the group and was producing the play, came to see a rehearsal. After watching the first scene, she made us all stop and sit down for what turned out to be the talk that made me fully recognize who I am.

"Do you all realize what this play is about? Have you thought about the issues this play addresses?" she asked.

April looked each one of us in the eyes. Silence filled the auditorium. I had never stopped to think at all about what the play meant.

"I just want you all to know that this play is about you and me. This play talks about the things that haunt our Latino community at home and here at school. We all know what they are . . . or do we?"

I still had no idea what to say. I only felt guilty for not taking the play seriously.

"Ernesto shows the problems within the Latino community. Ernesto deals with an issue we all hate to talk about and even think about, but one that we all have to deal with. Ernesto talks about the issue of skin color in our own community." April continued to stare into our lowered gazes. "Ernesto speaks about what it means to be black in the Latino community, and how we ourselves are ashamed of our own African roots. Do you all even realize that we have a black Latino in our cast?" April looked at me and I stared back at her. Never had I even heard those two words together: black and Latino. Until April said it, I had never recognized the color of my skin as being part of my identity. I looked around and realized that I was the only black Latino on stage in the auditorium and, with the exception of my own brother, on the campus.

After April's final question the whole cast fell silent, and I knew I had to break the silence. "I guess I've never thought of myself as a black Latino. When I was young, my mom always took my brother and me to the barber to get our monthly haircuts. She always said that we looked better with short hair and that way we wouldn't have to deal with our Afros," I said. Since I was a young child, my mother raised us to believe that we were Latino above everything else. She never mentioned the fact that two of her children were light skinned and two were dark skinned. Skin color had never been an issue when I lived on a Caribbean island. Until I reached the United States, and particularly college, I was not aware of the politics of skin color. Even in the Latino organization and community, I noticed I was the only dark-skinned male in the group. I didn't quite fit in the Latino community that was supposed to be a support group for me. The only other person in the Latino community at college who lived and understood what I experienced every day was my own brother.

As I began to meet students outside of the Latino circle, I found the friends who have given me the confidence and the courage to go after what I wanted. When I joined a black fraternity, I found friends who pushed me to my limits but stood by me at all times. The brothers of the fraternity made me see myself in a new light. One night, a brother asked me to stop by his room to talk. As he walked up and down the room, he just smiled. "Have you ever looked at yourself, I mean really looked at who you are?" he asked. I just stood quiet because

I didn't know how to respond. He said, "Look at yourself. You are a Latino man at one of the best colleges in the country. You have a good GPA, you are doing a sport, and you have a job. Not many people can do all that at this place." I guess I have always done whatever it took to make it. In prep school, I had to stay home in order to keep focused on my academics and avoid the elitist attitudes of the students. In college, I had to focus on academics by keeping myself busy in different areas of work and study. I simply stared at him blankly. He realized he had not gotten his point across, and said, "I guess I'm going to have to break this down for you. You have the height, the body, the face, and the mind to get anything you want on this campus. You have done it in class and on the field. And the only thing that's stopping you from going after women is your self-confidence. I'm here to tell you that just by looking at you, there is nothing that can stop you. When you realize that for yourself, you will understand what I have said." I left his room with a silly grin on my face. I knew I had received good news about how others perceived me, but I had no idea what to do with it. My first instinct was to run and tell my friends, but my friends might have thought I was incredibly conceited. "He's so full of himself," they would have said. And that's exactly how I felt. I felt full of my "*self*." That brother made me step out of my body, look at, and judge myself. As a friend and a brother, what did I have to offer? I had more than I had ever imagined.

As I look back, I now know that I stood in between the black fraternity and the Latino community. My worst fear came true: I was not part of any one group and never will be. As a black Latino on a small campus, I found a way to define and redefine my identity by the perspectives of both the African American and Latino communities. In my journey, I followed the voices that helped me reevaluate myself. Through those voices, I saw another piece of my "self," another piece of what it means to be a black Latino. I just hope I can be a new voice for those who live between the lines.

4

I Reconcile the Irreconcilable

ROB

This 20-year-old African American describes his determination to be a leader of men. The death of Rob's father when Rob was 8 led his mother to relocate the family to the South, where she had grown up and would pursue a medical residency. Concerned about the lack of male influence in her son's life, she introduced Rob to a number of institutions that were predominantly white and predominantly—or entirely—male: a military academy's summer camp; the Boy Scouts; a prep school. The author followed the pattern, joining a fraternity when he entered college. Active and successful in student government at college, Rob now has his eye on the presidency of the student body as he seeks to reconcile within himself those "seemingly contradictory experiences and paradoxes of race and privilege, disadvantage and advantage."

One of my first memories is my father teaching me how to spell my last name; "D-A-N-F-O-R-T-H," he would say over and over again, and I would repeat the letters until I had memorized them. My last name held a fascination for me. It is sufficiently rare so that I have never met a Danforth who was not in my family. I also was struck by the way that my family used our name; when they spoke it they always changed their tone, as if it was the most special word in the English language. Members of my family have always carried themselves with a certain sense of arrogance, and I do not mean this in a bad light. I have found that America's most successful blacks are rarely modest. Arrogance or cockiness is used as a sort of drug to combat the sense of inherent inferiority that America places upon blacks. In my experience as a black person who deals in the white world, all of my peers who have demonstrated the so-called virtues of modesty and humility have, in almost every case, failed to achieve their desired goals.

From what my relatives tell me, my grandfather was an arrogant man. He was born in North Carolina into a family of landownership that could also read and write. His father had attended college, graduating sometime before 1920. He went on to get a degree in dentistry and, like so many black men of his era, moved to the North. In the thirties, after a first marriage failed, he moved to New York where he met and married my grandmother. He set up his dental practice, and they had four sons; my father was the third of these. My grandfather would always make a distinction between other blacks and himself. As far as he was concerned, his education and profession put him in a separate class. He passed this attitude on to his sons to a certain extent. Although I never heard my father articulate this sentiment, I could tell the difference in the way that most other blacks carried themselves and the way that my father and his friends carried themselves. My parents' friends were all college-educated blacks who seemed to be still celebrating the gains of the 1960s, which is appropriate since they were the ones who had benefited the most. I was expected, as these people had done, to take advantage of the new-found educational and social freedoms to the fullest. This meant college definitely and graduate school most likely.

When I was 6 my mother entered medical school. A few months later my father was hospitalized for cancer of the colon. My mother hired a live-in housekeeper to take care of my sister and me; we would have such help around the house for the rest of my childhood. When I was 8 my father died at age 41. My memories of this are images of lots of people being around the house for several weeks. I understood what had happened, but my father had been gone for so long in the hospital that the situation seemed somewhat removed from me. I do remember my mother's grief, but I was so young that my emotions were not developed enough to understand anything more than the concrete changes in everyday routine. My mother graduated from medical school and decided to pursue her residency in North Carolina, where her mother and younger brother lived and where she had grown up. I felt indifferent to the move except for the fact that I had just recently learned that North Carolina was a slave state; I was wary that there would be racists down there. I was 9 years old.

My mother's family in North Carolina was quite different from my father's. My grandmother worked as a waitress in a downtown department store, my maternal grandfather was a mailman who died soon after I was born. My mother had grown up relatively poor, though not impoverished. I did not see much of my mother, since she was completing her residency as a pediatrician. We lived in a suburban home in a predominantly white neighborhood that had a few blacks. The house was larger than our first home and better appointed. I attended the public schools but didn't like them at all. They were large and impersonal, and it seemed the teachers really didn't care about the development of students. One positive aspect was my inclusion in the district's Talented and

Gifted Student Program. I also served as the treasurer of the elementary school's student council. In middle school I became involved in the public-speaking program in which we would choose poems or speeches and practice for the countrywide competition at the end of the year. I won 2 years in a row, once in poetry and once in prose. During my time in public school in North Carolina, I felt awkward and out of place. There were no other kids in the school who had a similar background. My earlier exposure to white kids in Connecticut contrasted with the starkly segregated world of my North Carolina town. The other black students teased me for not speaking in the "Black English" dialect. The middle-class white students did not really associate that much with the blacks. Maybe once a year I would hear an insult of "black boy" or an occasional "nigger." By the end of 7th grade my marks in school were dropping, and I felt as if I was learning nothing. When my mother offered me the chance to go to private school, I jumped at it.

My mother was always afraid that my development would be adversely affected by having lost my father at such a young age, so she was determined to provide other strong male influences in my life. Partially as a result, I have always been exposed to institutions that were predominantly or entirely male. These include my attendance at a military academy's summer camp, the Boy Scouts, prep school, and my college fraternity.

My mother got the idea to send me to a summer military academy from my father's older brother, my Uncle Bill, whose son had also gone to this camp. I spent the four summers following my father's death at this military academy-turned-summer camp where all the traditional American values were stressed. We were awakened every morning by bugle and had to assemble in military formation. The days were filled with athletic events such as horseback riding, riflery, and archery. In the evenings we saw movies like *True Grit* and *Patton.* During these four summers I became accustomed to spending long periods of time in an entirely male environment. I also learned at an early age what it meant to be independent from one's parents. However, there were some corresponding disadvantages to the experience at the camp. It encouraged the boys not to be dependent upon parents or other adult figures and to look with disdain at such needs for nurturance or guidance. Leadership and responsibility were emphasized at the camp. As each camper would return for another year he was moved up a notch in military rank. After 4 years I was made a second lieutenant. My duties included assembling my group of 100 campers, who would report to me and salute in military fashion. By the end of my last year I had become so enamored with the place that I wanted to return there and go to the military academy. My mother was not about to let me go that far.

When the decision came to send me to prep school, the fact that it was an all-male school did not matter. The school was undoubtedly the best college preparatory school in central North Carolina. The surroundings at St. Andrews School were so much nicer than public school that I was too dazzled to worry about the lack of women. Also, the work was so much harder that I spent much more of my time studying than socializing. The structure and atmosphere of the St. Andrews program appealed particularly to the male psyche. Almost all of the teachers and administrators at the school were male, athletics were mandatory, and success in sports was heavily stressed. Time and again it was emphasized that we were the future leaders of our community. Since there was not a woman among us, this message also carried other connotations. As we entered the 9th and 10th grades, girls from our sister school, St. Anne's, began to attend classes with us. They came to St. Andrews to take math, science, and English, although we were not allowed to take such courses at St. Anne's, since it was generally thought that the girls' curriculum was watered down. There were only two or three black girls at St. Anne's, and my contact with any of them was rare. After 5 years of this situation, I became used to functioning in an all-male academic environment. It seemed perfectly normal to me to attend meetings or plan activities that were entirely devoid of any female participation.

My first day at St. Andrews was rather strange. I noticed first the difference in the way students dressed; they were all wearing pastel-colored "dress shirts." There were no blue jeans allowed, but the students did not seem to care. In class, I was struck by how much control teachers had over their students, who simply didn't act up as much. Out of my 8th-grade class of 65, 4 of us were black. Three of us were new students and the other one, Jonathan, had been at the school since 4th grade. I ended up in the same class with him. Though he seemed pleased that there finally was another black person in his class, his attitude toward me was somewhat patronizing. He would constantly stress to me the difference between St. Andrews and my previous educational experience.

One day not long after I had first started at St. Andrews, the teacher arranged the seating. I ended up sitting next to a boy named Scott, a typical West End white kid. I noticed that he stared at me constantly. I got the feeling he was staring because he didn't think I belonged there; he did not stare at the new white student in the class who also sat near us. Another incident also clued me in to the way that things worked at that school. Members of the class had to give an oral presentation. One student named Ben gave his talk and he stuttered very badly. No one laughed or even flinched, and at the end he was congratulated as if he had given a flawless presentation. Next, a student named Louis went up to give his speech and he also stuttered badly. This time the members of the class chuckled and made faces. After the class most of the boys, including Ben, made fun of Louis. I questioned Jonathan about the double standard, and he explained to me that it was "not cool" to make fun of Ben because he came from a very wealthy and prestigious family, and his father was a respected alumnus. Louis, on the other hand, was Jewish, and his family owned a discount furniture store. Also, Louis had only been at the school for 3 years, whereas Ben had been at the school since kindergarten.

I soon came to understand that the boys of St. Andrews were taught that there was an ideal best exemplified by members of the community's elite society. These men were always white, always wealthy, and always Protestant. There was only one black teacher at the entire school, and he was too immersed in his religion to worry about social concerns. The only other blacks at the school were the kitchen and janitorial staff; not just particular members of the support staff were black, but the *entire* crew. The only white who worked for the school in this capacity was the supervisor. The students would always call these maintenance employees by their first names, no matter how old they were. The janitors would simply nod their heads in response. To call any other member of the staff by their first name would be grounds for severe punishment.

At first the students in my class did not know exactly what to make of the black students, but by the end of our first year opinions about us had begun to gel. Al was the most popular black member of our class. He was a gifted athlete, and this immediately gained him considerable respect from our classmates. He was middle class and did not live in a very fancy neighborhood but every weekend a different white guy would invite him to spend the night. I was treated quite differently. In English and history classes I was beginning to show a remarkable amount of verbal ability. This shocked the other students in class; they had expected me to be slightly below par, at best. Another thing that shocked them was my accent. Within a year I had so immersed myself into the life of St. Andrews that I had donned a near flawless southern gentleman's accent. On the other hand, my athletic skills left something to be desired. The other boys dealt with this by coating me in humor. I began to notice that many of my habits were being ridiculed. This would continue in earnest until the 10th grade. I was constantly questioned as to why I did not possess greater athletic skill. When I showed skill in the classroom they said the only reason I did well was that I had somehow been able to shirk the curse of ignorance placed upon my race.

Early in 9th grade I was confronted with overt racism for the first time at St. Andrews. A student named Tim came up to me and for no reason said, "Nigger, nigger, why so tall? Nigger, where's your basketball?" He then proceeded to laugh and walk away. When I told another classmate about this incident he dismissed it as not being so much a racial attack as a personal one. He pointed to the fact that Al was one of Tim's best friends. I was later to find out that Tim said that he just wanted to see what my reaction was, and that he would never have done such a thing to a "normal" black person. When I went to my faculty advisor to explain my problem to him, he asked that I not tell anyone else and said that he would handle the problem himself. I never got any sort of an apology from Tim. During my freshman and sophomore years I was a target for racial harassment. Guys would say things to me just to get a reaction, and often I supplied them with it. During this period my grades, particularly in math and science, began to fall. I failed two terms of chemistry and one term of trigonometry.

During the last month of my sophomore year we held elections for junior-class leadership positions. When the nominations came up for student council, a kid named Tom decided it would be funny to nominate me. There was no way that I could win such positions, which were reserved for students who could act as role models. When the time came to give the speeches, I argued that the people who had held the positions of leadership so far had rested on their laurels and had looked upon their positions as honors rather than jobs. People were surprised by this tactic; it had previously been unspeakable to condemn our class leaders. When election day came I actually had much support. I won my position handily, to the surprise of the students, faculty, and administration of the school. I therefore found myself in a very different position to deal with my junior year, and my self-esteem rose considerably.

During the following summer I spent most of my time working out in the school weight room and became close friends with Jonathan, the black student who had first greeted me in 8th grade. Now he had a new sense of respect for me due to my election as a class leader. Jonathan was the eldest son of wealthy physicians. His wealth did not in any way prevent him from acknowledging his black identity, and "blackness" was often a topic of conversation between us. By the time junior year began we were definitely the best of friends. Both of us had the desire to complete St. Andrews as successfully as possible, and we were willing to do anything to make this wish a reality.

As junior year began, I was hungry for opportunities to get involved. I entered the tryouts for the school's team for "Battle of the Brains," a TV quiz show in which area high schools competed in tournament-style competition. I did not make the competition team, but I did make first alternate and I practiced with the team and went to all of the matches. The coach, Mrs. Morgan, took a personal interest in me and valued my capacity to learn and understand facts, especially in the area of history. By the next year I was to join the television team and I soon became a major force. Many people were surprised to see a black guy on the team from St. Andrews. We did very well, making it all the way into the semifinals. I even sent my tapes to the admissions committees at the colleges I applied to.

I didn't really search for all of the activities that I became involved in. When sign-ups were announced for the drama club's play, Tom, the same guy who had jokingly nominated me for a position on the student council, took the liberty of signing me up. To the surprise of many, I actually went ahead with tryouts for the play. I became involved in several productions during the course of my junior and senior year, which brought me into contact with the women from St. Anne's for extended periods of time. Jonathan and I began to go to the parties of our wealthy white friends. These parties were comprised of the "popular crowd" of the St. Andrews and St. Anne's students. These people began to take a new attitude toward me; I was no longer simply someone to make fun of. I had finally begun to turn my experience at St. Andrews into a positive one.

In the spring of junior year I found out that I was accepted by the AFS intercultural program and went to Israel to stay with a family for the summer. The group with which I traveled was a diverse mix of people from around the United States. About half of the students in the group were Jewish, and I was the only black. This was the first time I had come into close contact with people from all over the country, and I felt as if I had been living in a closet; the closed-mindedness of North Carolina had left its mark. We arrived in Israel and were taken to a youth hostel in Tel Aviv where we underwent further orientation. As we traveled around Tel Aviv, I remember feeling self-conscious because I was black, though this feeling left when I saw that there were actually a fair number of black Israelis. After I had been in the country for several days, my host brother, David, came to pick me up with a female friend of his. As I talked with them, I began to notice the differences between them and my peers at home; these people seemed to be a lot more mature and less materialistic. I also felt that they did not notice that I was black, or that if they did notice, it made no difference.

In all of my travels around Israel, I never felt that my race was an issue or a problem. I was referred to simply as an American. I remember only one conversation that concerned race. My host father had heard that things were pretty bad for black people in the United States and he asked me what my experiences had been. I told him that in my hometown there were still many problems that revolved around race. However, I explained that things were much improved since the days when my parents were my age. He replied that to his people, race itself meant nothing. He noted that when distinctions were made, they had more to do with religion than race. But what he told me and what I observed were two different things. The family that I stayed with were of European descent, and every once in a while they would make derogatory comments about Jews of Middle Eastern descent. I also saw the way Arabs were treated within Israel. Their neighborhoods were some of the most impoverished places that I had ever seen. And the Israelis to whom I spoke believed that if the Arabs wanted to live better they should go to another country. My eyes were opened to the fact that people could oppress others for reasons unrelated to race. I had heard that this happened around the world, but I had not seen it up close. I left

Israel feeling that I understood much more that people had different perspectives on life, and that no one perspective was necessarily better than any other.

When the time rolled around to start thinking about college, my initial reaction was to apply for early admission to the University of North Carolina. However, this attitude changed when I noticed that Jonathan was looking at an entirely different set of institutions. His football prowess, along with good grades, had assured him of acceptance to most of the Ivy League schools. This sparked my interest in these schools, and when it came time, I applied to them. Most of the guys in my class thought that I was taking a shot in the dark; there was no way that I would ever get in. In the end, however, I was successful and was accepted into every school to which I applied.

The reaction by some to my acceptance into a top college was that I would soon fail or disappear into the woodwork. This seemed to be the attitude of the St. Anne's girl who was also accepted to the same college as I was. She had been part of the crowd that had given me such a hard time during high school. Whenever she and I would talk about heading off to college, she behaved as if the two of us were going to entirely different schools. I got the feeling that she could not imagine that our college experiences would be at all similar, primarily because I was a black student and could be expected to separate myself from the college mainstream. However, my stock did go up among the faculty of the school. I was encouraged warmly by faculty who had been cool toward me in previous years. The teachers even went so far as to award me an honor prize for outstanding citizenship at graduation, the culmination of 2 years of surprising people by succeeding where I was not expected to.

The fact that my Uncle Joe attended this same college has much to do with the attitude that I have developed toward it. Samuel Joseph Danforth, my Uncle Joe, was the oldest brother of my late father. He enrolled in my college as a member of the class of 1954. This was years before this college had any thought of diversity; there were only three blacks in his entire class. He even joined a fraternity. After graduating, he went on to medical school where he did well enough to earn a fellowship in research.

When first coming to college I sensed that, as a black student, I was expected to look upon the past of this institution as something that should be alien to me. I was supposed to reject its traditions and reactionary fraternity system. However, my family's connection did not allow me to take this stance to the extent that some of my fellow black students did. I was aware that in the past my college had many problems and prejudices; my uncle had been excluded from a fraternity that had an open policy of excluding blacks. However, I did not treat the past of this institution with the loathing which I sensed from other black students, and which I felt some administrators expected me to espouse. For some reason, I felt connected to that part of my college's past that my uncle represented. Part of this was a sense of pride in being a black second-generation Ivy Leaguer, and a fourth-generation college undergraduate. For this peculiar reason, I wished to experience that side of college life that most black students feared or even hated.

I lived my freshman year with two roommates from very different backgrounds. Phil was from the Midwest; he came from a wealthy background and had attended an exclusive day school, as I had. Jim was more middle class, his father was a football coach, and he had come to college primarily as an athlete. Interestingly, I was the intermediary between these two. Phil and I shared the same tastes in clothes and had shared a similar educational experience in high school. Jim and I could talk about football, had similar attitudes toward women, and enjoyed rap music. Phil and I developed the closer relationship. Jim did not drink, and alcohol would soon become a large part of my life at college. I also found it difficult to discuss my career goals and plans with Jim; he knew little, if anything, about corporate law or investment banking. On the other hand, Phil's experiences and aspirations were more congruent with my own.

During my first term at college, alcohol became the means to purchase my popularity. This popularity would make possible attainment of most of my student leadership positions ranging from class council representative, to student assembly representative, to class president. The college had a policy that excluded freshmen from the fraternities during their first term. As a result, wherever alcohol showed up, large groups of freshmen were sure to follow. One Friday a couple of my hallmates and I decided to buy a few cases and invite some people over. We set the beer out in a trash can with some ice and soon a crowd of about 50 to 70 people had gathered in our hallway. Phil suggested that I go around and collect "chips" (small donations of one or two dollars to help defray the cost of the beer) and, as a result, I met more people in 1 hour than I had met during my entire first 2 weeks. Later, as people were beginning to file out, I heard people saying, "You guys are really ballsy" and "when's the next rager." We had these parties for the next 6 successive weekends. We started to buy our beer in kegs and people began to depend upon us for their weekly entertainment. Within 3 weeks our parties were 150 strong, and even upperclassmen were beginning to show up. I began to achieve widespread recognition, at first as the "big black guy who collected the chips." Eventually people whom I did not ever recall seeing before began to call my name around campus. I began to realize that if I had anything going for me, it was the fact that I had an image that stuck in people's minds.

Elections for class council were announced about the fifth week of the term. I decided to run and produced only one simple campaign poster. It used photographs from our several parties and the caption read, "Let's keep the tradition going." Therefore, in my first student government election I ran on a platform of "free beer" and parties. It worked, and I went to my first class council meeting the next week.

By the second term of my freshman year the fraternity system had become a major mental preoccupation of many of my fellow classmates, as well as myself. We had abandoned our weekly parties on the hall and had begun to consume beer at the expense of fraternity brothers. The Zeta Upsilon house had a reputation for being a haven for the wealthy and powerful. This reputation was taken seriously by the campus, and an article on this particular house had appeared in *Playboy* magazine just a year before. This did not intimidate me or my roommate, Phil. One Wednesday night early in winter term we went into the basement of Zeta. It was filled with about 30 guys wearing Brooks Brothers shirts with ratty jeans and dingy baseball caps. The Grateful Dead played in the background. I went over to a guy who appeared to be wearing a sweatshirt from one of St. Andrews rival schools. It turned out he had actually gone to Exeter, but he got excited when he found out that I had gone to a private school and he invited me to come back the next week.

Phil and I began to go to Zeta U on a regular basis. We became good friends with most of the brothers and we began to spend time outside the house with those guys whom we expected to become members of our pledge class. At the beginning of spring term, rush came around. Both Phil and I were let into the house, and I began to spend all of my leisure time there. I would get up and go to class, eat, and then go straight to the house. For a relatively small fee each term, I would have all of the beer that I could drink, not only at my own house but also at most of the other houses in the system. I began to partake of the system on a regular basis, but I did not feel that I would be any more productive if I was not in a fraternity.

The women who hung out at our fraternity were basically the female counterparts of my brothers. They were all white and wealthy and knew it. They were much more civil toward me than were the St. Anne's girls, but they were extremely image conscious. One thing that really struck me was the fact that I received odd looks from these people when they discovered that I was in Zeta U. I was the only black person in the house, and at many of the "social set" parties that I would go to, I would almost always be the only black person in the room. The one thing about the fraternity that would often cause me stress was the every-term chore of finding a formal date. Usually the only women who were interested in going were white sorority girls. I often shied away from asking black girls because I was afraid that they would not feel comfortable. I often had to reconcile within myself the fact that, as a black person, I belonged to this organization that made no effort to include blacks.

During the entirety of my sophomore year, I was the only black member of the house. When rush for the next class came along, I felt obligated to ensure that another black member got admitted. One black guy, whom I did not really know, rushed. When the time came for deliberations, I made a passionate plea for this person's acceptance as a member of the house. Several of the other brothers felt that I used "racial guilt" to force this member into the house. Therefore, they put pressure on me to ensure that person would become a good member. I felt that such an attitude was inherently wrong, but it is representative of what I have often had to deal with as a member of this fraternity. Even though I have been exposed to several incidents of racial insensitivity, to question these events usually brings about vehement denial of any racist motives. Often these incidents are passed off as jokes, or simply a matter of objective, intellectual fact. The style of racism may be different from the more blatant form I had to deal with at St. Andrews. However, the end result is the same; I am made painfully aware that I am different from those around me. One fear that I had when I joined a white fraternity was that I would be shunned by other blacks on campus, but this has not come about because I always made a point to speak to black students whom I know, especially when I was in the presence of my white friends.

The experience of being in a fraternity has opened my eyes to the true nature of this college. Though the administration preaches a "principle of community" that promotes the toleration and celebration of diversity, the student body is allowed to maintain an elitist structure. Most of the people in my fraternity are white and wealthy. The people that they eat with, socialize with, and compete with in athletics are also white and wealthy. I am the only black friend that most of these guys have, yet I do not bring them face to face with the poverty and injustice that most blacks must labor under. This causes me to wonder whether I am giving these people a false sense of security about their dealings with black people, and whether I should be more persistent in voicing black concerns in my dealings with my fraternity brothers. However, I believe that I should not seek to place a special burden upon myself to "educate" my white friends. To do so would reduce my ability to function and, hence, succeed.

Rushing my fraternity was rather easy; 10 years in predominantly male environments allowed me to take to Greek life like a fish to water. By the beginning of sophomore year, as my skills as a student politician increased, I began to realize that it would be to my advantage to reassess my views toward women. I began to use the word "girls" less and use "women" more. My politician friend, Randy, persuaded me that my attitude was eventually going to get me into trouble. However, inherent in his criticism was a basic misunderstanding of why such attitudes had developed, his having always been in a coed environment where parity between the sexes was stressed. Even now, however, the part of student social life to which I belong is rather divided along gender lines. All of the major positions in student government, with one exception, are occupied by men. So my involvement in a male-dominated environment still continues, though my awareness and perception of this situation has changed.

My career in student government has, in several ways, been tied to my fraternity experience. First, I realized that if I was to assert myself as a leader at the college, it would be necessary for me to join a fraternity, which had to be well respected and traditional. Second, my closest partner in student government was also a fraternity brother of mine. Third, my fraternity experience has constantly brought me into contact with more and more people. Being in a fraternity such as Zeta U also has an effect upon my campus image. Just as black print is most distinctive against a white background, I, too, stick out in my college environment. This makes me more recognizable and, hence, more viable as a campus politician. There are also some drawbacks to my unique position. There are many on this campus who thrive upon their differences with other people, whether they be racial, socioeconomic, or religious. Many of these people have used their situation to gain prominence and power within the community. To many of these people, I represent a dangerous element because I reconcile the irreconcilable. By virtue of who and what I am, a Zeta U, a class president, and a black person, I mix experiences and attitudes that many in this community contend cannot coexist. If anything can, these attitudes can eventually hinder my progress in this community.

My associations with whites are a result of the institutions and experiences that I have been exposed to. I never set out with the purpose of associating myself with the wealthiest, "whitest" people that I could find. I do, however, show great discretion in choosing the educational and social institutions in which I become involved. Blacks have traditionally been excluded from such organizations, but in the late 1960s a conscious decision was made to allow blacks access to these places. This is the situation into which I was born. The earliest decisions about whom I would associate with were made by my parents. They decided to settle in a predominantly white neighborhood because of certain perceived advantages. These reasons further led them to place me in a white nursery school. As a result, I learned from earliest childhood to be most comfortable in a predominantly white environment. My parents saw no harm in this, since they understood that the recognition of racial differences would come with age.

The motivation for associating with whites was not a desire to stay away from blacks. The minute number of blacks at traditionally prestigious schools and organizations forced me to modify my patterns of association and socialization. I had to associate with whites in order to have any social life at all. There are very few blacks who have shared my set of experiences, and to find someone similar to me who is black is rare. I guess that these shared contradictions and experiences form the basis of my friendship with Jonathan. Most of the time we spend together is consumed with the discussion of race and class . . . and women.

My relationships with women, or the lack thereof, are a result of my unique situation. Just as I am hampered by the lack of other black males who have shared my experiences, there are even fewer black females that I have come into contact with. This is not to say that I haven't met a few, but the field is very small. It is unrealistic to believe that I will be compatible with every upper-middle-class black female that I meet. To limit my relationships with women to one race is therefore foolish for me. In dealing with white women, another set of factors comes into play. Even in the 1990s it is not fully acceptable to have interracial relationships, especially for those women who are conscious of their class and position. They care about what their peers will think, as well as their parents. This is especially true in a conservative town like the one I grew up in, or the small, sheltered community of my college. When I have tried to initiate such relationships, I have encountered the barriers that society has erected.

As I look beyond my upcoming final year at college (with an eye on the presidency of the student body) I feel I have a good idea of what it is that I have to overcome. I must be sure that I have reconciled within myself these seemingly contradictory experiences and paradoxes of race and privilege, disadvantage and advantage. I am a young black man, socialized by elite white institutions, very aware of the racism that surrounds me; yet my perspective on life is one of empowerment and unfettered opportunity. If I do not reconcile these contradictions, then those goals that I have set for myself shall be much harder, if not impossible, to reach.

PART II

Identity

The Social Construction of Race, Ethnicity, and Culture

JEWELLE TAYLOR GIBBS

In the twentieth century, no countries have been more obsessed with race than the United States, South Africa, and Nazi Germany. In their obsession with race as the most distinguishing characteristic of different groups, social scientists, leading intellectuals, and politicians in these three societies have systematically classified people according to phenotypical traits such as skin color, hair type, and facial features. In the process, they have distorted this pseudoscientific concept in order to create and maintain a social hierarchy, cultural hegemony, political dominance, and a system of socioeconomic subordination based on the presumed natural superiority of those individuals classified as "white."

Notwithstanding the fact that these historical developments assumed different forms in these three societies, the similarities among them are striking in terms of the dynamics of promoting racist propaganda and fostering racial divisiveness as well as the terrible consequences of implementing racially discriminatory laws and social policies. The Third Reich in Nazi Germany deliberately and falsely manipulated the concept of race in order to stigmatize and demonize Jews and Gypsies, initially to justify their social and economic exclusion and ultimately to implement the "final solution" in the concentration camps of World War II. The Afrikaners of South Africa, in contrast, invoked Biblical scripture and nineteenth-century social Darwinism to justify their brutal conquest of South Africa's indigenous peoples and their subsequent policies of apartheid and oppression.

In the United States, people of color have experienced a variety of oppressive, discriminatory, and exclusionary strategies from the colonial era to the current post-civil rights era. Black Africans and their descendants were enslaved for nearly 250 years, from 1619 to 1865. Once slavery ended, they were subjected to another century of "Black Codes," "Jim Crow Laws," segregation, and discrimination. Still today, after 30 years of civil rights legislation and affirmative action programs, black Americans are oppressed by unequal treatment in education, employment, housing, health care, and the criminal justice system (Hacker, 1992; Jaynes & Williams, 1989). Native Americans have been victims of extermination campaigns by the U.S. government and have been forced to relocate from their ancestral territories to barely habitable reservations or lands. Their children were sent to off-reservation "Indian schools," which led to near total destruction of tribal cultures, and Native American communities have generally suffered woeful economic and social neglect (Jacobs, 1985).

Hispanics/Latinos, who are recognized by the U.S. Census as an ethnic group but treated in U.S. society as a racial group, have historically been exploited as migrant farm laborers and are frequently deprived of their basic civil rights in areas of education and employment. Even second- and third-generation Hispanic Americans are often marginalized socially and treated as undocumented aliens (Shorris, 1992). Asians who were first encouraged to immigrate to the U.S. in order to provide low-paid labor, for example, to help construct the nation's railways, have since been subjected to political exclusion and interred as enemy aliens during World War II. Today they suffer frequent economic scapegoating and media stereotyping (Takaki, 1989).

Thus, in all three of these societies race or ethnicity has been used not only to classify people according to a set of superficial characteristics but also as a marker for social stratification and selection. This process has served as an insidious and irrevocable tool for assigning privilege and prestige to groups based on measures established by the white majority or ruling elite and as a way to control access to the opportunities, resources, and rewards of the dominant society.

As the contributors to the following section so clearly express, the socioeconomic consequences of racism have significant implications for the social status and psychological development of people of color in U.S. society, particularly for the process of racial identity development and racial identification among children and youths of color. The quantifiable impact of racism may be easier to measure in terms of its broader consequences, such as higher rates of poverty and unemployment among African American youths, higher school dropout rates among Mexican Americans, higher rates of suicide and substance abuse among Native American youth, and increasing gang membership among young Asian immigrants (Gibbs & Huang, 1998). However, racial discrimination, exclusion, and marginalization may have a much more subtle yet complex impact on the psychological development and psychosocial adjustment of children and youths of color, particularly in terms of racial identity development. As the personal narratives in the following section illustrate, youths of color develop idiosyncratic strategies to cope with racism and attempts to marginalize them, and their efforts to construct a racial identity reflect some common themes and dynamic processes.

Common themes expressed in these case studies include the young people's growing awareness of racial, ethnic, and color difference; their search for self-definition, social acceptance, and intimacy; and their efforts to consolidate a biracial and bicultural identity by the time they reach young adulthood.

These youths employ dynamic processes that represent both conscious and unconscious strategies to cope with the challenges they face. In some instances they reveal healthy coping mechanisms, such as sublimation and intellectualization, while in others they use more immature defense mechanisms, such as denial, isolation of their feelings, reaction formation, displacement, and identification with the aggressor. They also use strategies, such as "switching" from one ethnic identity to another in appropriate social contexts, or choosing alternative identities that transcend race or ethnicity and allow them to affiliate with another peer group (e.g., athlete/jock, punk rocker, counterculture hippies).

In the past decade, the issue of racial identity development has moved from the margins to the mainstream of academic research due to a number of converging factors. First, demographic trends indicate that the United States will have no clear racial or ethnic majority by the middle of the twenty-first century, when white Americans will constitute approximately half of the population and people of color the other half. Second, the fastest growing group of children in the population are those from interracial and interethnic families, which will make them more difficult to categorize racially and to stigmatize socially. In fact, these families have appealed to the U.S. Census Bureau for a new category that will allow them to specify all of their racial and ethnic heritages, but the Census Bureau rejected this request in favor of allowing people to check all categories that apply (Root, 1996).

Why is the issue of racial identification still relevant and significant at the end of the twentieth century? To what degree is this topic simply an ongoing elitist debate among a small group of minority researchers—an issue they perceive as critical and address in an attempt to understand the contemporary conflicts between racial and ethnic groups in U.S. society? How does this issue inform the phenomenon of "identity politics," that is emerging as demographic trends show an increasing proportion of people of color and a decreasing proportion of whites in the United States as the millennium approaches?

The process of racial identity development is inextricably entwined with the issue of racial identification, an identity that is involuntary for most people of color, socially constructed for others, and irrelevant or insignificant to an increasing number of racially mixed people. However, racial identification as an external validation of an essentially internal self-perception goes far beyond personal issues and merges inevitably with political issues. Insofar as racial labeling has important implications for public policies, social programs, legislative and judicial decisions, the personal becomes indistinguishable from the political. Racial demographics are manipulated to set goals for affirmative action in college admissions, employment, and government contracting; they are invoked in voting rights and other civil rights cases; they are used to justify bilingual education programs; and they can determine the allocation of funds for government research, health care, job training programs, public housing, and a host of private and public social programs. Thus, any major change in the way race is conceptualized and categorized in the United States would likely result in numerous unintended consequences if applied to the implementation of public policies and legislative initiatives, including the current proposal to create a new census category for biracial and multiracial individuals.

IMPACT ON THEORY AND RESEARCH

As Robinson points out in this section, racial identity development theories have been evolving since they first emerged in the early 1940s. Kenneth and Mamie Clark's racial preference theories, which were based on experimental analogue doll studies in preschool children, were linear, unidimensional, and static, focused on the formation of racial identity at a preoperational level of cognitive development.

Decades later, an Afrocentric perspective, fueled by the Civil Rights Movement and the Black Power manifesto, influenced the more complex racial identity theories presented in William Cross's Negro-to-Black Conversion Experience in 1971 and Parham and Helms's Racial Identity Attitude Scale (RIAS) in 1985. As Robinson notes, revisions to the RIAS by Parham and Cross in 1991 recognize that the process of racial identity development continues throughout the life cycle and that there are enormous individual variations in its timing, expression, and qualitative dimensions.

Concomitant with the growing ethnic consciousness of Asian Americans, Latinos, and Native Americans in the 1970s, new models of ethnic and cultural identity development began to emerge in the 1980s, including Arce's Model of Chicano Identity Development in 1981, Phinney's 1989 Model of Ethnic Identity, Sue and Sue's Racial and Cultural Identity Development (R/CID) in 1990, and Huang's model of Asian American identity formation in 1994.

An element of this burgeoning ethnic consciousness was an emphasis on biracial/bicultural identity development. In his 1982 doctoral dissertation, Kich proposed such a model. Three distinct stages were delineated: (a) the young child's first awareness of his or her differences and dissonance; (b) the struggle for acceptance; and (c) self-acceptance and the assertion of an interracial identity in young adulthood (Kich, 1982, 1992).

Reflecting the increase in interracial families, Poston proposed a five-stage biracial identity development model in 1990. This model offers a conceptual framework and heuristic rationale that takes into account the unique factors that influence the identity development of ethnic minority youths and adults.

Most of these theories share some common assumptions about racial and ethnic identity development and similar ideas about dynamic processes. For example, all are stage related and assume that racial identity development follows a logical sequence of stages until the individual arrives at a healthy resolution of his or her racial identity. Another underlying assumption these theories share is that biracial and bicultural individuals will inevitably experience some level of stress, conflict, or discomfort as they move through these stages of self-discovery and self-definition that will be reflected in maladaptive behaviors, immature defense mechanisms, or dysfunctional modes of adjustment. However, there is also growing evidence that the identity development of some biracial individuals does not conform to this rather rigid sequence of stages, which may indicate that there is greater variation in both developmental processes and identity outcomes (Root, 1992, 1996).

As the case histories in the following section clearly reveal, youths who are both biracial and bicultural are faced with a number of essential issues in integrating their personal, social, and sexual identities. In my own empirical and clinical research with such youths, I have found that even the most well adjusted must work through at least five major issues in sorting out their dual racial and ethnic heritage in relation to (a) their personal identity (Who am I?); (b) their social identity (Where do I fit?); (c) their sexual identity (What is my sexual role?); (d) their relationship with their parents (Who is in charge of my life?); and (e) their career aspirations (What are my options in life?) (Gibbs, 1987; Gibbs & Hines, 1992).

Results from our study of 12 biracial adolescents and their families in the San Francisco Bay Area suggest that a young person develops a healthy biracial identity in the context of a supportive family that openly discusses racial issues, a racially heterogeneous school and neighborhood, racially diverse social networks, and exposure to multicultural activities and educational resources (Gibbs & Hines, 1992). Conversely, biracial adolescents who exhibited psychological or behavioral problems were more likely to come from dysfunctional families that avoid discussions of racial issues, to be reared in racially isolated neighborhoods and schools, and to have limited exposure to or involvement in multicultural social networks or activities (Gibbs, 1987; 1998).

As an example of being color-blind and avoiding race themes, Robinson presents the case of Christine, a young biracial woman whose parents rarely discussed race or its implications for her identity. Although she finished college and appears to have good relations with her parents and female friends, her narrative reveals a great deal of denial and isolation about her feelings, relatively limited heterosexual experiences, and social marginalization throughout her adolescent years due to her inability to confront her mixed identity.

Liz, an African American woman, had the benefit of her father's racial socialization messages. However, as a sophomore at a new high school, she too engaged in her own form of color-blindness. She decided that since she could not be white, which was easier, she would wear a blindfold regarding being black.

IDENTITY AS SOCIAL CONSTRUCTION

The social construction of racial identity is a contemporary issue in the social sciences. However, within the literature and performing arts of African Americans, Asians, Latinos, and Native Americans, this fact has been long understood. The tragic figure of the mulatto mistress, the sexually exploited Eurasian bar girl, the Latina entertainer passing for white, the drunken half-breed Indian—these images abound in the pages of second-rate novels, in B-movies, and in urban folktales. Most of these stereotyped images represent the persistent ambivalence, denial, and displacement of the negative attitudes toward interracial and interethnic sexual relationships throughout U.S. history (Nakashima, 1992).

The concept of "social construction" implies that racial identity is an interaction between an internal psychological process and an external process of categorization and evaluation imposed by others. Helms (1990) has proposed that racial identity is a composite of three components: personal identity, reference group orientation, and ascribed identity. For racially mixed individuals, these three components are presumably more ambiguous, fluid, and complex and are also heavily influenced by physical characteristics, family attitudes, community norms, and multiple contextual factors.

These contextual factors can include the racial composition of a child's neighborhood and school, their parents' social networks, and their own peer networks. Experiences with employers, community leaders, and the police can also significantly affect how a youth defines himself racially, as well as how he is defined by others (Gibbs & Hines, 1992; Pinderhughes, 1995). As Root (in press) has recently suggested, other factors such as hazing by peers, parental neglect or abuse, and the race and class of a biracial child's custodial parent can be "color-coded" positively or negatively through the child's perceptions of his experiences, then subsequently be displaced onto members of the same race. Under these circumstances, a biracial youth would be more likely to reject the racial identity of hazers and that of an abusive parent or devalued noncustodial parent. The race of biracial children's mothers may explain biracial childen's racial identity preferences.

In my recent research on black youth in England and Canada (Gibbs, 1993, 1997), I found that race, culture, and class contributed in different ways to the self identity of these youths but that these demographic variables were filtered through a broader prism of immigration patterns and the history of race relations in the two Commonwealth countries. Black youths whose families immigrated from the Caribbean to England and Canada after World War II, who retained their cultural identity and who were working-class, viewed themselves primarily as Caribbean blacks. In contrast, those whose families were descended from African sailors (in England) or African American slaves (in Canada) and were more often racially mixed identified more closely with Anglo-Saxon culture and viewed themselves primarily as British or Canadian blacks. However, in both England and Canada, black and biracial youths who were more acculturated, upwardly mobile, and involved in interracial schools, neighborhoods, and peer networks reported that they experienced less racial stigmatization, exclusion, and discrimination.

However, biracial youths in these studies reported feelings of racial and social marginality to blacks and whites, ambiguous personal identities, and pressure to define themselves in opposition to the norms and expectations of either group (Gibbs & Hines, 1992). These same phenomena are reported in clinical case studies, autobiographical accounts, and personal narratives of mixed race people who identify themselves as Creoles, mulattos, mixed blood Indians, mestizos, and Eurasians or "hapas" (half Asian Pacific Islanders) (Njeri, 1997; Root, 1992, 1996).

The narrative of Scott, who is biracial and bicultural, aptly illustrates how these youths can "switch" social identities to fit in with blacks or whites, depending on the situation. His story also shows how he could define himself "outside the borders," subtly simultaneously identifying with a nonracial group as an athlete while reinforcing a positive stereotype of black males as superathletes. Susanna, a biracial female, also chose to identify with "punks" and "skaters" as an alternative to choosing a black or white racial identity—this, after being reared as a Buddhist and being expelled from a private school where she was the only student of color. In an effort to hide his homosexuality from family and friends on his small Dutch Caribbean island of Curaçao, the adolescent Claudio "switched" his sexual orientation in order to fit in with a heterosexual and homophobic society. Amidst the hiding, he pretended to be what and who he was not.

The case of Steve represents an example of cultural and ethnic identity confusion. This young man had internalized ambivalent or negative images of African Americans, yet his dark skin color caused him to be perceived by others as black. After experimenting with other identities (as a soccer player), he began to address his feelings of marginality and alienation during the college years, seeking to resolve the tensions of his bicultural identity.

One insight that emerges from these narratives is that mixed race youths often embark on a journey of self-discovery that can be circuitous, emotionally exhausting, and painful. This process of self-discovery may be facilitated by intrapsychic exploration, interpersonal support, or counseling, or it may be impeded by self-destructive behaviors, lack of peer and family support, or hostile environmental factors. It is also clear from these narratives that the development of racial identity is a lifelong process, one that evolves as an individual interacts with broader social networks, experiences diverse environments, and negotiates new challenges in personal relationships, family, work, and community activities.

FUTURE DIRECTIONS

Recent demographic changes in the United States have been accompanied by political and cultural changes as well. In the political arena, several state and federal government initiatives are attempting to bring about draconian changes in immigration policies, to cut back on bilingual education, and to reverse affirmative action policies and programs (Gibbs, 1998). All of these political developments can be construed as a backlash against the growing political and economic power of people of color in U.S. society. While these initiatives are usually framed in terms of eliminating unjust racial or ethnic preferences and promoting democratic principles, they impact negatively on opportunities in and access to education, employment, and economic development for people of color. Moreover, many of these programs are targeted at specific ethnic minority groups who have used racial identity politics to pursue their own agendas for achieving equal opportunity.

There is also increasing income inequality in U.S. society, where class and race have historically been always inextricably connected. However, recent evidence suggests that education is a stronger factor than race in socioeconomic status; thus, college-educated people of color, particularly those with professional and technical degrees, have gained and will continue to gain increasing access to economic opportunities and social mobility that have traditionally been associated with the white majority (Lerman, 1997). As this trend accelerates, it is conceivable, as Wilson (1978) predicted in his controversial book on race and class, that social class identity will be a more salient variable than racial or ethnic identity in determining a person's status and lifestyle options.

In the cultural arena, there has been a great deal of blending of racial and ethnic themes in literature, the performing arts, fashion, food, and the media, which has blurred the lines between race, ethnicity, and culture. This trend will likely accelerate as families become increasingly multicultural and multiracial, thus reducing the power of racial and ethnic labels to stratify and marginalize groups. The thriving "crossover" phenomenon in American culture—Afro-Cuban music, French-Asian food, Spanish-English dialect ("Spanglish"), and black-white urban music and clothing styles—not only serves to reduce the gap between whites and people of color, but also to challenge their preconceptions about themselves and each other and to foster, albeit subversively, increasing interracial and interethnic socializing and heterosexual relationships.

CONCLUSIONS

In his recent book *Postethnic America*, Hollinger (1995) has predicted that by the middle of the twenty-first century, the U.S. population will be so racially and culturally diverse that labels will be meaningless, and American society will finally lose its obsession with race and ethnicity. Hollinger and others suggest that racial identity will become more situational, fluid, and pragmatic, that individuals will adapt their racial or ethnic identity relative to varying contexts (family, work, community), relationships (friends, lovers, parents), and goals (economic, political, cultural).

As the United States continues to receive and absorb immigrants of color from around the world, color as an indicator of race or ethnicity will become increasingly less accurate. Thus, the use of racial labels to rationalize and reinforce social distinctions will become more difficult and will, no doubt, be replaced by other extrinsic measures of classifying individuals and groups. Moreover, as these new immigrants intermarry with people of other races or ethnicities, the cultural diversity of American society will be increasingly enriched and an entirely new consciousness of racial and ethnic identity created.

However, the emerging consciousness of biracial and multiracial people as a distinctive group seeking their own racial identity label could pose an even more serious challenge to the future of U.S. race relations. As the white population shrinks proportionately in the twenty-first century, white politicians and power brokers may attempt to expand the definition of "whiteness" in order to maintain their economic and political power. One obvious way to expand the "white" population is to be more inclusive of light-skinned Hispanics, Asians, and other racially mixed people who can "pass for white" in physical appearance, thereby conferring a more privileged social status on people of color who are perceived as acculturated and eager to be assimilated.

If this scenario were to occur, the United States would follow the example of Brazil with its mulattoes and South Africa with its "coloreds," wherein a sort of racial and social "buffer" between dominant whites and subordinate blacks exists. Such a policy would, in essence, reward racially mixed people in order to maintain and extend white dominance. Since in the African American community, blacks with lighter skin historically have been accorded higher status and have had access to greater educational and economic opportunities, this possibility is fraught with the danger of creating a permanent black underclass that would suffer the double disadvantage and discrimination resulting from low socioeconomic status and darker skin. As Robinson underscores in the next chapter, "colorism" has an unsavory history in U.S. society. It is a persistent factor in the social relationships and aspirations of African Americans, but it can also be a double-edged sword for youths seeking to define and internalize a positive racial identity (Haizlip, 1994; Root, 1992, 1996).

The following section presents narratives of individuals' adaptation to various racial and cultural heritages. These young people have negotiated the challenges and resolved the dilemmas of growing up and developing healthy identities in a racially and culturally polarized society. Their struggles provide insights, and also generate crucial questions about the broader issues that will confront a multicultural, multiracial American society in the twenty-first century.

The Intersections of Identity

TRACY L. ROBINSON

A primary theme in the following chapters is that all of the narrators' identities are multiple, simultaneous, converge with one another, and exert a powerful influence on their development. *Identity,* in this context, refers to both visible and invisible domains of the self that influence self-construction. They include, but are not limited to, ethnicity, skin color, gender, sexual orientation, nationality, and physical and intellectual ability. In different contexts, various facets of one's identity may dominate in self-definition.

Six narrators are featured in this section: Scott ("Lost in the Middle"); Liz ("Walking a Thin Line"); Steve ("Caught between Two Cultures"); Susanna (Becoming Comfortable in My Skin"); Christine ("Color-blind"); and Claudio ("Becoming Myself"). Each is of African descent, a child of the diaspora, representing various ethnicities from the United States, the Caribbean, Canada, and Europe. Three of the six narrators are biracial, one is bicultural (a child of immigrant parents), one is Dutch West Indian, and one is black American.

While I state these racial designations, it is not my intent to locate people into mutually exclusive racial and gender categories in an effort to conceptualize race and other identities in binary terms. From the perspective of biracial or bicultural people, having to choose a fixed identity negates their other identities that, while perhaps less visible, are substantial parts of their self-definition.

This chapter presumes that neither race nor ethnicity alone is capable of explaining or predicting racial attitudes, experiences, and cognitions. As a means of describing variations in racial identity attitudes and behaviors, various racial identity development models will be referenced in the next section. First, there is William Cross's model of Nigresence, or Black Racial Identity Development. W. S. Poston's model addresses biracial identity development. Janet Helms's White Identity Development Model is presented because the mothers of the biracial narrators are white. Vivian Cass's Gay Identity Model is included because homosexuality is a prominent identity for one of the narrators.

Following the identity models, I consider three subthemes that I have identified from the six featured narratives. They are (a) factors that delay racial identity development, (b) racial signifiers, and (c) psychosocial passing. Throughout the discussion, the multiple, shifting, and intersecting nature of identities will be integrated.

RACIAL IDENTITY DEVELOPMENT THEORY

Three decades ago, Erikson (1968) introduced an eight-stage psychosocial theory of identity development which purported that identity is comprised of the individual and society, is historically contextual, concerned with the present, and linked to the future. Identity, he argued, is also based on an epigenetic principle that refers to timely, orderly, and purposeful growth among living organisms.

Largely influenced by Erikson, a number of researchers presented identity models that sought to explain human beings' psychosocial, cognitive, moral, and ego development (e.g., Piaget, 1972; Kohlberg, 1984; Loevinger, 1976). An implicit assumption in each of these models was that identity is unidimensional, linear, and progresses in normative patterns, usually referred to as *stages*. Steeped within a modernistic tradition based on empiricism and monocultural-ism, most of these stage models were developed in the 1970s and normed on white, middle-class populations, paying little or no attention to race or gender diversity.

Racial identity development theory has also been in existence for several decades. Within this time, numerous models have been developed for diverse racial, ethnic, cultural, and biracial groups (Cross, 1971; Hardiman, 1982; Helms, 1990; Poston, 1990; Sue & Sue, 1990). While given different names, racial identity development models assume within-group heterogeneity and maintain that lower levels of development have the potential to change over time when individuals encounter dissonance to existing cognitive schema.

CROSS'S NIGRESCENCE MODEL

As the most widely applied racial theory about African Americans, Cross's Negro-to-Black Conversion experience, or Nigrescence, has been extremely influential in the development of models related to racial identity among European Americans (Helms & Parham, 1984; Sabnani, Ponterotto, & Borodovsky, 1991), other people of color (Sue & Sue, 1990), and women (Ossana, Helms, & Leonard, 1992). Cross's work has also contributed to a heuristic body of research among various populations, particularly among college students.

Within Cross's theory, racial identity development is a maturation process whereby negative external images are replaced with positive internal conceptions (Helms & Piper, 1994). His five-stage Nigrescence model includes (1) Preencounter, (2) Encounter, (3) Immersion and Emersion, (4) Internalization, (5) Internalization and Commitment. Nigrescence refers to "a resocializing experience" that "seeks to transform a preexisting identity (a non-Africentric identity) into one that is Africentric" (p. 190). Africentrism involves an awareness of black identity, knowledge of cultural customs and traditions, liberating psychological resistance strategies, an understanding of oppression, and strategies to resist it (Dana, 1993; Robinson & Howard-Hamilton, 1994). Because Cross (1991) made a distinction between personal identity (PI) or self-esteem and reference group orientation (RGO) or racial identity, Nigrescence has both personal and interpersonal implications.

At Preencounter, the first stage, a black person views the world through the lens of the dominant white culture. When asked to describe themselves, people identify with factors other than race, such as work, church, or club affiliation. Cross maintained that many Preencounter blacks are psychologically healthy and that antiblack attitudes among African Americans in this stage are rare. Despite indices of psychological health at this stage, Cross (1991) stated that "Preencounter Blacks cannot help but experience varying degrees of miseducation about the significance of the Black experience" (p. 192) and are more likely to operate from a Eurocentric cultural perspective in evaluating beauty and art forms.

At the second stage, Encounter, blacks develop a new view of the world, usually due to a shocking personal experience, that is inconsistent with the old. Cross said there are two aspects of this stage, first experiencing an encounter and then personalizing it. Despite the myriad of daily experiences that could encourage a person to move from Preencounter to Encounter, a failure to internalize and personalize the experiences can hinder movement up to this next stage.

In the third stage, Immersion and Emersion, individuals focus on being black and exclude others, particularly whites. This transitional stage has two phases. In the first Immersion phase, individuals are immersed in blackness and "group think." White people and the white culture may be avoided in favor of blackness. The second phase of the third stage, Emersion, is less volatile, with fewer boundaries drawn across racial lines.

Internalization, the fourth stage, is more peaceful and calm. At this juncture, individuals have resolved any dissonance regarding their emerging identity, evidenced by high regard for blackness.

Internalization/Commitment is the final stage. It is characterized by a long-term interest, commitment, and a greater ability to conceptualize the self beyond the narrow confines of an oppressed identity. In this stage, people often seek to eradicate oppression for all people.

BIRACIAL IDENTITY DEVELOPMENT

Poston (1990) developed a five-stage Biracial Identity Development model to address the growing number of people who identify as biracial or multiracial. Because many of the existing models assume racial exclusivity, Poston sought to create a biracial model that reflects positive changes in self-definition. Poston's five stages are (1) Personal Identity, (2) Choice of Group Categorization, (3) Enmeshment/Denial, (4) Appreciation, and (5) Integration.

The first stage, Personal Identity, occurs when people are very young and awareness of membership in an ethnic group is new. Reference group orientation attitudes are virtually nonexistent; instead the emphasis is on issues of personal identity, such as self-esteem.

Choice of Group Categorization is the second stage. In order to have a sense of belonging, people may feel pressure to choose an identity, often that of one ethnic group. The status of parents' ethnic background, acceptance within a particular culture, and physical appearance are factors that influence choices about seeing the intersections of one's many identities or choosing one parent's race as dominant.

The third stage, Enmeshment/Denial, describes those who feel confused and guilty about the perceived need to choose one identity over another.

Appreciation is the fourth stage. In this stage individuals have begun to appreciate the multiple identities that comprise their existence and to broaden the range of those with whom they identify.

The last stage is Integration, which describes a coalesced self-concept, a sense of wholeness, and an ability to value one's diverse identities.

WHITE RACIAL IDENTITY DEVELOPMENT

Although traditional conceptions of race refer to people of color, white Americans also have a racial identity. It is, however, rare that a white person has an experience that causes them to assess their attitudes about being a racial being (Pope-Davis & Ottavi, 1994). It is easy for a white person to live without having to examine the meaning of being white. This neglect of racial significance can impede a white person's self-awareness, a crucial factor in racial identity development. Helms (1990) has been the primary voice in the theory of White Racial Identity Development. Her six stages are (1) Contact, (2) Disintegration, (3) Reintegration, (4) Pseudo-Independence, (5), Immersion-Emersion, and (6) Autonomy. According to Helms (1990), "the evolution of a positive White racial identity consists of two processes, the abandonment of racism and the development of a nonracist White identity" (p. 49). The first phase begins with the Contact stage and ends with Reintegration. The second phase begins with Pseudo-Independence and ends with Autonomy.

A white person enters the first stage, Contact, by encountering the idea or the fact of black people. Their family environment usually affects whether their attitudes toward blacks are characterized by fear or naive curiosity. In the Contact stage, whites unconsciously benefit from institutional and cultural racism, and tend to be idealistic about the equal treatment of blacks. During interactions with blacks, whites may experience some anxiety as they come to realize that, independent of economic conditions, there are clear distinctions in the treatment of people across race. Continuing social experiences with blacks will move a person into the Disintegration stage, which is characterized by a conscious dissonance and inner conflict. Whites in this stage realize that African and European Americans are valued differently in society.

In the third stage, Reintegration, a person recognizes the covert and overt belief in the dominant culture that whites are superior to African Americans. What is important about the Reintegration stage is that whites acknowledge having a racial identity. In this stage, individuals tend to protect their sense of white privilege, even though it is unearned. They take the attitude that people of color are not entitled to privilege because of their inferior social, moral, and intellectual status. Because honest dialogue about race between racially different people does not often take place, it is fairly easy for a person to remain in this stage, the height of white racism. However, a jarring event can trigger movement into the next stage.

According to Helms (1990), "Pseudo-Independence is the first stage of redefining a positive white identity" (p. 61). In this stage, which is primarily intellectual, a person acknowledges responsibility for white racism. Although the negative aspects of the earlier stages are absent, white norms continue to be used to interpret cultural or racial differences. A person in this stage is often met with suspicion by both whites and blacks. Discomfort with their ambiguous racial identity may help move the person into the next stage.

The fifth stage, Immersion/Emersion, is characterized by replacing old myths and stereotypes with accurate information. It is essentially a period of "unlearning." A person in this stage may participate in white consciousness groups where the goal is to abandon a racist identity. The attention, then, is not on changing black people but to change whites. The successful resolution of this stage requires the individual to re-experience earlier emotions that were distorted or repressed.

Autonomy is the last stage and is an ongoing process. Race is no longer perceived as a threat, and a person continues to internalize and apply the new definitions of whiteness that they developed in the earlier stages.

CASS'S MODEL OF GAY, LESBIAN, AND BISEXUAL SEXUAL IDENTITY FORMATION

Sexual orientation exists on a continuum that includes varying ranges of homosexuality, bisexuality, and heterosexuality. To assess the growth, development, and awareness of gay, lesbian, and bisexual individuals, Cass (1979) developed a six-stage Model of Gay, Lesbian, and Bisexual Sexual Identity Formation. The Cass model provides a guideline for assessing a person's level of development. It is important to note that a person may remain "stuck" in a given stage, skip certain developmental levels, or may regress from a higher stage to a lower stage depending upon the events that occur in her life. An overview of each stage is provided below.

The first stage is Identity Confusion, in which a person has a growing awareness of thoughts, feelings, or behaviors that may be homosexual. These self-perceptions are incongruent with their earlier assumptions of their heterosexuality and according to Cass, represent a developmental conflict.

In the second stage, Identity Comparison, the individual further investigates the feelings first experienced in stage one. As they gather more information and seek more contact with gays, they develop increasing congruence between their self-perceptions and behaviors but experience increased conflict with others. As a sense of conflict heightens, they may move to stage three, Identity Tolerance.

This third stage is marked by increased contact with the gay community, leading to a greater sense of empowerment. A person may now have a strong homosexual self-image but continue to present themselves outside the gay community as heterosexual.

It is at the fourth stage, Identity Acceptance, where an individual encounters intense conflict between their self-image and the perceptions of nongay others. This conflict may be resolved by either passing as "straight," having limited contact with heterosexuals, or selectively disclosing their orientation to significant heterosexual others. Those who find these strategies effective may stay at this level comfortably; otherwise, the continuing conflict pushes the individual into the fifth stage, Identity Pride.

In this fifth stage, an individual manages the conflict by fostering a dichotomized homosexual (valued) and heterosexual (devalued) worldview. They have pride in the gay community and in their personal identity but also anger at an alienating heterosexual society. The responses of others to their new identity, particularly those who are not gay, influence whether an individual moves to the final stage, Identity Synthesis.

An individual moves to the final stage if they have positive reactions from non-gay others. They note both similarities and dissimilarities with homosexuals and heterosexuals and see their sexuality as just one part of their total identity. Although some conflict is always present, it is at the lowest and most manageable point in this stage.

DELAYERS TO RACIAL IDENTITY DEVELOPMENT

I have identified three subthemes in the six featured narratives: factors that delay racial identity development; racial signifiers; and psychosocial passing. Connections between these themes and the preceding section on identity development will be made.

Factors that delay racial identity development reflect dominant discourses that can arrest conscious awareness of race matters. They include continuous isolation from racial and cultural community, parental silence about race, and dominating identities. Discourses refer to ideas embodied in structured statements that give meaning to social practice (Monk, Winslade, Crocket, & Epston, 1997). Racist discourse, for example, alleges that being white is superior to being black. A discourse of the American "melting pot" that espouses ethnocentric homogeneity might address the question, "Why do African Americans have to be African? Why can't they just call themselves American and be Americans?" Numerous discourses around race, gender, sexual orientation, and other identities result in people being evaluated on the basis of how close they are to being white, male, middle class, Christian, heterosexual, English-speaking, young, and mentally, physically, and emotionally able bodied (Reynolds & Pope, 1991). Such an evaluation of people's worth creates a culture that is often uninviting for those who are deemed different and fosters class elitism, religious bias, homophobia, racism, sexism, and prejudice against persons with disabilities (Robinson, 1998).

CONTINUOUS ISOLATION FROM RACIAL AND CULTURAL COMMUNITY

Advances in educational and occupational attainment during the last three decades have resulted in greater economic success for many black Americans. One indicator of this prosperity is growing numbers of middle-class black Americans who reside, work, socialize, and are educated in predominantly white communities. This raises the question, however, of what effect continuous isolation from people who are culturally similar has on the healthy development of racial identity among adolescents of color.

Some of the narrators indicate the effect predominantly white environments have had on their awareness of race, racial identity, and racism. Steve, the son of Trinidadian parents, said that his predominantly white neighborhood was very quiet. Steve learned how to be quiet and he learned to be quiet about how he was different. Steve's predominantly white middle-class setting was silenc-ing to dialogue about racial and ethnic differences that may have been per-ceived as divisive or even threatening and thus were rendered invisible.

Given Steve's neighborhood, school, and social experiences, white people served as his reference group. White students were all he knew. His continuous isolation from other blacks prevented him from developing healthy images of black people and of himself, and did not allow "them [sic] to convince me of myself." Consequently, his sense of self as a racial being appeared confused. As an adolescent, Steve accepted the same media stereotypes about black people as many whites did who lacked meaningful contact with blacks.

In addition to the racial differences between Steve and his predominantly white neighbors and schoolmates, he was also mindful of the ethnic differences between himself and native blacks. Steve's narrative explores the multiplicity of his identities—American born, first son of successful and strict West Indian parents who resided in predominantly white neighborhoods with similar schools. This multiplicity afforded him varying degrees of power (depending on the context) but it also may have delayed his racial identity development.

Both Christine and Scott also had prolonged isolation from blacks during their childhoods. Both were raised in predominantly white neighborhoods and are children of white mothers and black fathers. In both cases, their parents seemed to deemphasize race, which impeded race becoming a significant part of their self-construction. Scott said, "My identity, even though it became an issue later on in my life, was shaped almost free of any notion of race in my ear-lier years." As a light-skinned person of color, Scott questioned whether his interactions with his white neighborhood friends gave him social privileges that darker-skinned blacks did not have. Thus, Scott's attitude about race and racism may have been formed by the fact that race was a negligible factor, due to his ability to blend in physically with whites.

Research on colorism suggests that African American adolescents at extremes of the skin-color continuum are less satisfied with their color than adolescents in the middle (Robinson & Ward, 1995). While this does not appear to apply to Scott, his light skin color did cause both Scott and other blacks not to regard him as black. In Scott's mind, his light skin color did not cause him to suffer the "burden of color," which isolated him from other blacks and height-ened his feelings of estrangement.

Christine's neighborhood, school, and community were also predominantly white. Her interactions with her black paternal grandmother were strained and minimal. It was not until her first year in college that she had her first black friend. Isolation from black culture, music, people, and history appeared to characterize Christine's existence and marginalized her sense of racial under-standing.

The inability to celebrate one's own culture and to practice it with others considered culturally similar can threaten positive racial identity development and the formation of strategies to cope with racism. Conversely, connections with a racial community can enhance one's self-knowledge, foster group belonging, and affirm one's racial self in community with others (Brookins & Robinson, 1996). Susanna is an example of this. Susanna is a biracial child of a white mother who raised her and a black father. Her neighborhood, when she was of school age, was comprised of people of various racial and ethnic backgrounds, and her school was in the middle of a predominantly black community. Seeing herself reflected in the faces of other brown children, she developed a sense of sameness with them. While she experienced bouts of isolation in college from some black women who didn't accept her white mother and white roommate, she developed connections with black women while at Spelman college that enhanced her self-understanding across her multiple identities (e.g., gender, race, ethnicity, intellectual interests). She said, "For the first time I made friends with people to whom I did not have to explain myself. Not only did the women look like me, but we had shared experiences."

PARENTAL SILENCE ABOUT RACE

Racial socialization learned from parents is essential in helping children develop racial understanding in a world polarized around race (Ward, 1991). Although their multiple racial and ethnic backgrounds should not relegate biracial and bicultural children to an exclusive category, society has a tendency to assign them to categories based on skin-color hue, hair texture, and facial features. It stands to reason, then, that biracial children need racial socialization messages from their parents that will help them address their and others' racial inquiries. So, how does parental silence about racial matters affect biracial and bicultural children? The reader should note that insight into the parents' identity issues is gleaned from the narrators' stories about their parents and not from the parents themselves.

Scott's mother, a white Canadian who was divorced from Scott's Jamaican father, raised Scott and his sister. Race played such an insignificant role in his early years that understanding himself as a biracial being was not an issue. Scott's parents were silent about race. They focused more on fortifying his self-esteem, raising him to believe that he could achieve anything he desired. They considered language (being bilingual) a potential buffer against racial discrimination, as in Canada, ethnicity, nationality, and language had greater salience than race.

Christine's mother is Austrian and her father is a black American from Alabama. During her childhood, race was ancillary, and Christine's narrative suggests that her parents gave her practically no racial socialization messages during her childhood and adolescent years. They emphasized other areas of development instead, such as citizenship, academic excellence, and sports. Christine admitted that she grew up color-blind in an ethnically nondiverse, predominantly white community. Although race was not an awkward topic for her family, if it was discussed it was more political than personal. The Personal Identity stage of Poston's (1990) Biracial Identity Model describes Christine. She had little sense of belonging to any ethnic group, and her family emphasized personal identity attitudes, such as self-esteem. Yet she did have reference group orientation attitudes, which were based on her predominantly white lifestyle, community, and school. Christine stated that identifying herself racially was inconsistent with who she saw herself to be. Her difficulty with racial self-definition appears to be related to her parents' relative silence about race.

When Christine was in high school, her mother broached the topic of race after viewing a television special. Christine suspected that her parents were unaware of the racial challenges she would encounter and did not warn her, before she left for college, of the difficulty she would encounter as a biracial person. Christine speculated why this was the case: "Perhaps as a white person, my mother could not relate, and therefore could not know what I would experience. As a black child of the south, perhaps my father found the issue of race too painful to discuss."

The process of critically reflecting on one's life stories, choices, desires, and options and making decisions that may contradict the wishes of valued others describes a crisis. Entering a state of crisis about race thus becomes a conscious act and is in stark contrast to conceiving race in a manner similar to prevailing dominant discourses. According to Erikson (1968), however, crisis is not like a catastrophe. Rather, it is a developmental turning point and represents a crucial period of vulnerability and heightened potential. During the many years when Christine did not think about race or define herself as a racial being, she experienced no observable racial crisis. Such upheaval came while she was in college during heated racial debates with black students. Christine was adamant that race was insignificant, given her "half-black" racial designation, but her sustained consciousness about and dissonance over race led to a crisis.

Parental silence about racial matters does not just affect biracial children. According to Steve, the American-born son of Trinidadian parents, his Caribbean-born parents were culturally naive about the racism Steve would encounter. Growing up as a racial majority in Trinidad did not require Steve's parents to question their racial identities as Steve was forced to. Essentially, Steve's parents were not able to socialize him about race in America because of their limited experiences.

Racial Identity Theory can illuminate parents' racial socialization behavior. According to Cross's Racial Identity Theory of Nigrescence, black parents at beginning levels of racial identity tend not to regard race as a salient factor in their lives. At Preencounter, the black person views the world through the lens of the white dominant culture. At this stage, a person has little awareness of racial oppression or racial pride, since race and racism have minimal importance in their life. A parent, then, at Preencounter is less likely than a parent at Internalization to provide their children with racial socialization messages, exposure to black history, or healthy psychological resistance strategies for coping with a discriminatory society. Instead, they cultivate school, community, and athletic interests. In contrast, Liz was given very clear racial socialization messages by her father, who told her to run hard in life as a black female, to be twice as good as whites, and to fight racism with self-knowledge and an understanding of world history.

Helms's theory on white Racial Identity Development offers insights to white parents' silence about racial matters. In the first stage, Contact, whites benefit from racism but are naive about both racial meanings and inequitable processes. White parents at beginning stages of racial identity do not understand the meaning of race for themselves, let alone its relevance for their biracial children. For instance, Scott's socialization that race was an insignificant theme is similar to that of many whites, who do not think about being white. As white women who appear to have been at beginning stages of their racial identity, the mothers of Christine, Scott, and Susanna, despite their intimate relationships with black men, lacked the understanding necessary to talk with their biracial children about race, racism, racial identity, and racial pride. Even the racial and ethnic differences that Susanna's mother exposed her daughter to did not encourage them to have explicit discussions about race.

DOMINATING IDENTITIES

Although the self is comprised of multiple, shifting, and simultaneous identities, a dominating identity represents a facet of the self that is most influential in self-definition. This identity can overshadow others and is influenced by the status of that identity, by reference group affiliations, and identity development.

Claudio's dominant identity was that of an out and proud gay man in an intensely homophobic society. Being a black Dutch West Indian gay male at a predominantly white college did not challenge Claudio nearly as much as contending with the ostracism and cultural isolation from his black peers who were unable to reconcile his homosexuality with their austere codes of blackness. Claudio's preoccupation with combating homophobia overshadowed his attention to racial identity.

Claudio's gay identity consumed his identity quest. Consistent with the early stages of secrecy and denial in Cass's model, Claudio, while a young adolescent in Curaçao, was confused and closeted about his gay identity. Discourses about the abnormality and immorality of homosexuality contributed to his silence. In time, he disclosed his gay identity to others at his boarding school and began to exemplify Identity Pride. Claudio's strong leadership in the gay community in college coupled with his disappointment and anger at an alienating heterosexual society demonstrates his management of conflict through a dichotomized homosexual (valued) and heterosexual (devalued) worldview.

Steve's dominating Western, middle-class identity, in which whites were his primary referent group and he was isolated socially from blacks, interfered with his establishing vital links to a potentially sustaining black community. In his case, it became more challenging to ascertain how his esteemed dominant identity (i.e., as a middle-class black he was superior to other blacks) was counterproductive to achieving self-understanding and a sense of community.

RACE SIGNIFIERS

Although multiculturalism is an ideal within society, racial boundaries in the United States are rigid. The narrators told of this "line in the sand," and identified what I call *race signifiers,* rigid criteria based on both physical characteristics (e.g., skin-color hue) and behavior (e.g., use of Ebonics) used within black communities, and occasionally by whites, to signify "blackness."

In these narratives, the young people identified traditional notions of blackness to include (a) keeping conspicuous and regular company with blacks; (b) having the ability to use language recognized as specific to the black community; (c) not using language recognized solely as specific to the white community; (d) nonparticipation in white academically gifted classes; (e) athletic ability; (f) having "rhythm"; and (g) being heterosexual. Nearly all of the narrators talked about being considered "different" because of the non-black ways they communicated, looked, and or behaved.

One discourse of racism is that academic excellence is the domain of whites. Many of the narrators who excelled academically said their academic programs physically separated them from black students. While the merits of excellence in education are not being overlooked, Liz told us that such segregation, particularly during adolescence, left her feeling confused, alone, and lacking in role models with whom to identify.

Race signifiers affected Steve in that he began to believe that being black was inconsistent with middle-class status, speaking Standard English, and being in academically gifted programs. He saw that blacks had their own language, which he did not speak, given his limited exposure to black Americans. His mother told him that he was different from American blacks and would proba-bly be more comfortable marrying a white woman someday. Steve's encounter with a black basketball player actively demonstrates the discourse that says blacks are better at sports than at academics.

Christine did not connect being biracial with being black. Her sustained isolation from blacks may not have equipped her to validate being "half black" and integrate this identity with other identities (e.g., being academically gifted, a gymnast, track athlete, school leader, and homecoming princess). However, Susanna, who is also biracial, chose to define herself as black. It is likely that her childhood encounters with racial diversity encouraged her self-definition. Scott's extremely light skin was not a signifier for being black but his ability to run fast certainly was. Scott felt that being black was coupled with a "particular code of conduct and attitude associated with it in order to be considered a mem-ber (i.e., speaking Ebonics)." In Scott's mind, being white was easier. His con-fusion about his black side seemed to delay his racial identity development.

Cross's Immersion and Emersion stage can help explain rigid and restrict-ing codes of blackness. At this stage, there is intense focus on being black to the exclusion of others, particularly whites. Cross indicated that in this third stage, which is transitional, "the person's main focus in life becomes a feeling of 'togetherness and oneness with people'" (p. 207). Stagnation at this stage may delay conceptualizing race from multiple perspectives. For example, the young black man who criticized Christine for being out with her white male college friend could be described as being immersed in his racial identity. In his mind, there is a narrow range of acceptable behavior for black people: They ought to stick together and avoid white people. Yet deconstructing race is essential, as is expanding meanings to be inclusive of multiple identities and the abundant ways in which blackness is conceived of and expressed in people's lives.

PSYCHOSOCIAL PASSING

The concept of "passing" within the black community refers to blacks who pass for white because of their light skin color. Susanna had this to say about pass-ing: "Although light-skinned, my appearance and features obviously belong to a woman of African descent. . . . Were I lighter skinned, European featured, and had I then chosen to pass, my life would be very different." Psychosocial passing refers to people who seek to render invisible the visible differences between themselves and a desired or chosen reference group. By behaving in ways that are consistent with other group members, they subconsciously seek to avoid having their differences noticed.

The desire to pass is a response to the hierarchical valuation and devalua-tion of certain identities over others and can be particularly stressful. Liz wanted to fit in and just be a "normal teenager rather than a token racial representative." She believed that if she could divorce herself from racial matters, and even deny that they existed, they would disappear and not continue to have such a strong hold on her life. Liz's goal was to become essentially raceless (see Fordham, 1988), to be an individual first and black second. To achieve this, Liz was not really able to identify with anything. She resisted being confined and stigmatized by notions of blackness and avoided having her race be the only characteristic that provided her life with meaning and substance. Yet she did not appear to fit in Cross's Preencounter stage. She had thought about race and experienced racial encounters. At the time, Liz did not realize that she did not have to disassociate from race in order to express uniquely her blackness and be accepted as an individual.

Scott alluded to the psychological stress of passing when he told how one of his classmates called him a "nigger." Scott's biggest fear was that others would also call him a nigger and that he would then be designated as "different." His precarious relationship with blacks due to the varied meanings he and they ascribed to his light skin color increased his need to identify with whites.

Scott's inability to acknowledge his racial difference from whites did not protect him. If anything, it trapped him with fear and intimidation. His silence on his race also surfaced during his adolescence in relationships with girls. Essentially, he was silent about being half black, since he knew that white girls were attracted to white guys. His goal, then, was "to be just Scott, the guy that was a part of the group." Scott simply wanted to belong and not be different. While it is developmentally consistent for an adolescent to want to belong, denying his identity was a huge psychological price to pay for fitting in.

In contrast to psychosocial passing, Claudio learned to honor his identity as a gay black man and came out to himself, friends, lovers, and his family. He redefined his identities from a "both/and" perspective rather than an "either/or." In doing so, he validated his multiple identities as male, black, Dutch West Indian, bicultural, gay, and academically talented.

CONCLUSION

Each narrator's life was rich with multiple, textured, and converging identities. As the narratives unfold, they convey a variety of attitudes about identity that highlight the individuals' growth and identity development. Although important to self-construction, race and ethnicity alone do not constitute all of one's attitudes, experiences, and cognitions related to the self. There is a need for all people to accept a multiplicity of identities and expressions that defy traditional, stereotypical, and dominant discourses.

5

Color-blind

CHRISTINE

The daughter of an African American father and white Austrian mother, this college senior had a childhood blissfully unaware of racial identity questions. As she entered college, however, she began to realize that there has been a powerful racial subtext to her relationships with white men. Realizing for the first time that some white men desire her because of her color and some exclude her for the same reason she began to question many aspects of what it means to be biracial in American society. Likewise, she experienced the condemnation of black students at college for her interracial dating. Caught in the middle, and now believing her parents' "color-blind" upbringing of her to have been naive and unhelpful, Christine engaged in a painful process of questioning her basic assumptions about race and identity.

My parents talk little about their interracial marriage and the difficulties they have encountered as a couple. My father grew up in Alabama, my mother in a small town in Austria. My father never shared with me his mother and sister's disapproval of his marriage to my mother. I am only aware of this because on one or two occasions, my mother had made a reference to their hostility toward her and me during the first two years we were in the United States. After being told of my father's intention of marrying my mother, my grandmother strongly opposed it and refused to welcome "white trash" into her family. And for a long time, I was not welcome in her home either, because I was the child of such a sinful marriage. Once, at about age 2, when I was visiting my father's stepsister, my grandmother allowed me into her home, though she still rejected my mother, her "white" daughter-in-law.

My memory of the visit escapes me, but according to my mother, all of the grandchildren were visiting my grandmother at the time. A cheerful and bubbly child, I had arrived at her house in good spirits, but when my mother had returned, I was extremely quiet and sad. My mother says that my grandmother had given gifts to all of her visiting grandchildren except for me—the granddaughter of a condemned marriage. That was the last time I visited my grandmother until I was much older. I visited her in a retirement home when she had Alzheimer's disease several months before she passed away. Despite my grandmother's inexcusable actions, I never hated her, nor did either of my parents ever speak negatively about her. My parents attributed her dislike for their marriage to her age and the cultural attitudes of the South.

My paternal grandfather, however, adored my mother. Though I was not extremely close to him, I did see more of him than I did my grandmother, from whom he was divorced. He had visited us occasionally while I was growing up, and my family had once gone to see him in Alabama when I was 16 years old. During our short visit to the South, my family noticed that people stared at us a little longer, both because we were strangers in the segregated town and we were an interracial family. Despite the stares and scrutiny we experienced, we dismissed the stares as the stupidity of the South. We did comment on the silliness of it all, but we did not discuss the social implications or the challenges we as children of a biracial marriage might experience as we got older.

Race was not an awkward topic for my family to discuss; we were comfortable with being members of an interracial family. It just did not make sense to dislike someone based on skin color. As difficult as it is to comprehend, I never looked at my parents as a black father and a white mother; they were simply my parents. I grew up "color-blind." I knew that they were black and white respectively, but I did not understand what that meant. I was unaware of the difficulties both the black and white communities could have with an interracial couple. I had not yet been personally touched by the hostilities and disapproval of the outside world.

My mother's family was not thrilled about my parents' marriage either, but for different reasons. They did not want their daughter to move to the United States. As a result of the distance and language barrier, I was not close to my mother's parents. Despite their disapproval, my parents were married. I know that my parents had gone through a difficult period during the beginning of their relationship as a result of family members and strangers disagreeing with their choice to marry each other, but my parents were able to weather the difficult times and, overall, they have had a successful marriage.

The eldest of three, I am a child of this Austrian and African American union. My sister is 3 years younger, and my brother is 5 years younger. My parents married in Austria while my father was in the service. Soon after I was born, we returned to the United States. Four states and two children later, my family settled in a small, predominantly white community near Portland, Oregon, when I was in the 2nd grade. My father had left the army and had taken a job in law enforcement, and my mother began a career in teaching. For the most part, my community was not ethnically diverse. There were very few African Americans in my public schools as I was growing up, and I was not good friends with any. Overall, my closest friends were white.

Before people knew me or my family in my new town, I sometimes had to answer questions about adoption and why my mother was white. I vividly remember in the 2nd grade, a friend asking me if my mother was my real mom. Even after answering yes, it was still unclear to her how it could be that I had dark skin and my mother had light skin. I had to explain to her that my mother was white and that my father was black. Sometimes classmates would look at my mother with her white skin and blonde hair, then look at me with my black hair and dark brown skin, and in a somewhat surprised and confused voice ask, "That's your mom?" Occasionally, children (and adults) would ask me where my mother was as she stood next to me. Someone had once asked me, "If your father had been white and your mother black, would you also be white?" I never took offense at the questions; I simply answered and tried to explain, though there were times when I wished I didn't have to. The one offensive comment I remember, which I did not think of as offensive at the time, came from a friend in high school. She had previously lived in San Diego and one day said to me, "You don't act like the black people I knew in San Diego." It did not occur to me to respond back, "Well, you don't act like the white people I knew in Boston."

My first discussion about race and ethnicity took place during an intense program the summer before my senior year in high school. In the midst of the emotional and mental stimuli during the program's week of "racism and oppression," I was forced to ask myself questions about my background and beliefs. The issue of race hit close to home when Greg, a student in the program and a child of a biracial marriage, shared his personal struggles of growing up in Portland, Oregon, and the difficulty he sometimes faced as being neither black nor white. As he spoke about his background, Greg had prompted questions I had never been faced with before. I found myself partly relating to some of his frustrations and not relating to others. For the first time, I wanted to examine my experience as a biracial child. However, in spite of my interest, I was hesitant and did not seize the moment. The social implications of being a biracial child was a new topic for me. I was confused and uncertain about my feelings. For the most part, I had always had a good sense of who I was, but that afternoon as I listened to Greg speak, I wondered. I was 17 years old and I asked myself why my identity was now being questioned. Planning to leave home for college after my senior year in high school, I could not afford to *not* know who I was. I sat there in silence. That summer, the door on race had been opened, but I had soon returned to my placidly comfortable home. It would not be until I entered college that the conversation would begin again, and I would be forced to explore the issues surrounding my biracial identity.

The issue of race was never really discussed in my home. Sometimes, we discussed it on a political level, referring to others, but it was never seriously discussed on a personal level in reference to my family. Only once, when I was in the 10th or 11th grade, did my mother raise the topic seriously. After she had watched a news program on biracial families the night before, she asked us at dinner if we ever had problems being children of a mixed marriage. We all answered no, and we moved on to another topic. I believe my parents had thought it better to wait until we brought up the issue of race, but after seeing the TV show, my mom thought perhaps she better finally raise the topic herself. Since none of us said we had any difficulty, she left it alone. I honestly do not believe that either of my parents were aware of the special challenges we were to face when we got older.

Overall, I was well liked and successful in school; I was ranked fifteenth in my high school class. I was an athlete on the state track and gymnastics teams, and as the junior-class president, I was very active in student government. I was also president of our honor society, was homecoming princess, and was voted "most likely to succeed" my senior year. I spent most of my time with a small group of close friends, but I also had other friends from many different cliques: the jocks, the stoners, the brains, etc. Although I was well liked, I never dated nor even kissed anyone in high school. In fact, when I was homecoming princess, I had to ask a male friend from out of town to accompany me to the dance. Though I was delighted and surprised to be given the title, I was also embarrassed and confused for not having a date.

While in high school, I never considered the possible effect race could have had on my relationships with boys. I guess I didn't consider skin color to be an issue because there were two interracial couples in my school, and my sister had also dated a white guy. I also wasn't really interested in dating, so I didn't give it much thought. The few times I did think about it, like most girls, I was more insecure and self-conscious about my body weight and appearance than my racial identity. However, I did not know what was in store for me after leaving my hometown.

The door of racial consciousness that had been opened a little the summer before my senior year was to be opened wide when I entered college. Before I left for college, my parents did not warn me of the difficulty I would encounter as a result of my ethnic identity. Whether because they themselves did not know what I would encounter, or did not know how to broach the topic, or were trying to protect me, I cannot say. Perhaps as a white person, my mother could not relate, and therefore could not know what I would experience. As a black child of the South, perhaps my father found the issue of race too painful to discuss. I do not know. In any event, the two extremes of their respective colors meant they would not be able to understand my experience as a mixture of them both.

During the first week of freshman fall, I met Vanessa and Shawna, who were to become two of my closest friends. It would be the first time in my life that I was to be good friends with anyone African American. I do not remember our first conversation about race, but I clearly remember debating and even arguing about the implications of being an African American in the United States. We argued about "imposed definition"—the way outsiders perceive each person—and "self-definition,"—the way one perceives oneself. I argued that since I was only half black, I could not align myself with one race or the other and, more importantly, that race was not significant. I frequently got the response that we live in a racist society that will never be colorblind. In shock and frustration, friends tried to tell me of the historical backdrop still affecting many blacks today. However, I did not care about ancestors from years ago. In my mind, my background was limited to knowing that my mother was born in Austria and my father in the United States. It was that simple. Even though it struck me as very interesting that so many African American students at my college thought their roots were very important and felt it crucial to strive to obtain more facts, I lacked any desire to do the same. I believe this attitude was linked to my parents' lack of encouragement during my earlier years to discover my heritage, though now they are very encouraging. My black friends seemed to have parents who strongly encouraged them to explore their past.

I was frequently told by friends and acquaintances that society will always label me as a black woman regardless of my mixed background. Sometimes mistaking my desire to claim my European background as wishing to identify with the dominant culture, I was questioned about my allegiance to the black community. In response, I argued that by identifying myself solely as black, I was denying a part of me. In addition, I found it unfair that blacks were given the right to claim their mixed ethnic-racial heritage, whether it be Cuban-African-American or Haitian-African-American, but as an Austrian-African American, I was challenged. My friends tried to reassure me that they were not trying to deny my Austrian heritage. They questioned why I didn't know more about my black ancestors. Sometimes I felt I had to recognize only my African American heritage in order to avoid being accused of succumbing to the dominant culture's pressures and beliefs. Regardless of others' definitions and explanations, I could never quite comprehend the importance of defining oneself by race or ethnicity. As a product of a family that did not stress race, it seemed odd to me for such emphasis to be placed upon one's racial background. I was criticized as being too idealistic for stressing the primary importance of regarding people as human rather than as members of a racial group.

Another point of tension was the role of ethnic affinity houses on campus. Confused and uncertain about the intent and purpose of these organizations, I often debated with Vanessa and Shawna about the purpose of these groups. Though I now understand the need for the African American organization and other affinity houses, at the time I could not comprehend the need for such groups. Why was it that a WASP-only organization would be considered racist, yet the college African American organization was not? I felt that these organizations negatively accentuated the differences between races and further secluded themselves from the rest of the college community. It was explained to me that the college African American organization was needed for some students because the college campus was not a diverse environment and the organization helped minority students adjust. In my opinion, the opposite was true. There were many people of color at my college, and I found the campus to be diverse.

The African American organization was a very uncomfortable place for me. I did not understand the slang being used, nor the hairstyles and products members referred to, or in some instances, even the food they were discussing. Needless to say, I was not active in the African American organization. The only organization presentation that I attended was on the topic of interracial relationships, or "Jungle Fever." The guest speaker was an actor in the movie *Jungle Fever*, directed by Spike Lee. He shared his positive experience of having dated a white woman, but his sincerity and love for her was challenged by some members of the audience. Theories on why this successful black man was dating a white woman ranged from his insecurities and self-hatred as a black man to his desire to have the "great prize" or "trophy" at his side. Although not everyone spoke negatively about interracial relationships, I left saddened, angry, and frustrated. I was upset with one audience member in particular. He criticized the black male who marries a white woman, concluding that such a man possesses many insecurities, and that a "true black man" marries his "strong black queen." This statement was made after I shared my experience as a child of an interracial marriage. I couldn't help but feel that his comment was directed at me.

Even at the time of the Rodney King incident when, ironically, I was enrolled in my first black history course, I was not active in "race politics" at my school. I remember gazing out of the classroom window and watching the protests and speeches on the quad, as my history professor spoke of the injustices and struggles of the past. I did not participate in any of the protests and marches; I was still determining my new identity as a minority and what it all meant. My sister, on the other hand, was very involved in the forums and speeches at her conservative college. Like many of the minority students at my school, she felt frustrated with her student body's general lack of concern and understanding of the sensitive issues surrounding the Rodney King case. She told me about her frustrations in trying to educate others on race, while also concentrating on her studies. She felt it should not be her job to enlighten the rest of the campus and that she might be happier at a historically black college. My sister came to feel so strongly about this that she left school to take time off. She is currently applying to schools and hopes to find a more intellectual campus with a strong black student body.

I cannot explain why my sister was able to find and cultivate a stronger tie to the black community than I did. During college, she and I have discussed the issue of race several times, and though we have similar opinions and viewpoints, we inevitably end up arguing and abruptly ending our discussion in frustration. I tell her I do not understand how she can feel a connection with the black slaves and experience their suffering anymore than I can understand how young Jewish people relate to the pain and suffering of their ancestors in the Holocaust. I can sympathize as a human being, but I can't understand how skin color can create a stronger link and greater understanding of other's suffering. I also do not understand her new belief that, except for our mother, she no longer has anything in common with white people. Our conversations usually end with her accusing me of being influenced by the dominant white forces. Ironically, of the three children in my family, she is the lightest skinned, yet she is the most "militant" in advancing the "black cause." I think her new attitudes are the result of her experience at her small conservative college and the influence of her African American boyfriend and other black friends.

My brother is a junior in high school and is coming to terms with his biracial identity 2 years earlier than I did. In general, we share some of the same experiences and feelings, though he is more enlightened than I ever was during my early stages of discovery. He has been confronted with race issues and has discussed the implications with my parents. At his predominantly white, well-to-do prep school, he has been challenged by a few of the black students. They question his allegiance to the black community and, on occasion, remind him of his skin color. In spite of our similar experiences, unlike me, my brother has become involved in his school's African American club. Always struggling to keep a foot in both communities, he sometimes finds the fight exhausting.

My most upsetting brush with racial conflict occurred one Friday night in a fraternity basement. I was hanging out and having a good time with a friend who happened to be a white male, when I noticed a black male across the room giving me disapproving looks. Uncertain as to what would warrant such stares, I ignored him and continued talking and laughing with my friend. Eventually the stranger approached me as I went to the bar to get a drink. Taking the liberty to judge my behavior, he informed me that it was wrong for a black woman to date a white man, that we need to stick together and keep the race strong; we cannot dilute it by mixing with other races. With his light brown skin, he looked like a product of a biracial marriage himself. Overcome with complete disbelief, I stood there numb. I was first overcome with shock and anger, which was followed by sadness, and then I was angry again. *No one* had ever told me personally that interracial relationships were wrong, and I had never been condemned for associating with white males. I was outraged at the stranger. First of all, the male whom I was talking with was just a friend, and second, race should not dictate with whom I will be intimate. Furthermore, I felt he was unfairly judging me and my family.

My friend took me outside to calm me down. He tried to comfort me, but neither he nor anyone could understand the anger and frustration I felt. I left the fraternity alone; I needed to reflect on what had just happened. After calming down, I thought about my parents' marriage and thought about the hardships they must have endured to make their marriage a success. I also wondered if they ever conceived of the hardships their children were to experience as products of their marriage. A few days later, I saw the same guy on campus, and he apologized. I later learned that he came from a very wealthy family and attended a predominantly white prep school. I also found out that his sister was to marry a white man in a few weeks.

Despite that very upsetting incident, I did subsequently have a five-month romantic relationship with a nonblack male at school. His name was John and he was Jewish American. During the time we were together, I never felt judged by the college community nor did I question the community's feelings on interracial dating. That is, not until I saw a fellow student's documentary film on interracial dating on my campus. I went to see the film with one of John's best friends and a friend of mine. After seeing the film, I was disappointed that John had missed it. I believed that the film would have prompted us to discuss our interracial relationship on a personal level that we had not done before. Now I wanted to know how his friends and fraternity brothers felt about him dating someone of a different race. Was he ever confronted by others with the issue of dating a black woman? Before the film, I would have definitely said no, but after the shocking testimonies in the film, I wasn't so sure. Although I ultimately knew that dating across color lines was not a concern for him and that what other people thought did not dictate whom he would date, I was still curious to know if, as an individual in an interracial relationship, he ever felt judged by others.

John and I had talked about race early on in our relationship. I was aware from the very beginning that he wanted to marry someone Jewish. On one of the first nights we went out, we talked into the early hours of the morning about his desire to marry someone Jewish. However, our discussion was not on a personal level; it had been a philosophical-sociological discussion, and we did not examine our potential interracial relationship. He tried to explain and justify to me his conscious choice to marry someone within his own cultural group. As someone who was struggling with self-definition and imposed definition and having never felt any strong feelings for one race or another, I found it was difficult to understand why and how at the age of 21 he could eliminate all women of races and cultures other than his own as potential partners in marriage. Although John himself had a strong sense of his Jewish culture and had strong ties with his background, his parents were certainly a powerful influence in his decision. I wondered if they were aware that their son was dating a black woman and what their reaction would be. I never asked him because I didn't want to put him in the awkward position of having to defend his parents. Also, I did not want him to get the idea that because I was interested in his parents' potential opinion of me, that I was therefore thinking about marrying him.

The following summer I spoke with a black woman who had a strong desire to marry an African American, and for the first time I had an understanding of why someone would prefer to marry within their own race and cultural group. She said that she would not rule out marrying someone of another race or background but believed that there were many things she experienced as a result of her race which could not be explained to someone who had not experienced it. Her potential husband would have to belong to the same group in order to understand this important aspect of her life.

I had many questions about race and relationships, and the documentary only provoked more. John was my first real boyfriend, and we had been dating for 4 months. I wanted to share with him my uncertainties about our dating. I feared being viewed as a mere "college toy" since, in his eyes, as an African American woman, I was not marriage material. I wondered why he believed he could only marry a Jewish woman, yet he dated women from other ethnic groups. His previous girlfriend was white. Though I was not in any way interested in marriage, after the film and the discussions I had with others about the issue of interracial dating, I was curious about the role I played for him. I never believed that John would date someone based strictly on skin color, and I never thought that he had an ulterior motive for dating me, but after the film I learned that some people are fascinated with skin color and consider it all a game, while others consider crossing racial lines a sin.

I had always found someone attractive based on their looks and personality and I never thought about getting involved with someone based on their skin color. After seeing the film and having a number of discussions about interracial dating, I realized that some people actually do think that way. All the faces in the documentary were familiar; they were faces I had seen in the library, the student center, dining halls, and at parties. I was surprised at the number of people, both black and white, who were opposed to interracial dating, and I was disturbed by the film's story of a failed relationship largely due to the external pressures of disapproving outsiders. With it already so difficult to find that special someone, why did some people feel adamantly opposed to interracial couples?

In the film, there were two white students who admitted to having "jungle fever." A woman spoke of the black male anatomy and said she had once begun dating a black man based solely on the old myth that black men were better endowed sexually. A white male spoke of his attraction for black women because, according to him, they were better in bed. I sat there disgusted. I could not believe my ears as I listened to their ridiculous claims. I was particularly disgusted with that same white male who, the term before, had told a friend of mine that he found me attractive. I felt disgusting and dirty as I sat in the auditorium and listened to him openly express his racist feelings and desires for black women. What I once thought to be a compliment was nothing more than attraction for my skin color, a false association with great sex. I sat there quiet. I did not want anyone to know that I had been an object of those feelings, that I had once evoked such sick thoughts. I knew I wasn't to blame for his offensive sexual lusts, but I could not help feeling dirty and ashamed. This is the guy who had smiled and waved to me crossing the quad on the way to classes. The same guy who was so nice to me in the library, cafe, and in the gym. I could not believe my ears. I kept asking myself if he was acting or were these his true feelings. I had believed him to be a nice and sincere guy. I had guessed that the reason he was extremely nice to me was that he liked me, but I would have never have imagined it was because of my skin color. As he continued to talk about how black women are great in bed, he made me feel like an animal. I asked myself how many other guys honestly believe in the myth. I never once considered that someone might be interested in me because they believed it would be "fun" to date a black woman. Was this guy's attitude the exception?

The documentary left me with a lot of unanswered questions. Following the film, I had an interesting conversation with a black student who was one of John's best friends. He desperately tried to describe his frustrations as one of only two black males in a predominantly white fraternity. He described feeling as if white women only wanted to be his friend. He attributed his lack of girlfriends to two things: Few black women came to hang out in his fraternity, and nonblack women were not interested in him since he was a black man. He asked, "You belong to a predominantly white sorority, don't you sometimes feel the same way?"

"It's not a white sorority. My house is ethnically mixed. There are women of many different backgrounds," I said.

"Whatever," he replied. "There are only what, three black women in your house?"

"To tell you the truth," I said, "I never thought about my skin color being an attraction or a turn-off for males. I understand the getting-a-date-for-house-function-blues, but I never attributed the difficulty to the color of my skin."

My thoughts on the issue continued to spin, particularly about the reasons and implications of crossing race lines. Why was it that I never blamed my skin color for not having a date, yet my friend did? Perhaps my European features "saved" me. The next week, after doing a lot of self-questioning and exploring, I brought the topic up at dinner with a group of black female friends: "Do you think some men are attracted to black women on the sole basis that the woman is black?" I asked. The question was greeted with a simultaneous "Yes!" I was surprised that without any hesitation or moment of discussion they all agreed. One woman stated, "I was told by a friend in a historically black Greek house that he has heard about a mainstream fraternity on campus that actually has a contest to see who can sleep with a woman of each ethnic/racial group. Each race is ranked, and depending upon the woman's background, the guy gains points. It's something like, if the woman is Korean, the guy gets 10 points, Puerto Rican 20 points, and so on. I don't know all the details, but that's what I heard," she said.

"Do you honestly believe that?" I asked in disbelief.

"Yes. It's definitely not something in which the entire house participates, but it's definitely believable. It's just a question of which house." I didn't know how to react. I was just shocked by the thought. I could feel chills down my spine and I was disturbed by the rumor.

It was nauseating to think that someone could become involved with someone else because of skin color and, worse yet, to win a contest. The male was considered the victor of a stupid and disgusting contest; the woman a mere victim. Was it possible that guys at school, supposedly intelligent males, would do such a thing? I called a friend, who is also a minority, and told her of the rumor. She didn't seem at all surprised.

"Do you think that story is true? Do you think there have been guys who have been attracted to me because of my skin color?" I asked.

"Yeah," she replied. "Not all guys, but I am sure that there have been some who liked you because of your skin. Not to say that no one has ever liked you for you, or that you are not attractive, but your combination of dark skin color and traces of European features are a combination of the forbidden and the embraced. Mike liked you for you skin color, and Billy once told me that it was obvious to him that you were not all black. He said he could tell by your nose, cheek bones and hair." I didn't understand her point. "And what are you saying?" I asked her.

"Well, in Billy's case, I got the sense that your European features assured him that you are not black; therefore, it is okay for him to like you. And as for the guy in the film, your black skin appealed to him, as it does to others who have 'jungle fever.' In both cases, race is an issue—in a negative sense."

For a very brief moment after that discussion, I thought about questioning the motives of all guys interested in me. I could never, however, bring myself to confront any of them with this serious question. I eventually abandoned my shaky belief that race affected my relations with males because it was difficult for me to believe or comprehend that anyone would date someone from a different race or ethnic group out of curiosity or because they thought it would be fun. It just seemed so ridiculous to me. It was not until recently that I began to contemplate seriously the role race has played in my interpersonal relationships.

John had gone to Israel during the summer before our senior year, and during his stay, his ties to his Jewish culture were strengthened. It was a day after returning for our senior year of college that we broke up. I wasn't devastated by the split. During the summer, I had also been thinking about breaking it off; I wanted to be able to spend as much time as possible with friends before graduating. John stumbled through the words when he broke up with me. He mentioned how spending time in Israel really confused him, his parents were pressuring him, he just needed to work through the garbage, and he thought it best if we broke up. Later, when I asked him to please better explain what happened, he simply said that he didn't want to be tied down and didn't want to be in a relationship. Nine weeks later, he started dating someone else. She was Jewish.

Although my experience as a biracial child has at times been difficult, I do not disparage interracial relationships. As a result of my parents' marriage, I believe I hold a unique perspective on the world. I have realized that my skin color may be an attraction to some men and a turn-off to others. I need to confront this issue and ask the next person I become serious about whether I am being ruled-out or ruled-in because of my skin color. I sometimes feel that as a biracial woman I have one more doubt to add to the list of insecurities most women experience when dating. "Does he have 'jungle fever' and like me because I am black? Or does he consider it a sin to mix the races and dislike me because I am black?"

I am still exploring and defining who I am. During my senior year in college, my younger sister wrote me a letter encouraging me not to worry about the future and "life after college." She wrote, "Gather your strength and confidence from our ancestors." With the letter, she included a short family tree. It was then that I discovered my great-grandparents were Native American on my paternal grandmother's side and that my great grandfather on my father's side was West Indian. It came as a surprise to learn I have even more "mixed blood" than I realized, but so, too, do many black Americans.

In retrospect, it is difficult for me to say whether or not I would have liked for my parents to broach the topic of race while I was growing up. I sometimes wish that they would have talked about the implications of being biracial. Other times, I am very thankful for the journey of self-discovery. I have come to terms with what it means for me to be a biracial child in this country and I am at peace with my self-definition. But I also realize that there is a continuous struggle between self-definition and the external perceptions and assumptions of others. People continue to make judgments and assumptions about my actions based on my skin color. It is usually very subtle, and I find it difficult to address. Recently, a colleague of mine at work told me she knew of a very attractive black man whom I should meet. After her comment, I questioned if she would have given the same offer to a white colleague. Did she assume that I would only date black men? Did she think I *should* only date black men? Would she have said to a white woman, "I know an attractive *white* man whom you should meet?"

I also have to cope with many of the same injustices from the white community as all minorities do. As a child of a black-white union, I carry a part of my white mother with me wherever I go, so it is sometimes difficult to feel aligned with the black cause when it requires taking sides between the white and black communities. I have come to define myself as neither black nor white, but as a union of the two. I am still exploring the definitions and implications of the terms black, brown, African American, mixed, mulatto, etc. I am definitely more enlightened than I was when I began this journey of self-discovery and definition, but I have much more to learn and sort out. I've begun to research my background and have contacted my oldest living relative on my father's side to find out more about my heritage. My grandmother on my mother's side is also helping put the pieces together. I want to be able to give my children the gift of the past. I realize now that my family does not just consist of my parents and siblings. Regardless of the questions in my own mind and that of others regarding my biracial identity, I know who I am and I am proud.

6

Walking a Thin Line

LIZ

Liz's parents, a dark-skinned man of West Indian background and a "barely beige" mother, emphasized the value of an education and the importance of "winning" for a black girl. Liz attended, first, an elite country day school with a predominantly white population, where she was confronted with the stark realities of racism and bigotry. At her second school, one of the top prep schools in the country, Liz sought to be seen as an individual ("me first, black second") rather than as a representative of her race. Happier and more confident at this school, she was nevertheless confronted with questions of identity and race by privileged white teenagers. "What is the price one pays if one is educated in adolescence isolated from those visibly like oneself," her story asks. Liz wrote this narrative in her senior year.

My father always told me that life is a race; you have to run, and run hard, or else you'll be overtaken. If you are black, he said, you can't let yourself be overtaken even once. Today was my day to prove that I was faster and better. We lined up for the 50-yard dash, my best event. I knew Karen was desperate to win, and everyone wanted her to win because she was pretty and popular. "Go!" The light breeze turned to wind against my face. I felt my feet stomping the squishy, almost velvet grass. I ran trancelike for a few blinded seconds, and then, ahead of me, I saw the finish line and I knew I would be there first. As I crossed the line, I heard the other girls thundering in behind me. The onlookers gathered around Karen to console her. In their eyes she should have won, because she was pretty and popular. I had taken the glory meant for someone else. I stood alone, half smiling.

That day was my day to play their game and win. In longer races I pretended to be tired or too slow, and then sprinted by the other girls to the finish. Shorter races were a mere dash to the finish line. At the awards ceremony, I repeatedly rose from my seat among the other girls to collect my first-prize blue ribbons. The only award I didn't win outright was for the all-round best girl of track-and-field day. Karen and I shared that award, though I had beaten her in every event. That was life at my private country day school.

I took the train home, across bridges and through tunnels, returning to the cold shelter of concrete that was home. My father applied his "run hard" philosophy to everything that concerned me. I was to practice the piano for at least an hour each day as soon as I returned from school, eat dinner when my mother returned home from work, and then study until I went to sleep. This was the way things had to be if I were to be successful, if I were even to cross the finish line at all. "You have to be at least twice as good" was his constant refrain. My mother would tell him to stop saying things like that. "That's right," he would respond, "I forgot that you're white." This was a big joke for him, but it really annoyed my mother and it confused me. My mother is a small woman, whose skin is barely beige. People often approach her and rattle off quick questions in Spanish, which she doesn't speak. Her hair is nearly black with deep waves. Her lips are small, thin, and barely noticeable. I often wondered how she could be my real mother. I came to understand the joke much later, when my grandmother died.

My father refused to attend my grandmother's funeral in Maryland, so I accompanied my mother. I was introduced to a relative in the church who turned to my mother and said, "Don't worry. I have a darkie like her too." I understood then why my father wouldn't go. Even after nearly 30 years, he could not pay false respect to the woman who did not speak to her own daughter because she married a "darkie." She had forbidden their marriage and excluded both from any activity involving her. Why should my father be involved in her funeral? Why should I? The seas of resentment ran deep.

My grandmother had in fact forbidden more than that. When my mother's uncle offered to pay her tuition to attend Howard University, my grandmother had not allowed it. Instead, my mother had to stay home and take care of her four younger brothers. Women did not go to college; they married and had children. After many wasted years, my mother left home, got a job, and returned later only to have my father rejected. They married anyway, and my mother spent 10 years attaining a degree from college at night.

Physically, I am more like my father, which had been made clear to me at my grandmother's funeral. His deep black skin produced fear and awe. He is only 6 feet tall, but his blackness makes him appear a giant to the world. His big bones carry at least 50 pounds of excess weight, which people wrongly assume is pure muscle. His deep voice can revert to a West Indian accent in midsentence, or sometimes midword. His parents immigrated to New York City from a remote island in the British West Indies. His father died in Harlem when my father was 12, leaving his mother to raise two sons alone while working as a maid. Her main concern was her children's education. Having served as a soldier in World War II, my father was eligible for the GI Bill, even though he never had to fight because they didn't generally send black soldiers to the front lines. "Racism probably saved my life," he laughs sarcastically.

After the war, my father obtained both an undergraduate degree and a master's in social work. His mother "scrubbed white people's floors" to help him pay for his education. He chose social work in order to make a difference for people and, thus, to be important. While his strong bone structure and deep voice gave him power and authority within our home, they earned him only prejudice in the outside world. He was always acutely aware of this, having lived as an adult well before the civil rights movement. He chose political action as his career and used education as a means to achieve his goals.

This focus on education and achievement is why, beginning in 2nd grade, my parents sent me to an elite country day school in suburban Connecticut. At school I started learning the ways of racism the hard way. When I would answer every question correctly day after day in class, my parents were called and told I was too aggressive. And even though I was always the best and everyone knew it, my grades were only slightly better than average. When the class was broken into groups by ability, I would always be placed in the second to highest group; there was no way they were going to acknowledge that I was smarter. There was always another excuse, a favorite being that my handwriting wasn't clear enough. When my parents demanded that I be placed in the appropriate group, their pleas were ignored; their money would never be as good as that of my white peers. At every turn, the deep seas of racism had to be beaten back, either by my parents coming to school, or by my spending summers learning SAT words that my school wouldn't teach me, or mathematics equations they claimed I wasn't ready to learn. Maybe the hate words themselves didn't harm me, but the prejudices they represented certainly did.

But finally, by 8th grade, I had actually forced my peers and teachers to be accustomed to the idea that I was smart. I took pride in this because I had accomplished two goals. First, I gained a certain amount of respect from my teachers who had placed me in the highest English and math classes. Second, with a change in my appearance (thick straight hair, carefully curled each morning) I had managed to sneak into a group of friends. And I still had Wendy, my best friend since 4th grade. We had both been isolated by our peers.

Wendy was a short, chubby girl who had a slew of learning disabilities and a mother with multiple sclerosis who was confined to a wheelchair. The kids laughed at Wendy's mother, and she was deeply ashamed of her. We had managed to defend each other against our evil peers until we made it into the second most popular group, and we even made several friends in the most popular clique. We had discovered the key to popularity as teenagers: clothing and music. Clothing and music denied Wendy's weight problem and denied my blackness. We were both ecstatic, though we never spoke of it. Throughout our time at Country Day we remained best friends and by 8th grade we had immersed ourselves in our clique.

Looking back, I realize that it was my friendship with Wendy that saved me from eternal misery. I realized this when, on the bus from a field hockey game, Wendy told me, "You know, a lot of people think it's amazing that we're friends, since you're black and I'm Jewish." At the time I was angered that she had so directly identified my blackness. No matter how popular I was, I was still black and that really made my experiences different from my peers. Later on, I realized the importance of that comment. Wendy was aware of both what it meant to be black and what it meant to be Jewish. She recognized our friendship as a statement of hope for the world. We had both benefited and we were both very happy, although my love for my private school didn't grow.

One incident in 8th grade that stands out in my memory is a history lesson on the three-fifths clause in the U.S. Constitution. Under the three-fifths clause, blacks were no longer to be "nonpeople," we were now considered three-fifths of a person! My history teacher did not discuss who benefited from this proposal, using it instead as a symbol of change and movement toward equality. History class was the last period of the day, and as class ended, we gathered at the door anxious to go home. "Don't forget to put up your chairs," the teacher said. We each put up the chair in which we had sat and returned to the door. "Who didn't put up their chair? Who was sitting in that seat?" Someone had been absent that day and so there was an extra chair. "Who's going to put up the chair? We're not leaving until that chair is up." We all stood silently. We had been accused of something no one had done, then ordered to do something that was no one person's direct responsibility. I let out a loud sigh and walked to the back of the room, put up the chair, and returned to the door. "Thank you, Liz. You see class, blacks are worth more than three-fifths of a person." I stood in shock, full of regret at putting that chair up.

At dinner, I told my parents what my teacher had said. My father was furious, as I had expected. He sat back in his chair, pursed his lips, and let out a long "well" that ended with a sharp breath: "huh." My mother didn't know quite what to say either. For 4 years my parents had countered subtle attacks, but never one so blatant. For 4 years I had tried to work myself into the mainstream—to be Liz first and black second. In one foolish comment, my teacher rebuilt every barrier it had taken me four years to tear down. No one in that class and no one who heard of her comment could see me as myself first, and black second. The meaning of race had been explicitly exposed and confirmed by laughter.

That evening, my father, who majored in history in college, tried to teach me a year's worth of history in 3 hours. His deep, powerful voice wove American history with his family history. In my supplemental lesson, he went from American slavery to British slavery, from the three-fifths clause to how racism saved his life in World War II. As he moved in and out of history books and in and out of family history, his voice held my attention with long pauses and quick repetitions. By the end of the lecture, he had placed my teacher within a particular history and me within another. He wanted to come to school with me the next day, but I adamantly refused. I was too old for that.

The next day history class was, as usual, chaotic and unfocused. Finally, the teacher reached her breaking point and began her pathetic speech with these ill-chosen words: "Why don't you respect me?" During her 5-minute speech of whining and pleading, there were smirks all around. Suddenly, I felt my hand rise and my chair rock back on its hind legs. "Why should we respect you if you don't respect us?" Faces were now pale. I had said the unspeakable. My three-fifths self had nothing to lose.

The teacher was obviously shocked. "But I do respect you." Suddenly, everyone else in the room faded out. It was just me and her. I continued, "How is it that you respect me when you make racist jokes? How is it you respect me when you ask only me what I think about slavery?" The list was nearly endless. "I didn't mean for you to take it that way." I heard none of her words. They were meaningless. The damage had already been done. She could not retract or recast her words, as I could not mine. Each time she jumped to defend herself, her words were ignored. I summarized my father's history lesson. I told her how my family was from the British West Indies and how there was no three-fifths clause there.

That afternoon, my advisor sat me down and informed me that my history teacher had resigned from her position. He told me how she had not meant to hurt my feelings and that she could not be racist because she had worked at a school for delinquent youths, most of whom were black. Therefore, according to my advisor, I should apologize to her. I resisted, but I knew that I would be threatened with a variety of disciplinary actions, so I accompanied him to a meeting with my now ex-history teacher. She began by apologizing to me, and I followed with an obviously insincere apology. She then told me that I had an inferiority complex. I sat quietly and listened angrily. This complex, according to her, was common among blacks. She must have assumed the existence of this complex because I defended myself against unequal racist treatment. Once her conscience was satisfied, she stood and hugged me as my body stood passive and limp. I saw my advisor outside the window, his thumb pointed up and hand bobbling up and down. He had "done good." I had done as I was asked.

After that, I knew I did not want to spend 4 more years at my school. To my amazement, my peers congratulated me for standing up to the history teacher.

Even so, I was tired out, beaten down, and definitely needed to leave that school. I wanted to find a more diverse environment in which I could be a normal teenager rather than a token representative of my race. I wanted to go to the parties, to hang out after school with my friends, to be me first and worry about being black second.

At the beginning of sophomore year, I began at the Hilltop School. It is among several top prep schools in the country and is therefore both highly selective and academically rigorous. It also represented a whole new opportunity for me socially. My goal was clear. I wanted to be "cool." My choice was made; I would rather be white as it's easier, but since I could not be white, I would simply not address or confront anything that concerned being black. I would wear a blindfold. I would refuse to see. It would be easier this way because I could feel a part of things. Discrimination would not harm me if I did not see it clearly.

Strangely, though I now try to shake that decision to be blind and to look honestly at my experiences at Hilltop, I cannot. The openness of my childhood eyes had vanished when I attended Hilltop. All of my experiences at Hilltop were colored by my experiences at Country Day. And so, in describing Hilltop, I cannot remove my blinders the way I can with Country Day, where I saw the world in a manner that I wanted to leave behind when I began at Hilltop. There I was looking for a new way to see the world without race as the primary lens. I was simply seeking the perspective most everyone else had. To achieve this goal, I had to reject the "black first, me second" identity that Country Day had given me, though who I am is not separable from being black. But being black at Country Day was a main component of my identity there. At Country Day, the world was decolorized because there were no shades of grey; the world there for me was either good or bad, peaceful or violent, happy or sad, white or black.

At Hilltop, I found the in-between shades of grey by never really identifying myself with anything. This way I could be an individual—me first, black second. Hilltop gave me this chance by setting up an environment, for better or worse, that allowed my full participation as an individual. Finally, there was room for me that didn't have to do with being black. While the issue of race sometimes came up in conversations with my peers, it was always about how awful the outside world was and how different we would be. The issue never came up in any institutionalized or unavoidable way, at least in part because Hilltop took pride in its diversity. It wanted to encourage every individual. There were always plenty of black teachers, even though I never took a class with any of them, and they were always the most respected and admired teachers. Although during my first year there was a "black spot" in the cafeteria, it had vanished by my junior and senior years. While maybe there was a covert expectation that black students would date each other, there was rarely any dating at all. Most of my friends didn't have "real" boyfriends until college, so that never really became an issue. More than anything else, when I look back at Hilltop, I primarily see my development as an individual. I see myself as a rebellious, fun-loving teenager who learned much more socially than academically.

I showed up for registration at Hilltop with perfect teeth and a new pair of contact lenses. I knew that contacts were the most important possession I could ever own. When I exited the optician's office wearing them, the first thing that happened was a man tried to pick me up. I knew that contacts would change my life. And they did. Now I could be pretty and popular, the most important things for a girl to be. Starting from the first day I went to Hilltop, instead of being told I looked like a ram, I was told how lucky I was to be so pretty. Still, when I looked in the mirror, I had to struggle to see beyond my invisible thick glasses; when I touched my hair, I had to struggle not to feel any kinks.

After being at Country Day for so long, it was far more important for me to grow socially than academically. I felt confident for the first time in both areas. I knew I was academically qualified and respected by my peers, so I did not have to study twice as hard or run twice as fast. And even when I nearly failed physics during my sophomore year, no one ever questioned my overall ability. Instead of others seeing me as qualified only by race and gender, the issue was simply, "Liz is not very good at physics." For the first time, I was allowed to feel that I could be excellent at some things and poor at others. Being black had nothing to do with my strengths and weaknesses. This pervasive attitude at Hilltop was encouraged. Once a week, we would meet as a school in the auditorium where we were told to think about the world outside of Hilltop, to consider how we wanted the world to be. Each week we were told to get to know our peers, to try to meet new people different from ourselves in culture, race, class, and so on. We were told that the opportunity for an education at Hilltop was a gift not to be taken for granted. We should try to use it to build the world we wanted, starting with our community at school. Somehow, we believed anything was possible and in our potential to make changes. I think it is because I know the world can be like this that today I have a strong desire to help make the world "a better place."

Two incidents occurred during my senior year that centered on the issue of race. My senior fall, we were all geared up to look at colleges. Victoria had just returned from visiting UNC-Chapel Hill and Duke. I had not considered applying to either school because I preferred not to attend college in the South. Still, I had faithfully read in my numerous college guides about both schools.

"What did you think of Chapel Hill?" I asked. "I read that they've had the highest number of black student body presidents in the country." I'm not sure what I expected Victoria to say. I certainly did not expect her response "Yeah . . . well . . . they really like their basketball team." I pretended not to be offended, making no comment at all. I later recounted the story to my friends. More than anything, the comment had made me sad. Her judgment was so quick and certain, her perspective so limited. It was simply sad.

Her comment didn't directly affect me. I did feel directly affected, however, when Joan, a white South African student, asked what was wrong with the comment. "That wasn't a really bad thing to say, though, was it?" We all just kind of sighed and ignored her, thinking, "She really couldn't understand, after all, what could we expect from a white South African?" Instead of just leaving the issue alone, she started yelling at us and crying, "Why don't you treat me as though I'm like everyone else? I can't help that I was born in South Africa!" We all sat in shock, not knowing what to say. She ran off, and the incident was just forgotten.

Later on, it occurred to me why she yelled at us like that. We deserved it. I should have known how she felt. I had acted as if she could not understand racism. I had treated her differently than I might have treated an American or any other peer of mine. If she had been an American, I would have at least been annoyed. I might have tried to explain to her what was wrong with the comment. But because she was South African, we felt she deserved to be ignored. Just like how because I was black, I could only become student body president through my skill at basketball. I realized that I should have explained to her what was wrong with the comment, that we all should have. By the next day, I was no longer sad about Joan's ignorance but, rather, about my own. So I apologized to Joan and explained the comment to her. Ironically, she still didn't understand at all and insisted that the comment wasn't really racist. Even so, she didn't deserve to be ignored because of our assumptions about what a white South African would think. She might just as easily have known more about racism than any of us. My conscience was satisfied. I had gone back and treated her as a normal individual.

The second incident occurred just before graduation. I was talking with friends about the "three-fifths" incident I had experienced with my 8th grade history teacher. Suddenly Eric blurted out, "Oh, my god! You're black!" Everyone paused and laughed. "I mean, I knew you were black but I didn't really realize it." I had no idea what he meant, but I just said, "Yeah, no. I understand." Looking back on that comment, I realize what a really wise thing that was for him to say. Everyone there was equally shocked by the history story. I questioned whether they were shocked because nothing like that had ever happened at their old schools, or because they didn't realize how much of my experience was different from their own. Eric's words may not have been well chosen, but their meaning was significant. Because I had been an "individual" at Hilltop, I hadn't been black. That part of my identity had simply been ignored, set aside. Eric had simply admitted that his perception of me was not balanced.

At the same time, my perception of myself was not balanced either. I had not allowed my insecurities and anger at my experiences at Country Day to be a part of the self-confident, easy-going Liz everyone at Hilltop thought they knew. This self-protecting reaction was also helpful because it prevented me from bringing my resentment and distrust to Hilltop. Putting Country Day in a hidden place allowed my identity to come through independent of race. I became confident in my appearance, in part because my friends had ignored its obvious tie to race. I became confident in my academic ability because I didn't have to work constantly to prove myself to doubting peers. All of a sudden, I was good looking, smart, fun loving, independent, compassionate, popular, and also black. Certainly, I still had my insecurities, but they were below the surface. If I had allowed myself to bring Country Day to Hilltop, my experience would have been much different, far less developmental.

As I now consider what has made me who I am today, with my college graduation 2 weeks away, I can't help but focus on how my early experiences with racism (and sexism) have shaped my life. So much of my identity revolves around my struggle to find an individual identity as a black woman growing up in a predominantly white environment. I know that many of my experiences have separated me from other blacks. I will always walk a thin line to maintain my racial identity, but race will always bond me with others. It was a constant struggle, sometimes fruitful, most times disappointing and confusing. My adolescence was spent isolated from those visibly like myself, without role models, with no paved road. I felt beaten down and I knew I was all alone, without a soul to share my turmoil. No one understood me, and I only partially understood myself. And so, though wearing thick glasses, I could not clearly see myself or the world in which I was so out of place.

As I look toward my future, I do not know exactly what to expect. I know I would like to make a positive change, but there are so many ways to do that. I also know that I have not yet explored many options I find appealing. Over the next few years, I hope to explore some more creative options and figure out what I would like to do most. As I face my future after college, I feel a burst of hope and new energy. I can envision the world as I would make it. I can see that I have a place. But I also remember running, and my father's metaphor of life as a race that has to be run hard. He was right. As a black woman, I cannot ever let myself be overtaken.

7

Becoming Myself

CLAUDIO

Claudio's experiences as an African Caribbean, homosexual man exemplify the clash of prejudices and challenges that arise in belonging to more than one minority group. The son of an absent father and often suicidal mother, Claudio demonstrated great resilience in the face of multiple prejudices: racial discrimination within his own family because he and his brother are too "dark"; and ostracism from black communities in the U.S. because of homophobia and divergent cultural backgrounds. Claudio overcame some of these barriers by coming out as gay, first to friends, then to family, and finally embarking on a path of vocal gay rights activism. Because of Claudio's success in espousing gay rights, and the supportive gay community he found, combined with the shame and rejection he encountered from black communities, gay identity seems to take precedence over racial identity as a developmental milestone. This essay was written at the end of his sophomore year.

When I was 9 years old, my best friend in the world was Ronnie. We did everything together and spent a lot of time at each other's houses. One day, we were at Ronnie's house playing in the pool. After swimming we were taking separate showers in the outhouse by his pool, when Ronnie asked if he could step into my shower because he didn't have any soap in his. I wondered why I couldn't just pass him the soap, but all of a sudden I found myself excited at the idea of showering together. I had always been attracted to other boys, but didn't know what that attraction was and had never had the nerve or opportunity to act on it. At that moment I knew that I really wanted him to come over into my shower and that I wanted to see his body. I told him to come over.

Initially I didn't look at him. My back was turned to his as we stood under the same shower, and I was extremely nervous lest we get caught by his father or someone else. After a little while I relaxed a little and began to enjoy our shower. But when he said: "Why don't you turn around? It's no big deal if we see each other naked," I was terrified. I didn't want Ronnie to know I was aroused; I was afraid that he'd get mad and I'd lose my best friend. Then I turned around and realized he was turned on too!

That day we didn't do much more than explore each other's bodies with our hands. It was a wonderful experience and I felt closer to Ronnie than ever before. That was the first time I ever fooled around with another boy and from that moment I knew what was right for me. Ronnie and I became steady partners and were together for almost 7 years until I left Curaçao to come to school in the United States.

In order to understand much of what I am going to write about, you need to know a little about my family background. My name is Claudio. I'm from Curaçao, a little island in the Dutch West Indies. My father's parents are from Bonaire, one of Curaçao's sister islands, and my mother's parents are from St. Vincent. I am second-generation Curaçaoan.

My father's mother is white and his father black. My father took after his mother, having very light skin, a big pointed nose, and light brown eyes. My mother, on the other hand, is very dark, as her father is black and her mother half-black and half East Indian. When my parents were married, my father's family refused to accept my mother, saying that he was marrying beneath his level, although my mother's family is one of the most influential and wealthy on the island. My paternal grandmother carried this prejudice on with her grandchildren, saying that she didn't want to have anything to do with us; she called us "the monkey's children." Even as a very young child, I could sense her intolerance and shame, her unwillingness to be seen with us, the offspring of her son's undesirable marriage.

My parents' marriage was very fragile, and after the birth of my brother Mario, it began to fall apart. I remember my parents arguing; knowing that my mother was suffering hurt me deeply. I would often go to my mother when she was alone in her room after fighting with my father; we spent night after night crying together on her bed. One night, after my father had gone to bed following a particularly incendiary argument, I heard someone quietly crying. I knew that it had to be my mother. As I approached where she sat in the doorway, I realized she wasn't wearing any clothes and that she was pointing a large knife at her chest. I started yelling for my father and ran to get my grandmother who lived next door. They eventually persuaded my mother to put down the knife, but that wasn't the end of the story. My mother had also taken a huge amount of Valium and she was hospitalized for several weeks.

While my mother recovered from her suicide attempt, my brother and I stayed with my grandmother. Life was so much friendlier there, free of arguments and crying: Life was what it should be for a kid. When my mom came home from the hospital we had a family meeting and my dad promised to change his ways. The perfect life we had once shared was back on track—but only for a while. By late summer things took a turn for the worse, and my mother again attempted suicide. But this time when my mother came home, my father did not.

Eventually my parents divorced, and I no longer had a father. He never came to visit his three sons, who missed him dearly. As a result, my brothers and I spent much of our childhood going to therapy sessions to help us cope with the questions and problems that resulted from our childhood years. Even today I still harbor a great deal of anger and bitterness toward my father—for the pain and suffering he caused me and my brothers, because he was never there when I needed him most, but more importantly for what he put my mother through in their years together. Three lifetimes would not be enough time for me to forgive my father.

During those turbulent years, there were only three places where I felt special and safe: in my own bedroom, at my grandmother's house, and at school. I was always the top student, and the teachers helped me feel proud of my intelligence. I think back and realize how obnoxiously arrogant I must have been when I was a kid in elementary school and in the beginning of high school. School was the only stage on which I could shine, and I made sure everyone knew it. I realized that I was worth something, and that even if things were bad at home, I always had the sanctuary of school in which I could learn to become a better and stronger person.

However, outside of school, I was very insecure, perhaps because I sensed from the start that I was somehow different and that this difference would set me apart from my peers. I've known about my homosexuality as far back as I can remember. I didn't always have a name for it, but since I was 5 or 6 years old I knew that I felt closer to boys than I did to girls. I also knew that there was something wrong about these feelings I had: They were considered wrong. I had many female friends during my childhood, but they never made me feel the way I did when I was around my male friends. Whenever I was with a boy I felt a certain satisfaction that I didn't feel with girls. I was very young and confused about it. As I grew older and started to have sexual fantasies, I realized what was going on and was terrified. I was only 9 years old when I truly admitted to myself that I was sexually attracted to boys, but I was going to change it. I had always heard that gay people were animals, that being gay was a sin, so I tried everything I could to suppress my attraction to other guys. But nothing worked. When I was 12, I decided to accept the fact that I was gay and I came out to myself.

By that time I had been actively intimate with Ronnie for almost 3 years. We saw each other almost everyday and we would often spend our time together in sexual experimentation. Although our experiences were almost all very positive ones, they were under the pretense that we were straight friends who did things with each other that simply felt good. We had never talked about being gay, and at 12 years old there was no way that I could tell anybody that I was gay, so I decided to pretend that I wasn't. I didn't think it would be that tough, but I proved myself wrong.

Having to live my life hiding in the proverbial closet, constantly lying about liking girls and trying to force myself to be attracted to them, was the worst part of growing up for me. People expect a young guy to talk about girls in an enthusiastic way, and I made sure that I did. I knew that I would have to live with the pain, the prejudice, and the lack of acceptance that I would face in my life if I ever decided to be out. I really wanted to be able to be myself, but I knew I would pay a high price so I kept my secret. I started to hate myself for being gay when I was 14. "Why am I cursed like this?" was the question that went through my mind most frequently. From when I was 14 to when I was 17, I did everything I possibly could to appear straight, yet I despised having to hide a part of myself that was as inherently me as the deeply dark brown color of my skin. I could never share my true feelings about myself and about my future with family and friends, and found myself constantly lying and making up stories in an attempt to hide my homosexuality. I spent those years pretending to be someone and something that I wasn't.

What really enraged me was always hearing people say, "Be yourself," when I grew up knowing that "myself" was something that people would not accept. Filled with self-hate, I turned to alcohol around that time and I started to think about suicide. One night when I was almost 15 I tried to kill myself. I locked myself in my room after taking many shots of vodka and several shots of drain cleaner and waited to die. The pain quickly became so intense that I started convulsing wildly and screaming at the top of my lungs. Fortunately, my mother and stepfather rushed to my rescue. As the medics put me in the ambulance, I saw my mother violently sobbing on the ground outside the front gate, and I knew at that moment that I would never try to take my life again.

Ronnie and I fooled around from the age of 9 until we were 16. We promised each other never to tell anyone about what we had done together. We had a 7-year monogamous relationship by default, as neither of us knew any other guys who would want to risk fooling around. And at the time we really didn't need anyone else. We were young and horny and had found the best outlet for our sexual energy. But the sex was just sex; Ronnie didn't allow any other attachment, any kind of intramale affection.

Ronnie and I never talked about being intimate and having sex with each other, though it happened almost every time we were together. The few times I brought up the issue Ronnie told me to shut up and quickly changed the topic.

He was afraid to talk about it, since we had always heard that gay sex was one of the worst things a person could engage in. We knew that if people found out, we would be alienated and ostracized severely. By never naming what we were doing, we also thought that we somehow avoided responsibility for taking part in such "deviant" acts. As we grew older though, I wanted to do more than just have sex. I wanted to know what Ronnie thought about us, but he wouldn't talk. I wanted to feel the romantic affection of another man. Instead, he became more and more ashamed of having sex with another guy, until he could hardly look me in the eye. Our friendship started to suffer as a result, and though we're still friends, to this day Ronnie and I have never talked about all those times we spent by ourselves, locked in my room or out in the woods. Last summer Ronnie got married to a long-time girlfriend of his.

When I was 16, I decided I wanted to broaden my horizons, to leave the limited environment of my island. My family could afford to send me to the United States, so I decided to apply to boarding school. One question on the application stands out in my memory: "Which one of the following best describes your ethnic background?" None of the possible answers accurately fit my background, so I decided to check "African American." But when my mother saw my check mark, she exclaimed, "Don't put yourself down as African American!"

"Why not?" I asked.

"Because you're not African American. You don't want to associate yourself with those people. When are they going to stop dwelling on the past and start working for their future? If they continue the way they are going, they'll never improve their situation. You're in a class above them and remember that. Check 'other' and fill something in there." I looked at her, wondering if she was kidding, but I didn't challenge her because I thought she was right. Growing up I was taught that African Americans were lazy and loved to live off of the government and that they only perpetuated their situation by feeling sorry for themselves. I thought it was their own fault for being in the situation that they were in. So, I checked "other" and wrote down "Dutch West-Indian/black."

I left Curaçao just after my sixteenth birthday for a new life, new friends, and a new school in Stowe, Vermont. I was going to be a junior and planned to go to college after I graduated in 2 years. I was confident that I would succeed in anything I aspired to. Nevertheless, I was scared beyond all imagination about arriving at Stowe by myself and not knowing anyone there. It was quite intimidating. It wasn't until the night before I left Curaçao that I realized how much it hurt my mother to see me go. She didn't want to lose her oldest son. "Are you leaving me because I left you when you were 10? Are you trying to get back at me for abandoning you?" she asked, crying loudly, "I should never have let you apply in the first place."

When I was 10 years old, soon after my parents' divorce, my mother decided to leave Curaçao and went to New York to get her college degree. My two brothers and I spent the next few years reconciling our feelings of desertion with our love for her. It took me a while to get over my feelings of abandonment, but by the time I was 14 I understood that my mother was doing something which would benefit us all in the long run. I harbored no hard feelings about it and that is why her words that night took me by surprise. I had never been accused in such a way before and I was stunned that my mother thought that I was trying to get revenge. I started to cry myself and assured her that I was not trying to get back at her. The next morning, as I was leaving my home, I could see all the pain in her eyes because we both knew that we would probably never get to live with each other again. "Once they leave, they never come back. I shouldn't have let him apply to school," I heard my mother whisper to my grandmother at the airport. Deciding to stay on Curaçao would have been the best gift I could have given my mother, but I was selfish and ambitious and I needed to get off that little island. I still sometimes think about the happiness I could have brought to my mother by simply staying put, but my life was just beginning; I have many years to make my mother happy.

I got to Stowe that afternoon. I wasn't ready to face new people, so I decided to stay in my room and unpack. A couple of hours after my arrival I left my room to roam around the dorm. In the TV room there was another black guy who had recently started the process of dreading his hair. His head was a farm for hundreds of little twisted clumps of hair that grew straight out of it.

By his accent and appearance, I assumed he was African American. He said his name was Kenny. I told him that my name was Claudio and that I was from Curaçao. "No way man," he said, "I'm from St. Thomas." From that instant, Kenny and I were good friends. Around Stowe we became known as the "Islandboys." Once I had met Kenny, it was easier to branch out and meet more people. It was the beginning of some great times at the school.

On Curaçao I was used to living in a society that didn't segregate on the basis of race or ethnicity. Everyone lived together in complete peace and harmony. But at Stowe things were different. I was struck by the extreme diversity of the student body, but what was more striking was how each group segregated themselves. Blacks hung out with blacks, whites with whites, Latinos with Latinos, and so forth. I had a hard time dealing with this phenomenon, although our dorm was the most integrated group on the campus.

One of the first nights at Stowe, I asked my friends to explain to me why people at Stowe chose to segregate themselves so much. They said this trend wasn't true only at Stowe but all across the United States and explained that people didn't necessarily segregate themselves by choice but that many groups feel unwelcome with people of other races or ethnicities. That night I had my first lesson in race relations and I realized how much minorities in the United States suffer on a daily basis, a very foreign concept for me at the time.

Soon enough, however, I began to experience some racism myself. And though I had a really hard time dealing with it, it didn't bother me as much as the discrimination I was experiencing from the black community at Stowe. People I thought of as my own didn't like me because of who I was. Looking for organizations to join at Stowe, I came across the Stowe Afro-Latino Society, a social/support group for people of African or Latino descent. Being of African descent, I figured I would have a lot in common with the members of the organization and decided to become a member. But I wasn't welcome. I didn't speak the African American vernacular, didn't walk like African Americans, and because I couldn't identify with their experiences, they labeled me a "sellout," an "oreo cookie."

The women in the group were more accepting than the men, who had a particularly hard time dealing with my sexual orientation, which some people had begun to speculate about. They hated the fact that I was gay, and most of them refused to speak to me. There seemed to be an underlying shame that a "brother" could be gay. Initially, I was deeply hurt by this treatment and couldn't understand how a group of people who, over the centuries, had suffered the pain of marginalization themselves could, in turn, marginalize me: another brother. This experience made me realize that, as a gay man, I would not be assured of any communal bond, except with the gay community, with which I had no contact at the time. I know now that homosexual prejudice transcends race, nationality, religion, and even friendships and family. When I realized that the black community at Stowe was unwilling to accept me because they thought I was gay, I decided that I didn't need their support. I looked for friends elsewhere and met some wonderful people in the process.

My dorm housed an incredible diverse mix of students from all over the world. We all liked each other very much, respected each other's differences, and learned about each other's cultures. I spent 2 of the best years of my life at Stowe, and one of the main reasons for that was how wonderful all the guys in my dorm were. During my first year at Stowe I didn't fool around with anyone. I was afraid to alienate myself from the mainstream in any way, afraid that if my dorm mates found out I would be totally ostracized. I decided to establish myself in my dorm first before I did anything that risked my being rejected. Being in an all-male environment made it quite difficult to control my urges and desires, since all kinds of homoerotic activities took place on a regular basis. Nevertheless, I wasn't intimate with a guy at Stowe until November of my senior year.

After a football game that November, I went back to my dorm room with a friend named Brian. He lived in my dorm and had just begun to hang out with my best friend, Jason. Beginning tentatively, we eventually shared a sexual experience. When we were done I asked him what he thought and he said: "That was great. I want you to know that I'm not gay though. I was just experimenting." I told him that I also had had a good time. I was really happy I had found someone to be sexually intimate with and someone who wasn't afraid to talk about it.

A few months later, in the winter of my senior year, I came out to Jason. Being able to muster up enough courage to tell Jason that I was gay was one of the most liberating processes I have ever experienced. For me, coming out was a way to show the enormous self-respect I had and a refusal to continue being ashamed of my homosexuality. Coming out was a lifelong process for me that began at the instant I realized that I was attracted to other guys. I finally reached the end of that process when I was a senior at Stowe. There were two main reasons I came out. One was to stop lying. By the time I was a senior at Stowe I had lied so much to friends and family about every aspect of my life that it scared me. Consciously denying the fact that I was gay was at the root of the deception. And from this lie more lies manifested themselves by force. Sometimes I would lie about an experience with a girl, for example, and a few months later when someone brought it up, I would have totally forgotten the details of my lie! The second and more important reason I came out was because I wanted to be myself. I reached the point where I refused to reject a very integral part of my being, refused to be ashamed. I was gay and was going to be gay to everybody. I no longer cared what people thought, as long as I knew that I was being honest to myself.

When I decided to tell Jason I was gay, it was easier said than done. I knew that he was gay-friendly, a straight member of the Stowe gay/straight alliance. Nevertheless, I was so afraid of his reaction that I had actual nightmares about telling him. But I was so close to telling him that I had to do it then lest I never get the chance again.

"Jason, there's something that I've wanted to tell you for some time now, but haven't been able to." I said. "It's still very hard for me to say this and I'm afraid." "What is it Claudio? You know you can tell me anything," he replied.

I looked him right in the eye and said, "Jason, I'm gay." He looked, smiled, and shook his head. "Is that all?" he asked. He walked over gave me a hug and told me: "It makes no difference to me, buddy. You're still the same Claudio. I'm honored that you trust me enough to tell me." At that moment I felt better than I had ever felt before. It was something I had never experienced before—Claudio, Uncensored. Someone else knew my secret; someone finally knew the true me. I felt closer to Jason that night than I ever had before. Because Jason was the first person I felt the courage to come out to, he became the most important friend I had during my teenage years. Without his support that night my life would have taken a different turn, and the story of my life would probably be different than it is now.

I had two other sexual relations at Stowe my senior year. Pete and I were sexually active for about a month early on in my senior winter at Stowe. He was Asian Caucasian. Even though he seemed to intensely enjoy our sexual adventures, Pete always made blatantly homophobic remarks in public, and I decided that I couldn't be involved with someone like that. He did change his ways once I came out to him, but whatever intimacy we shared came to an abrupt end.

Sangick was very different. Sangick was the first guy I ever made love to. It was more than just fooling around, it was love. A gay man never forgets the first time another man tells him that he loves him. The night I heard those words from Sangick was one of the most special nights of my life. Sangick and I were lovers for the rest of my time at Stowe. Telling him good-bye was one of the toughest things I've ever had to do.

My graduation from Stowe was especially hard for me. In my 2 years at the academy I had formed the closest friendships of my 18 years, and in the span of 2 days, the 45 guys who had been part of my everyday life for 2 years slowly disappeared. My 2 years at Stowe were the only time of my life that I have ever been truly happy. I had gone to Stowe a young, innocent, undefined 16 year old and left having learned to accept and love my newfound self: I found the true Claudio in those 2 years. The school had been a safe haven from my unhappy past, and I was about to leave the sanctuary of that place for college.

I decided to attend a prestigious college in New England because it seemed to be so much like Stowe. It was a relatively small school in a rural setting with a beautiful campus and a reputation for having the friendliest people. When I visited my future college for the first time, the beautiful architecture and the green campus grounds reminded me of Stowe in every way possible. It seemed to be just what I wanted.

The summer after I graduated from Stowe I came out to my parents. It was the day of the World Cup finals. I had planned to tell my parents that I was gay that summer, but I had no idea how to go about it because I was afraid they would react badly: "Hi mom. Did you see the game today? Brazil won and I'm gay, by the way." How do you break such news to your mother? I was very concerned about loosing my family's love and support. I was still financially dependent on my parents for everything I needed and I wanted to go to college! If my parents decided to disown me, who would pay my college tuition? Where would I live? Where would I call home?

That summer I had started hanging out with some gay teenagers. They showed me the ropes about gay life on Curaçao. I had never had gay friends before, and my mother became a little curious. That day at brunch my mother dropped the bomb: "OK Claudio, I have a question for you," she said. "Why have you started hanging out with all these gay guys?" That was my cue. I thought, "Claudio, this is your chance. Fucking tell her!!"

"Because I'm gay," were the words that fell softly from my lips and spilled all over the table.

"Are you serious?" She asked me earnestly as she picked up her glass of champagne and took a giant sip.

"Yes, I'm gay."

My mother looked at my stepfather and then back at me. My heart pumped as she searched for words, but I tried to seem calm.

"So what do you think?" I asked.

"Well, what can I do? If you're gay, then you're gay. I can't change that. You're still my son, and I still love you more than you can imagine." There was a tone of disappointment in her voice, and her eyes filled with tears. I understand how hard it must have been for my mother to hear what I told her that day and I really couldn't have asked for a better reaction. I am really proud of my parents and family and very relieved that I'm able to be myself around them. They have been extremely supportive of my decisions in life, including my lifestyle as a gay man.

My grandmother has also been very supportive. She once told me, "Make sure that when you have a boyfriend that you bring him to visit me so that I can meet him. I want your boyfriends to be as big a part of my life as your brothers' girlfriends." Those words probably carry the most meaning of anything I've ever been told. I love my parents, grandmother, and brothers dearly for having accepted me as a gay son, grandson, and brother.

Before I knew it, I was getting ready to leave for my freshman year in college. As September drew nearer, I became increasingly concerned about my prospects as an openly gay man in college. My parents were also very concerned, due to the college's conservative and homophobic history. The biggest problem I had to face was my own courage and integrity. I had just come out of the closet and I promised myself that I would never go back into that darkness. But all of a sudden I went from being out and proud to being horribly afraid and unsure about being openly gay in a new environment. I had heard horrible things about my college's past and feared becoming another victim of the school's history of hate.

My freshman year started out pretty rough. Many people told me I was the first person they knew who entered his freshman year at the school openly gay. I was surprised, but I loved wearing that crown, and was proud that I had broken new ground. Still, I was confused. Everyone was really supportive and accepting, but they all talked about how unaccepting this college was and how brave I was. A few weeks after I arrived on campus I met with Ted, the head of the gay organization on campus. Ted also painted a bleak picture of my collegiate future. He basically said that because I am openly gay I would never be accepted into the mainstream, that I would be extremely alienated, and that I should be ready for many personal attacks, both verbal and physical. I left the meeting feeling scared, disappointed, and distraught.

Ted's prophecy of verbal attacks proved true almost immediately after people found out I was gay. Accepting the fact that my social options were diminished, I decided to find my place within the gay community at my school. But I soon realized there really wasn't one. There were no more than seven people on campus who were out. Wanting to find a sense of community, I turned to the African American organization on campus. I had met two black women who accepted my homosexuality and decided to go to them for advice. They told me there was no way I would be accepted by the men in the group, and it hurt me very deeply that I was, once again, turned away by my own people because of my sexual orientation. That fall I stayed in my room for the entire term, depressed and angry, not leaving except for classes, meals, and rehearsals for my singing groups. I called up every other Ivy League school asking them for transfer materials. I wasn't going to take 4 years of this crap. I was getting out. At Christmas break I told my parents that I was planning to transfer, and they were very happy with my decision.

But, when I returned to school in the winter, I started to have fun. I started hanging out at a fraternity and became good friends with four brothers who were gay. They introduced me to the drug culture at my school. For a while I had fun smoking pot every day, but soon it annoyed me that having fun always entailed smoking pot. I got my break from marijuana when I met Clive.

Clive was a member of a gay youth organization at another school in the region and he was beautiful, intelligent, funny, interesting, extremely charming—in short, everything I wanted. That spring everything was great because I was in love. Being with Clive took my mind off the oppressive atmosphere at my school.

Toward the end of spring term I ran for the cochairmanship of the gay organization on campus in a campaign I named "Becoming Visible." My goal was to get homosexuality more visible on campus. I won the election and was suddenly extremely visible. I was very excited at the time and had no idea of the adversity that lay ahead. Through my work with the gay group on campus, I really started to grow up. I didn't take little things for granted anymore. I had to watch my back constantly, because of my position as "big gay man on campus." Throughout the spring and summer, my relationship with Clive was the one thing I felt I could count on. When I felt the relationship start to fade I fought to make it work, but it ended soon enough. The pain was immense; the love I had counted on to survive had left me again, and my life started to go downward.

When my sophomore fall started, I began to hate my school again. Most of my time was dedicated to the gay organization, and I was also active in numerous other political groups on campus. As chair of the gay organization, I took on the task of changing the school's two centuries of homophobia. I realized early on that I would be fighting a virtually impossible war. The students simply don't care about the issue, and though the administration is concerned, it's afraid of the financial repercussions of dealing with issues of homosexuality on a large scale. As a result, an entire group of people is left feeling they have no place on my campus. My school is often said to have the highest student satisfaction rating in the country. I ask myself, "Who are the people that are so happy?" I know that it's not the gay men and women who attend this school.

In a recent letter to the student body about four suicides on our campus within one school year, the dean of the college said that the school did nothing that lead these students to kill themselves. True. The school truly did nothing, absolutely nothing to make this campus a better place for these students to live, learn, and grow in. My school has a long history of discrimination against anybody untraditional and a "culture of apathy" that discourages any significant change. At a well-publicized discussion to address a rash of rampant homophobic activity on campus, only 14 people showed—2 reporters, the 5 organizers, 2 gay college officials, and the invited guests. That proved to me that people here just don't care about minority issues. They are privileged to the point where they don't have to, I guess.

In the past 2 years I have been the target of homophobic harassment on campus. I've received threatening messages on the phone and on e-mail, and people yell homophobic remarks at me when I walk across campus. I can't go anywhere on campus and feel safe. What kind of college experience is this? The college has a "Principle of Community" that states that all students have the right to live in a safe, comfortable, and respectful environment, but that hasn't been my experience. In my 2 years here, I've seen the administration try to assure the safety, comfort, and respect it claims to be a basic right of all students, but the majority of the student body still harbors a lot of hostility toward minority students, especially those that are gay and lesbian. I look back at my first 2 years and see how much I've grown because of the adversity I have faced.

All resentment aside, I feel like I have accomplished much. I have exposed everyone on this campus to issues of homosexuality by being out and visible, which I believe is imperative, and I've answered thousands of questions, hoping to foster a better understanding. The level of tolerance for gays and lesbians on this campus has increased to a more reasonable level, but much work still needs to be done. More and more people feel free to come out of the closet and the gay community has grown to a number which no longer makes me feel like I'm the only gay person on campus. My political career has come to an end though, at least for the rest of college. I need to fight my own war. I am going to spend my junior and senior year taking care of myself, spending quality time with my friends, and having a good time. I need to take advantage of the little time I have to just be myself.

8

Becoming Comfortable in My Skin

SUSANNA

Susanna, the only child of a white Swiss mother and an African American father who divorced when she was a child, grew up with little awareness of race in a multi-ethnic neighborhood. Living with her mother, a practicing Buddhist, at a Zen center after the break up, Susanna found herself the only black child at the local public school. This confirmed for her a growing sense of being an "outsider." Though in adolescence she came to embrace her identity as a black woman, she moved in white circles and had two important friendships with white women—one a "punk" at the private alternative school she attended, and the other her college roommate, who was Jewish. Intense and rewarding though the relationships were in many ways, Susanna concluded that these white women could never fully understand her experiences as a woman of color. An exchange term at a prominent black women's college in the South enabled Susanna to feel respected, understood, proud of her black racial identity, and ready to take on the challenges of graduate school. At the time of writing she was completing her final term of college.

I'm tired of explaining. I often wonder why more black people haven't gone into international relations; we have more practice at diplomacy than anyone. Our relationships with whites require such constant diplomacy that we should get diplomatic immunity from the U.S. government.

I'm tired of explaining. I'm sick of being the spokesperson for all black people. How should I know why black people rioted and destroyed their South Central home? I can guess, because I know history, but why does my hypothesis carry more weight than someone else's? I live 3,000 miles away and have never been there, but white people are ready to take my word over that of a white person who grew up in L.A. Why?

I'm tired of explaining . . .
My hair: Why is it braided?
Music: How can rap be called singing?
If they sample, isn't that stealing?
How can you buy an album with two men talking and another simply play-
ing someone else's songs in the background?
Why do you all sit together? (Excuse me, but why do you all sit together?)
Why do you get so out of control in church?
Why do you all talk like that? Don't you know how to speak "correctly"?
Why are so many young black men uneducated, incarcerated, addicted?
Why are so many black girls mothers?
Who is Malcolm X?
Why don't you love Dr. King? J.F.K.? Lincoln?
Why do we need a black history month?
Why do you want to be called African American instead of black?
Why do you always have to bring race into it?
WHY, WHY, WHY?

It seems that I am supposed to have all the answers. I don't. Because I'm black, I'm an authority on "Being black in America." I therefore have enormous power—and responsibility.

There is a certain paranoia built into my consciousness, bred from years of explanations and condemnations. "What are you?" they ask, as if my race defines me. If I say that I am African, Swiss, and Cherokee, does the listener gain some intimate knowledge of my mind or heart, or do they simply know my genealogy? How does my genetic code set up my social realities? I've grown accustomed to the questions, and most answers are by now memorized and routine. Recently, however, I was caught off-guard when a white friend of mine decided to set me up with one of her boyfriend's friends. As we talked about the upcoming blind date, all that kept running through my mind was, "I hope she told him I'm black." It was such a simple thing, really, just two words, "She's black." I felt unbelievable relief when she said that she had told the boy that I was black.

This situation, in various forms, is played out over and over during my life, and I find I have become uncomfortable in my skin. My white friend would never dream of having to explain her skin color. As my friend told me about this blind date, I rubbed my skin and looked down at my shuffling feet. I often experience this discomfort in my own skin, when I walk through the mall, or stand in line at the bank, or enter a white bar, when I drive through white neighborhoods, or sit in a restaurant full of white people. I become uncomfortable in my skin and want to rub it off. The rubbing action is usually not apparent to those around me, but it reveals my paranoia.

I know that I am a human being and I have as much right to be in these places as white people. But I'm not white and it matters that I'm not. Every one of those faces that watches me as I sit down to eat, or follows me up the aisle as I pick out jeans, knows that it matters. I know that all of those people are not Ku Klux Klan members or Nazis. I realize that some of them may even be dating or married to a person of color. I try to keep an open mind. I try very hard to appear comfortable. But I know that even one racist among them could cause me a lot of trouble. In the extreme, I could die because of their paranoia. More likely, I may not be served promptly, or the clerk might triple-check the items I take into the dressing room. It all has to do with my skin, so I feel uncomfortable because that is their only basis for judging me. What they react to is my genealogy, not me. My genealogy is inescapable, and in this society it defines me.

My mother was white and my father was black. As a child, I viewed them as equals, regardless of their gender or skin color. They were both my parents and exercised equal control over my life. Since they were both equally in control in our house, I naturally assumed that this equality extended into the world beyond our front door. This assumption was confirmed by the neighborhood in which we lived. My friends were black, white, Hispanic, Jewish, Catholic, Baptist, American-born, and foreign. By age 6, I not only spoke English but also understood some Spanish and Hebrew. One of my favorite playmates was a little black girl named Brooke who, along with her baby brother, lived in the home of her adoptive white parents. All of this seemed perfectly normal to me. I had no idea that my neighborhood and life were different in any way.

I didn't know that there was a difference between being black or white until I was 7 years old. I didn't wake up one day and exclaim "Hey, I'm half black and half white!" It was a gradual process of self-discovery and definition that I don't believe has ended or ever will end. I'm constantly trying to figure out who exactly I am and how I fit into the larger American society.

Although my neighborhood was inhabited by people of various backgrounds, the school I attended was right in the middle of a predominantly black area. Except for the Jewish kids who went to Hebrew school, every child on my block attended the same school. Classes consisted of about 20 black students and 3 or 4 white ones. Some classes were all black, simply because there were not enough white kids to go around. My homeroom was one of these all black classes.

One day our teacher introduced a new student to our class. We all turned around and found, to our horror (myself included) that he was white. The poor boy was not just white, but *white*, practically albino. He had extremely pale, almost translucent skin, blue eyes, and the blondest hair I had ever seen. As we stared, some jaws dropped and there was a sound, something between a snicker and a murmur, but definitely an inhospitable menacing sound. Very quickly this new boy's face went from vanilla to cherry. My immediate reaction was that we were invaded by something foreign. This boy was not like us. I knew for sure whatever we were, he wasn't.

I'm not sure I realized at that moment that I was not white or if it was more a matter of realizing that this new boy was white. I knew that I belonged in this class, in this group of people, and he didn't. I didn't hate him, but I couldn't understand why he was in our class. Where exactly I expected him to be instead of with us, I really don't know. I had other classes with white students and I had never felt this way toward a fellow student before. It seems my racial identity was discovered and defined by recognizing someone else's race. To see myself, I had to see someone else.

As I matured, I began to see the complexities inherent in defining oneself in this society along racial lines. This definition was even more difficult for me as a biracial child. On the one hand I have a certain freedom of movement single-race people do not have: I move in white and black groups with equal ease (and equal difficulty). To a certain extent both groups accept me, yet they also reject me. I am at once black and white, and neither black nor white. However, it has become clear that I will always be treated as a person of color. I cannot "pass" as a white person; though light-skinned, my appearance and features obviously belong to a woman of African descent. I choose to identify myself as a black woman because that is the contextual reality of my life. Were I lighter skinned, European featured, and had I then chosen to "pass," my life would be very different. I cannot escape my ancestry; I am reminded daily of my history every time I have to explain or defend myself. I have chosen, therefore, to love and celebrate my African past. I am still defining myself. It matters that my mother is white; my Swiss immigrant ancestors set me apart from other black people who have no white ancestors (or none within recent memory). However, none of us arc treated with complete equity or respect by white America. This, I believe, binds us together more closely than our distant or not-so-distant ancestral blood.

My parents argued constantly and seemed incompatible opposites during their marriage. They had separate bedrooms; my mother was at her best in the mornings; my father loved the night; she took me to the beach; he taught me to draw. Rarely did the three of us do anything as a family. When I was 7, my parents divorced. At this time my mother was a practicing Buddhist. She and I moved in with a family who were also Buddhists who lived right next to a Buddhist center.

After a while the Zen center moved to a small town outside the city, so we followed. Until that point I hadn't paid too much attention to the Zen center other than occasional visits during ceremonies. While my mother and the other adults went to morning or evening Zen practice, the other kids and I hung out together playing games or watching TV. I was the only black or biracial child. The family we lived with was white and had two sons, and there were two Japanese girls living at the Zen center who had been adopted by a white couple. Once we moved to the country, however, my mother's Buddhism became more of an issue.

The Zen center bought an old nursing home and began building around the existing structure to suit its needs. Everyone living at the center participated in the construction. We had licensed electricians and plumbers living there, and every person had a job. Men, women, and children pounded nails, rolled out insulation, swept plywood floors. Working together we raised the walls and attached the roof. One of the principles of the Zen center was to work together and develop a community that was as self-sufficient as possible. We grew our own food and built and maintained our own buildings. Eventually, we added the meditation hall, a dining room, a fitness area with a hot tub and sauna, a library, an office, a pagoda, and, in the woods, a separate monastery for monks and nuns. I was again immersed in a diverse community of people: wood carvers, potters, jewelers, singers, a belly dancer, a nurse, a couple of sailors, business-men and women. I met people from all over the United States, as well as Canada, Japan, Korea, Laos, Cambodia, Vietnam, China, France, Germany, and Poland, among others.

I was usually one of a very few black people at the center, though I never felt out of place or alone. There was always something to do, either exploring in the woods, doing chores, or playing with the endless stream of children that passed through, especially at ceremony times. Most adults worked outside the center. Food was cultivated or bought collectively, though you had to pay room and board and rent. Any additional food, personal items, or clothing were bought by each individual. My mother worked (as she had since my birth) at a hospital in the city as a chemistry lab technician. Child care was never a prob-lem as there were always plenty of older children and adults keeping an eye on the youngest kids.

While life in the Zen center was fun, exciting, and safe, I found public school to be one of the most horrible experiences imaginable. I was the only black child in the entire school. I was a minority for the first time. The rest of the students were overwhelmingly of French Canadian descent and white. I remember being constantly aware of my dark skin, my Afro, even my height. I was tall for my age, which had never bothered me before, but in this new setting being tall only seemed to make me stand out more. I learned to slouch down in my chair in an attempt to go unnoticed. I had friendships with a few of the girls in school and in the neighborhood, but these friendships never lasted. I believe the prejudices of the girls' parents were mainly responsible; I was black, and my mother was a Buddhist. Whether one or the other of these facts was more responsible, I don't know. The combination kept me from forming lasting friendships with any of the other kids.

My father, who was an artist, stayed in the city, never became a Buddhist, and didn't like the idea of me growing up in a Zen center. Like most of our neighbors, he thought of Buddhism as a strange cult. Eventually, he realized that neither my mother nor I was being brainwashed in any way; so instead, he worried about "practical" things, like my ability to eat at a dining room table. I had grown up like most other Americans, eating meals at a table with silverware. At the Zen center, all meals were vegetarian (my father worried about my health, too) and we ate out of bowls with chopsticks or spoons (no forks or knives), while sitting on the floor. I visited my father every other weekend, and he took these opportunities to give etiquette lessons. It was my job to set the table correctly, and he supervised the way I held a knife and fork. He always served meat that needed cutting so I got protein and practiced using a knife all at once. It was several years before he became convinced that I was in no danger of wasting away, that vegetarian diets are often healthier than meat diets, and that I knew how to handle myself at a dining room table.

During my visits with my father I had access to his extensive collection of books. I read voraciously about black and Native American history, especially since he was often in his workroom creating his art or filling out grant applications. He quizzed me on the books I read and in the process, taught me to question whatever was presented to me as a fact. Largely self-educated, he showed me how to learn and to think for myself, though he was still determined that I get the best education he and my mother could afford.

At this time my natural shyness intensified, and though I kept trying to make friends during the next 3 years, I always felt like an outsider. There were times when I was happy, when I had a couple of friends, when I had someone to sit with at lunch. Most of the time, however, I was lonely, dreading going to school each day, hating having to put up with other kids' ignorance and cruelty. This period of my life was the beginning of the paranoia that I believe all black people, to varying degrees, carry with them in this society. I recall thinking that every whispered joke and every giggle was somehow related to me, to my appearance, to my skin color. This paranoia has followed me and has become such an integral part of how I live my life that I cannot remember how light and free I must have felt as a small child.

By 7th grade my parents and I chose a private school back in the city where I had lived previously. Though I was still shy and distrustful, I was also hopeful that the new school would be a better, more positive place for me. Compared with the students in the small town, these kids were worldly, intelligent, and open-minded. I assumed I would not be the only person of color in my class.

By 9th grade, however, it became clear that the one other black girl in my class was there only because her white stepfather was a longtime member of the administration. Two of the black boys in the upper grades were there on scholarships only because they agreed to play on the school's basketball team. I had thought that I made friends with a number of students, but only one or two of them ever invited me to their homes, and I was never invited to any weekend parties that everyone else seemed to know about.

Because I was becoming more aware of my history and the manifestations of racism, I rebelled. I suppose I didn't rebel in the most responsible or thought out manner, but I was 15. I stopped doing my schoolwork, skipped classes, and started hanging out with punks and skaters—the people we were expressly warned to stay away from in morning assemblies at school. I tried to dye my hair purple (the color didn't take), wore combat boots and ripped stockings, as much to fit in with my new friends as to break the dress code and upset the teachers and administration. All my efforts did not go unrewarded: My guidance counselor wrote my mother a letter suggesting that I was insane and needed treatment (not as an outpatient) and the headmaster kindly suggested that perhaps I would be happier somewhere else and offered to do anything he could to help me get there.

My parents were understandably upset that I had sabotaged my chances of graduating from the best private high school in the area. I'm sure neither of them knew what to do with me, nor did I at the time explain all the reasons why I felt I had to get out of that school. I knew what hope and promise they had in my graduating from that school, and that they fully believed the hype about its greatness as an educational institution. I wasn't sure my mother could understand precisely the atmosphere I was trying to escape. At the time she and I had never explicitly discussed race.

My father had built his life and professional career as an artist and educator on combating racism. The image of himself he presented to me and to the world was that of a civil rights activist, constantly fighting racism, never backing down or running away from a conflict. I did not think he could understand my desire to simply get away from that school rather than change the system. From various things each of my parents had said and done over the years, I knew there was a very good chance they would insist that I stay in the school despite the racism, simply because the reputation of the school would help me get into a good college. I got myself expelled rather than being forced to stay in the school. I then immersed myself in the punk subculture.

Looking back, the time I spent deep into the local punk scene was not all good. I did dangerous or just stupid things I probably would not have done otherwise. When I felt as if my parents did not know me, the punks were my family. A group of us hung out together constantly, sharing money, cigarettes, places to sleep. I soon found out that all the punks my age went to the same private alternative high school.

My mother wanted desperately for me to graduate from high school, any high school, though my father was only satisfied with a top school. He thought that the alternative school I chose was full of freaks and idiots. Only two things finally changed his mind: my absolute refusal to go any place else; and the fact that his current girlfriend, a well-adjusted and intelligent woman, had also graduated from that school.

This new school marked a turning point in my life. For the first time in a classroom I was exposed to black history and literature. We read Malcolm X, Maya Angelou, and Alice Walker. I was encouraged to write and to speak. I went from being a silent child slouched in a seat in the back of the room, to becoming a vocal member of my class. I even took a debate class and won my debates. I finally had real friends whom I still occasionally see. I began to write seriously and share my writing. And I had my first real boyfriend.

He had long, wavy brown hair and pale skin. He was the lead singer of a hard-core band, smoked Marlboro Reds, and wore a leather jacket. We knew each other from classes and through mutual friends. We debated each other in class; I won because my argument was logical, he was the star because he was loud and funny and made the most ridiculous assertion sound like the Word of God. One day he started telling people he loved me. He told all the students, every teacher, every administrator. He told all of them to tell me. He wrote it on the chalkboards of classrooms he knew I had to go into. Finally, he started telling me directly. I thought he was out of his mind. He invited me to watch his band perform, to watch them practice, to lunch at a local diner. At some point I became his girlfriend.

When he met my mother he flattered and charmed her. Even the cat loved him immediately. Then we went to meet my father. So far as I know, my father had only dated white women, and interracial dating was never an issue in my family. My parents felt that compatibility and mutual respect are most important in a relationship and that these things can be found in individuals of any race. I therefore knew my father would not disapprove of Anthony because he was white. The problem was that my first real boyfriend was a long-haired rock musician. My mother has always been the more calm and realistic of my parents. She thought it was great Anthony had a hobby and she knew he was essentially harmless. Although many famous rock stars have bad reputations ("sex, drugs, and rock'n'roll"), she recognized the fact that Anthony was first and foremost a 17-year-old high school student and not a depraved rock star. She also gave me more credit than my father did; she knew I wasn't foolish enough to drop out of high school to be some boy's groupie. My father, on the other hand, had very definite ideas about rock stars, even nonfamous teenage ones. One of the things I've never understood about my father is how, as a champion of human rights, he could at the same time be very closed-minded. Although he confronted anyone who tried to ignore the individuality of each black person, he nonetheless was perfectly capable of lumping all of a certain group together and then affixing a stereotype to them. On different occasions he did this to gays, Puerto Ricans, and long-haired rock stars.

At that first meeting with my father, Anthony and I sat at the dining room table waiting for my father to return from his back room. He came up behind Anthony with an enormous pair of gardening shears and said, "You seem like a nice young man, but I think you need a haircut." He didn't actually use the shears, and we all laughed at his little joke, but the attitude was clear. I stayed with this boy for almost a year. He did drive 3 hours with me to an art exhibition my father had in another town, but he never agreed to go to my father's house again.

After just a few weeks with Anthony, it became clear that although he did care for me, his greatest love was for his music. Throughout our relationship, most of our time was spent doing things related to his band, which required my driving him everywhere. He didn't drive and I had my own car, so I willingly became his chauffeur. Ironically, my father never drove, so the women in his life (including me) became his chauffeurs. I believe this made me more willing to accept my role as Anthony's driver. My mother's vocal unhappiness and ulti- mate rejection of her role as my father's driver undoubtedly brought me to the realization that I did not want to remain in a similar relationship. I drove Anthony to his practices, his shows, to buy equipment, to and from his house and school, and everywhere else he wanted to go. My growing resentment at my role as his driver expanded when I realized that while I was spending all this time helping him pursue his music, I was doing nothing for myself except the bare minimum I had to pass my classes. This inequity finally broke us apart, though mutually and amicably. I learned that it's important for the men I am with to have a passion outside our relationship but that his goals should not and cannot overshadow or replace my own.

After my experience with Anthony and my father, I decided not to intro- duce my father to any boyfriends until I had been dating them a while in order to avoid unnecessary gardening-shear-type incidents with boys who would be out of my life the next week. I thereafter screened my boyfriends' introductions to my father very carefully. Guys with shaved heads, tattoos, or no high school education did not get mentioned at all. Skateboarders and musicians were men- tioned but I never explicitly said I was dating them. On the other hand, my mother met just about everyone I dated, or at the very least she heard about them. This was because we lived together and so she was more intimately aware of my social life, and because I knew that she would judge them individually rather than on the basis of rumor or appearance.

My best friend from the time I was 15 until I was 18 was a white teenage punk. We had an instant connection. The first day we met she invited me to stay at her house. At that time I was unhappy at school and I wasn't getting along with either of my parents. I ended up spending almost every night of the next 3 months at my new friend's house. We spent summer days hanging out with other punks and going to hard-core shows. We shared clothes, money, friends, and ideas. She was the person who first told me about the alternative high school where she was a student. She was the first white girl my age to really treat me as an equal.

I never paid any attention to the fact that she was blonde and blue-eyed, though I knew she had never experienced any kind of racism or discrimination and could not possibly know what it really meant to live within my skin. But she was my best friend, and I tried to talk to her honestly about my feelings and experiences. I told her about how when my father had his first art show he was not permitted to attend because of the color of his skin and, to add insult to injury, about how someone liked his piece so much that they stole it right out of the gallery. I told her about my people, stolen from their homeland, enslaved for hundreds of years, segregated, lynched, disenfranchised. We read together black poetry and novels. We both watched the tape of Dr. King giving his "I Have a Dream" speech and sat through Alex Haley's *Roots*. She could not *know*, but I thought she understood.

For 2 years we were inseparable. Darleen and I went everywhere together, shared money, clothes, even our cars. For 3 months I lived in her house, slept in her bed. We went to the same school, had all the same friends, hung out in the same clubs. But then some people we knew decided that it would be really cool to become skinheads. Darleen has always been the type of person who needs to surround herself with a group of people, preferably the newest, strongest group of the moment. So when she shaved her head, I laughed because she looked like a fool but I was not worried about the future of our friendship. I took it for granted that this was just another one of her phases, like when she became a punk, grew a Mohawk, and dyed it pink. The skins, in the beginning, were simply a conglomeration of the local misfits. They had no direction, no philosophy. All they had were their bald heads, their Doc Martens, and each other. I continued to be friends with Darleen and with the rest of the skins. But then the inevitable happened. One day a man showed up who recognized an untapped resource when he saw one. Within a very few weeks he had transformed these wandering lost souls into an army of hate.

A few of the original skinheads left the group when neo-Nazi doctrines were incorporated into this newly coherent organization, but Darleen was not one of them. If she had tried to convert me to their way of thinking or denounced me as an inferior savage, a traitor to my race (as a biracial person), then my choice would have been clear and immediate—I would have told her to go directly to hell. But she didn't. She spent most of her time with the skins (I had since found other friends as well) but when she did meet me and she was alone, she was always glad to see me. She continued to treat me like her sister, the same as she had for 2 years.

I was 18, getting ready to graduate from high school, trying to find my way and myself. I had not yet become comfortable with myself, my abilities, or my skin. I was facing an enormous transition, from youth to adulthood and I was still unsure of myself and what I wanted for my future. Darleen had helped me through innumerable crises over the previous 2 years, and I needed her still. She had always had faith in me, picked me up, told me I was worth something. I needed that still and so I didn't want to end our friendship. I hung on to her and waited patiently for her to come to her senses. I tried to reach out to her and tell her how I was feeling, how hurt I was that she could be friends with people who spread nothing but evil hatred. But she didn't listen anymore. I spoke and she looked at me and nodded, but she didn't hear. As long as she was accepted by her band of Hitler wanna-be's, she was happy.

I came to realize that although she didn't use racist jargon against me personally (as far as I knew), the fact that she did not speak out against it and befriended those who espoused it, made her just as guilty as the most vocal members. I also realized that she was no longer my friend. Whatever we had shared in the past was lost and could never be retrieved. She had turned her back on me and all that I was. I could not, and will not, attempt to maintain any sort of friendship with someone who has so little respect for me.

Darleen is no longer a skinhead. Due to constant police harassment and the subsequent arrest of their beloved leader, the skinhead organization fell apart and its members have, for the most part, returned to their former wandering misfit lives. Darleen moved to Florida. She comes to visit her family every once in a while, and I have run into her a couple of times. We have talked about her time with the skins. She denies any racist behavior on her part and seems to blame me for the dissolution of our friendship. Last time I saw her she said, "I can't believe you're mad at me about all this. I love you. You're my sister, and you always will be. "

There are things which only she would understand. Sometimes I run into someone I haven't seen since I was 15 or 16 and I want to tell someone, but Darleen is the only person who has known me that long and would remember. I sometimes get an almost unbearable urge to call her and talk about our growing up, the crazy things we did, the dreams we had, the insignificant things we thought were matters of life and death. But then I think about that last conversation and find that where our paths had once been parallel and adjacent, they are now miles apart and heading in totally different directions. Her time with the skins caused an impassable rift between us. We no longer understand each other and have given up trying. I am no longer her sister, and she is no longer my friend.

My experience with Darleen did not keep me from becoming friends with white women later on. But from this experience (and other less dramatic ones) I've lost some of my naiveté. I have learned that there is a limit to the depth of my friendships with white women. There is a point at which they cannot understand my life as an African American woman; there is a part of me they cannot know. Our relationships can be very deep and loving but I have learned that there are some truths that they do not *want* to hear, and there are some things that they *refuse* to hear or believe. I can never again have a relationship like the one I had with Darleen. I cannot take a white woman's friendship at face value or her understanding for granted.

In high school I found and began developing my talent for writing. To my parents' relief and delight, I also discovered a love of learning and a particular interest in African American history. I decided to attend an all-female, predominantly white college. Although I had some reservations about choosing such a college, I felt that my experience in predominantly white schools, the urban setting, and the self-confidence I gained in high school would keep me from feeling the isolation that I felt so deeply earlier in my life.

The first person I met at college was my roommate. She was a white woman from my home state, and we found we had several mutual friends and acquaintances. We hit it off instantly and over the course of the year, became very close friends. Today, 4 years later, we have both just graduated, and I still consider her one of my best friends. Claudia and I have always been able to talk honestly with one another; I think she's learned a lot about what it is to be a black woman from me and I know I've learned about being a Jewish woman from her. We recognize the limitations of our relationship. Our differences matter, there are things that she cannot know because of her skin, and things I cannot know because of my religion, but our friendship is built on respect. I have learned over the years (especially after Darleen) that I can't expect any white person to understand how I feel or think in every situation. What I can and do expect is that the person does not dismiss my reactions as insignificant. I expect to be taken seriously and for them to at least try to understand my point of view. In return, I give them the same respect.

Unfortunately, my relationship with Claudia is the exception, not the rule. The college I attended was full of people who are, in various ways, racist. Of course there are many who are not and with whom I have been able to forge friendships. Outward, blatant racists are in the minority but they do exist and in some cases thrive in that school. More common are those who don't even recognize their own ignorance. I met administrators, faculty, and students who fall into this category. From my first day until my very last class, I came across this ignorance. I have learned from both my parents that you have to choose your battles. My mother has practiced this philosophy while my father never has, and as a result, he has never known peace. In college, I chose my battles. To say nothing, ever, would be to give up my pride, my dignity, and would be an affront to my father's lifetime struggle. But to fight every tiny injustice would consume me and be a rejection of my mother's wisdom. Small things—being singled out as the spokesperson for my race in an otherwise all-white classroom, having white students not see me as they physically pushed their way past me in the halls—I would discuss with my friends or my mother. I would really let my emotions out in my writing, in my journals. The more important issues—a racist supervisor or professor who let their prejudices interfere with their jobs and their treatment of me and other women of color at the school— these I chose to confront directly and fight.

My relationships with black women in college were equally complicated. Many women did not accept me because my mother is white and because I became so close to my white roommate. I tried going to Black Student Organization (BSO) meetings but I found myself being constantly ignored in discussions. I also thought the BSO members spent far too much time arguing amongst each other and the elections were really popularity contests. I suppose all political organizations are plagued with similar problems, but I felt that these problems coupled with a general lack of respect for me was too much to deal with. I stopped going to BSO meetings, opting instead to concentrate my energies on my schoolwork and fighting ignorance when I encountered it on my own. Not participating in BSO further alienated me from the black students. I made friends with a few of them, but my deepest friendships with black people my own age are with people I knew before I entered college and a couple of people whom I met who worked at the school.

As an escape from the daily struggle of life at my college, I spent the first semester of my senior year on an exchange program at Spelman College in Atlanta, Georgia. I had never before been so far from home, never traveled farther south than New Jersey, nor lived in a predominantly black area. I knew no one and I felt scared and alone, but I quickly met other exchange students. I have always felt uncomfortable ("paranoid") in the North, at college, in my neighborhood. Suddenly, I was among people who looked like me. Of course there were differences in hair or skin shade or body type. But I could recognize myself in almost every person around me, in students, faculty, locals.

In the past I gave lip service to the idea that black people need to see other black people in positions of authority and power. I have advocated the recruitment of black faculty and students to predominantly white campuses. However, all of this for me was theoretical; an idea, a vague concept based on the real need for equality. At Spelman I learned the reality. Not every experience I had was positive, and I don't necessarily believe black people should be educated only in all-black settings. But the impact of being taught almost exclusively by black people was intense, consciousness altering, and awesome. All for such a basic and deceptively innocent reason; simply because everywhere I looked I saw images of myself. Ironically, I thought about being black less than I have ever done in the North. More precisely, I didn't have to think about my blackness because it was taken almost for granted.

Within the group of friends I made, complexions varied enormously, from the slightest hint of tan to deep brown. But we were all black women. For the first time I made friends with people to whom I did not have to explain myself. Whatever the differences in our backgrounds, we shared this one crucial trait. Not only did the women look like me but also we had shared experiences. My fears, paranoia, and confusions were finally understood, and I found other women who had the exact same feelings. I could express myself without having to worry about offending anyone or being labeled as crazy.

I left Spelman having made lifelong friends with black women my age for the first time. I have graduated from college and am now looking forward to attending graduate school in California. I plan to study African American literature and to continue with my own writing. After I earn a Ph.D. I would like to teach at the university level. Moving 3,000 miles away from my friends and family was a huge decision. But the school I will attend has one of the best African American studies programs in the country, and I also feel I want to get out of the Northeast. I've lived here my entire life (with the exception of 5 months in Atlanta) and I want to see what else is out there. Going to Atlanta taught me that I can survive away from home and whetted my appetite for adventure. I am looking forward to meeting people of various backgrounds and making new friendships. I am also prepared for the struggles which are inherent in being a person of color in this society.

9

Caught between Two Cultures

STEVE

The son of Trinidadian parents, Steve grew up in an affluent suburban set-ting. While he interacted primarily with white peers, Steve was painfully aware of the cultural and experiential gap between his background and that of black Americans. His parents openly reinforced these differences, encouraging Steve to fraternize with and even date whites. Steve realized his own stereotypical perceptions concerning blacks, while attempting to forge some relations, however tenuous or superficial, with a black community. He strove to define himself in his own terms, as an intelligent, athletic, black man, despite the limiting forces of a hard-to-please father and a seemingly nonreceptive black peer group. Steve wrote this essay in his senior year.

I grew up in suburbia, the elder of two children. My brother Drew was always at my side. I was used to his presence, although he was more like a sad-dlebag than anything else. The neighborhood was very quiet, very residential, and very white. I was always conscious of that fact, but Drew and I always played with the white kids on our street and never really said anything. We would occasionally play with the other black families a few miles away, but usually we played with white kids. I never made a fuss, never asked why I was the only kinky-haired boy in my class. Kinky hair and dark skin didn't matter when I was 5 years old.

My dad grew up in Trinidad under the stern eye of my grandfather, a very strict man who wanted his children to obey his every command. He wasn't harsh; rather, he was incredibly demanding. I don't believe my grandfather was any different from his Trinidadian comrades other than he kept after his chil-dren a bit more to achieve. Dad followed grandfather's directions to the letter. He attended one of the more prestigious secondary schools in Trinidad and he excelled. Dad wanted to become a politician, but grandfather frowned upon that and told dad that he should become a doctor, so that is what he did.

When it was time for my father to continue his education, he took the general placement test that everyone on the island had to take. He had the second highest score on the exam and had the choice of going to three different American schools: Harvard, Yale, and Howard. According to dad, the choice was simple. The prime minister of Trinidad had gone to Howard. Furthermore, Howard had a very large Caribbean student population so my father would feel more comfortable. The famous names of the other two schools didn't matter. I emphasize that it was not because of any sense of black pride or black consciousness that my father chose to attend a predominantly black institution; it simply made sense to him. Growing up in an all-black environment, my father had no sense of a rabid, collective enemy.

Dad succeeded at Howard while he worked as a janitor at the Trinidadian embassy and as a cab driver. It was while dad was in Washington, D.C. that he met my mother. Mom, too, was from Trinidad and had left home at 17 to go to school in London. Eventually, she moved to Canada to work at the University of Toronto. She happened to be in Washington, D.C., visiting a friend when she literally bumped into my father. From the stories they tell, it definitely wasn't love at first sight. In fact, their initial meeting foretells a great deal about their future together. Dad was drunk at a graduation party and tried to get fresh with Mom. She slammed Dad about his being drunk and acting so stupid. Basically, they were arguing from day one. Nevertheless, love must have been there somewhere. They were married during my dad's second year in medical school. After my arrival 2 years later, my parents relocated to Nashville.

My general consciousness of my place in the world began in the 4th grade when my best friend at the time, Bill, asked me when I first knew that I was black. To a 9 year old, whose mind was focused on when the next soccer game was, that was an extremely stupid question. I told Bill that I always knew I was black, but his question remains one that I strive to answer daily.

Another struggle to define who I am has been my lifelong attempt to gain my father's unconditional approval. Even when I entered St. Christopher's, the private middle school my family chose for me, I was competing less with other students than for my father's approval. I think the reason I tried so hard to please my father simply came from my wish to impress everyone: the popular students, the coaches, and teachers. I desperately wanted to impress my father. I should have realized that all attempts to impress my father would be in vain. For example, I recall one Thanksgiving my parents had some friends over, and my usual straight-A report card had just come. One of the guests commented on how wonderful it was that I was doing so well. I was just starting to feel good until dad cut everything by saying, "It's not wonderful; it's expected." I slumped in my chair and started thinking to myself that I shouldn't have tried so hard; I should have done poorly so that there would be no expectations.

At St. Christopher's, I was part of a small band of outcasts. My friend David, who was Jewish, introduced us all to a girl named Sara from his synagogue who had just moved to town and would start at St. Christopher's. She and I hit it off instantly. We would eat together, talk to each other on the phone, everything. We simply liked each other's company. When she started to wear my number for volleyball, a bond between us was confirmed. I always wore the number four for the sports I played: soccer, football, and basketball. It was the first number I had when I started playing soccer at 4 years old. It seems silly now, but it mattered to a lonely and isolated middle schooler. The number was always special to me, and when Sara said she wanted to wear it, I felt very close to her and felt as if I meant something to someone other than my mother.

In the eyes of everyone at the school, we were a couple. Even my parents thought we were going steady. They didn't care that Sara was white or that she was Jewish. At her Bat Mitzvah, I was allowed to sit with her family, and they didn't seem to mind either. Nobody said a word. It was driving back from a dental appointment that the first real words were said about my relationship with Sara. I was talking to mom about my day at school, and she asked how Sara was doing. After I told her, she started talking about marriage. That genuinely confused me since that was one of the furthest things from my mind at that age. Mom said that it would probably be easier for me to marry a white American than it would be to marry a black American since I had had a completely different experience and upbringing and therefore I wouldn't relate as well to American blacks. At first I was confused and hurt. I was black; I was supposed to see black women and marry one someday. Now, mom was telling me that wasn't necessarily the case. Then everything started to make sense.

Mom was right, at least in some respects. I was different from all the other black children I had ever met. I was from a different culture. My difference wasn't a result of my brains; it was a result of my parents. There is a significant difference between West Indians and black Americans, as demonstrated by the fact that all of my grandfather's children were driven since childhood to achieve at the highest levels. Everyone I've ever known from a West Indian family has had the exact same upbringing; strict parents who focus on education, not "the man" keeping them down. In the Caribbean, blacks dominate so there is no sense of a common enemy, nor is there a real concern about racial identity. Groups commingle. In the United States, there are very well-defined racial boundaries. People are brought up black or white. My parents, drawing upon their own backgrounds, ignored racial identity questions because to them they simply did not exist. They were black and they knew it. It was different for me. I was caught between two cultures.

At age 12, I had already been playing soccer for 8 years. I was a star from day one. I felt natural with the ball, and my athleticism didn't hurt matters. Once I had reached St. Christopher's, I was playing with a local club team. Everyone in the area knew of me and my soccer prowess. I found that on the field I could exact all the pent up revenge I had for being considered a nerd off the field. People always wanted me to be on their team. In fact, the "cool" kids automatically wanted to be my friend and even wanted me to sit at their lunch table. I never went. I always felt a certain kinship with the nerds. Since I was isolated in general social circles, the outcasts were the logical group with which to remain. I figured that the day I had a bad game would be the day that all these "cool" people would turn on me.

I recall an incident that heightened my sensitivity to the question of my racial identity, especially in the eyes of my peers. My friend Sara was having a birthday party, and I brought along my younger brother Drew, who was then also attending my school. At that time, the song "Jungle Love" by The Time was out. Drew and I would often dance throughout the house as we listened to it. It got to the point where we had memorized all the dance steps in the video. Pretty much everyone from St. Christopher's knew that "Jungle Love" was my favorite song so when it came on at the party, Drew and I immediately started to dance. Suddenly, the floor cleared and it was just Drew and me shaking and wiggling on the dance floor. Everyone else just stood and stared. We kept going until the song finished. Everyone clapped and then Madonna or some other artist came on and people came back out on the floor. I remember another social outcast came up to me and asked if Drew and I would perform at parties as "an attraction." I remember feeling very weird when he asked me that. I also remember feeling quite alienated on the dance floor. Drew was pretty much oblivious to all that was going on since he really didn't know anyone and had had his eyes closed while he was dancing. I, however, had had my eyes open and saw everyone staring at us. I felt like a trained animal, there for the pleasure of those who watched it move. The song didn't help. In the background, there were ape noises that increased my uneasiness about the whole situation.

In a way, I think that everyone felt that my dancing to the song and my liking The Time was a verification of my blackness. And I believe that I meant for that to happen. In elementary school, I had tried to fit in with everyone by listening to Duran Duran and Def Lepard. However, near the end of my career there, I started listening to Prince and The Time both because I enjoyed the music and because they were black groups. I thought that by listening to black music I would be associated more with black people. Basically, that's what happened at the party. The people there expected me to dance to that song, not because I liked the song but because it was by a black group. Furthermore, people expected me to dance because I had "rhythm" as all black people supposedly do. Once again, I fell into their little trap of what was expected of me.

I was never a great shooter in basketball, probably because I was a right-handed kid who shot left-handed. However, my speed and agility helped me where my skills weren't necessarily up to par. I played basketball in a league with only one other black kid. The first time I played against him in a game I was so paranoid I couldn't even concentrate. I was scared of him because he was black. I was scared because I bought into the stereotype that blacks were better athletes than everyone else and that basketball was a black sport. I wasn't really black. I had the skin color, but my family acted differently and I lived in a white neighborhood where I had mostly white friends. Therefore, I wasn't *really* black and couldn't compete against him. I didn't even talk the way other black people whom I knew or saw on TV talked. I wasn't the same and I was afraid that I would be considered a fraud. I had the skin color, but I wasn't truly black.

The weird thing is, I never saw myself as a fraud. I was black and I never doubted that. I just felt that I was perceived by the whites at St. Christopher's as not being black because I was the son of a doctor and privileged. And even though I never asked, I felt that because of my somewhat privileged life and because of where I spent most of my time (i.e., suburbia) I was not black to them. My fear kept me from interacting with the black kids that I did know and it caused me to stereotype my own people. I was confused; in addition to being privileged, my upbringing was different. My parents never really concerned themselves with surrounding me with other black children. Again, race wasn't an issue for them, but it had to be an issue for me because I was being raised in this country, yet I didn't know where I fit in.

Basically, I bought into white stereotypes of black people. I really had no clue as to who I was and what it meant to be a black American. Since I spent so much time around white people, I figured that I should concentrate on being accepted by them on their terms. I didn't have any real contact with black people other than the ones at dad's office. They never treated me any differently, and I always felt accepted by them, but I never spent enough time there for them to influence me. Even at this writing, I'm afraid I still buy into the stereotypes. It is a perpetual concern that I fear may remain with me forever.

When I look back on my St. Christopher's years, I realize that there was a significant amount of pressure toward assimilation. I don't think that it came intentionally from my parents, or that they had been brainwashed. Their mistake was being culturally naive in this country. That is, they had never experienced during their development what I was going through in mine. They had grown up in an all-black environment where identity questions were moot. They had experienced racism in this country, but since dad had come from Howard, he spent most of his time in an environment in which he was isolated, almost protected, from full-blown racism. They underestimated the amount of racism I would encounter.

My problems were further exacerbated by my parents' upbringing. Trinidadians are very much immersed in British ways of thinking and acting. Speaking with a slight British accent or in Queen's English was the norm. In the States, however, blacks speak their own language. With my limited exposure to black Americans, I never picked up on the language. I was speaking "proper" English at all times. Therefore, when I found myself surrounded by black people, they always thought I was trying to be white. I was "too proper."

The greatest evidence of brainwashing is apparent in my own ways of thinking. I really believed that black people were supposed to be better athletes. Even though my athleticism helped me socially, I am not sure whether I was naturally athletic, or since I am black, the white kids' expectations that I would be a good athlete explains why I dominated their leagues. My own stereotyped perceptions of black athleticism are hard to dispel and will probably always be with me. I bought into the vision of what TV and my schoolmates thought black people were supposed to be. Some people may think that my explanation is a cop out. But when your black parents are one way and you have no other black people to contradict that way, then inevitably they play a role in shaping you and your mindset.

Ironically, I got a chance to begin to feel comfortable with black people when a predominantly black high school in the inner city with a "magnet" science program came to St. Christopher's to recruit more white students. On my first visit to their program I saw nothing but black people. Some people were running around the halls boisterously and watching the girls walk by. Others were casually leaning against the wall talking with friends and being "cool." Definitely a different "cool" that I knew from St. Christopher's! I remember feeling for the first time that I was home. I have no real explanation for that feeling. Maybe it was less a feeling of home, and more a feeling that maybe this place can help me get in touch with my "blackness." My parents were quite skeptical, in spite of the school's electron microscope and advanced curriculum. They wondered whether a city public school had a strong enough program for me and whether colleges would look down on a public school. I know they were also concerned about drugs and violence at this school. I think it's possible they were aware of the cultural differences that existed between me and other American blacks and didn't want me to associate with people not as focused or driven as I was. Mom would sometimes say that I had very little in common with other black kids and that it was pointless for me to be in groups with them. But I couldn't back down; this was my last chance to salvage any relations with black people.

I thought that once I immersed myself in black culture, I would have no problem finding my identity; it would be as easy as switching schools. Of course, I was wrong. I spent all of my time with the white students that I had known from elementary and middle school. I rode the bus with them, had the same classes as they did, and ate lunch with them. These white students and their ways were all I knew. Furthermore, the magnet program's accelerated course load segregated the school. Spending all my time with white students made me into an "incog-negro"; I existed, but I wasn't down and I didn't matter.

I decided to change my insignificant status by playing soccer. I figured that the easiest way for me to meet people and gain some level of respect was to play a sport, but I soon came to another jolting realization. I was one of three black guys on the soccer team. Soccer was basically a white sport—at least in the States. When I went to Trinidad and played, I was considered part of the group. But in the United States, especially in the South, football was king and if you didn't play it, you didn't count much. I never gave up soccer, however, because I enjoyed it too much. I ended the season as the leading scorer and had some level of notoriety within the small circle that hung around the soccer team. Although once again that group of people was predominantly white, it was a group to belong with and feel accepted by, so I never complained.

I was dying to get into a relationship, primarily to show myself that I could kiss a girl the way I saw other girls being kissed. I wanted someone with whom I could spend a lot of time. At that point, I didn't really consider black girls to be an option. In all honesty, I was afraid of black women. My mother, to that point, was the only black female example I had in life, and no other black woman I knew acted like my mother. To some extent, I was intimidated by the attitudes that I saw in so many of the black girls that went to our high school. I remember one party where a black girl asked me to dance. I had been hanging with the white people for most of the evening, and she came across the floor to ask me to dance. While we danced I really didn't pay her much attention, partly because I was all nerves. After a few songs, we separated. She was quite pretty, and I really wanted to talk to her some more, but I was afraid I was going to be "called out" and ridiculed by other black people. We looked at each other across the room, but the barrier my mental distance imposed kept us separated. We never danced again.

About this time, I wanted to get away from my family because I thought they gave me more stress than help. My parents' relationship was tenuous and even frightening at times. Mom and dad argued about everything—from clothes to work. I was growing closer to my mother since she had started refereeing soccer, but we were still eons apart when it came to many ideas. Dad was as distant as ever, and Drew was still too young. Dad was the worst because he always told Drew and me that he wanted to be "pals" with us, he wanted to be someone we could talk to. However, dad was the one who always maintained an emotional distance and demanded that we do the same. We always had to present a public facade as the perfect family. We knew we weren't, but we were always told to never let other people see that. Drew and I were supposed to display the straight-A student, superathlete, socialite mask. I felt that in dad's eyes, we were "show-niggers" on display to impress other people.

Continuing on the track my father set for us, I attended a summer program. Early in the program I invited Roger, Wanda, and the rest of the black people from the program over to my house for a barbecue. My mom arrived at the dorm and drove us back to the house where we swam, ate barbecue chicken, and watched "Hollywood Shuffle." I remember overhearing my dad say how shocked he was that I had brought home almost all black people. "I was expecting a whole bunch of white boys and out pops all of these black people," dad commented approvingly. I found that remark particularly strange. If dad wanted me to hang out with black people, why didn't he give Drew and me an atmosphere in which to do so? If it bothered him that I only had white friends, why didn't he say so? I couldn't understand him and I never made an attempt to ask him these questions. Dad and I were too locked into the superficial roles of "supportive father" and "achieving son." Beyond that, there was no communication between us. I never got answers to my questions because I didn't think it was my place to question him.

Junior year in high school was a time of complete acceptance. With Wanda, my new girlfriend from Memphis, making occasional appearances, blacks accepted me as one of them. I still was able to associate with people of other cultures. My two closest friends weren't black. Lisa, a close white friend from my elementary school years, had reappeared at the magnet program, and we picked up where our relationship had left off. Marisa, a Latina girl, became a friend through Lisa. I had very few male friends. Women were the people I found easiest to be close to as friends. I wish I knew the reason behind this. To this day, my interactions with women are puzzling. I've never questioned my sexuality in regard to being homosexual or heterosexual. I am definitely heterosexual. However, I have experienced some awkward relationships with women in my growing up.

This was also the year that I decided to educate myself on African American history. Before I left for another summer program, I looked around my parents' library and picked out *The Autobiography of Malcolm X* and *Malcolm X Speaks*. All the music I had been listening to—Public Enemy, Living Colour, Ice Cube—always mentioned Malcolm X, but I felt really stupid because I knew nothing about Malcolm's philosophy. I chose Malcolm X because he stressed that blacks weren't Americans. I made the connection that if blacks weren't Americans, they were closer to me and that would be our common bond. I now had to go out and prove this to people so I would have a bond. The more I read the books, the more I felt justified in my feeling of alienation. Malcolm said in one of his speeches that blacks can't call themselves Africans because they were too far removed and can't call themselves Americans until they are no longer second-class citizens. Therefore, they are people without a country. That was exactly how I felt. I took this newfound knowledge with me wherever I went, believing its message wholeheartedly.

In the presentations I made to the summer group, I spoke of how blacks weren't Americans. I wrote about Malcolm X in my final paper. My consciousness was finally making itself evident. The one good thing about this arising consciousness was that I wasn't carrying a chip on my shoulder. Everyone in the group felt comfortable around me, and I had become the center of the social life. I was the one everyone asked to play pool, volleyball, or ultimate frisbee. One girl commented that I was the first black male that she had met that wasn't ultramilitant or a sellout and she respected that in me.

While I was away, my father seemed to miss me, and I wanted to see him. I thought that my absence from home had made him realize that I was someone to care for, not order around. I did not only resent dad for not letting me choose my own direction in life. There were many separate events that brought a lot of stress to our household. One occurred during my sophomore year when I suddenly heard my mother screaming Drew's and my name across the house. I rushed into my parents' room. My father was standing over my mother with his hand raised to hit her. I dove in front of Mom, and Drew grabbed dad and pushed him back. Dad shoved Drew off him and told him not to touch him. I shielded mom with my body and told dad to calm himself. I found out later that the argument was over money and my mom's charge account. Drew had panicked and wondered how I had remained so calm during all this turmoil.

I needed to talk to someone but there was no one in the house to talk to. Drew was too frightened to confide in, and I couldn't take something like this to my friends at school. It was simply too personal. I went to my soccer coach, who had always treated me as a second son and whom I had thought of as a second father. He told me that my parents were both very independent people and sometimes their personalities clashed. Everything he said made sense. This was one of the few times that I felt good about talking to someone. Then again, it was the first time I had ever opened up to anyone. I had been repressed for so long in my own home that being able to speak my mind freely, without worrying what the listener would think, made me feel good about myself.

All this stress hadn't created a close relationship between my father and me. When I came home and began my college applications, I decided I would try to concede a few things to dad. I asked him if he wanted me to apply to Howard. He quickly and sternly told me no. Stanford was going to be my school. When I look back on some of the conversations after my college decision, I realized why dad didn't want me to apply to Howard. Mom told me of all the trouble dad encountered immediately out of medical school. He couldn't get a residency at the main hospital in Nashville because Howard was seen as a predominantly black institution that either gave my father an insufficient education or made him into a Black Panther. In a "fine, upstanding Southern town" in the late '70s, a black man with a conscience couldn't and wouldn't be tolerated. Dad had struggled initially and he didn't want me to go through the same thing. He wanted his sons to attend institutions that would have automatic name recognition and universal respect.

Returning to high school, I felt it was my school now. Everyone knew my name, even people I didn't know. Blacks and whites, students and administrators respected me. I was a leader at the school, local, and state level; I was a student of national caliber. I had arrived. Socially, I moved in circles both black and white, although I still didn't feel completely comfortable at black parties and I avoided them with excuses such as, "I have too much work," or "I had a meeting out of town." When I had parties, most of the people there were white, although as time passed more black people came. I just didn't associate with black students enough to invite them to my parties. Maybe I moved only superficially in black circles. In the end, I guess I just wasn't down yet. Because of my upbringing, I don't think I ever will be down completely.

As graduation approached, I was inundated with praise from everyone. When I was named a National Merit Scholar my father told me how proud he was of me for the first time. The words never came out of his mouth. He sent me a card. Normally, if I got a card from mom and dad, it would be in mom's handwriting, but this one was in dad's. There was a 50 dollar bill inside the card, but I didn't see it. I was so happy that my father had actually said he was proud of me that I began to cry ecstatically. I showed the card to Drew and ran to give dad a hug. I still have the card framed.

The counselors at school also lauded me. The one thing that I kept hearing was how strong I was. They kept talking about my cousins who were both struggling in school, and the teachers commented how strong in character I was to overcome the stigma in black society that to be smart was to act white. At first I thought that my counselors were making racist statements. But when I thought about it, what they were saying was true. Some black people did get on your case if you studied too much or made high grades. But for me, it wasn't a matter of peer pressure. Desire to succeed and achieve at the highest level was what drove me. I always wanted to be better than the best and that kept me going. I wasn't going to let someone tell me that I wasn't who I was—a black male—just because I sat with my books a little longer than everyone else did. I guess hanging a bit more with the white students, I was able to avoid some of these pressures. I certainly didn't act white, but I carried myself differently and had different priorities. The same went for Drew. The Trinidadian upbringing reinforced our priority on education.

As I write this I am 6 months away from graduating from college and heading toward a career in medicine because it is the one career in which I don't think I have to sell myself out to the majority (white) community in order to succeed. However, after my college experience, I call into question my decision to enter into this field. I ask myself whether the black students made me an actor. Do I claim to dislike white people, corporate America, and other such institutions in an effort to fit in? I know that I don't dislike all white people. I also know I can talk the game of everyone else on the campus, the talk about "the man keeping us down." I don't know if I believe it, but I may have said it enough to hypnotize myself into believing it.

I also find myself heading into medicine partly because of my father, who guided me in this direction. However, since I am now seen as the rebel of the family for calling into question some of his statements and directions, I do feel that I could have gone in any direction I wanted. I greatly admire dad for his work in the black community at home. In his office, I saw that he could be expressive—not emotional, but genuinely caring. I do want to emulate my father in some ways. I would love to do what he did for the Nashville black community. Nevertheless, I don't want to become jaded and out of touch like him. I am significantly more expressive than my father; I listen more closely to those around me—especially family—and I examine and question myself constantly.

Make no mistake; I am far from being an extrovert. I hide my inner feelings from those closest to me. I still see that dad's teachings have caused me to be distant from other people. It is extremely rare that I communicate my thoughts and feelings to other people. I am trying to hide my "weaknesses" from them. But I'm learning and trying. I find it difficult to communicate with people who are not similar to me. Not many people have a trinity of identities: Caribbean, American, and black. And by not communicating and not finding someone similar, I sometimes feel abandoned. My parents can't understand because they only understand one aspect of me; most of my friends here can't understand because they understand only another aspect of me. Only my brother Drew actually understands because he is living the same experience. For this reason, we have become much closer as we have gotten older and struggled with the same problems of identity, although I lean to the black side and he leans to the Caribbean. In the end, I'm just who I am and I try to improve my understanding of my identities and myself each day.

10

Lost in the Middle

SCOTT

Scott, a biracial child of a distant Jamaican father and an overprotective Canadian mother who divorced when he was a child, recounts his struggles to integrate racial identity into his self-image. Growing up, Scott gravitated to a white peer group, acknowledging his black half only to capitalize on the stereotype of the outstanding black athlete. Because of his light complexion and his belief that he has not "suffered the burden of color" he felt a complex ambivalence toward, yet desired to be accepted by, the black community. Only after he resolved his relationship with his father, and befriended another black athlete who likewise fell through the racial cracks, could Scott begin to consider a racial identity as a defining feature of himself, as opposed to allowing athletics to eclipse all other aspects of his identity. This essay was written in Scott's sophomore year.

I was born biracial—the son of a black Jamaican father and a white Canadian mother who eventually divorced. In their eyes I was not a half-black/half-white kid who had to be warned of the prejudices I might encounter in society. They raised me as someone who could achieve anything he wanted. Therefore, my identity was shaped almost free of any notion of race in my earlier years. I saw myself as no different from anybody else, and therefore I was able to discover for myself the meaning of life and who I was. Once I had discovered that my natural athletic ability could make me stand out as an individual, it became very easy to define myself mainly in athletic terms. Thus, since race did not play a major role in my earlier years, understanding myself as biracial was not a central goal. Not until I realized that skin color could make a difference in how I was perceived in my relationships and how I saw myself, did I really begin to explore who I was.

When I was between the ages of 4 and 8, I was just like every other little kid on the block. Race, religion, and, to a certain extent, age made no difference in determining who my friends were. If there was a kid down the block who was around my age and whom I could play with, he or she was my friend. Furthermore, if we somehow shared some things in common (like climbing trees), then we were best friends! In fact, one of my closest friends when I was young was a French-speaking white kid named Mathieu. Since he was in all my classes at school and lived just up the street we saw a lot of each other. The common need to be bilingual in the province of Quebec made Mat one of my best friends. I was raised in an English-speaking family and he in a French-speaking one. Therefore, when Mat's mother proposed that we become good friends because we could learn from each other, we took that as the foundation for a close friendship. Those were the simple rules to my childhood friendships and they were all I needed to feel a sense of belonging.

I remember playing with a lot of kids, but since only a small percentage of my neighborhood was black, most of my memories are of playing with whites. I also believe that those few black kids were raised with a greater awareness of their skin color and thus didn't experience the freedom my lighter skin color allowed me in mingling with whites. I often wonder if my childhood friendships would have been any different if my skin color had leaned more toward black than white. I don't think my parents would have raised me any differently, but the way people treated me, especially my friends' parents, might have been different and I'm sure some kids would have been steered away from me. Then again, I might have bonded more with black kids if I felt I was being treated differently by white kids because of my skin color. I may have felt more confident in my later years expressing myself as black, instead of being fearful because I have not suffered the burden of color. One thing is for sure; I would not have been the same. Our North American society puts so much emphasis on physical attributes (e.g., nose shape, skin color, hair texture), that the slightest change in one's appearance can lead to a different life experience.

The first time I remember experiencing the feeling of difference was when I was about 9 years old. I was walking through the shopping center with the Jamaican mother of the family who lived next door to me. When I told her about how I was upset at this kid at school and referred to him as nothing but a "nigger," she reacted with shock. As soon as I said the word "nigger" she stopped and looked at me, surprised, and said, "What did you just say?" Not expecting that reaction, I immediately thought she was upset that I was disrespecting someone by calling him names. The word "nigger" was just something I had heard once from some kid when he was referring to someone else. Therefore, I treated it as just another derogatory word like "fag" and never imagined the word had deeper meaning. When she asked me if I knew what "nigger" meant, I just shook my head and said no. I soon found out there was a particularly degrading aspect to the word that applied only to people of color, which meant me.

From that day on, I was more attentive to that word because I wanted to make sure no one would disrespect me in that way. In fact, this one kid whom I took to calling "le gros" ("fat guy") started retaliating by calling me "nigger." He obviously also knew the significance of the word because he would stand up to me as he used it and then look at me expecting a reaction. When he first called me a "nigger," I remember acting upset because I felt that it was expected but not really getting into it. I believe that this initial reaction to the word was enough to convince the kid that he'd somehow found a way to get back at me for calling him fat. Therefore, he began using the word more frequently and with much more fury. The more I heard the word, the more it got to me. The fact that this kid threw the insult at me because he knew its secret made me feel trapped. There never seemed to be any proper response to this insult because it had to do with something I couldn't change—my skin color. It was like suddenly being told I was never really part of a group—just a tag-along. One of my biggest fears, in fact, was that other people would start calling me "nigger," so every time he said the word, I would always lower my voice in hopes that he would not shout it out. After all, why would I want people to know I was different!

As I was being forced to deal with racial difference, I was also compelled to accept the fact that I was the son of two very different people who were going separate ways. Before the divorce I had seen myself as part of an indivisible family, like every other kid. Afterward, I suddenly became part of a single parent family run by my mother with only occasional visits from my father.

I was 13 years old the day I walked into our kitchen to find my mother crying in my father's arms. I was immediately concerned for my mother, but something about the way she was crying made me hesitate to question my parents. I had never seen my mother cry before, so witnessing it for the first time scared me. My father's dazed look was discomforting and eerie. After a few seconds of staring I summoned the courage to ask my grandmother, who had been living with us for as long as I could remember, what was happening. She looked at me sadly and told me my mom and dad were having some problems and were going to need to spend some time apart. At that age I did not yet understand what that meant, so I questioned my grandmother again, and she told me they were hurting because they still loved each other. I figured that was a satisfactory answer and went back to watching TV, figuring things would work out. Looking back, I'm surprised it never really occurred to me that that night would lead to a divorce and a complete change in my relationship with each parent.

My mother has always been very protective of my sister and me, but I think the divorce increased her motherly concern. At a young age, my mother's attention was very important and extremely comforting to me. When she hugged me,

I felt as if nothing could ever hurt me. I was always the absent-minded type, so my mother would do her best to make sure that I left the house with my head on right! She would double- and even triple-check that I had everything I needed before I left for school. Nowadays, however, her constant questioning and double-checking really irritates me. She somehow still feels that I am not responsible enough to take care of myself. She may be right, since I tend to leave things to the last minute. Even though I owe her a lot, the one thing she never managed to teach me was how to be independent and responsible. Knowing that my mother would be there to ensure things got done never inspired me to take any initiative. Furthermore, not having to suffer any consequences of my actions made me apathetic about my vices. The more she wanted me to do something, the less I cared to do it. Ever since the divorce, I get the feeling that my mother has refocused her life around my sister and me. Losing my father has made her want to tighten her grip on us and, even though we are no longer children, she seems reluctant to let go.

My mother will always be the central person in my family because she is the responsible and take-charge type. She made sure everything was done, even my father's little "favors" that she put up with throughout their marriage. However, she has always felt very strongly about the way my father delegated his responsibilities. Her dislike for his apathetic and irresponsible attitudes (the "island ways"?) has made her fear that I will become just like him. From a young age, she preached responsibility to me and made sure I knew how to take care of myself. Nevertheless, despite her efforts, I seem to have turned out a lot like my father. My relationships with women have never really been successful because as soon as I feel like I am getting tied down I feel trapped and lose interest. In addition, I share my father's laid-back attitude which sometimes goes so far that I will not do anything unless absolutely needed. This upsets and worries my mother. On one hand, she feels the need to have me learn responsibility by making me do things for myself. On the other hand, since she is extremely concerned for my well-being and does not want me to have to suffer the consequences of not doing something important, she ends up doing a lot of these things for me anyway.

I would describe my relationship with my father in one word—"subtle." When I was young, I rarely went to my father with problems. There are few instances, in fact, that I can remember of my father and me actually spending time together. My father never really learned how to relate to young kids, though I am amazed at how easily he befriends everyone else. In fact, apart from my mother and my sister, I have never heard anyone ever say anything negative about my father—everyone else seems to love him. He goes from not being able to play with his sister's young kids (because usually when the kids try and get him to play with them, he is so uninvolved in the game that they quickly lose interest!), to knowing everyone in his department (including the parking attendant) on a first-name basis and having them talk to him like he's one of their best friends. That he could cajole his former secretaries to spend hours working for him when he comes to Montreal is pretty impressive! The unfortunate aspect of his manipulative ability is that it's made him a notorious delegator. At home, as in the office, he was accustomed to having people do things for him. When my sister or mother would raise a complaint, he would give them a disgusted look and grumble, "Don't be absurd—I'm just asking for a small favor." That he couldn't really relate to his own kids and didn't contribute much to the family atmosphere were some of the major factors that led to the divorce.

Even though my family situation continued to confuse me, my racial identity was gradually beginning to resolve itself. Once I became more comfortable with the idea that I was not like everyone else, I began to see my black half as my defining feature. Even though I still did not appreciate being called a nigger, it no longer seemed like my difference was a secret. In fact, in most circumstances, it became a source of pride. Since I was half black, I saw myself as having access to all the attributes that blacks were renowned for. Being able to run fast was one of those attributes that I was particularly happy about having. I was not ashamed to be only *half* black because being half white allowed me to keep my place in a white group while still being somehow different and, as I saw it, better.

As I used to say in high school, I had the best of both worlds. Even though I still did not identify myself as solely black, I was content to be the guy who hung out with whites, but had something to him that didn't make him an everyday-white guy. Depending on which side put me in a good light, I allowed myself to swing both ways along the black-white continuum. For instance, I used to be exclusively interested in white girls since the girls that my friends and I spoke about were almost always white. Furthermore, since I didn't see many interracial relationships (I never really saw my parents as the white woman with the black man and I certainly didn't see them as role models for relationships), I naturally assumed that white girls were attracted to white guys and that if I were ever going to get a white girl, then I should not try to be a black guy. So, instead of claiming myself as a half-black kid, I kept quiet about it and tried to be just Scott, the guy that was part of the group.

When it came to playing sports, however, I always played as Scott, the black kid among whites. I always attributed my skill in sports to my athletic legs given to me by the black half of my genes. I have long legs and a short torso, which are, as my father once told me, characteristic of black people. If someone were to ask me during a basketball game or track meet whether I was black or white, the answer would always turn out to be "I'm black." In this context, my being black would make sense to people and would make them look at me with awe. I was proud to be able to do things my friends could not, and amazingly enough, my source of pride somehow increased when other black athletes recognized me as black.

Since athletics were highly regarded in high school, my seemingly natural ability to run fast and pick up sports quickly made me a cool friend to have. When I discovered how much respect I could get from being a good athlete, I automatically started to emphasize that part of me. While being biracial may well have made my identity task complicated, it added to the respect my athletic ability was accorded. Once kids would figure out that I was half black they would automatically assume that I was a good athlete and, thus, someone to look up to. Furthermore, not only was I a good athlete but also, apart from a very slight skin color difference, I could have been white. This may have been the reason why I had never really suffered much racism at a young age because my skin color was close enough to be in the white majority group and I was a good enough athlete to be one of the elite. Athletics was my talisman against anything bad that could happen to me. As a kid, it only made sense to me to let everyone see who I was by setting my best foot forward—my athletic one.

Even though my athletic talent was always my most definable feature because it seemed to overshadow my biracial physical features, it was also a defensive weapon. On many occasions, my speed, the source of my pride, was tested by being challenged to a race. Since I was seen as the fastest guy in school (one girl called me "Ben Johnson"), people would measure their worth by comparing their speed with mine. In essence, the challenger had little to lose while I, on the other hand, had everything to lose. In fact, even though I did not lose often, I can still remember the first time this white guy beat me. I felt like I had somehow lost my identity. I was terrified that everyone would treat me differently. Until recently, every time I competed in track I was overcome by a big rush of fear, as if my status as a revered person depended on this one athletic test. Once I learned to channel the fear, and later on change it into anger toward my competitors, it gave me the boost I needed to run faster. If I won, then I would mostly feel relieved. If I lost, then I would feel that sinking, shameful feeling that would send me back into an abyss.

It took me a while to build up my athletic name, but eventually I was known as a good athlete not only in my neighborhood but also by the coaches and athletes involved in track-and-field. Once people started coming up to me before a race and treating me like I was a celebrity; the wonderful feelings of acceptance and dominance became addictive. I felt that the better I got, the more I was becoming someone special. To keep that status I had to overcome all rivals, including a longtime friend and competitor in hurdles. Unfortunately, this competitor is one of the most talented athletes I know and he repeatedly beat me in hurdles for 6 years straight (we always finished in first and second place, even when put up against the rest of Canada's top young hurdlers). Beating him became an obsession, and the fact that I was consistently narrowing the gap gave me enough motivation to keep training. He had the ultimate respect, and I wanted it! I can honestly say the day I beat him was one of the best days of my life. I was overcome with happiness and pride. I had always known that I could beat him, but it was not until I actually did that people started paying any attention to my talents as a hurdler.

It was easy to masquerade as a black man among whites because, to them, I was not fully white. On the other hand, I always felt awkward calling myself black in front of full blacks because I knew that, to them, I did not look fully black. It seems to me that being white is not really a hard category to be a part of because there are no special entry standards. Being black, however, always seemed to have a particular code of conduct and attitude associated with it in order to be considered a member (i.e., speaking Ebonics). Unless I got the nod of approval by a black guy, I was on shaky ground with my black identity. Being able to get a "hey" or "what's up" when I pass a black guy on the street gives me some reassurance that I am at least viewed as potentially black. I feel true acceptance by the black community when one of my black friends refers to me as black. I recall when one of my black girlfriends came by looking for me in my room, and I wasn't there. She decided to e-mail me jokingly: "You dirty little Negro, how dare you not be there when I come over!" The fact that she called me a "Negro" was an affirmation that she believed I belonged in the exclusive black group. It made me feel happy and reassured that I was not being perceived as a phony to the black population—even though I felt like a phony!

I came to see the word "nigger" not as an exclusive word but an inclusive one. Even to be called a nigger from a white guy would not disturb me as much as it did when I was a kid. In fact, the last time I can remember being called a nigger was last year. One of my girlfriend's ex-boyfriends was upset that she had decided to see someone else and got a friend to find out about me. Apparently, once he found out that I was dark skinned, he came to the conclusion that it would never work out because I was "only a nigger." His remarks may have shocked my girlfriend, but they had a more humorous affect on me. I had not been called that maliciously in a long time, so I didn't take the word seriously. I knew that my outward appearance had never really caused me any severe prejudice. I had faith in the fact that, even though there might be people out there who still believe in the natural inequality of the races, there were so many more who would not discriminate—at least in my neighborhood. I actually felt more sorry for the guy's prehistoric ignorance than angry at the intended insult. In addition to my feeling of amusement, I also felt some pride—as if he had unintentionally complimented me with the word "nigger."

The history of blacks in North America is a tale to be admired because, in a world of hate, they have found ways to survive. They have produced so many strong, verbally expressive leaders like Martin Luther King to defend the rights I feel so strongly about (i.e., liberty and equality) that to be considered a part of this race of freedom fighters was a great compliment. The word "nigger" no longer embarrasses and degrades me; rather, it has become my ticket into the exclusive black group.

Just as I was gaining pride in my black heritage, my father and I started to get along better with each other. It had always been easier to relate to other people's fathers because I never knew where I stood with my own. It was not until I was old enough to travel with him at the age of 17 that I began to understand that some of his attitudes that I did not like were widespread.

That summer my father suddenly decided we were both in the need of a break (me from track and him from work) so he bought us two tickets to Jamaica, his birthplace. It turned out to be a memorable experience. I got a better understanding of my father's attitudes and the similarities between his personality and my own. Two months prior to the trip my father began to treat me warmly—a significant improvement from the apathetic attitude he usually took toward me. Previously, the only time he would get really animated about anything was when we spoke about track, or when he wanted me to do something for him. Once we got to Jamaica, however, he began to treat me like an adult. He spoke to me as if we were best friends instead of father and son. I relaxed around him because I no longer felt as if he expected anything from me. I was surprised to find that the resort we stayed at was for single women and men to vacation and meet new people. I felt like my father and I were good friends just hanging out, as if I had finally achieved a bond with my father because he was now treating me more or less like an equal.

An increasingly warm relationship with my father enabled me to see that, unlike my friends, I hadn't entered into relationships properly. Making friends at college has been a difficult process because it is hard to find people who have shared my experiences. Furthermore, I wanted to have friends with whom I did not feel obliged to hang out; I was tired of being the fake friend. My first friend at college turned out to be my best friend. Drew was someone I had met on the track team and, unlike most of our track team, he was black. Even though he was black, he did not act like most black people I had encountered. He was open, friendly, and did not talk with the usual black slang that I always felt was another divide between the black community and me. I soon discovered that Drew, even though he was completely black, viewed himself in much the same way I saw myself. He recently told me about an experience he had when visiting his girlfriend that describes exactly what I had been feeling. His girlfriend was black and mostly hung around with other blacks, especially black guys. When Drew first got there, he said he was surprised by how fast he was accepted into the group. He immediately felt like the others treated him with as much respect as they would a close friend. However, after spending so much time at college mostly hanging around whites (because he never really felt like he was vocal enough about issues to be part of the African American group), he had developed a lot of white mannerisms and ways of expressing himself. Instead of using typical black slang, he expressed himself with proper English. Consequently, when he hung out with these black guys, he felt like he was acting completely different from them. In his own words, he felt like he was "Carlton" (a fictional character in the TV show "The Fresh Prince of Bel Air"). Carlton is the stereotypical assimilated black kid who speaks proper English, is rich, and dresses like a preppy. He does not really fit into the expected black male role and is consequently made fun of by Will Smith (the "Fresh Prince"), who is supposed to be representative of the real black man coming from a poor neighborhood, dressing like a rapper, and speaking with black slang. The Carlton image that Drew brought to mind was almost a perfect reflection of what I feared I had become. Drew and I were scared of being seen as outsiders. For the first time, I actually found someone who felt the same way I did. While the majority of my friends are white, Drew is the only friend I feel a connection with. The fact that he's black plays a role because he experiences the same racial issues that I deal with (i.e., being accepted or not), but his skin color is not the main reason for the connection. Even though Drew is black and I am biracial, somehow we find ourselves lost in the middle, and our shared understanding of this feeling provides the connection.

Unlike me, my sister has always been vocal about racial issues. Even though we both feel strongly about issues of discrimination, she would always be the type to take a stand against injustice. I, on the other hand, usually wait until an issue emerges and then attack it if the opportunity is available. I recall one time my sister managed to get my father to vocalize what he actually thought of all the radical blacks who made public disturbances to draw attention to inequalities. My father was of the opinion that all the fuss was ridiculous. He felt that if you just concentrated on what you wanted to do in life, opportunity could be made for anyone. My father seemed to be basing his argument on the fact that he was black and successful, so others could be, too. My sister jumped at his seemingly ignorant attitude and expressed her discontent with some counterarguments. The amazing part was that even after my father had given her his typical disgusted look and stopped pursuing the matter, she continued to try to argue with him. If the matter had came up between my father and me, once I figured out my father had no interest in pursuing it, I would leave him to his own ignorance. This different level of commitment made my sister much more black than I am; she is not afraid to identify herself as black. Her outspokenness on race makes me feel like I am not doing justice to my own identity. I know that if she can call herself black, though she is even lighter then I am, then I should be able to claim my blackness too. Unfortunately, I was not then convinced that I needed to address the issue of a black identity because my athletics were still allowing me to achieve success and recognition without any issues of race interfering.

Reflecting on the different ways in which my sister and I integrate race into our respective identities has helped me to understand how much athletics can influence racial identity. When you have an outstanding ability that not only overshadows your other characteristics and abilities but also seems to impress most people, you tend to answer the question of "Who am I?" in terms of what you can *do*. In my sister's case, since she chose to stay away from athletics, she seems to have pondered the question of identity in a much more psychological fashion. I have been easily categorized as "Scott the track athlete," while she became more aware of her race and incorporated it into her identity. The older I get the more I realize that although athletics has always been a big part of who I claim to be, I can no longer identify myself as just or primarily an athlete. Knowing that athletics are temporary has allowed me to step outside myself and see what else there is to me.

A pivotal moment in my life came when I first realized that I was using athletics as a cover because I thought there was nothing else worthwhile about me. This turning point happened in a philosophy class when one of my teachers began the class by asking several students "Who are you?" When people would answer with such responses as: "I'm a student," "I'm a happy person," or "I'm an athlete," the professor would get a disappointed look on her face and say: "No! That's *what* you are, but *who* are you?" I sat there amazed and scared that she would ask me because my answer would have been as unacceptable as all the others. When the professor finally got fed up with asking people the question, she finally revealed the answer that the class would ponder in the coming months. Apparently, she was looking for an existential answer to the question: "I'm nothing." I realized that I really was nothing more than what I had set myself up to be—an athlete and nothing else. Even though I realized that I was forcing myself into the one-dimensional figure of "Scott the athlete" which could never reflect everything I was, I did not know what else could be added to the list.

Being at college has forced me to become relatively self-sufficient. I have learned the consequences of not doing things on time and this has made me a more responsible person. My mother has just recently begun to realize that I need to be trusted with making my own decisions. She therefore does not question me as much as she used to. Unfortunately, the damage seems to have already been done. The constant nagging has strained my relationship with her, and this break will take a while to heal. I no longer feel the urge to tell her anything because she usually asks too much. She feels like she needs to ask me things because otherwise I won't tell her. My hope is that if my mother would just let go, then someday I might be able to open up to her and have her completely trust me to make my own decisions. As for my father, at the present time, we have a good relationship, but it somehow lacks the substance that it would have had if he had been there to watch me grow on a daily basis. Again, I hope that someday when I get to spend more time with my father we will be able to talk about things other than track and generalities.

My identity is still a mystery to me, except that it seems to be shaping itself in a more defined way. I have been eliminating things from my life that I don't like and keeping those that I can tolerate. I do many things because I have to and not because I really want to. For instance, engineering is my major because I see it as one of the only worthwhile professions that can assure me a financially stable life. It may not be the best way of deciding my major but I figure being financially successful will alleviate the burden of having to do many of those things that I just don't care much for. Athletics is still a part of my life but it is no longer the center of my existence. Now I can find joy in improving rather than just winning. I no longer fear losing to others; I now try to focus solely on myself. Nevertheless, I still have the fear of not succeeding because I dread the day when I might be forced to quit track for other occupational responsibilities that I do not really care for. The scary reality of track-and-field is that only the top few in the world will make enough money to support themselves through the sport. It is far more likely that I will have to give it up (especially since my talents seem to lie in the decathlon—the event that is often overlooked and, thus, not as well funded!). The only comforting thing is that at least I will be ready for that day because I am not clinging to any false hopes.

The fact that I am only now at college beginning to understand myself as a half-black man is pretty amazing given our society's numerous prejudices against those with different ethnic, religious, and racial backgrounds. However, apart from my athletics, which may have diverted most of the racial slurs, I strongly believe that being raised in Montreal may have also had its own impact. Montreal has always been a very ethnically diverse city where difference may be more tolerated because it is encountered on a daily basis. Most importantly, the biggest issue in Montreal, which can be traced all the way through the history of the province of Quebec, is language. I grew up having to learn both French and English because not knowing both would have certainly led to being discriminated against by either the Francophones or the Anglophones. Consequently, my parents thought it much more valuable to educate and protect me against the language prejudice that I was more likely to encounter than racial prejudice. The fact that language was such an overwhelming issue throughout my childhood may have significantly decreased the chances of racial discrimination. In fact, I remember many more instances when I was confronted about being an Anglophone in a so-called French province than being confronted about being a half-black kid among a white majority.

I am not quite sure why I feel that I do not fully belong in the African American category, but it might be because I do not feel like I have been put through the test of discrimination. If I have not suffered through the prejudices of being black, then how can I really be expected to connect with black experience? Somehow, being black has become more than just skin color to me. Being simply dark skinned is not enough to be a member of an exclusive black group because you may not have been forced to internalize your blackness. Until you internalize it by being forced to accept the responsibility of being on the front line in the fight against prejudice in any form, then you can afford to simply wear your color as an article of clothing, to be taken off and put back on at will. Although I do take a stand on prejudice and the equality of human beings, I have never really felt the need to fight it beyond my own experiences. I do not attend things like rallies against racism and do not actively participate in the affairs of the African American organization at college. Even though I feel I should, these things do not seem important to me, which leaves me with feelings of guilt. My efforts to fight racism have occurred on a small scale and that is partly why I do not feel like I belong in the exclusive black group. Being half black, however, is not something I can change about myself, so there will always be a part of me that will feel neglected if I do not have the guts to affirm myself as black or assert my right to be black. As a 20 year old today, I am following in the footsteps of my sister and gradually beginning to incorporate race into my identity. It is a very slow process, but accepting myself as being black gives me a feeling of wholeness, and I know that without it, I am nothing more than a white guy with a tan.

PART III

Resilience and Resistance

Resilience and Resistance

JANIE VICTORIA WARD

Most American teenagers adapt adequately to the normative stressors in their lives: the biological changes of puberty; the various school transitions they must go through; the increased importance of their peers; and their changing relationships with parents and other adults. Some children and youths are overwhelmed by the stressful environments they live in, which are characterized by crime and violence, drugs, high rates of teen pregnancy (Scott-Jones & White, 1990), poor schools, and unemployment. Over time, these multiple stressors prevent them from attaining the expected developmental outcomes of adolescence, thus leaving them ill equipped for the challenges of adult life.

Researchers who study African Americans draw specific attention to conditions associated with poverty and economic disadvantage, citing these as the most challenging threat to the successful psychosocial development of African American families and adolescents (R. D. Taylor, 1994, p. 121). Children under stress are the least likely to master the psychosocial tasks in each developmental period (Comer, 1995). Overburdened, stressed-out parents, whose hypervigilance is critical in counteracting the negative environmental forces influencing their children's lives, are frequently unlikely to be patient and provide the close supervision their children need. Fortunately, many black children and teens coming of age in socially stressful situations are able to resist environmental risk factors. Black youths who effectively resist and persist can be considered resilient. The narrators in this section shed light on factors related to resilience in black youths and how psychological resistance facilitates processes of resilience.

Resilience is often defined as the ability to withstand and rebound from crises, adversity, and the risk factors known to effect negatively developmental outcomes. Werner and Smith's exhaustive and influential longitudinal study of 700 children on the island of Kauai, Hawaii, has helped us understand the role of environmental stressors and their impact on individual development and family functioning. They cite poverty, perinatal stress, family discord, and low parental education as primary environmental liabilities (Werner, 1989; Werner & Smith, 1982, 1992). Other scholars of resilience have added childhood circumstances such as having an ill parent, a chronic illness, being a teen mother, a child in institutional or foster care, delinquency, criminality, and maltreatment to the list of risk factors (Masten, 1994, p. 8–10).

In an effort to identify the factors that influence resilience, researchers tend to focus on people who beat the odds and on individuals who adapt well within stressful, adverse situations (Rutter, 1987). This emphasis on the factors that help individuals cope under stress has led to the conclusion that resilience is primarily due to a constellation of personality traits, including a strong, hardy personality, high self-esteem, a sense of hope, optimism, and a realistic belief in one's own ability to control life's events and overcome adversity (Rutter, 1985, Walsh, 1996). Other researchers suggest that having activities that one feels connected to and involved in appears to alleviate stress and facilitate coping, as does the belief that life changes are important to individual growth and development (Kobasa, 1985).

Along with specific personality characteristics, factors in the social environment contribute significantly to resiliency. These social assets include supportive family relationships that promote self-esteem and self-efficacy and provide needed emotional and social support, particularly during times of stress (Werner & Smith, 1982, 1992). In a number of studies of high-achieving African American adolescents (Clark, 1983; Scheinfeld, 1983), parenting practices that include warmth, firm control, and close monitoring appear to encourage self-motivation and autonomy in adolescents (Hauser & Bowlds, 1990). Similarly, Gramezy (1984) states that black inner-city children who exhibit resiliency despite their often difficult communities are likely to live in orderly homes, and to have parents who are actively involved in their children's psychosocial development, build on and guide their children's interests, and encourage mature behavior. In addition, these parents provide access to other adults outside of the home who can supply and sustain supportive relationships with their children. Finally, high self-esteem, positive self-image, and a sense of social responsibility were found to aid the development of successful coping attitudes and behaviors.

Despite advances in civil rights legislation and enforcement, racial inequalities in American social, political, and economic structures continue to have a negative impact on the lives of black people. Racism operates at both the individual and institutional level. Overt and covert acts of discrimination in housing, education, employment, health care, and social services place burdens on black families differentially across the social-class spectrum; such discrimination continues to be a major stressor for blacks and potentially compromising to their mental health. Racial bias and discrimination, when compounded by long-term poverty, can prove particularly disturbing to black children and youths, leading some to become hopeless and desperate when faced with unrelenting economic deprivation. Though economic success may mediate its intensity, no dark-skinned individual is completely immune to racism, whether it be individually directed or institutionally sanctioned. Middle-income blacks residing in racially integrated neighborhoods, attending integrated schools, and employed in integrated workplaces often find that assimilation produces a unique bicultural stress (Pinderhughes, 1989; Tatum, 1987), one that can bring about good or bad results. Pinderhughes states, "biculturality can cause strain and take a heavy toll in emotional stress and identity confusion, but it can also create exceptional strength, flexibility and tolerance for diversity" (p. 113). Psychiatrist Chester Pierce posits that when we view stress as resulting from an individual's lack of support, then for victims of racism and sexism, "clarifying and reinforcing the types and sites of needed support offers preventive, intervening and curative possibilities" (1995, p. 277). Pierce calls attention to the multitude of "microaggressions," those slights, putdowns, and subtle, perhaps unconscious, degradations, aimed at black people that wear on one over the course of a lifetime and which require time, energy, and psychic strength to deal with and endure. Despite this reality, the child development research has little to say about the stress associated with the effects of minority status and racism.

We do know that race-related socialization, the transmission of knowledge about race—racial identity, racial discrimination, and race relations (Ward, forthcoming)—buffers some of the potentially harmful effects of the stressful experiences associated with racism. The lessons learned, adapted, and passed down in black families guide black children's interpretation and negotiation of their social environment and prepare them to meet the goals of adult social and civil life. I argue that a successful racial socialization is one that prepares black children psychologically to resist their racial subordination by learning how to identify racism and when, where, and how to develop the appropriate strategies needed to withstand, endure, and overcome the unpredictability of contemporary manifestations of racial oppression. These messages about *race* and *place* not only shape the black child's identity but also initiate black children and youths into the current race game, helping them to understand which "moves" they can make toward their intellectual, academic, and monetary success as well as to understand which "moves" can be made against them. Generally, these messages about race are passed on directly or indirectly through parents, teachers, friends, extended family, and others black children regularly encounter. Racial socialization serves to forewarn children about the nature of their racial reality—teaching them what to expect and how to develop adaptive techniques to resist the negative forces of racial devaluation. In essence, racial socialization buffers racism by fostering resistance, and this resistance is a protective factor that buffers the effects of stress associated with racism.

The adversities faced by the following six autobiographers—Chantal, "Gotta Keep Climbin' All de Time"; Viola, "Finding Zion"; Rick, "Feeling the Pressure to Succeed"; Stacey, "Running Hurdles"; Malik, "Reflections on My Survival"; and Denise, "Quest for Peace"—encompass many of the vulnerabilities traditionally associated with growing up in low-income communities, i.e., poverty, substance abuse, violence, and crime. Three of the authors lost a parent to early death, and one initially dropped out but later reenrolled in secondary school. Such normative stressors could have derailed these vulnerable children and ushered in individual psychopathology. Why and how these teens found the strength to overcome are linked to a variety of protective factors that are also evident in the autobiographical statements presented in this section. For Malik and Denise, attending and excelling within high-quality academic programs mitigated the negative effects of family poverty and drug addiction. Both students learned to direct their energy and focus on schoolwork and achieving academic excellence. Strong and cohesive family relationships and high parental expectations appear to have held Chantal and Denise together as each grieved for and eventually overcame the death of a parent. The fact that Malik's father returned to the family and took custody of him after his mother's downward spiral into crack addiction undoubtedly saved Malik from a life of unrelenting misery. Malik's and Chantal's personal characteristics fostered the requisite inner strength needed to sustain resilience, despite sustained periods of poverty and drug addiction in Malik's case, and premature death in Chantal's. Moreover, they were both fortunate to have plenty of people in their lives who lifted them up, helping them to tap sources of collective strength. All of the authors in this section mention, either directly or indirectly, specific messages they received from family members regarding the value of educational achievement. This is further testament to the critical function of family support in helping black children adopt attitudes and behaviors conducive to overcoming risk, independent of the parent's display of counterproductive behavior.

In reflecting on the adversities they faced and the interpersonal relationships that either enabled or at times constrained their agency, the six narrators in this section shed light on a number of tensions in the conceptualization of resilience as (a) a unipolar construct, (b) a "bouncing back" phenomenon, and (c) in binary terms. With specific reference to African American children and families, viewing resilience as an unipolar construct, that is, seeing it solely in psychologically positive, health-enhancing terms, may be limiting. Likening resilience to strength and durability tends to obscure the price that being and becoming resilient exacts on some people. In this culture, the Protestant work ethic, with its emphasis on self-sufficiency, productivity, and competition, privileges and encourages the attitudes and behaviors associated with resilience without giving adequate attention to its hidden emotional costs. Individuals may bear up for a long time (thus looking like they are resilient) and yet be emotionally compromised along the way. While it might not kill him or her, the hardship may still take its toll, making the distressed individual *stranger*, as opposed to *stronger*. For example, in his narrative, Malik writes powerfully about his painful past, a time in which he was "preoccupied with a struggle to survive," which forced him to develop survival skills well beyond his years. To survive growing up with a desperately drug-addicted mother, he admits, he had to distance himself psychologically from her. Years later, as a young man negotiating adult intimacy, he looks back at his past and wonders whether his fear of being hurt by those he loved may have left him unable to care for and love another. "Can I still feel the love I once felt toward my mother for any other? If I do learn to care, will my emotions be like a ball of glass, ready to shatter at any moment?" Malik's survival strategy kept him afloat in childhood, yet this same strategy appears problematic for him as an adult.

The notion of "bouncing back" that is often associated with resilience implies a return to a state that already existed, but in reality this return may not be possible. Indeed, successful resilience would seem to shape a sense of the self that is very different from what existed prior to the crisis. If one has been truly resilient, he or she is not quite the same after a crisis. Yes, core aspects of the self are still recognizable, but it appears that the individual is significantly transformed in the process. Walsh calls this "scarred, yet strengthened" (1996, p. 264). In his narrative, Malik tells us that when living hand-to-mouth with his addicted mother, he experienced hunger, physical abuse, and neglect, yet somehow, despite being dirty, exhausted, and ill fed, he had enough in reserve not only to attend school daily but also to keep up with his schoolwork as well. Eventually, once he was "rescued" by his father and sent uptown to live, Malik's resilience was most apparent, allowing him to excel both academically and athletically in high school. Similarly, Chantal's story exemplifies this "bouncing back" quality. Death changed Chantal's outlook on life, and although she was at times overwhelmed with sorrow, depression, and responsibility, Chantal was able to withstand her mother's death and the early responsibility of having to support her grieving father and raise her younger brother. Chantal recalls being strengthened by her memories of her mother, a strong, forthright African American woman from whom she learned the bitter but powerful lesson that black people, particularly black women, must work twice as hard to get half as far. Her mom encouraged her to strive, to take pride in herself and her heritage, and though the effort was at times nearly unbearable, Chantal's desire to work hard and stay focused was a testament to her dead mother. As she grew older, these messages of strength, survival, and racial pride were echoed by the significant adults in her life, particularly the members of her black church family, who rallied with their support. Chantal looks back in her narrative and appreciates how the experience of loss and recovery made her mature, responsible, and determined, ultimately leading to her present-day success.

We see a process taking place in Denise's narrative which is similar to Chantal's, yet different in at least one important way. At the start of her story, Denise appears to withstand and move beyond the shock and pain of her father's senseless murder at the hands of the police by focusing much of her energy on schoolwork. Like Chantal, Denise heard and internalized the supportive encouragement of caring adults (particularly her mother) who reinforced in her the idea that she was intellectually gifted and could, despite her impoverished beginnings, be the first in the family to attain a college degree. As her story progresses, Denise provides a dramatic example of the bipolar nature of resilience. Her coping strategy, placing all of her psychic energy into repressing her father's murder, suppressing her own feelings about the trauma, and staying totally focused on academic achievement resulted in good grades, but at the expense of her emotional well-being: A pyrrhic victory, to be sure, since we find Denise in psychological turmoil toward the end of her story, overwhelmed by a series of devastating crises, a sexual molestation, and the death of her beloved grandmother. These cumulative losses compounded her vulnerability: "I wanted to be invisible . . . I wasn't sure how much more I could take. I wanted to scream NO at the top of my lungs to let out the pain that I was feeling. I didn't want males looking at me . . . I kept to myself, I felt trapped in a body that no longer belonged to me. I felt trapped in a life that I didn't want." Denise had become a master of denial—unwilling and unable to share her pain, which subsequently exceeded her ability to cope.

Traditionally, in discussions of resilience, risk and protective factors alike tend to be seen in binary terms: In other words, a situation or status is assumed to be either risk provoking or to protect against risk. Within the sociocultural context of the lives of many African American adolescents, not only do risk and protective factors operate simultaneously but also some risk factors may actually maximize opportunities to cope effectively with and overcome adversity. For example, in Malik's case, growing up with a drug-abusing mother put him at serious risk, yet this same mother provided, albeit tenuously at times, shelter, food, and encouragement for doing well educationally. Indeed, in her healthier moments, Malik's mother was able to offer important guidance such as giving her son a respect for authority, discipline, and a strong work ethic that Malik believes inspired his determination to survive. In this section, all of the narrators' African American parents gave important racial socialization messages that were intended to prepare their black children for individual prejudice and systemic racial inequities. For example, when Chantal told her mother that her teacher, in commenting on Chantal's strong academic status, had told her she was "different," her mom admonished Chantal not to accept this backhanded compliment as flattery and warned her to be careful of those who wish to see her as a "token nigger." Chantal's mother, like many other African American parents, taught her child how to identify and resist negative appraisals from the wider society, how to debunk its myths and filter out racist messages. Other race-specific messages authors recall include emphasizing the value of hard work, maintaining a fighting spirit, and refusing to let your mind get caught up in the pain.

Because the identification of resilience tends to be made after the potentially harmful effects of a stressful experience have been endured, the literature on stress resistance knows little about what resilience looks like in the moment. For example, we do not yet know the degree to which being resilient is a conscious act. Similarly, the process by which someone effectively interprets and negotiates a social environment may also be unconscious. Ossana, Helms, and Leonard's (1992) study of culturally diverse college women found that women at higher stages of "womanist identity" (Helms appropriated the term "womanist" from black feminist writers to emphasize an identity that is flexible, self-defined, and may or may not be consistent with feminist beliefs or social activism, 1990, p. 403) were less aware of gender bias on campus. Her work suggests that resilient individuals may be less in touch with the tenuousness of their situation or less mindful of how much energy is being invested in negotiating the stress they are confronting, while simultaneously capitalizing on critical resources of support. Requisite naiveté and the denial and suppression of emotional pain may serve to help the psyche's resistance from being destroyed by the adversity faced. Individuals who succumb to adversity may well be more aware of the extreme energy needed to resist its destructive effect (Debold, 1995). They may feel unable to weather the storm as they are overcome and immobilized by pain, confusion, and fear.

RESISTANCE AND RESILIENCE AS MUTUALLY REINFORCING PROCESSES OF STRENGTH

Robinson and Ward (1991) argue that African American teens must learn to cultivate healthy psychological resistance in order to withstand and oppose the reality of racial oppression and to take a stand for that which affirms personal self-worth and self-determination. African Americans have a long and informative history of resistance. The civil rights movement of the 1960s and 1970s is perhaps the best-known contemporary example of collective social resistance. The marshalling of inner strength to survive physically, psychologically, and spiritually through centuries of intense human degradation and subjugation—

from chattel slavery through the decades of Jim Crow—exemplifies the historical legacy of psychological and social resistance at both the individual and collective levels. Though racism in the post-civil rights era is far more subtle, the sociopolitical environment continues to be demeaning and judgmental toward people of African descent. For African American adolescents today, resistance includes the refusal to accept the credibility of external sources of knowledge and the creation of strategies to counter the cultural forces that undermine self-confidence and compromise healthy growth and development.

Stacey provides a dramatic illustration of resistance in her narrative of struggle to overcome the obstacles in her way. Stacey grew up in a family that passed down its knowledge of black history, black cultural traditions, and its own familial history. She was always a good student; when she met educational challenges along the way, she would recall the advice from her uncle to "remember who and what has helped you get where you are and hope to be." With these words in mind, Stacey would self-motivate, tapping into the stories and collective memories of a cultural legacy of struggle for educational access and equity. These messages reminded her that the challenges she now contends with are a testament to those who came before her and paved the way for her success.

Resistance is about how African Americans respond to race-related pressures and stressful experiences of racial prejudice and discrimination. African American parents know that they can respond effectively or ineffectively to these pressures by creating and executing healthy resistance strategies. Rick stood up to the stereotype that blacks were less intelligent than white people. His resistance strategy was to refuse to internalize the "rumors of inferiority" that followed him through childhood. Rick exhibited resiliency in his educational endeavors. After beginning with a sense of academic inferiority, he overcame his low academic self-esteem so successfully that he became high school class valedictorian. Much of his social support was derived from family, friends, athletic coaches, and members of his church community. Predominantly black churches provide basic theological instruction and far-reaching moral education. They not only teach the children in their congregations why and how to learn to get along with one another but also help disenfranchised black people cope with (and change) the realities of the American political, social, and economic structure (e.g., the civil rights movement was born in the black church). Most important is the supportive network of the church family, which can be seen as part of Chantal's, Rick's, and Stacey's extended families. Stacey says that her family stressed the importance of their spiritual beliefs, believing that God made it possible for them, indeed for all black people, to overcome. She believes that God provides direction and purpose in her life. Finally, we see in Rick's story how using one's own life to oppose and disprove racist stereotypes can fortify an individual and facilitate healthy coping and resiliency.

There is a dialectic between resistance and resilience, in that resistance fosters resilience. The resilient individual is able to negotiate hard times by resisting effectively and that successful negotiation facilitates further resilience. Resistance in the black community and family provides a preventive psychosocial intervention that boosts hardiness and psychological resilience of black children. Optimal resisters are, in turn, resilient. That dialectic is an integral part of African American tradition.

Resilience, therefore, can be seen as a by-product of black parents' interpretation and construction of their social reality. Black parents, in teaching their children how to interpret, evaluate, and react to their social reality, fortify their ability to withstand and rebound from normal and race-related adversity. They teach resistance as an ethical principle, instilling the belief that blacks as a people can and must resist at all levels—psychological, social, and spiritual (Ward, forthcoming). In many African American families, children are taught implicitly or explicitly such strategies of resistance as the necessity of being forewarned about and adequately prepared for possible encounters with racial discrimination (Peters, 1985; Ward, 1995). Chantal's mother, her grandmother who was a repository of traditional black culture, and members of her church family passed down race-specific knowledge, culture, and political perspectives that helped Chantal recognize and cope with racism. Before she died, Chantal's mother emphasized the subordinate position of African American women in the United States, information Chantal used to stay focused and determined through all of her life trials. "Remember this if you don't remember anything else, Chantal," her mother would say. "You have to be twice as good as any white person to get the same recognition. None of them will expect you to succeed, but do it in spite of them." These messages about power and social position taught Chantal powerful lessons about racial connection and solidified her identity as a black woman. We learn from Chantal's story that racism not only plays a role in the construction of one's identity but also that it can help shape one's vocational aspirations. Chantal has decided to become a teacher. Drawing upon her own social and intellectual needs as a smart, low-income black girl, she hopes to be a formidable role model in the lives of low-income black children like herself. The intergenerational transmission of historical resistance illustrates to black children that the sociopolitical environment in the past was much worse, that much has improved, and yet they must keep striving to make life better. Chantal says, "I have used her thoughts to push me even further when racism hits me in the face." Chantal's and Rick's families provide examples of how supportive adults attempt to inoculate their children against discriminatory mistreatment by promoting self-esteem, self-confidence, and racial pride and by stressing the value of perseverance and struggle. Bowman and Howard's (1985) study of race-related socialization messages found that black children whose parents discuss with them the nature of race-related barriers to social mobility perform better in school. Openly acknowledging and addressing racism, race relations, and racial identity are key components to resistance and in many cases provide a preventative psychosocial intervention.

It is no surprise that two of the authors in this section refer to old Negro spirituals. The messages of these songs speak to the spiritual legacy of African American resistance, which embodies the "power of moral and spiritual sources of courage as a life-sustaining force of conviction that lifts individuals above hardship" (Dugan & Coles, 1989). Chantal writes that gospel music lyrics like "Gotta keep on climbin' all de time" gave her the strength she needed and reminded her that though the struggle never ends, odds can be surmounted, and "trouble don't last always." African Americans pass down their history of resistance via the oral tradition. Making each song their own, black individuals rejoice in and share their lived experiences of overcoming adversity by continuing to sing the spirituals and gospel songs that have sustained them over time and by telling and retelling personal stories of perseverance and resistance. Stacey, who begins her story with a familiar verse from a popular gospel tune that ends saying, "Nobody told me that the road would be easy—but I don't believe he brought me this far to leave me," makes its message of resilience her own. Later, when a publication at her college callously demeaned black students and faculty, Stacey drew the strength to resist effectively from the words of her song and was able "to turn her resentment into a force that propelled her to protest," a resistance strategy that was smart, self-affirming, and ultimately liberating.

Chantal, Rick, Malik, and Stacey provide examples of effective resistance in the black community. Presented together, their stories illustrate how resistance occurs within a collective and fluid context of past and present histories, wherein stories of struggle and triumph are transmitted via a cultural backdrop of spirituality and family connections that provide an anchor for mediating inevitable injustices due to institutional oppression. However, not all resistance strategies adopted by African Americans are liberatory and psychologically healthy. Some strategies are what we call resistance for survival (Robinson & Ward, 1991), which are transient, crisis-oriented, short-term solutions that blacks mistakenly adopt to endure the stress and consequences of their subordination. These survival strategies, though they may feel appropriate at the time, are seldom in the black individual's long-term self-interest.

Denise's and Viola's stories are especially interesting in that both women have managed to develop a repertoire of resistance strategies, some of which served them well psychologically and socially. Both internalized a strong sense of themselves as smart and capable and held fast to this belief. Denise was also able to fall back on powerful support from the church (particularly gospel music), her own poetry, her academics, and her strong relationship with her mother. Viola was saved by her intense relationship with her mother as well, a woman who aided and encouraged her intellectual development and ultimately supported the hard decisions she felt forced to make. However, Denise and Viola also provide some examples of unhealthy resistance strategies, which both women eventually came to see as shortsighted and ultimately psychologically damaging. Viola grew up in a racially isolated area where there were few brown-skinned, biracial children who looked like her. Raised in intermittent poverty by her white mother following her parents' separation, Viola suffered painful racial taunts and disabling abuse from the white children in her school. Their negative comments about her looks led her to feel ugly and alienated, "skulking around corners, avoiding their gaze." The white teachers ignored her predicament and provided no protection. Unable effectively to resist their devaluation and exclusion, Viola spent much of her school days fluctuating between rebellion, frustration, and emotional pain. Eventually she became depressed and physically ill and was angry and mistrustful not only of the white children who hurt her each day, but of all white people in general. Unlike Chantal and Stacy, who describe being surrounded with messages that helped them to interpret racial animosity and affirm their identity and self-worth as black females, Viola writes little about her mother's efforts to prepare her young biracial child for her racial reality. Though the extent to which a white mother can effectively prepare a biracial child for race-based discrimination and marginalization may be limited, Viola's mother attempted to fill the void left from years of rejection by her peers, actively encouraging her daughter to travel to and embrace the Caribbean island of her father's birth. Later, when her deep disaffection from school led Viola to threaten to drop out, it was her mother who arranged a private tutor in Caribbean literature—a black mentor whose assistance ultimately helped to turn Viola's life around.

Although intellectually gifted, Viola was scorned and excluded by her white peers. Isolated, lonely, and depressed, she eventually joined up with a group of underachieving black students, educational outcasts who turned their back on schoolwork and school rules. In early adolescence, she adopted two ill-conceived "resistance for survival" strategies—academic underachievement and sexual promiscuity. By age 13, she had begun socializing with a group of teenage Caribbean boys as an antidote to her miserable school situation. Unlike the white kids, these young black men accepted her into their group, seeing her as one of them. Soon she came to see that for these boys, beauty was linked to skin color, and that her light skin afforded her a higher status. She discovered a new source of power—her sexuality, which she used to attract and secure male attention and maintain some sense of racial connection with the only group that would let her in. Even after she was sexually assaulted by an acquaintance in a date rape, she continued on her path of unhealthy resistance. She writes, "A path of unhealthy relationships was easier to follow than to allow the powerful emotions around being violated to bleed into my sex." Strikingly, Viola's mother did instill in her daughter a solid foundation that Viola was finally able to build upon. By age 15, Viola could no longer endure the conflict between her identity and her schooling. Bored with the Eurocentric curriculum and ignored and stigmatized by her white teachers and peers, she saw no reason to stay enrolled in a school system that refused to motivate her or even acknowledge her existence. Completely drained by her negative school experiences, Viola chose to resist by dropping out, in effect "de-victimizing" herself, holding fast to her own self-concept as an intelligent black woman with integrity. By the end of her story, Viola, who had been regularly visiting the Caribbean island of her father's birth, expressed her strong desire to connect with her culturally black self, sensing that it could be a helpful ally to employ in her self-defense. She ends her narrative proud of her heritage, which she will use to forge her own individual identity.

Viola became temporarily derailed by choosing to resist rejection and devaluation by engaging in sexually irresponsible behavior and academically dropping out. In her narrative, Denise describes adopting two resistance-for-survival strategies that also proved problematic. The first was designed in response to her being rejected by her siblings and black school peers. Accused of "acting white" in terms of her extracurricular choices and academic success, Denise began to doubt her own self-worth and became fearful of racial disconnection. "I began to believe that I could not accept myself until other black people accepted me," she writes. Constantly fearful of reprisal and rejection, Denise adapted a self-imposed silence around her black peers, an action she described as defensive, reactionary, and emanating from her desperate need to be accepted.

Her second psychologically unhealthy resistance strategy was a response to the race-related anger and frustration that began to consume her following the murder of her emotionally distraught father by a group of overzealous policemen. This strategy was to deny these powerful feelings, and thus emotionally distance herself from her fury. Discussing the details of her father's death, which she describes as a "police assassination," was declared taboo by her mother. So with a resigned silence, Denise suppressed her emotions and used achievement as a coping strategy. She threw herself into her schoolwork, excelling academically while unwittingly sinking deeper into an emotional abyss. It didn't help that her seven siblings, envious of Denise's "smart label" and academic success, denounced her use of Standard English, teasing her endlessly, questioning her blackness, and accusing her of trying to be white and proper. Denise writes that unlike other blacks, who learn "anti-intellectualism" from their peers, it was her siblings who taught her that being intelligent means automatic rejection by black people. Having learned not to share her emotions about her homosexual feelings, her sexual molestation, and her grandmother's death, Denise used writing as an emotional outlet, pouring her thoughts and fears into her essays and poetry. But in college she stopped writing, and as college life became increasingly stressful, "breaking her spirit," Denise was left with no outlet. Finally, at the end of her narrative and following an emotional breakdown triggered by a TV broadcast of the savage beating of Rodney King by white police officers, Denise is slowly coming to terms with her psychological pain, allowing herself to finally mourn her father's death. The repressed and cumulative trauma from her multiple losses were too much to contain. Ultimately, a breakdown also triggered Denise's breakthrough.

Though Denise exhibited unhealthy strategies of resisting through self-silence and denial, it must be noted that Denise is also a survivor. Undoubtedly, her ability to persevere is at least in part derived from her ability to find her strength in the messages of hope and tenacity that she grew up with. The stories of black resistance shared within her family and community stayed in her heart, and despite disagreement with the church over issues of homosexuality and gender roles, Denise had become "dependent" on gospel music—frequently drawing upon its powerful messages.

Chantal, Rick, Stacey, Malik, Viola, and Denise provide dramatic illustration of the ways in which black and biracial families live with and respond to the stress associated with racism and minority status—stressors made more devastating when compounded by poverty and economic uncertainty. These six young adults exhibit resiliency in different domains of their lives. We see that for some their ability to be resilient is uneven—allowing them to cope well in some aspects of life, yet offering minimal protection in others. Resistance, defined as the ability to stand up to negative cultural forces of oppression by promoting and acting on attitudes, behaviors, and values that are self-affirming and self-determining, fosters resilience in black and biracial children. These narratives uncover vivid examples of healthy and unhealthy strategies of resistance, which expand our understanding of racial socialization and its role in the process of resilience building in black and biracial children and youths.

11

Gotta Keep Climbin' All de Time

CHANTAL

Just as Chantal was entering adolescence, her mother died suddenly. She was left bereft of her mother's frequent insights and suggestions about how to achieve in a world that is often patronizing or hostile to successful black females. Recalling her mother's frequent admonition that she will have to work twice as hard as white students to be successful, she did just that, with the constant support of her father, and was accepted into an elite college. There she encountered more subtle forms of discrimination but was able to equip herself intellectually through courses which explored race, class, and gender in ways she found transforming.

Writing as a junior in college, Chantal describes her decision to become a high school teacher despite being told often that she is "too good to teach." She describes a journey of hard work, loss, intellectual growth, and a spiritual and political commitment to dedicate her life to the young people in her community.

"**M**om, Mommy!"

"Call the ambulance, Chantal! Tell them your mother can't breathe. Give them our address!"

My footsteps shook the glassware on the buffet table as I ran to the phone. After hanging up, I returned for more instructions. My mother's body lay on the floor, her back against the flowered love seat. My father, with his arms around her, knelt by her side talking nonstop.

"Stay calm, Anne, you'll be okay, don't worry. Chantal, go get Mrs. Smith, tell her to come over right away!"

Pain shot through my cold knuckles as I knocked on the wooden door. "It's Chantal," I said to the groggy voice that answered the door. "It's my mom, she can't breathe. We need your mom to . . . I, I." Tears rolled down my face as my body lost its strength and fell into a chair in the house.

The next thing I remember is kneeling next to a bed in the Smith girls' bedroom. One of the girls tried to reassure me, "Don't cry, Chantal, God will take care of your mother." The girls prayed with me, and I prayed by myself. I cried myself to sleep at the Smith house that night.

Early the next morning, I woke my younger brother (I cannot remember how he got to our neighbor's house) and walked back to my house. My uncle was inside on the phone, and my father sat in the back of the house. He stood up and said to me, "We lost her Chantal, she's gone." He embraced me as I stood motionless for a few seconds, then I returned the embrace and said, "Well now, she won't have to worry about the folks at church anymore." No tears fell from my eyes, yet something inside me had changed. I felt empty, incomplete, and numb.

Against my father's wishes, I went to school that morning. In the middle of 8th-grade algebra, it hit me. I went to the bathroom and cried without ceasing. One of my best friends followed me into the bathroom, where I told her of my mother's death. She told my algebra teacher, who was a pastor at a local church. I will never forget how he took me into the computer room and talked with me. He explained what God had planned for my mother and how I must understand God's will. I told him that last night while I prayed, I knew she would die; God had told me. I was now afraid of what life would be like for my family and I was angry that this had to happen to me. God had something in store for me, my teacher said. I now believe that He does.

My father's mother helped me to understand the death of my mother, and her guidance and wisdom influence many of the ways that I look at life and our existence on this earth. She told me often that we all must die and that God has a time, place, and reason set for our death. One must not try to defy God's will, but to be thankful for all the other blessings that he bestows upon us daily in both small and big ways. My grandmother was a symbol of stability in my life; I could always count on her, she would never leave us. Of course, I realized as I grew older that she, too, must die, but I felt that one of the reasons that God kept my "granny" alive was to help us survive this tragedy in our lives. She was also the repository of traditional black culture in our family; her cooking, folktales, and stories about the past grounded me in my heritage when I was being attacked by nonblacks in my life. This knowledge and pride remains with me today.

I only survived these past 6 years through the grace of God. I owe all of my success to Him and to my parents. My mother gave me the foundation of my first 13 years, from which I draw most of my values, while my father reinforced those values as well as supporting, advising, and loving me. My father and I did not have a close relationship before my mother's death, although I loved him dearly. However, since her death we have become best friends. We talk about everything: politics, religion, people, relationships, the world. And although I have learned to disagree respectfully with him, our talks strengthen my character. My mother's death caused my father to be more attentive to the needs of my brother and me and to play a more active role in our lives.

My mother's death has changed my entire outlook on life. I feel I skipped my adolescence, a time, in my eyes, of careless abandon, silly mistakes, and independence. Instead, I found myself overwhelmed with sorrow, depression, and responsibility. My brother, who was 6 at the time of my mother's death, and my father, who was psychologically devastated by it, both depended on me. I resented having this responsibility during my teen years; I felt that it wasn't fair that I had to clean up "all the time," that I had to worry about my brother's clothes, homework, and discipline while the majority of my friends did not have to deal with these issues. In retrospect, I realize that I was exaggerating my plight. Mrs. Smith, our neighbor who helped us during the night of my mother's death, worked for us as a sort of housekeeper. She cooked breakfast for my brother and me, washed our clothes and dishes, and cleaned house for us for the next 4 years. Until I could drive, she drove me to my numerous school activities. Yet I perceived myself as the new woman of the house, therefore causing myself undue emotional stress. I pitied my father for having to work so much in order to compensate for the loss of my mother's income, so I cooked dinners whenever I could and tried to keep all domestic needs in check.

My brother, Ryan, also became my son. In effect, I tried to take my mother's place in my brother's life, while simultaneously trying to forget her absence in my life. In hindsight, I realize that I was probably overbearing, almost paranoid, about my brother's life. However, at that time I felt that I had to ensure my brother's success for the sake of my mother, for she would have made Ryan a success. Now I appreciate my higher levels of maturity and responsibility, which in part have enabled me to be so successful. At present, I have a unique position in my family. I am at school for three-fourths of the year, so much of my influence occurs over the phone lines. I think that I have gained more confidence in my father since I have been at college. My college experience has helped me understand many of the things with which my father struggles. Therefore, we talk at length about subjects he cannot discuss with many people. For my brother, I try to be a cheerleader, a friend as well as an advisor. I tell him if he needs me, I'm only a phone call away. I scold him if his grades fall and I encourage his athletic pursuits. I still feel a large responsibility for my family and I ensure that things I do at college will not jeopardize my family's economic status nor bring shame to my family in any way.

I learned my sense of family responsibility from my parents. I learned that what I do in society reflects on my family, particularly on my parents. I work to succeed because my parents taught me to always do my best. I want to make my family proud and to become a success to honor my mother. My mother incul-cated this ambition in me throughout my first 13 years of life by pushing me beyond my limits. Her description of the subordinate position of African Amer-icans and women in the United States forced me to realize that I would always have to fight in this world, but that my battle could end in a much sweeter suc-cess through hard work. I will never forget one of my mother's first long lec-tures about being black in the United States.

I thought that earning a spot on the National Junior Honor Society would disprove those teachers who doubted my ability because I was black. When my mother and I left the induction ceremony, I felt wonderful. My mother, how-ever, looked disgusted. During the ride home, she told me why she was so angry. She had spoken to my math teacher, Mrs. McGuire. "She was just *so* impressed with you. She said, 'Chantal is so polite and intelligent. She's a hard worker and doesn't give me any problems in class. She's so *clean* and dresses so well.'" My mother's face wrinkled, and her voice cracked when she said, "*What did she expect?* Did she think you would come to school dirty and badly clothed! Did she think you were stupid and undisciplined?! No, I *know* what she thought! She saw your little black face on the first day and thought, 'Here comes another one of them niggers.' It is unbelievable to her that you, a black girl, could be as good or better than those white kids! She kept saying, 'Chantal is so *different,* she's not like the other kids.'" She meant you're different than those other black kids or what she thought other black kids were like. Tell me white folks ain't a trip!"

Then my mother turned to me and said, "Remember this if you don't remember anything else, Chantal. You have to be twice as good as any white person to get the same recognition! None of them will expect you to succeed, but you do it in spite of them. They'll call you nigger, jiggaboo, blackie, pick-aninny, and anything else, but you fight them tooth and nail, and make them know that you deserve a place on top as much as, if not more so, than they do. Don't ever stop fighting for your people, because they have never stopped fighting for theirs." I didn't quite understand her anger then, but I will remem-ber the incident always and I have used her thoughts to push me even further when racism hits me in the face.

Thinking back on this incident helps me realize that one of the many char-acteristics my parents instilled in me was racial pride. I knew from childhood that I was different from the majority of my classmates, who were white, and that this difference made me special. My classmates made my difference known to me almost daily, through their endless questions about my hair, church, music, and other black students. To combat the frequent cruelty and ignorance, I used my brute strength. I was already a "tomboy" and one of the tallest children throughout my elementary years, so I acted tough and pushed some people around occasionally in order to prevent any incidents from occurring. I would blow my top over "the N word" and anyone who criticized black people. I don't think I changed many minds regarding blacks, but I thought that at least I had shut them up. Now I fight my battles with knowledge and words. Life as a black girl was hard where I grew up not only because I was one of a few African American kids in my school system but also because the area contained white working-class people. I was thus also a part of the "white trash" school system—I was the nigger among them.

There were never many African American teachers in my primary education (I remember only one African American male teacher in elementary school), but this did not seem to bother me. I was fighting students' racism too much to worry about the teachers. Once I established myself as a good student as well as a tough girl, I focused my attention on what type of education I received and from whom I was receiving it. However, that did not occur until junior high. Establishing myself was strange because I always had to either prove that I was "really" black (because I didn't "act like black people"), or prove that other black students could also do well and that I wasn't just "different" from other black people. My mother had warned me of this when I told her that during my first day of junior high, two or three of my teachers already knew who I was and smiled approvingly. I couldn't understand how they knew who I was, or why they didn't express their approval to other students. My mother replied matter-of-factly, "You're one of the few good *black* students they've seen in the junior high." She added a word of warning, "And you be careful of them, too. They'll be the same ones that will talk about black folks like dogs and tell you, 'Oh, we're not talking about you, Chantal, you're different.' You let them know that you're no different than any other black person, you just work harder than most people, black or white. Don't you let them make you into a 'token nigger.' You are where you are because you *deserve* it, not because they needed a black face in the classroom." The next day I went to school with a new sense of dignity and resolve. I looked around my classroom and recognized that in four of my six classes I was the only black person and in the other two I was the only black female. I realized at that point that my next 3 years would be tough. Not because I hadn't been in this situation before, but because for some reason junior high seemed more hostile to me. The feeling makes me think of a phrase in a gospel song: "It's an uphill journey ya gotta keep climbin' all de time."

My mother's prophesy came true. White students and teachers treated other black students who did fit their stereotypes ruthlessly—by name-calling, jokes, and more severe punishments than for whites committing the same offense. Many of my black friends suffered from the looks and comments of whites in our school, who told me that I was "different" and therefore didn't treat me that way. I won the presidencies of both student council and national honor society and earned various athletic and academic awards. However, this charade of acceptance and harmony put on by many of my white classmates did not change their thinking about all African Americans. I was still "different," and "not like those other black people."

Throughout high school I had to prove myself again and again. I put more pressure on myself than even my parents did. My mother gave me only one guideline and one condition, "Always do the best that you can and know that you'll always have to be twice as good and work twice as hard as any white person to get the same amount as them." I still follow this golden rule. My mother's death, which occurred when I was in 8th grade, caused me to push myself as a testament to her memory, as well as to make my father proud of me. I have always thought that God had a plan for my life since He prepared me for my mother's death that night the ambulance took her away. These factors gave me the motivation to succeed, through high school and to the present day.

Unfortunately, even in the leadership positions that I earned in high school, my ethnicity still held a negative connotation. During the selection process for some positions, I heard rumors that "she only got it because she's black." Such statements disappointed me because I thought that, especially in these two organizations, I had overcome such stupidity. I really thought that I had made an impact that transcended race. Unfortunately, what I found out reaffirmed my parents' adage that no matter how much money, power, or friends you have, or how hard you try, white people never get around the fact that you're black and that before they get to know you, they'll see your black face and already have opinions, usually bad, about you. My schoolmates' comments and attitudes undermined all that I thought I had done to change white peoples' ideas of black folks and to make the way easier for other blacks.

I received support from my church family in dealing with a white world that refused to accept me for what I was: an intelligent, motivated, hard-working black girl. Members of my church always encouraged my efforts, pushed me to do more, and told me they were proud of me. I was one of the few young people in our congregation who had succeeded in organizations outside the black community, which made me even more "special." Older people in my church thought it was great for me to be able to relate to white people, that it would be necessary to succeed in the "real world." My personal relationship with God became the most important factor in my success and in the preservation of my sanity and self-esteem. This relationship mandated that I be faithful, patient, relentless, humble, caring, honest, and tough. Much of my character was shaped according to what I thought my responsibilities were as a faithful Christian.

My experiences in high school were similar to those I would have in college. I began to learn about the inner workings of the complex system of discrimination and oppression against my people that originated hundreds of years ago. At times, my very spirit felt attacked by the traditions and networks that many of the students at my college had and which placed me one step behind them in the beginning of our college careers. *Daughters of the Dust,* a movie by an African American woman, reminded me of the privilege and heritage of many white students, as compared to mine. The movie showed how ex-slaves survived and passed African traditions and survival skills from slavery on to their descendants. More interesting, though, is that the movie centered on the lives of females and their relations with each other and to men.

I called my father to talk to him about the movie. I told him:

In many ways, it made me angry and sad. The movie told stories from slavery and it made slavery so alive in my mind. The writer, an African American woman, traced her family to the Gullah people who were taken to an island off of the coasts of South Carolina and Georgia. I was angry because I will never know the African country of my family, my ancestors. It makes me angry that even after all that those women and men endured, we as black people aren't fully accepted in a society we helped build into the industrial power it is today. My friend Joanna has relatives in Poland, my friend Christina in Puerto Rico. I don't have any of that, and I'll never find it either. I don't know anything about my real culture, or history.

I stopped talking. Tears ran down my face. I panted lightly. My hands squeezed my pillow. The calm, though slightly worried voice on the other side said:

Chantal, calm down. Like I've said before, we and the American Indians are the only true Americans. White folks made us into true Americans. They stripped us of everything we had: language, clothing, relatives, religion, tradition. But they will never and have never taken away our pride and our will to survive. We have created our own culture: our own dance, religion, music, language, clothing. Yes, we are of African descent, but we can't trace it. If we go back to Africa today, we wouldn't know where to start. Africans would call us foreigners because we don't know our tribal affiliation. Many of us don't know anything about Africa, because that's the way white America wanted it.

"I know," I said, "but I feel so rootless, so unattached to any specific country. I know I don't fit into USA, baseball and hot dogs, and the Grand Ol' Flag."
My father replied:

You're right. Your culture is part of the family traditions that we practice: baking cookies and cakes with Grandma in December, barbecuing
with the family on Labor Day, cooking and eating certain foods:
greens, water bread, hamhocks, dirty rice, pig's feet, chitlins, black-
eyed peas, sweet potato pie. It's being involved in the black church
every Sunday. It's listening to black music and learning our dances. It's
listening to what your grandmother has to say about her life and how
life was for black folks in her day. That's the black American culture
we know and we must save. Be proud of it, because it's made by us, for
us, and it's all we got.

I vowed then to learn more about my history and culture, and to continue
the tradition of perpetuating my own culture apart from mainstream American
culture.

I realized how much some of my classes at college changed the way I
viewed the world. Few of my courses at college were riveting, but I must admit
that the majority of them exposed me to new perspectives that I have found
quite fascinating. The few exceptional courses I have had in my college career
have changed the way I view my life and society in terms of gender, education,
and class. One of the most eye-opening courses I experienced was an African and
African American studies course, which increased my awareness of some African
cultures which made me more sensitive to, and more protective of, my African
American heritage. Through this class, I learned about parts of the African culture
that American slavery prevented me and millions of others of the African diaspora from retaining, thus affirming my need to protect what few cultural roots
African Americans have in the United States.

Another cultural difference I recognized in contemporary African American society is our social behavior. We love to laugh, talk loudly, and joke. Many
African societies do the same. Conversely, Western European societies find
such behavior rude and barbaric when done at "inappropriate" times. In perfor-
mances, African performers and spectators interact to make the performance
successful and enjoyable. Spectators talk to the performers and clap, sing, and
dance with dancers or instrumentalists. Similarly, African Americans shout
"Amen" in traditional black churches, sing spontaneously, talk to the movie or
TV screen and to actors on stage—all actions that European Americans usually
frown upon. This course opened my eyes to many aspects of African American
culture that I had known existed, but could not see any reasons for. I realized
that I should not try to change these aspects of my culture because the majority
considered them inappropriate, but that I should retain them in order to keep my
African American heritage alive.

My sophomore fall, I took a course on contemporary issues in education. I remember one particular week when the other students in my discussion group disgusted me with their naiveté about inner-city schools. Being one of only two people in the group who had attended a city school, or had firsthand knowledge of city schools, I naturally spoke up in class. One of my classmates, whose comments drew a few nods of agreement from others in the class, said that inner-city schools needed parents who cared about their children's education, school boards who weren't just in education for status, and better police enforcement of drug and weapons possession. I answered, "No, what we need is for someone to go to the suburbs and say, 'Look, *you* must help to: (a) redistribute the money for education across property tax districts more evenly; (b) invest in renovating and repairing these old schools; (c) buy books for these children; (d) pay teachers higher salaries with more benefits; and (e) invest in making schools safer places. Otherwise these same children whom you are trying so hard to keep away from your suburbanite kids will grow up with little or no education, which will lead to few or no job opportunities. They will come to your neighborhoods to rob and sell drugs. Do you want preventative medicine? Give kids a chance to do well by themselves. You can invest in them now, for schools, or later, for prisons.'" I spoke with a great sense of urgency in my voice and raised my hands at the end as if to say, "What's your decision?"

One woman in the class commented that my position would scare more people than it would get to help. I disagreed, saying, "No, I don't think so. If that community is close enough to the school district in trouble, then they will respond in some way. You see, people in the U.S. don't respond unless it affects them directly. As long as the poor minority kids are miles away in the inner city, it is considered their problem. People say, 'We (upper-middle-class whites) can't help it if the local government is corrupt and the teachers don't care. They should have a higher value on education.' But the minute those poor kids start bothering the suburbanites, *then* it's a *problem* and *something must be done about it*. It's a sad situation, but true." One young man asked me if I wanted to work in an inner-city school, to risk my safety and sanity there. I replied that I would if that's what I had to do to help students who did not have teachers or parents or school boards who cared. I would have to take some risks. Then I rhetorically asked the group, "Why are we in the business if not to help kids?"

I recognized that even in this education course, many of the students either did not want to become teachers, or may have fancied the idea but only wanted to teach in the elite private schools that many of them had attended. Putting themselves on the line was out. Giving too much time and energy was out. Risking a nice, well-paid "real" job for the sake of some unknown children was out. The course made me see the inadequacies of my own primary and secondary education and it also made me see the dire need for teachers who are bright, creative, and, most importantly, who love to teach. I was convinced that

I was one of those teachers and that the children back in my hometown, especially the children of color, needed someone like me.

I realized also, through another exceptional course, that girls and women of color in particular really needed caring support. I learned that women cannot be viewed as one monolithic group who have similarities just because of their gender. The professor of this class challenged my ideas regarding women, particularly how different classes of women have shaped feminist thought. She taught me that the feminist movement is not just a fight by women but also that men must play a part in it as well. The course taught me that history cannot be analyzed without examining issues of race, class, and gender and that studies which ignore these aspects miss a whole set of factors pertinent to whatever the subject may be. I have come to accept and advocate this position when dealing with issues specific to women, as well as other issues.

These classes forced me to think of all these issues daily. I knew that my view of the world was changing when a statement by a speaker at a conference I attended revived all of the analytical skills that I learned in my best classes at college. The speaker, an African American male, said that the black feminist movement was destructive to the African American struggle for equality and self-improvement. He said that because the black feminist movement is based on the white feminist movement, it is centered in the Eurocentric idea of individualism. In his opinion, black feminists were against the family and were most interested in themselves. I thought to myself, "In many cases, without us, the black family could not have survived!" He continued with the "fact" that the issues facing black women were nothing compared to those faced by black men (incarceration, murder, drug usage, etc.). I tried to argue with him, but I had no knowledge of black feminism, so I floundered in my words.

I knew something about his statements was not right, but I didn't know what. His comments led me to the study of black feminism in the United States. I visited the African American women "expert" on our campus. I told her my story, and she gave me a list of 20 or 30 books on black feminism, its beginnings, its criticisms of white feminism, etc. This reading finally gave me the words, thoughts, and theories I needed to explain and discuss all of the issues especially relevant to women that I had been unable to discuss because of ignorance. My vision of the world has since become even more analytical. Knowledge truly is power.

I read throughout the summer of my sophomore year while I worked at a summer camp. The readings on black feminist literature and theory helped me to understand the complexity of the fight for "women's equality." I found that black women have, throughout our history in the United States, fought for fair treatment for themselves and other African Americans. I learned that, in many cases, black women viewed white women as oppressors as well and that white women's ambivalence about and frequent perpetuation of racism within the lives of women of different races separated women of color from "mainstream, white feminism"; thus the usage of the term *womanists* has increased recently. I realized that only through discussion and arguments within the women's movement could a more comprehensive agenda be formulated that would include many women previously excluded from the feminist movement, which will hopefully strengthen the movement as a whole.

All of these discoveries (I call them *discoveries* because I know that these feelings and ideas existed within me, but that I could not recognize them due to my ignorance of the theory and terminology needed to express them) heightened my awareness of my femaleness and of all the positive and negative situations that this femaleness placed me in. I scrutinized men's and women's comments about women more carefully, trying to assess their ideas about women from these comments. I became aware of how the media portrays women and how women view themselves in American society. I see how these issues affect the way people view me as a woman. Now I am trying to deal with this heightened awareness of myself and the difficulties of being a double minority—African American and female.

This heightened awareness of my femaleness caused me to reflect on the few relationships I have had with men in my 20 years. In high school I felt that I didn't have time or "didn't want to be bothered" with a boyfriend; I was too busy with all my activities. However, I had two very close male friends with whom I spoke about everything. One cared for me deeply, but I put him off because I wasn't ready for a big commitment, and we didn't see each other often because he lived 15 to 20 minutes away. I became attracted to the other young man, but he didn't want a public relationship; he wanted a private, sexual one. I refused to be someone's "mistress," so I had to say no. Also, this type of situation would go against my feelings at that time against premarital sex. Turning him down was very difficult (my mind said no, while my body said yes), but I wouldn't have been able to live with myself had I compromised.

Other boys in high school seemed too immature and unmotivated. They had no idea of what they wanted in life—they just wanted to have fun. Not having a boyfriend did not bother me; it was not a priority. However, once I arrived at college, I thought I could find a mature, ambitious young man. Unfortunately, I guess I was "too something," and I didn't get any offers. I had a conversation with Hezekiah, a black male friend, during our first year of college. He told me that black men did not want women to be "complaining, correcting, and checkin' them all the time. Black men want peace in a relationship. Guys hate to be rejected. Black women at this college dis' us so quickly that we are sick and tired of being rejected." I could not understand. When guys don't ask women out, is that not a form of rejection to the women? I know many of my female friends on campus thought so. We often do not feel acceptable to men because no men respond to us. He told me that my confidence and independence scared some men off. If that was true, then I would just have to deal with not having a man. That was my attitude throughout my college years; I decided I would have to wait until graduate school.

My double minority status as an African American woman caused people in my community to expect me to do certain things to prove my ability and to take advantage of opportunities that I could not have had a generation ago. When I explained in my senior year of high school that I wanted to become a high school teacher, people, men and women, black and white, could not believe it. When I then returned home for a teaching internship my sophomore year at college, these same people seemed surprised that I still wanted to pursue a teaching career.

Many people felt that "I was too good to teach," or that "I could do so much better than just teach." I didn't dare tell them what I really felt, that if we, "the best and the brightest," did not help educate their children, then to whom are we leaving our children's learning? To people who do not care about either our children or their education, people who are just picking up a check and enjoying their summers off? How are we to inspire our children, especially minority children, to strive for excellence when they cannot find one teacher of color in their school, let alone teachers worth admiring? Our children need role models, and pushing good college students away from teaching as a career will not put role models in our schools. I took these attitudes into my internship at a university laboratory school and decided to get the most out of this opportunity.

At one time I doubted my desire to teach. I began to believe all the negative things my friends, family, and other teachers told me about the profession. Throughout my senior year of high school I wrestled with the question of whether or not I wanted to teach. I tried to convince people that through teaching I could help black children and thus the black community. Several older people said that I could do that through engineering, the sciences (particularly medicine), or law. I continued to hear comments such as, "Why are you going to an elite college if you're only going to teach? You can go to a state school to become a teacher!", "It doesn't really matter what school you go to if all you're going to do is teach."

One evening, during my senior year of high school, when I began to doubt my own choice of teaching as a profession, I asked my dad about my plans. There was a time when my father felt the same way about my career plans as the people at church and my high school teachers. He and I had some arguments about the same issues the other people brought up, but he finally began to understand when he knew that I was serious and adamant about what I wanted to do. I told him that I was sick and tired of people questioning my life. Every time I told people what I planned to do, they told me I could do so much better than to teach. I was sick of having to defend my decisions. I didn't know what to tell them. Why couldn't people be more understanding of what I wanted to do? My father told me:

> There will always be people who will doubt you and try to turn you away from what you want to do. They don't understand that you want to give to your community, because they don't give to theirs. They are too concerned with material possessions, so they want you to become something that will make you money. Many of them are jealous that you have the chance to go to such a fine college when they didn't, or their children didn't, and now they want you to do something *better* with that chance since you have it. People don't value their education, so they don't see the need for you to go to college to learn, not just to prepare yourself for a job, but to attend school for the sake of learning something. And because they don't value education, they don't see the need for well-educated teachers in the classroom. Any ol' dumb teacher will do. Don't worry about them, Chantal. You do what you want to do, and what I am able to do for you, I will. You see, most of those people would not go into debt for their kids' college education. They want to wear wing-tipped shoes, fart through silk, and drive Cadillacs and BMW's. Your mother and I made a promise that when our children were ready for college, we would do whatever was necessary to send them there. So you can go to your college, because I will make the sacrifice.

I hugged him with tears in my eyes. I thanked God for a father so caring and understanding.

Later, as I tried to decide which high school to select for my teaching internship, I struggled with the idea of whom I wanted to teach. A conversation with one of my college friends caused me to question my choice of schools. I had decided to teach at the lab school of a prominent university in the Midwest, where the students were predominantly white and relatively affluent. Was I "selling out" so that I could have the experience in an affluent private school that would not help black students? One of my goals was to help minority students through my teaching, and now I was taking a position at a predominantly white institution. Why? Was I being selfish? I talked to one of my former high school teachers, Ms. Powell, one of only three African American members of the faculty at my school. I visited her every college break to talk to her about what was happening to me in school and to ask her advice on many of the decisions I made in my life. I told her I was unsure about my decision to go to the lab school. She told me:

Chantal, take this opportunity to do what you *want* to do. Once you enter the work force, you probably won't have that choice. Your talent will not be wasted no matter where you teach. Students of all colors need to see a bright, talented African American female teacher. You will help your community if there is only one student of color in your class because your enthusiasm will spread to the students. You will give them a perspective on the subject that other teachers cannot. Don't you let others sway you from your decision. You are making the right choice.

I thought about what Ms. Powell had to say and I realized that she too had to deal with that question. She is in a predominantly white, public high school with few minority faculty. She has been there for many years and still enjoys it. I know that many students of color, especially African American students, have looked to her for advice and friendship. If she had not been there, many students would have been lost. Looking at her choice to stay and teach made me realize that minority teachers are needed everywhere and that my going to a predominantly white school would not mean that I am shortchanging my people at all. In fact, the few minority students in my high school needed the Ms. Powells much more than students in a majority setting. I could not abandon the few for the sake of the many.

I chose my teaching internship for many reasons. I knew that the majority of the students that attended the university's lab school wanted to learn and took their education seriously. I visited the school and received a warm reception from the administration and faculty. Teachers, administrators, students, and parents wanted one thing: the best education for the students. All of the branches worked together toward that end.

In 1 of the 3 days I led the classroom toward the end of the internship, we discussed whether or not the novel *The Dragon's Village*, a work about a Chinese woman who fought in the Chinese revolution of the 1950s and who helped in the Communist reforms following the defeat of Mao Tse-Tung, could be considered a "woman's book." The students grappled with the question, and I used much of the feminist writings I had just begun reading to bring into the discussion issues involving women. I told them that girls have typically been required to read books written, for the most part, by and about men and that they did not have the option of not reading a book because they did not enjoy the issues it addressed. None of the boys in my class thought of that. I tried to make them think differently about applying labels to people and objects without analyzing why we apply those labels. I hope that I changed a few attitudes that day.

I learned that many of my students didn't think beyond their own communities or experiences. Although the school promotes respect for diversity, many of the students do not try to learn about the different cultures found within the school. And although many teachers say they integrate minority groups into their classroom curriculum, the teachers' ignorance often hinders them from being able to present material relevant to a particular gender, class, or ethnic group to the class. I heard one English teacher say that "the classics" in literature are more important than others because once students understand the classics they will be able to read anything on their own. I suggested to her that without presentation of "the others" in class, the students will not be as likely to read them on their own. The U.S. educational system needs to include those people who may have been left out of history, literature, or science for whatever reason. If it does not, we will lose many students to disillusion, boredom, and disappointment because they will feel that only certain people (in this country, Anglo-Saxon males) do anything of importance in the world. That is not true, and we should not teach our children that.

I wanted to uncover these issues for many of my students and I think I did so many times during the term. This feeling affirmed my choice of the lab school for my internship, because my experience taught me that I not only want to influence minority children (African American children in particular) but also that European American children also need to know these things, and without teachers to expose them to such ideas, they may never consider them.

As I look at myself now in light of my own life story, I see myself as an African American woman who has grown through hardships and triumphs to gain a better understanding of herself and her role as an African American feminist in American society. I am coming to understand and to accept many different viewpoints within the African American community and within American society. What is important, however, is that not only can I acknowledge different viewpoints, but now I can also argue against them and defend my own views. I am able to stand up and fight to change the problems within this society. I am beginning to understand how to simplify and combat the complex network of discrimination. I always knew I wanted to help the African American community, but now I have reasons and goals for my work: to combat the continued ignorance, segregation, and prejudice that prevents equal opportunity and peace from existing in this country. I see my goals as trying to change the way people view themselves, each other, and the world, so that we all can work to end the system of oppression and discrimination that American society was founded upon. I know that the eradication of this system will mean a transformation of our society. I also know that there are others who are working toward the same goals, so I am reassured that change will come.

Through the educational system, I can give students the opportunity to think about their lives and the inequities of American society and instill in them a sense of social responsibility toward humanity, expanding their knowledge so that they too can fight with words and encouraging them to be transformers of society. Right now I am grappling with how far I want to take my own formal education. I know that whatever my educational level is, I must teach high school. Then maybe I can save a few students that would otherwise be lost, as well as push a few who may not have motivation.

No matter where my education or career takes me in my life, I know that I will work for my communities—African American, female, working class, Christian, and global. I owe this work to my mother, my father, my God, and myself.

Although my life has not been much of a struggle when compared to those African Americans who have lived in a different place or another time, the difficulties of growing up African American and female remain. Our mothers bear us into a hostile world that they know cares little about our existence. Our mothers whisper, shout, signal, and symbolize what we as women of our race must do: *fight, survive, grow, excel!* Throughout our childhood they guide and teach us how to adapt and adopt in order to accomplish. Their prayers ask God to bless, punish, and protect us. Our lives are full of tears, laughter, anger, fear, joy, and despair. But throughout our lives we have hope—hope that will take us through all the hardships that our mothers warned us of toward a place where African American women and others who have unnecessarily suffered lifelong trouble can live in peace and harmony, with freedom of choice.

My mother instilled in me all of these characteristics and much more. Her life and her death have marked me forever. Moreover, my father—not the stereotypical irresponsible black father—has refined my attitudes and challenged my assumptions. He serves as a model of what, in my opinion, I am looking for in a man with whom I would want to share my life. He has never claimed to be perfect, but his sacrifice, love, understanding, and endurance have affected the way I view men and society. I also cannot overstate how much the church has influenced my life. My relationship with my God, my spirituality, and my church family implanted in me a certain joy—a joy about life that enables me to survive the hardest times. They love and comfort, support and lift me when I need it.

These people and communities, in addition to my peers, have helped me to reach the twentieth year of my life with many sad stories, but many happy ones, too. Unfortunately, many of my race, gender, and class do not have this kind of support. Parents who physically, mentally, and emotionally abuse young African American girls, and institutions and peers who prevent and limit girls from progressing, hurt not only the African American community but our entire society. Much of the intelligence, creativity, and talent of young African Americans have been lost to stereotypes, assumptions, greed, ignorance, fear, and hate. Until more people realize this, more will be lost. We have a responsibility to save those who have been lost, to end the system that attempts to push others to the margin of our society. In my own small way, I intend to fulfill my responsibility.

12

Finding Zion

VIOLA

In the following narrative, Viola traces her evolving relationship to a distant culture and an even more distant father. Though Viola lived in Canada with her white mother, where she suffered under the oppression of difference among her peers, she was drawn to her faraway heritage and father in Jamaica. Frustrated that she couldn't look like, or fit in with, her prejudiced schoolmates, Viola believed that her racial identity and beauty were, to a large extent, defined by her connection to Jamaica. She craved sexual affection, which ultimately "backfired" in a date rape, to fill the emotional void left by her father. With the death of her father, and her introduction to feminist ways of thinking, her idyllic vision of Jamaica eventually shattered, her eyes opened to the island's tradition of sexism and violence. Viola wrote this essay in her senior year.

I have never lived in a household with both my parents. The most obvious part of their relationship was that they were apart . . . far apart. My mother raised me by herself. Even when given the chance to care for me during visits, my father never struck me as a parent. In my mind, his presence during my childhood was blurred into a general sense of mystique about his position in our lives. There was a large contrast between everyday life with my mother and the times I spent with my father, when elegant meals out and shopping sprees at his expense were the norm. However, when I was small I couldn't see that he was leading a comparably privileged life and that being without him added to my mother's financial struggle.

My maturation and the progression of poverty in my home eventually caused me to resent my father's lack of support. A few years before he died, a complex war began between my father and me that shaped my adolescence. This was much different than the friction I experienced with my mother. We were close, sometimes too close to work out our problems, while my father was a mythical and, at best, a magical figure in life. He was capable of appearing and transforming parts of my life (at least by providing material souvenirs of our relationship and puzzling words of wisdom) and then disappearing for extended periods of time. This fluctuation made me feel only half visible, so that, by the age of 13, I had pretty much given up on getting to know him.

Sometimes I felt pushed and pulled by my mother, too. Because of our closeness—to the point of sharing dreams and telepathy—my mother's problems often spilled over onto me. It is important to say that through all the bad times, what has kept us, and will keep us able to understand each other deeply is my mother's persistence in a world of obstacles. Ingenuity with scarce resources and pride in my voice are things I learned from my mother. A key part of her determination to be herself was refusing to depend on a man in any way. Another part was working hard to accommodate her desire to be a writer. But my mother also struggles with the scars of mistreatment that stem back to times far before she had me. Ironically, the strength I admired often put a strain on our household. She was a practicing alcoholic until I was 8 years old. Although I am thankful that she only drank when I was in bed at night, I do remember terrifying experiences like not being able to wake my mum at noon on weekends.

For the most part, the earlier years of my life passed by with ease. I remember living with my mum and my grandmother, whom we call Pedey, in a tiny apartment when I was 3. I knew that Pedey thought I was special and I loved her very much. My mum moved in with Pedey because she was having financial problems. My dad had left her pregnant in Toronto, forcing her to move back east to New Brunswick. When my dad left to return to Jamaica, he promised to be back every month for a year, and then we would all live together again. (During the next 17 years, he never came to Canada for more than a week). My cousin Sophie also lived in the same city. We were like sisters, since I was born only 3 months after her. We used to take off our clothes and dance for an admiring audience of three: her mum, my mum, and Pedey. There I was, a little brown body, dancing among all the white bodies. I never imagined I was different.

When I was 3, Mum and I went to Jamaica to visit my dad. We had been there once before when I was 1, but what I mostly remember from that trip was more the feeling of Jamaica than my father. I remember sitting in the backseat of the car, my eyes softened to the somehow familiar air. I saw the white face of my mother and the dark brown face of my father side by side. They were smiling as my mother fed me little bits of spicy Jamaican patties. I remember slowly grasping the little pieces and enjoying them both for their taste and the way in which my mum carefully handled them. My eyes watered from the spice, and I reached for more. The sound of my mother and father laughing together made the car seem an insufficient container for our happiness.

My second trip to Jamaica, when I was 3 years old, was quite different. I really recognized my dad. The smell of sugar cane in the heat and the black leather of his car were signals for me of his identity. But these elements didn't make me feel very much a part of this man. I still didn't see him as my father. I was living in a temperate world where fatherhood was defined by bedtime stories and next-door neighbors. My mum reminds me of periods of time I would spend, when I could just barely speak, saying over and over: "Ted? . . . Ted? Dad, Ted?" Because my pronunciation was not so precise, she would desperately explain that no, my daddy was not *dead,* but in Jamaica, and she would take me to the map and show me where it was.

For a long time my father would remain a tenuous connection to a part of me which was hard to articulate. This connection was not yet a negative thing. My mum encouraged me to accept my Jamaican as well as my Canadian blood. Some days she would set me up finger painting to reggae, other days to Beethoven. As I grew from toddler to child, I'm sure I tasted the soil of another land on my tongue and I perspired the salt water of the "likkle rock" when I ran. These sensations were home to me, as were wintry air on my cheek and dandelions. But because they were so familiar, I didn't differentiate between the two. My world as a child was comfortable, home-oriented, and private. I could play out the extent of either culture without interference. What triggered the sense of separation was the awareness and comprehension that my father was not around.

Starting school for me was the entrance into a period of malaise about my home life. I used to print "I don't have one" on personal information forms for school when asked about my father's name or occupation. I figured that a daddy must be something like a dog. I didn't have one, and whether it got hit by a car or ran away didn't matter because it happened before I was born. Friends started asking me where he was from. "Jamaica," I replied. I could point it out on the map for them. I didn't get offended when they asked if it was like Hawaii.

One girl at school used to think it was just the best joke to ask me, "Are you black or did you just take a bath in really dirty water?" I was honestly perplexed by this at first, thinking how could dirt be compared with having darker than white skin? Then it hit me that each time a kid looked at me they saw my difference as negative. When a girl befriended me, I began to feel that it was only because she felt pity on me. When the boys locked me in their playhouse or pushed me off the swing, I felt that they were trying to somehow modify me. I began to feel too exposed. I didn't like to be where everybody could see me.

I got into biking everywhere, so that no one could look at me for a very long time. I would even have my mother stuff my bicycle into the trunk of her car each day so I could bike around at lunch and to after-school care. I was beginning to be embarrassed by my faraway father because he represented a large part of why I didn't fit in where I lived, and he wasn't even around to help me with it. There were numerous times when my parents would talk about living together again, which would make me ecstatic. Not only would I be part of a "normal" family but I would also have some clout behind my skin color. My community would recognize us as unit and be less likely to mess with me.

There were limits to how much my mother could help me deal with racism as a child. The primary reason for this was that I hadn't yet learned concepts like discrimination. But another reason was my sense that my mum had never had to endure what was making me feel so out of sorts. I was around 4 years old when I began to notice the differences between Mum and me. She didn't have as much trouble as I did combing her hair in the morning. One day in the sun would turn me a deep brown, whereas she would redden. And there were other things I couldn't quite pinpoint until I was older. She seemed very at ease with other people and would often invite women over for tea. An acquired mistrust of white people caused me to skulk in corners during these visits. My mum would have to urge me to "Come and say 'Hi,' Viola."

I changed schools in second grade because I was so unhappy. In my new school, I finally found a real group of friends. But gradually, throughout elementary school, they lost interest in me as they learned what was "cool" and what was not. To deal with the cues that I was not quite right I gravitated toward the other outcasts: an Indian girl who bought me a bag of chips every day to guarantee my companionship; an Egyptian boy; a Jewish boy; and a girl with a learning disability. However, I did get on the good side of one "regular" girl. Her name was Penny. She was tormented by boys because of her daring nature. She was small and fast enough to carry out any stunt she could dream up. I admired Penny and took the chance with her to express my naturally outgoing personality. We were the leaders in kissing tag or Chinese skipping and we managed to be the loudest girls without being considered "conceited" in the judgmental eyes of the other school kids. We were among the few girls who could adeptly play rebound with the boys—no matter how hard the ball was whipped at the brick building.

The only thing was, Penny was pretty and I wasn't. She had straight, fine hair, and when all the boys called her "fountain head" I knew it was a compliment. She was shorter than the guys, so they took her seriously when she asked them to the dance. Whenever I "asked out" a boy he would answer, "Why would I go out with you, you're just another boy. You play with the boys, you have short hair—it would be like me going out with Jeff. Hey Jeff, come here! Will you go out with me, Jeff?" I tried to blend in by adding to the laughter, but every comment like that took chunks out of my ego. These white guys were telling me that I had no beauty. If I had beauty, it wasn't decipherable to them, and therefore I wasn't recognizable as a female. I was generally seen as a tomboy.

At that point, I would have given anything for a friend who cherished me as much as I did her. I began to spend more time with my best friend, Jan, whom I had met when I was 6. I was devoted to her for years. I didn't branch out at all in junior high. I wasn't provided with very many opportunities to make new friends. I certainly couldn't fit into any of the many cliques that formed at my new school. The kids would gather in the parking lot at lunch hour, forming tight circles according to who belonged to what group. These groups didn't budge unless someone passing by was recognized as a member and allowed to shuffle in. There was a sense of urgency about their huddle. If I ever tried to talk to anyone in a circle, I was physically elbowed out without a word. No explanation, just rejection. My cousin Sophie, the one I used to dance with, participated in this. Alone she was great. Thinking back, I find it ironic that this experience in the parking lot that I found so shocking was going on inside the building in more subtle ways.

I think in my attempt to mask my insecurities, I probably came across as a confident adolescent. That's how I got through junior high. In class when I practically whispered "j'ai dix ans" everybody chimed in with "You're only 10?!" I didn't look like the other girls at all because I couldn't afford their clothes and makeup and because I didn't know how to make myself appear like the others. They were all white, except the one Indian girl with whom I had been friends in elementary school, but she had given up on talking by this time. In fact, I could count on my hand the number of people in my junior high school who weren't white. Out of 900, there was one Egyptian girl who was very popular and looked white, one well-liked black, one delinquent black, one East Indian, and a handful of Aboriginals.

The alienation was too much to cope with. I began to suffer periods of depression. Probably the things that kept me going, besides Jan, were my abilities to write, paint, play violin, and dance. My mum encouraged me to work hard at my extracurricular activities because she knew how unhappy I was at school. Thinking it was simply due to boredom, she fought hard to add enrichment to my school life, which is why I ended up skipping the last grade of elementary school. Nonetheless, for half a year, I spent many of my school days in the health room with the lights out. I felt like my intestines were being eaten away. When I was in class, I'd daydream constantly. My marks stayed slightly above average, which I suppose gave the teachers reason not to worry too much about my state. I survived by fantasizing. I'd think about where I would go if I wasn't stuck in New Brunswick, if one of my mum's frequent plans of starting a new life would really happen. What would happen if we actually had enough money to act like a normal family, or even what would I do if any guy saw me as attractive.

But I was a nerd. And because my sexuality was becoming a stronger and stronger force inside me, it was a particularly terrible time for me to feel disliked. Not one guy took me seriously. I couldn't always connect it consciously with racism, but I often could. I heard a lot of "psss sss . . . that nigger" when I walked the halls. One day I was walking home when I heard a shout from above: "Hey Oreo!" which was engulfed by laughter as the window slammed shut. I looked around and didn't see any walking cookies, so I continued on. I was enraged that a guy who claimed he was my friend called me a nigger.

"Don't call me a nigger, Jamie. Don't call me that!"

"Nigger! Nigger! Nigger-nigger-nigger." His laughter made me dizzy.

"Don't call me a nigger, JAMIE. Please, don't call me that!" I was almost crying by now. "If you call me a nigger, Jamie . . . I'll kick you in the balls! I'll kick you in the balls. I'm not even black, don't you know . . . "

"Nigger! Nigger! Ha ha. Nigger!"

He thought it was a game to dodge my swinging book bag and laughed all the way out of the building. He wouldn't stop even when the teacher passed by us numerous times, seemingly oblivious to the savage attack. No matter how often this ritual occurred, I could never bring myself to kick him in the balls. I thought it would be too painful; I could empathize with pain all too easily. Because he was my friend every other minute of the day, I thought my anger and humiliation were irrational. Not only was I dumbfounded by the behavior of my peers but I also couldn't justify my own feelings.

In grade 9, I really wanted to visit my dad again. It had been 5 years since I'd been to Jamaica, and I was becoming increasingly geared toward that part of my heritage. I was hooked on the reggae albums my dad had sent me when I was little, but I needed to hear live Jamaicans speak to me. As my marginalization in school became unbearable, my instinct was to explore what made me different. I hoped to find sameness, or at least a nicer kind of different. I wanted to be a part of a culture so that I had something to defend myself with, a base from which to grow. I feared losing my authenticity if I didn't know anything about Jamaica.

My father didn't spend very much time with me when I arrived in Jamaica because, as usual, he was working frantically on a project, so I hastily took advantage of alternative welcoming arms. I met two guys on the beach in Ocho Rios, and we arranged to meet later. We walked through the streets of the city and talked into the night. The flood of attention unglued my strong grip on my behavior. In fact, I initiated sneaking onto the beach. I abruptly hopped up and scaled the fence, ending up suspended on the barb wire, anxious to get down before the trotting security guard arrived from down the path. Rowan gracefully unhooked me, and we decided to call it a night.

Later that night my boldness grew even greater. "I was aiming for your mouth," I said, when he turned his cheek to my kiss. "Oh! In that case, come over here," he replied. We moved behind a bush for a real kiss. This was my first taste of what would become my drug of choice: sexual affection. As we kissed, I wondered what that hard thing digging into my pelvis was. It must be his belt, I thought.

I literally stumbled back to the hotel room, arriving 45 minutes before curfew and feeling satisfied. I felt so female! I slept like a baby and woke up the next morning to find blood on the crotch of my bathing suit. I assumed it was a hormonal reaction to getting my first kiss. I didn't understand that I had gotten my first period until I reached home and Mum explained. I was relieved she didn't slap my cheeks so they would be forever rosy like I'd seen on a foreign film. That trip was very important. I began to see myself as attractive. After all the guys who had yelled out, "Cris chile! Can I talk?", how could I feel undesirable anymore? I categorized my beauty, though, as solely measurable in Jamaican terms. Only Jamaican guys stared at me like that. When I arrived back in New Brunswick, nothing much had changed. With a bit more gusto, I shook my braids around in gym class and gave presentations and speeches on Jamaica. Some students did react to me, but they seemed both annoyed and surprised that I dared to insist on a foreign identity.

I was beginning to see my relationship with Jamaica as separate from my relationship with my father. I had a physical, genetic, and psychic connection with this island and I wanted to consider myself Jamaican. I started listening to reggae a lot more. With every drum beat and every touch of a guitar string, my soul ached to go back. I was a wailer, just like Bob Marley, whose songs of being separated from his motherland were always on my tongue. I could allow myself to detach from my father when he hadn't written in months, yet to stay in love with a culture that I thought I could count on.

This perspective would become even more useful through my years in high school. I adopted Jamaica as my sexual medallion, relying on my color and appearance to attract guys' attention. I went for the ones I knew I could snag. To Jan and me, the next best thing to Jamaicans were Africans, and we started seeing two university students from southern Africa. Hardly a weekend went by when we weren't attending some function for international students at the university campus.

Johnson was my boyfriend, a skinny, decrepit-looking guy with an apologetic smile. In retrospect, I view the 9 months I spent as Johnson's girlfriend as a period of time when I was most openly degraded because of my skin color. At first Jan and I didn't take any of it too seriously. One day at Johnson and Oliver's apartment, as we sat draped over their furniture lazily peeling oranges, Jan rolled her eyes to signal she was bored. I twisted my face in empathy. We stuffed the whole oranges in our mouths and had a fit of muffled hysteria while the two guys looked on in perplexity and eventually left the room. To us, they were regular sex, headaches, and free tickets to meet real men. Jan and I were only putting up with them in hopes of finding more fulfilling relationships. In the end, my position in that community would backfire.

By 15, my life seemed to be opening up. I was hanging around a crowd of people who were mature enough to talk to and also had apartments and cars. Being surrounded by so many black people made me delirious. At Caribbean Night, I would become a different person. But sometimes a woman's voice or a hand gesture would make me homesick and I would look at Jan and realize she was still white. If I behaved the right way, I could be at best inconspicuous. It had never occurred to me before that the person I was closest to rarely had to deal with what plagued me daily. To socialize with these people she didn't diminish her differences, as I did. She had a more casual attitude toward it and was probably drawn toward these activities out of thirst for exoticism. However, her friendship and our new pastime were making life exciting for the time being.

After a couple of months, my relationship with Johnson was doomed. I couldn't put up with his possessiveness any longer. When Johnson sensed I was losing interest, he did everything he could to gain control. He let loose a temper I had never seen in him before. Even though I risked being cut off from the community I had joined through my relationship with Johnson, I decided to break up with him. A while later, I went to a party on my own, but he was living close by and when he heard where I was, he traced me down and chased after me. I pleaded with the host of the party, a guy from Kenya, for some help—I was scared. He told me with a smirk to go hide in the tree outside. Suddenly, it hit me that I couldn't count on any of these people. After I found a dark room to lock myself up in, I gave into the realization that if I wished to have any relations with these guys it would only be on a very superficial and unequal basis. I shrunk back into the bed as Johnson began to pound ferociously on the door. This time, he was threatening to kill me. The wood was cracking, and with the music now turned down, I could hear the splinters land on the linoleum. When he got too disruptive, a group of guys pinned him to the wall, and I escaped home.

From then on, I continued my attachment to that crowd in a less visible way, through almost purely sexual relationships. I wanted to be less a member of the community by interacting in private. Of course, there is always a system of gossip that makes it hard to maintain privacy in any community. I don't know how much that played a part in my denigration, but I was "put in my place" in the most effective and harmful way possible.

Immediately after Johnson, I was date-raped by a 27 year old from St. Lucia. My denial of having been raped, which lasted for weeks, was proof of how dependent I was on the attention and pseudoacceptance of my little community.

I continued to see the guy and acted as though nothing had happened. I didn't even tell Jan or my mum. Even now, after counseling sessions and vivid flashbacks, I can rearrange my "No" and his intimidating coercion into an almost normal scenario. It comforts me like a horror movie with a happy ending. That assault marred my sexuality with a tangle of confusion, remorse, and often unmanageable anger. It was easier to follow a path of unhealthy relationships than to allow the powerful emotions around being violated to bleed into my sex.

Around that time, the scene at school didn't offer many alternatives for socializing. Even more exclusionary than junior high, my new environment offered me one niche: a member of "the black table" in the cafeteria. We would all gather there at lunchtime to discuss our dance club practices and joke around. When the principal walked by, he would send an unforgiving stare our way as if trying to decipher our next planned act toward the school's demise. We were all supposed to be failures and troublemakers. Unfortunately, some of the black students bought into this stereotype. After so many years of reinforcement from their teachers and friends, they acted out the expected part of the inarticulate jesters. I can think of only a few black students who weren't either in dance club or on a sports team; many took more than 3 years to graduate. Their stereotyped characters, their energy and loud humorous ways of interacting with other people, allowed them to be a part of the school social system. Some were better than others at behaving this way, and they became the most popular black people around. Although I was perceived to be black in this group, I knew I was different from them. Not just because I was a "cafe au lait"; I didn't walk the walk or talk the talk very much beyond dancing and laughing. Additionally, I had constant encouragement at home to expand my knowledge and artistic expressiveness. I know I had a better base from which to modify my situation than did the other black students who came from less-educated, even poorer families.

For example, at one point in grade 11 when I was threatening to leave school, my mother arranged a private course with a Jamaican African man at the local university. By guiding me in my exploration of Caribbean literature, my new mentor taught me how to answer some of the important questions I had about my race. I began to understand why I was often perceived as superior to the darker, full-black Jamaican. Quite a paradox for me to swallow when so often I had been feeling not black enough. The times when Jamaican men ran up to my dad, complimenting him on his "beautifully complexioned daughter," now made sense.

My feelings toward Jamaica changed. In light of its sexist, patriarchal organization, my Jamaican identity became less of a mental solace. I was in the middle of defining my feminist beliefs and coping with my anger toward the male culture. Jamaica has such a blatant tradition of degrading women, which is clear in many pieces by its female writers.

The course also triggered a lot of disgust for my father. Since he had never explained himself, I could only assume that his behavior as a father was a simple product of his culture. And how could my mother have been so naive, I wanted to know. I began to ask her more about the conditions of her relationship with my father. Her responses never satisfied me: It was the seventies, a stronger atmosphere of interracial harmony, and they were deeply, deeply in love. Being the living outcome of all this, I was cynical. I felt more independent from my mother because I could understand her less. A violent defiance awoke inside of me.

By the time I was in grade 12, I felt ready to explode—a new emotion for me, as I had generally been "in control" of my feelings. I had put up with too many abusive relationships between the racism at school and my unbalanced social life. I was through with feeling like my insides were boiling away; I needed to take care of myself. Without warning, a crisis occurred. I wrote about the experience a little while after it happened:

> This morning the grayness of my town rode with me on the school bus up the hill. I thought it was going to be just another day of numbing myself in order not to explode.
>
> I got my books easily; there isn't much of a locker crunch on a Tuesday morning. I made it easily to my homeroom. I didn't even bother to walk along "Main Street" to see who had made it to school. I knew Jan was probably at home sick again. During the monotonic announcements, I prepared myself for the cold day ahead and then set off for math class, excited about getting back a test I thought I had aced.
>
> When the tests were being passed back people were smiling so I felt optimistic. When I got my paper back, I stared at my mark, practically a failure. I had studied so much. I could only concentrate on one sentiment: *No matter how hard I try to be recognized and commended I never am.*
>
> I needed to get out . . .
>
> From the top of the hill I could see the gray water and my house seemed miles away. It was the longest walk ever down Fern Street. I wished I could just fall and cry and pull my hair and roll and trip all the way down. When I finally reached home, I fumbled with the screen door in a mess of fresh tears, and Mum greeted me through the glass. She opened the door and extended a winglike arm. She uttered a phrase of receptivity and hung my coat on a hook. "I'm never going back there . . . I refuse to go back there." She knew me well enough to realize I meant it.

Dropping out of school seemed arrogant and senseless to many people, but even though she didn't understand all the social turmoil I was experiencing, my mother was always behind me. She sensed that I deeply needed to grant myself the sense of dignity that I had been denied over the years in school. Being expected to shovel in loads of ethnocentric material and to contort myself in a constant effort to be inoffensive had damaged me. This point in my life, where I refused to take anymore, is something I'll always be proud of. I certainly would not be who or where I am today if I had not done it.

At the time, however, it was unrealistic to think about going anywhere without a diploma. I was lucky enough to be invited to spend a term as an auditor at an American college by a family friend. Taking university classes, where the pace was fast and the material intriguing, proved to be highly therapeutic for me. After taking classes in feminism, science, and moral development, I knew more clearly what I wanted to study. My time off allowed me to learn much. I did a lot of good for myself, but I also got into bad situations with alcohol and guys. I was still reeling from an emptiness inside me. By standing up for what I needed, I had distanced myself from others. For instance, things were never really the same with Jan, because of our now-divergent life goals. When I did return to New Brunswick to attend a private high school for a year, it was in a different city.

This school was supposed to be geared toward people who needed more academic challenge and who had faced various social problems in public school. I was awarded a half-tuition scholarship, and my father agreed to pay the rest. Once I adjusted to the new environment (I had gone from the largest high school in Canada to the smallest), I was faced with the extreme measures of control imposed on the students' lives.

What I will always refer to as "corruption" was engrained into this institution and could never be explained in a few lines. My friends and I put up with basic injustices on a daily basis. I did make really close friends, which was the only worthwhile part of that year besides my diploma. We helped each other get by. I stuck it out because I so desperately wanted to get away, out of the Maritimes to study at a university.

Then something happened that depleted my psyche so immeasurably that I would be changed forever. I was feeling particularly deserted by my father. When would be the end of this sense of desertion? I wanted to end my foreigner status in my father's world. It was time; I was about to begin the steps into an adult lifestyle.

Every step I took on that manicured high school campus reminded me of how I would soon live. I would be so much happier as a university student. At the same time, I was often haunted by images of my mother coming to my classroom to tell me my father was dead. It made each sinew of my body vibrate with tragedy. Any chances of us having a meaningful relationship would be shot. I also think I imagined his death because I resented my dependence on him financially. Attending university, which he had agreed to pay for, would necessitate even greater reliance on him, but I didn't like feeding off someone who was merely an occasional voice on the phone or a signature on a birthday card.

My father had not been in touch since our last visit. As with my other visits to Jamaica during high school, I went with Jan. Normally, we had a lot of fun, and my dad's preoccupation with work didn't bother us since we had other things to fill our time with. But in my senior year, we spent 2 mind-boggling weeks on the island. My dad was acting deranged. He would sleep at weird hours and not wake up even when we pounded on his bedroom door. He went to meet people in deserted places and kept thousands of dollars under the mat in his car. He seemed to have lost his appetite and forgotten about ours. He wouldn't take us to eat for days at a time. Since he didn't keep much food in the house, we went hungry. After a few days, we became delirious and exhausted. One day we even set out to walk to the nearest town, which was at least 25 miles away, to go to the market. We didn't even make it out of his village and when we returned we began to panic. But the real conflict started when my dad announced we weren't acting appropriately in front of guys. We demanded to know what he meant. It turned out that our clothes were too revealing and that basically a woman was responsible for the way men acted toward her! I had never heard such a derogatory comment from my father. I lost it. The rage was consuming. I screamed that he wasn't even around to protect me from all the things guys did to me, he didn't even know what happened. Jan asked him if he thought it was a woman's fault if she was raped. I tore the banister off the new attachment to his house and threw some stuff around. Then we told him to take us to Ocho Rios and leave us alone, which he did for a whole week. In the midst of all this Jan and I both caught a tropical disease and wound up in the hospital when we finally returned to Canada.

Needless to say, I was not particularly receptive to my father after that visit. He wrote me a letter expressing a desire to form a more compatible relationship, but his tone was so condescending that I crumpled it up. Anyway, it was too late. I was rude about taking money from him and never spoke to him on the phone. The 3,000 miles between us complicated communication in the best of times; now I used it to distance myself from him emotionally. My love for him was interwoven too tightly with pain. I tried to let myself despise him.

So it was in this frame of mind that I sat in math class 7 months after my last encounter with my dad. There was a knock at the door, and my teacher sprang to answer it. It sounded like Mum to me; I knew her whisper. But why would she have traveled a hundred kilometers to see me just after I had been home for the long weekend? My teacher beckoned me to the door. I stepped outside into the dark hallway to meet my mother. She spoke, confirming my terror, "It's your Dad." I walked toward her as she backed weakly away from the classroom. "He's dead," she said to me. I was gazing at her face for any sign of reality, and it came crashing toward me. Her skin was as white as smoke except for the deep red rivers where tears had been staining all morning. I looked away and knew that this was real. I felt the ground plunge away from me and my heart seemed to suck in all the energy in my body. I would have to teach myself how to move again.

In the days that followed, I was unable to follow a train of thought or even turn on the water faucet. I couldn't even find a way to recall the deep anger I once had. It all flew away from me the minute he was murdered. What a sickening culture. That distant place that I spent half my youth trying to embrace had killed my father.

I had been aware of the thread of Jamaican society spun by overly aggressive males. It was what left women and their kids alone. Men killed men of their own race. I could explain it through the need for males to hold their expected place in society which was never met throughout the years of political upheaval. This kind of frustration is easily internalized. You could smell it mingling with ripe fruits in the shady marketplace heat. It was on every man's face who walked the streets. It had torn through the philosophy of early *ska* and created a *raga* of violent musical themes. I listened to it and danced in the island's roughest clubs, where the glint of steel was almost as noticeable as the scent of rum. It was inconceivable to me that all of that had put an end to my father's life. The Kingston newspapers called it the death of "the Gentle Giant." Although I knew another side of him, he was a man who expressed a need for serenity in life. He didn't deal well with conflict. As could be expected, the newspaper write-ups concentrated on my father's career. In one lengthy article, one line was allotted to mention his three children. When I read it, I was surprised by the pathetic gesture. I read photocopies of these papers at a table surrounded by relatives whom, for the most part, I had never met. A few hours earlier I had arrived in Jamaica in a trance. When I peered into the dark humidity for the people who were supposed to pick me up, my surroundings were devoid of mystery. Jamaica was banal, unexciting. Even my new relatives were not part of the island, they were mostly guests. In my father's home, his absence made me feel aloof, as though I had no reference point.

The days I spent in Jamaica to bury my father granted me closure to one thing and one thing only: my father's living days on Earth. Many other things, however, were opened up at that time. My half-sister Shauna and I met for the first time. Initially, we were too overwhelmed by it all to talk much, but eventually she spoke a bit about her life and filled me in on my half-brother, who hadn't come to the island. The high point of our bonding was probably the night of my dad's funeral. A group of family members who were around the same age went out to the bars. When we arrived home, drunk to the point of slurring, Shauna and I wrestled with the car key in the ignition until we practically wet ourselves in a hysterical release from the day. I actually felt a closeness to her that I had never had with anyone else; it was subtle, sorrowful, and full of relief. She reminded me of a part of myself that I didn't consciously know was there. I guess that is because we shared a father. But at times when we had to take care of the business concerning my father's estate, like sifting through his chaotic house for life insurance policies or any other important belongings, I was struck by how different my sister was from me.

My sister is 8 years my senior. My brother is 5 years older. Their lives intercepted with my father's at a different time than mine did. He was married to their mother Joan and was a part of their family until he and Joan separated when Shauna was a toddler. I certainly do not know the whole story of their relationship, but since my mother was involved with my dad just after he separated from Joan, I have heard some of my mum's perspective. She told me that Joan wanted to continue the marriage and was deeply resentful of my mother. After much turmoil (which included Joan entering my father's and mother's apartment one night threatening to kill), an agreement was reached: My dad would give Joan a second child and she would promise to leave them alone. This event is such a part of my heart even though it happened outside of my lifetime. I am appalled at these three adults for making that choice. On the other hand, I understand my mother's consuming love for my father, a Jamaican woman's claim on the ideal of a Jamaican family, and my father's fragmented devotion to both. Out of this was born a boy, my half-brother, who remains a surreal figure in my life. I have yet to meet him.

Returning to Canada after burying my father brought a sense of relief. I sat in the plane draped over the arm rest, watching the red earth plunge deep into the panorama. As the misty vegetation and hints of motion tipped away from me, I blocked out the sounds of Kingston that trickled through my swollen mind. I was becoming set on making my life whole. The hours I spent flying gave me a chance to let go of a lot. The sun was an exquisite reassurance among the clouds, but I felt no sorrow when it was time for it to disappear. Things would eventually be fine, even better than I could have imagined. I no longer had an unattainable life to entice me when I wasn't fulfilled. It would be impossible for me to be a part of Jamaican culture, both because I now despised it and because my dad was gone.

I haven't been back to Jamaica since my father's funeral. Four years later, the grief over my father's death is still a factor in deciding what to do with my future. It sometimes determines what kind of day I have and has given me an increased sensitivity to violence in society. I get angry with my dad, mostly when I feel the financial strain of my life closing in on me and realize that a lot of it could have been relieved if he were alive. Whether it would compensate for the pain he added to my life I can't answer, and I will never know how our relationship would have evolved. I do feel a deep connection to him, sometimes through an almost tangible presence that feels like him, but more often through the work I do and want to continue doing.

Environmental engineering was my dad's field. He did some very important things for the protection of Jamaica's nature, and it makes me sad that he can't continue his important work. I am comforted by my own interest in environmental protection; I know I will make changes. I am also scared because my passion is often powerful and I don't want to end up submerged in my career with no room for anything else.

It's funny because I'm also following in my mother's footsteps through my writing. Encouraging a child to express herself is the best gift a parent can give. My mother is always interested in my creative side, and I in hers. We still have fights, but we also share joy and humor that more than makes up for it. When I am too hard on myself, she can help me put things in perspective. My mother is a sometimes wildly emotional person and she has a core that is stronger than iron. She gets things done through thick and thin and has an amazing capacity for empathy. The pros and cons to this I know well; she gets tired and ill. But I accept the power she has bestowed in me as a great tool for my future.

I am open to the future and I feel more directed than I have in a long time. I know the way that life can surprise us. I have a lot ahead of me.

Unfortunately, the family I come from is split right now. There are relatives on both sides with whom I have rocky relationships at best. On my father's side some have shown no interest in finding out who I am, and others send me cards once in awhile. I haven't heard anything from my sister in months. I don't even know for sure where she and my brother are.

By looking at my life as a product of two ethnicities, I have learned about what ethnicity means to many people and I have learned what it means to me. I know racism; I know how many mixed people choose to be black because it's easier. I know white people who prefer it that way too. I am reluctant to resign myself to one side or the other, which shows up in many aspects of myself. I am neither black nor white, but I can be both. The strongest ethnic ties I feel are to others with the same heritage.

13

Feeling the Pressure to Succeed

RICK

Possessing all the "risk factors" for a poor outcome (drug-infested neighborhoods, dangerous schools, etc.), this sophomore describes a number of factors that helped him achieve success. He recounts his mother's determination that he do well in school despite his tendency to be a disciplinary problem in middle school, where the principal's patience and belief in him built up his belief in himself. Similarly, he developed a mutually supportive bond with his best friend in high school, which helped him avoid the temptations of the street and stay focused on school achievement. Finally, success in high school football along with outstanding grades opened doors to the best colleges, which he walked through proudly yet feeling the need to redeem the image of the young black male.

During my junior high years, I was often the only African American male in my classes. Other African American students ridiculed me for being with the white kids all day. I felt as if I had to prove my "blackness" when around my black peers. I learned early that black people and white people interact differently. I had to change my personality depending on my company. I would even change the pitch of my voice and language I used. I was often teased because I "sounded like a white boy." Looking back, I believe this hindered my ability to develop socially. I never was really comfortable with myself because of the constant changing of personalities.

I have always wondered if my brother had the same problems. Stanley is 7 years older than I. He went to college when I was 10 years old, so we never really were able to talk about things we had in common. My brother had always been my second guardian when I was little: I went on one of his first dates because there wasn't anybody home to baby-sit. He had to bring me to his junior varsity games because my mother worked on Saturday afternoons. Stanley did more for me than any father could do in my first 11 years of life. We always shared the same room, so there was normal sibling conflict but nothing unusual. I didn't realize that we didn't have the same father until much later in life. I think my mother mentioned his father once in my lifetime. I haven't the foggiest idea of what happened with Stanley's father, whether my mother was married to him, or if the man died. I also haven't a clue about the circumstances surrounding Stanley's birth.

After I turned 11, I didn't have a lot of contact with my brother. He left for college and only returned home on short vacations. He found other places to go in the summer. Stanley and I aren't people who pick up the phone and call every week or every month, perhaps because I spent so much time growing up without his presence.

While I attended middle school, I was threatened to be kicked out of the "gifted program" several times. Mr. Taft, the principal, and I spent many hours in his office discussing why I caused trouble. He knew a little Italian like most people in the industrial city in Connecticut where I lived and he would refer to me by the Italian word for irritation—*agita*. He would always tell me about his Irish descent and the problems and prejudices he faced growing up as a child. Looking back at those discussions now, I think it was his way of telling me that he understood some of the things that I was going through.

He usually listened attentively as I complained about teachers with whom I had conflicts. Many times he agreed that a teacher was wrong, but he would always say that was no excuse and would explain where my course of action was wrong. I don't ever remember Mr. Taft yelling at me in private. When the teacher with whom I got in trouble came in to watch me be reprimanded, Mr. Taft might yell, but it was only for show. This told me something about how things worked in the world. You have to try to appease everybody. Even though he didn't particularly agree with the teacher, he had to take her side so their professional relationship could continue smoothly. I learned a valuable lesson about politics.

Every teacher I had, at one time or another, said that they were done with me and never wanted to see me in their class again. They said they couldn't deal with me. One time I threatened violence against a teacher, Mrs. Sloan, and she was actually pretty shaken up. She said that she would slap me if I ever repeated "Fuck you!" in her class. I told her that if she hit me that she better duck because I would be swinging back as quick as possible. Before the words left my mouth, I was on my way out of the class. I knew it was serious when she got up and left the classroom and returned with the principal with tears in her eyes. I wasn't able to attend her class for a week. Mr. Taft, my mother, and I all had to beg this lady for her forgiveness. She finally gave in when my mother broke down in the principal's office. Mrs. Sloan saw my mother in tears and knew she was the only one that was able to help her. She told me that she was letting me back in class because she hated to see me treat my mother this way. She said that I would not receive any attention from her. I was to sit in the back, not talk to anybody, and if I attempted in any way to be a disturbance in her class, I would be removed immediately and permanently. I knew Mrs. Sloan and I knew that she wouldn't talk to me for a couple of days, but that eventually things would work out. Mrs. Sloan had too big a mouth and too big a heart to watch me sit there in her class and not learn something.

Seeing my mother in tears did stir remorse. I didn't want to cause her so much additional stress in her life. I had never seen her cry in front of anyone before. I realized that I was pushing the limit of our relationship. I think her tears were from frustration and I feared she would eventually tire of me and give up hope. Reflecting back, I would have to admit that she had good reason.

It is not that I didn't care and wanted my mother to come to the school every week, but I just wasn't concerned with succeeding academically. I didn't have a good self-image when I came into the classroom with the other kids. In fact, I was intimidated by them. I felt that I couldn't measure up when it came to academics. The other kids would study every night and have well-prepared notes. They were always ready when called upon to perform. I probably could have done the same but I wasn't that committed. In the back of my mind, I was scared that if I really tried my best and didn't receive an A like the other students, that inferior grade would reflect my real standing relative to my classmates. It was much easier slacking off and using laziness as an excuse.

I think that I had a prejudice when I was in middle school that continues somewhat today. I was intimidated by the other kids in an academic setting because they were white. I would not let one of those "nerds" beat me in any game in gym class from hockey to basketball, but if it was a science test, I didn't mind not being the best. I bought into the stereotype that society portrays of blacks and whites in the United States. Though I knew I was intelligent, I still felt as if I couldn't measure up. At home, I was always told that I was just as good as anybody, but I didn't think I was able to combat the prejudices sometimes perpetrated by society. When I ended up at the bottom of the class, I felt that it wasn't that bad because I was competing against the "best and brightest," but a better interpretation would suggest that I found comfort in scoring the lowest because this class was the "whitest" in all the city. I accepted less because I thought that was the way things tended to be. Though my thinking was naive, I think that a lot of African Americans in my position fall into it. Even at a predominantly white college, I tend to cut myself more slack, but if I were at a predominantly African American university, would I do the same? I am not really sure.

I think my inferiority complex becomes less distressing every day in some respect. Being in college, I see all the advantages white kids had growing up that I didn't. The reason why they always seemed smarter than the average black kid was that they had the computers, a desk to study at, tutors, and other things. It wasn't that they were smarter, it was just that they had a lot of things that I never knew about. It wasn't the racial differences that made them inherently smarter. In many cases, it was the economic class difference. I knew that I could pick up concepts as well as anybody; the difference was that in many instances, some of the materials had already been introduced to them. The stereotype that whites are inherently smarter than blacks can easily be accepted by some when you aren't aware of the two distinct playing fields.

Though the teachers always seemed to hate me, they all made sure they introduced me to the material and worked with me if I had trouble. When I needed to come through on a test to pass the class, I would always study, and though my algebra teacher never said anything, I could tell the way he flipped the paper on my desk he was proud. He would say, "Happy Birthday," or "How lucky!" when I did well. The fact is that he noticed and if he really didn't care, he would have totally ignored my improvement.

I think the only person in that school who thought I would succeed was Mr. Taft. He told me that I had a knack for pushing people's buttons. He would say that if I spent half the time in class instead of in his office, I would be a great student. There were kids in my school that he would suspend with regularity because they were always up to no good. Though I was up to no good most of the time, he knew that there was "something" good inside me which hadn't surfaced yet. I think every teacher I had in junior high school would be astounded that I made it to a good college. The only person who would not be surprised, though he might be amused, would be Mr. Taft. All he would say is, "It's about time, damn it!!!"

Through my years growing up, I have always had a male role model. People like Mr. Taft have been in and out of my life. For some reason, people want to help me. I don't latch onto people because I can be painfully shy, but adults have always taken me in. From the 6th grade up until my college years, youth pastors, people in the community, and coaches have always lent me a hand. It was a friend of my mother's who took me to basketball camp in the summers. One of the leaders of the religious youth group I attended took me hiking. My high school coach called around the city doing everything in his power to get recruiters to come see me. It could be that people helped because they always saw my mother working so hard to raise me. All of these people still come to my college football games. There isn't much that I have to offer these people, yet they still give to me. I hope one day I can influence somebody's life the way they did mine.

I went through 2 very rough years at middle school. I had in-school suspensions and even out-of-school suspensions, but I eventually made it through in one piece. My school troubles carried over into my personal life at home. My mother and I were at odds for the 2 year period. While I was attending middle school, my mother must have made 10 trips to the school in 2 years. She hated with a passion having to come up to the school to see about my behavior problems. "See, this is a reflection on me and not on you. All this is my fault because I let you have things too easy, but I will fix you because I will not allow you to embarrass me in front of those people." Television and contact with my friends was taken away when behavioral problems arose in school. Home life was miserable when things in school were bad.

My mother grew up in a family of eight on a small strip of land that my grandfather rented. She told me how she was allowed to take baths only twice a week and all the other horror stories of being the poor daughter of a sharecropper. She always told me how she had to miss school during certain seasons so that she could pick cotton for her father. She would show me all the corns on her feet from wearing shoes that were too small as a child. I think her work ethic is definitely derived from her childhood. She wanted to see both her sons succeed and saw education as the best avenue. She worked to pay for schooling at her state's black college. She definitely defeated the odds.

I think this work ethic has finally become more engraved in me since I came to college. I came into college with the attitude that I wasn't going to miss a single class, and if I didn't do well in a class, it was not going to be because I didn't do enough. As a sophomore, I still feel the same way. I think I am able to focus on goals somewhat like my mother does. We both feel that if we want to succeed at a particular thing, we are going to give ourselves to it fully, and we refuse to leave it to chance. I think that we have always been similar in this respect, but I never applied this value toward education until later in life.

Ever since I can remember, my mother expected the best from me. "I don't accept Cs" was the statement put on my 4th-grade report card. She repeatedly refused to sign the card, saying, "I don't want my name next to any Cs and you shouldn't either, Rick." Grades and in-school behavior created quite a distance between my mother and me. She has told me on several occasions that anybody can get a C. "You don't have to go to classes to get a C, it takes effort to not do well in school." I do agree with my mother to some extent, but she seemed to be fanatical about my grades. I remember as a little boy when we used to read together, she had little patience with me, though she had been a teacher earlier in her life. I dreaded reading time because it seemed as if she constantly scolded, "I just told you that word, how can you forget? Well, we will just wait here until you figure it out, 'cause I'm not going to tell you."

When I was in the 8th grade, Pop Warner Little League football was the only thing that I lived for. I couldn't wait for Sunday afternoon to play the other local teams. We practiced in the park that was a 15-minute jog from our apartment building. I would relish going to practice so I could get out of the house for a few hours. I felt comfortable and secure when I had on my equipment because I knew that this was something that I could do and do well. I remember the first day the team met at the park. All the fellows bragged about their expectations for the upcoming season. This was the first time that I had ever played organized football. I was nervous, but at the same time confident, because I had loved the game as early as the age of 5. I remember watching football with my mother while she explained the rules to me. She explained how many chances a team has to gain 10 yards, and so on. I sat at the edge of the bed as we watched the Steelers, her favorite team.

During my 9th-grade year, my mother and I moved to New York City, where she teaches middle school today. I spent a lot time in the parks hanging out until my mother came to pick me up. I got to see all the best players that the West Side had to offer. I saw playground legends such as "Pooh," who would play in his dirty work boots. He would come straight from his job at a gas station to the park to play basketball. Though he would be in work clothes and filthy work boots, he would out-jump anybody at the park. Between scoring points, he would take a time-out to sell or buy some drugs. "Hold up! I gotta get paid!", he'd say. He then would walk over to the gate, remove a small package from his pocket, and exchange it for a roll of crumpled bills from a "crackhead." Every day I would see the same tired people visiting Pooh for some drugs, whether it was the woman with the red bandanna along with her little son, or the old man who used to live upstairs from me.

One particular day, waiting for my mother in front of my apartment building, I saw our superintendent selling drugs. I was scared but I walked right up to him and asked if he could help me out.

"Yo, I need a job, think you can help out?" I asked.

"Don't you live in this building?" he replied warily.

"Naw, we just finished moving out."

"Yo, troop, I can't help you out now, I ain't got no jobs now, but I'll look out if something comes up."

"Okay, thanks anyway."

I wasn't sure if I was relieved or disappointed with the result. I understood what kind of dangerous lifestyle selling drugs entailed and the damages to others and to yourself that occur with drug abuse. I guess I had become desensitized to the effects of drugs on people. I had always been taught that drugs were trouble, and it was obvious to me that drugs were not going to get me to all the places that I wanted to go. I knew that a lot of the "crackheads" were ex-drug dealers who were tempted to experiment with drugs. I had seen the cycle these guys had gone through, but I needed to find security in something. I believe that

I still equate money with power and control, which isn't always the case. Football season had ended, and it was difficult to find self-worth in the other prominent things in my life. School was horrible at this point. I thought that selling drugs would give me the self-worth that I desired, that perhaps I would catch respect from everybody if I were able to flash a bunch of money all the time.

I think that the money gained from selling drugs would have only been secondary. I would have had to spend cautiously if I didn't want my mother to find out. I wouldn't have been able to show off my money; the respect would have had to come from the reputation that I would build. Living in the projects, the question wasn't *would* you sell drugs, it was *when* would you sell drugs? It was a sign that you had reached a certain level of influence. It is unfortunate that that mentality exists and that it is so prevalent. I think that it was only chance that prevented me from selling drugs. I didn't come into such close contact with drug dealers again until much later. I think that if at that time I had been presented again with the opportunity to sell drugs, I would have taken advantage of it. Luckily, I began to see a future in school and football and couldn't let drugs ruin that opportunity.

The motto in our family is: "Ignore problems and they will go away." I don't know why we do this, but I think it explains why I have a problem expressing myself even with family. I have never had the practice of talking about touchy subjects. In my family, we do not say "I love you" after long stints away from home. The last time I told my mother that I loved her, I was in the 9th grade, and she looked surprised. When subjects really hit home, the members of my family kind of put up barriers to protect ourselves. I don't even know the circumstances surrounding my brother's birth or what happened to his father. I don't know how anybody would react if I brought up the subject. In my family we don't talk about the past when it relates to us, so I really didn't know the circumstances of much of my family history.

My high school in New York City was unlike any other school I had attended before. When we first arrived in New York, I would see kids standing outside the school and I realized that I didn't dress like them or talk like them. Everybody had the latest and best sneakers, while I still had last year's style. I could see the gold chains gleaming in the sun. A lot of the students had gold rope links around their necks with Mercedes Benz emblems or other such things. The black denim jean suits seemed to be popular among the students, and I could see that I did not have as much money as they did. How could these students afford to dress so lavishly yet live in a terrible neighborhood? I heard the girls string four-letter words together with the greatest of ease. I could hear the New York accent in their voices. Despite what anyone says, there is a special aura that New Yorkers have like nobody else. That is why natives can always tell newcomers. There is a New York attitude that one must display in order to fit in. Everyone in New York walks around with a disgusted look to ward off confrontation.

People would come to school without backpacks, pencils, pens, paper, or the other essentials for being a student. Rudy would ask me every day in history class if he could borrow a pen and one sheet of paper. I obliged every day in amazement that either he had a terrible memory problem or he didn't care about graduating. I had been a student who didn't care for the rewards of academic achievements, but I always did enough to pass with a C. Rudy didn't pretend to care; he walked in and out of class as he pleased and cursed the teacher if he questioned his behavior.

I remember once during the first few weeks of class, a situation begged my attention. We sat listening as the teacher had each student read a paragraph from the ancient world history textbook. As one student began his turn to read, another student began talking to her friend about her escapades of the night before. Though her adventures were quite interesting, it was neither the time nor place to talk about them. Further, she was talking in a normal tone of voice, which made it next to impossible to hear the reading. Though she sat in front of the teacher's desk, he said nothing. Finally, after the competition of both voices, a third student could no longer bear it. "Shhhhhhhh!" he insisted. Though she was in midsentence, she quickly turned her back and stared at the person asking her to be quiet with a look that could kill and said, "Is there something wrong with your lips?" She had become offended by someone's audacity to tell her to be quiet. What nerve he had, he was trying to learn something in class!

I look back at my situation and I think that what most frightens me was that the students were all African American. This was the first time I had to interact with all black people besides my family. I had attended an all-black Southern Baptist church when I was younger, but I preferred going to my brother's predominantly white church because it was much more fun. Being at a New York City high school forced me to interact with black people on another level. I began to question whether I was prejudiced against my own people. I had so much hate for the school that it had to be a reflection on the people. I told myself that I had a major problem with ignorance in the school, not with the color of the students. I can't count the number of times that people said that I "talk funny," or said, "Stop trying to sound white." Outwardly I made no response, but to myself I would say, "I am only using correct English, thank you." I felt out of place and out of touch in an all-black situation. I would walk around scared, hoping that I wouldn't be harassed for the way I dressed or simply because I was a new kid in the school.

When we moved to New York, I got a chance to see my father more often. When we lived in Connecticut, I saw him three times a year. He never came out to our house; I always took the train and the subway to Brooklyn. Being in New

York, however, didn't actually increase meaningful communication between us. I had grown up my whole life without ever relying on a father, so I really had nothing to say to him. We would chat about school or sports, which was about as in-depth as we ever got. The more I saw the man, the less I liked him. He acted as if we should be the best of buddies, as if the first 12 years of my life didn't matter. The man didn't know me. Even to this day, he doesn't remember the name of the college I attend. Every time I see him, he asks me the name of my college.

He would say the divorce was the fault of my mother. I hate to hear excuses, and it makes me angry that he would try to turn me against the person who took care of me. I also hated it when my mother called my father a jerk. I felt as if it was a reflection on me. I know that isn't true, but I still felt that you shouldn't disrespect another person's father in front of their face. It would be fine for me to talk badly about my father because he is *my* father. I do not expect her to have respect for him, but she should respect me enough not to talk badly about him. She thinks it is a big joke when I complain, but I am serious. I don't think she understands that it hurts to hear those things, that if she did understand, she wouldn't do it no matter how bitter she was toward him.

I plan to get married only once in my life and to be a father to my children, which I think involves spending time with your child out of enjoyment, not out of obligation. I think that a father should be excited about being with his children. I hope that the family I create will be more open than my family when I was growing up and that my children ask me about things they are confused about. I hope that my family will say "I love you" to each other a lot more than we did. I think "I love you" is one of the most beautiful things to hear when it is sincere. I want to be much more in tune with my children's feelings than my father was with mine.

I was very thankful for football at this time in my life. Being an athlete allowed me to relate to my peers. Academic honors brought little acceptance at my high school, but athletic achievements truly won praise. I played junior varsity my sophomore year and was a standout. I knew my way around the football field so I felt comfortable. I still stuck out from my teammates when interacting off the field, but I was a good player so it really didn't matter. The fact that I didn't know the area or half the people in the school that they talked about didn't make a difference. Football not only enhanced my self-image but also gave me a circle of friends.

Through football, I met my soon-to-be best friend, Todd, who played tight end on the team. Our interaction throughout the season was minimal; we exchanged pleasantries but nothing more. After the season, I decided to run track to improve my speed for the next season at the varsity level. At the first track meeting of the winter term, I saw Todd. We began to reminisce about the past season and talk about the upcoming season. I had never run track before, and as this was Todd's second season, he showed me the ropes. Our school didn't have an indoor track, and since it was too cold to run outside, we ran in the building.

Every day Todd and I would discuss football, politics, religion, or anything else that was on our minds. We came to discover that we had a lot in common. We both came from single-parent families, though his father played a more active role in his life. I also learned that Todd had a strong commitment to Christ. At that time in my life, Christianity played a significant role. I attended a religious youth group regularly and eventually began to invite Todd along. Each day we discovered the similarities that we had. Todd had encountered some of the same problems when he first attended high school. He was a very bright math student. He placed out of freshmen math and was assigned to a sophomore class. Like me, he was the brunt of ridicule because he cared whether he passed a class or not. As the track season progressed, Todd and I became closer. We began to annoy the other team members because we were chatterboxes. The team would have to meet early Saturday morning in front of the subway station. Todd and I would begin a conversation at 8 in the morning and continue on the train all the way to the meet, whether in Manhattan or Brooklyn. The captain would threaten to separate us because he couldn't stand for two people to talk so much. I can't even recall what we talked about that was so important.

Todd and I spent much of our time in high school together. We worked at a Christian camp together in the summer for 3 years and really began to share with each other. I learned about his aspirations to be an accountant in one of the "the big five" accounting firms. I told him I wanted to be a senator or possibly president. That is not something that you want to tell people because they think you are either immature or crazy. He saw life as a set of events that were meant to happen whether or not one attempted to alter the course, so you might as well not worry about tomorrow. I was the total opposite. I thought if you worked hard enough at something, then there wasn't any reason why you couldn't change fate. To say the least, he was much more relaxed than I was. I think we complemented each other well in this respect. There were times when I would worry about his schoolwork or college applications and begin pushing him. I had to ride him every year to send his work application for camp because he never would get around to it. I remember the time he sent Christmas cards out in March because he "never could come around to it." At the same time, he wouldn't let me get too worked up about SATs and other academic tests. His favorite question was, "What is the worst that can happen, Rick?" Many times, I sat down and agreed I had blown things out of proportion.

I remember when Todd had to leave camp early our senior summer to go to football camp. His father came to pick him up. Everybody at camp was consoling me about losing my twin, but I just shrugged off the comments. "It isn't like he is going to war, I will see him before he dies fellas, relax." I had to keep the tough guy image up to other peers because it was not cool to be emotional about another male. His father emptied out his room while Todd and I went for a walk down the path. We were kind of quiet and really didn't know what to say. This was the first time that we were going to be separated for more than 2 weeks at a time. We walked down the path and sat on the bench next to the tennis courts. Though at times it seems that I was the person in this relationship with insight into the future, Todd was the wiser of us. I was going to an elite college, I was class valedictorian, I was going to play Division I football, but Todd was the one who carried me. I might have had a lot of things going for me, but I would have traded places with Todd any day. I would have been a miserable person if it hadn't been for Todd. He showed me the ropes at high school, he kept me from talking to the hoodlums and going to the wrong places. In any social situation, he was the icebreaker; I didn't have to say a word. I was his tagalong. If I was Todd's friend, then I must be a good guy. We made some small talk, but before he left he gave me some advice about going to college: "Be yourself because you might forget who you are."

Though I had seriously considered leaving my high school in New York to go to Chicago to live with my aunt, the principal persuaded me to stay. There were days when I thought I had made the wrong decision. I remember once watching another member of the track team get severely beaten by a mob of kids because he had spoken to someone else's girlfriend. After seeing this, I wondered about my decision. I realized you could die in this place for the stupidest things. When Robert, who sat behind me in advanced English, showed me his .22-caliber pistol, I freaked out. I thought to myself, when students are playing with guns in class and showing them off to other classmates, things are out of hand. I forced him to move from behind me because he obviously did not know how to handle a gun: Pointing it in every direction and playing with the chamber was behavior that made me feel queasy. I told him that if he didn't move at that very instant, I would tell the teacher. Possessing a gun in New York City public schools can lead to banishment from public school education for some students. He quickly complied with my wishes.

When my senior year rolled around, I was one of the happiest young men. I knew that if I survived one more year at Andrew Jackson High, I would soon be at college. I had one of the best seasons at my position in football. I was written up in the paper on a weekly basis. I even made the back cover of New York Newsday. I was nominated for the all-city team by several papers. I could not have asked for a better season. I had rushed for more than 800 yards and 10 touchdowns. Soon after the season ended, recruiters came knocking at my door. I knew that wherever I was going to go to school, I wanted to play football. It seemed as if every other night, a recruiter was calling my house: "My name is Joe Smith. I represent such-and-such college and I would like to congratulate you on the wonderful season you had this past fall and I would like you to know that we are very interested in you and that we would like you to consider our school." This seemed like a television episode with the celebrated recruit coming out of New York City and everybody putting in their bid to get him.

I look at how far I have come and I smile. I took the most roundabout path, but I made it to college. I learned that life is going to throw you a bunch of curve balls and that the people who survive the best are the ones who have the ability to adapt. I didn't do much adapting earlier in life, but I see myself changing every day. I think that change was a result of the people who played significant roles in my life like my mother, Todd, and my football coach. Everybody needs somebody, whether we like to admit it or not.

I think I struggle with "needing" people. I look at my relationships with the other students across the campus; I have a bunch of friends, but I don't really depend on people. I can't say that I have a relationship with another person that will continue after college. Needing people makes me feel vulnerable in a sense. You permit the person to have control of your emotions to a certain extent. I think that my fear of meaningful relationships is a result of fearing the pain that one might incur. Although I have had people that have cared for me in ways that I didn't deserve, I still don't trust people and their intentions. I definitely think that I am missing out on the college experience due to my superficial friendships with others.

I am not anything special. I am an African American who got a chance. I sit here today as a successful sophomore in a highly competitive college because I had a mother who pushed me beyond my limits. If I could have one attribute like my mother, it would be her ability to cope with any situation. She is the most resourceful person I know. I never went hungry and I always had a coat to wear in the winter. She always came through when I needed money for something. I learned from my mother that I, too, can handle any situation. I also believe that football has carried me distances that I probably would not have reached otherwise. Things could have worked out where I ended up on a corner selling drugs or working in McDonald's; instead I find myself with a good head on my shoulders and a lot of opportunities.

Being a black male doesn't seem to be as horrible as everybody makes it out to be. I find many people in the community pulling for me because I am a black male in college. Before my first term at college, I was at the local barber shop getting a haircut. The barber decided to give me a free cut when he found out that I was on my way to school the next week. The local sororities took a collection and gave it to me as a going away present. I find a lot of support for black males going to college. At the same time, I feel the pressure to succeed.

People are always talking about how the young black male is becoming extinct. Sometimes, you feel as if you have the weight of the community on your shoulders. Then, I look at how far I have come and I smile.

14

Running Hurdles

STACEY

This autobiography focuses on the author's determination to overcome obstacles in the way of becoming a doctor. Stacey, currently a college junior, describes a regimen of self-improvement begun in junior high school and carried on through college. Though she had many successes along the way, her status as a premed student in a highly competitive college brought her up against the fact that she could not maintain the high grades she had been used to in high school. She also reconsidered her single-minded striving for academic achievement as she became active in demonstrating against racism on her campus. Though shaken in her belief in herself, Stacey invoked religious faith as the means for survival. Her experiences at college emerged as a means for her to take a larger perspective on the philosophical notion of the good life and the meaning of personal success. Though her ambition remained, she moved toward a deeper understanding of her own fallibility and a spiritual acceptance of life outcomes beyond the grip of self-determination.

> I don't feel no ways tired,
> I've come too far from where I started from.
> Nobody told me that the road would be easy,
> but I don't believe He brought me this far to leave me.

As I think about the words in this gospel song, I can only look upon my past with relief and anticipate the future with hope. I ask myself what it is that has guided me to this, my junior year in college and my twentieth year in the world. The answer is, in short: motivation; hard work; determination; love; and, of course, God. There have been frequent ups and downs—times when I did much soul-searching. During these periods I learned to dig deep. I tried to understand why what was happening at that particular time was so important to me and then plan my future course of action accordingly. I was not always sure that the steps that I was about to take were the right ones. However, I did know that no matter what the outcome, there was a lesson I could learn. Often there were tears that could flow river-deep. Nevertheless, I knew that I would never give up on a dream, for my faith and hope reached far into the sky. Barriers became temporary hinderances which, once overcome, would make me a true victor—fit and able to handle future problems.

My mother often explained to me that I must never let others set limitations for me. She said that if I believed with all my heart that I could do something, I shouldn't let anyone tell me that I can't—at least not without giving it a try first. She added that only God knew what was to become of my future, not men. My mother believed in me, and more important, I believed in myself. I started to read books on how to succeed in high school and, using a self-teaching guide I got at the thrift store, I worked hard on doing algebra problems. Despite the teacher believing I was not yet ready for the challenge of the algebra course, I took the class in the summer and got an A! This experience helped me to learn a lesson of self-confidence and determination that I have never forgotten.

In high school I encountered new battles. Even though I had an A average and was taking a couple of honors classes, I realized that my English class was far from honors level. I remember talking to a teacher who said that the level I was on was *average*. That was difficult for me to accept. My 8th-grade teacher once said, "You should always strive to be above average and should never let anyone consider you average." Oh, no, I was not going to let someone look down his nose at me; I was just as capable of excelling as anyone else!

I used another self-teaching guide to aid me in preparation to take a placement exam to move to a higher level class. My book bag went with me everywhere: on long trips to grandma's; to my parents' meetings; to church; and even on the way to shopping centers. During this time people thought of me as a "little brain." I didn't pay much attention to this, because the only thing that concerned me was getting ahead. I was not going to let those who teased me distract me from the tasks which would one day help me become a great doctor. I knew that once I had accomplished my current academic goals, I would have time to move on to other things. Sure enough, I was put in a higher level English class after passing a placement exam.

Having realized that I was academically sound, I then went out for track where I made only a small contribution, but I still remained dedicated. I enjoyed getting to know upperclassmen on the team and began to look forward to going to practice. I felt that by talking to older students I was taking a sneak preview of possibilities for my own future. More and more I wanted to complement my academic success with other types of accomplishments; therefore, I added reducing my hurdle times to my list of goals. The feeling of being down in the starting block, waiting for the gun to sound, gave me a sense of perfect concentration. I was filled with excitement as I cleared the hurdles and passed the finish line. I was inspired by the senior awards ceremony where I saw students acknowledged for their outstanding achievements in academics and athletics. I wondered if the same types of honors were to be a part of my future.

In my sophomore year I challenged myself by taking mostly gifted-and-talented courses. My enrollment in these classes was a result of careful planning. Freshman year I had looked though the course guide and noted all the honors classes that I wanted to take before I graduated. I talked to teachers about the courses well ahead of time to see how I could best prepare. If I was to be a doctor, I knew that I would have to start working at it then. While I still continued to play sports, I managed to keep my priorities straight and maintain an A average. However, that year I failed the state writing test. I cried and never told my friends because I knew that I was the only one who could correct the problem. Because passing the exam was a graduation requirement, I had to figure out my next plan of attack. Recalling that some members of my family couldn't read or write very well, I knew it was important for me to work hard to overcome these deficits in my basic skills. With all this in mind, I worked diligently and passed the test the next time.

I didn't have a sibling at home to whom I could express my frustrations. Because my brother was 10 years older, I didn't get to know him well until he was in high school. The next thing I knew, he left home, got married, and had kids. The good things in life always seemed to be at the *next* stage of life or educational level. My boyfriend was the only person other than my family members with whom I felt comfortable sharing my goals, dreams, and frustrations. I never thought that my friends at school could understand my tendency to think so far into the future. They knew that I did well in my classes, but they really didn't know how hard I worked and why. Jason, however, was aware that I wanted to be a doctor and that it was my first priority. I had fun like everyone else, but whenever I had the chance, I read books on study skills or about being successful. Jason and I became very close, probably because he was a little older and was thinking about life plans as well. I learned to trust him in a way that I had not known before. I learned to love and to be loved and thus felt good about myself. Jason was there for me throughout many ups and downs until my senior year.

Stories about how difficult it had been years ago for blacks to obtain education of any sort made me strive even harder toward my goals. I knew that my grandmother, as brilliant as she was, didn't have much education. Even though she was the most insightful and loving person that I had ever known, it hurt me to know that she did not have the same opportunities that I had. It was almost as if she, along with many others, had been cheated out of something that they rightfully deserved. Although no one in my family ever pressured me to set high standards for myself, I knew that they hoped that I would succeed. Through much support and encouragement, they made me believe in myself to such a degree that I felt nothing was impossible for me to obtain. I never wanted to let opportunities pass me by; so many people had sacrificed so much so I could have them. Deep down inside, I knew I was able to overcome academic obstacles just as my family members had endured hard times in their lives. My family has always stressed that God made it possible for them to overcome prejudices and other barriers they encountered. I knew that if I continued to encounter academic stumbling blocks, I needed God to guide me through any problems that I might encounter.

During my senior year in high school, I spent most of my free time in the lab at the state university. Having participated in a fellowship program the previous summer, I developed a project that I could work on independently for a science research class. I had a key to the lab and was allowed to work there whenever I could. During the times that I processed rat nerve tissue until midnight, Mom or Jason stayed in the lab with me. Having such strong support from the people I cared about was crucial; I was able to develop the self-confidence and skills which made my interest in science increase. Filled with energy and enthusiasm, I felt a sense of satisfaction in knowing that my classwork had some practical applications in the real world. As senior year came to a close, I had succeeded in meeting most of my academic goals. I presented my project at a science fair and gained assurance that my skills in science were apparent in the work that I produced. I received many awards and scholarships at the senior awards ceremony, which made both my parents and me proud. However, in spite of all this success, I had failed to strengthen my relationship with God. I realized this to be true when I became haunted by Jason's words "You need to have God in your life" and a recurring nightmare. The nightmare horrifies me today as much as it did years ago. I dread the thought that my fate in the nightmare could ever take place. If by chance it did happen, I would know that I was in Hell or some other inferno.

In my nightmare, I find myself on a ship looking out at a dirty brown-gray body of water divided by a large brick wall. Boundless, the wall stretches as far as I can see up into the sky and out in every other direction. As I look into the water, I notice an object floating in its center. A strong and powerful force then pushes me forward, making my body press close to the ship. As the pressure intensifies along my upper spine I begin to feel weak against the force but somehow dominant over the unknown floating object. As the force increases, I am able to dive in the water and swim toward the object. Swimming fast causes my back to ache and arms to tire. Each stroke, though painful, seems to take me closer to the object. However, this feeling changes after about a minute. Suddenly it seems as though the object is moving away from me and toward the brick wall, which now seems more vast and blocks all light. I try to swim faster, but it does not seem to make much difference in the distance that I am from the object. Tired and puzzled, I stop swimming and reach out toward the object expecting to grasp nothing. Immediately I feel myself sinking. There is nothing that I can do to save myself; therefore, I take one last look at the object and the brick wall. I have arrived at the end of my journey.

As I now look back upon the dream, I can understand why I consider it infernal. In my interpretation of the dream, the ship that I am standing on is my home. The force coming from my home represents my parents and other role models. They are trying to lead me toward the distant object symbolizing my goals. Those who support me are trying to make me see that my goals are real and obtainable. Their belief in me gives me confidence to dive into the world, symbolized here by the water. Unfortunately, once I am on my own, I begin to take on too many tasks without really knowing what I am getting myself into in the long run. As I begin to think that I am reaching my goals, I find out that times have changed. My goals are leaving me and are about to crash into a brick wall. I begin to believe that my goals are now unobtainable, but I reach out in vain, feeling that I still might have some dominance over them. After doing this, I begin to sink into the lower parts of the world. By losing hope of obtaining goals, I become a victim of my own efforts. Because of this, I enter the bottomless lower world which is indeed Hell.

My worst fear has always been to have goals and not be able to obtain them. At the time when I had the nightmare, I never considered the possibility that it could come true, nor that God was a possible savior. I had not yet found the connection between my goals and Him. It was only while in college that I began to understand what a relationship with God could mean. Before then, I remained confused about how He would affect my personal development.

I am the daughter of a preacher. Though my father works many long hours in the church each week, he also has another occupation to help support us. As a preacher's kid (P.K.s, we call ourselves), I came face-to-face very early with many special expectations and problems. Most of the time I was puzzled by church members' inconsistencies and seeming hypocrisy. The biggest problem was watching people criticize one another. Being present at most of the church events, I became increasingly aware of jealousy. I have seen people upset with others for holding a particular office in the church, for singing too many solos, for dressing differently, and even for trying to become "buddy-buddy" with the pastor and/or his wife. This has always bothered me because, in seeking to learn more about God, I became more and more confused by the actions of those who claimed to be Christians. Inconsistencies became increasingly apparent as I became aware of these people's testimonials about how much the Lord had done for them. How could it be that these people could be so unkind to one another? Weren't these people supposed to be kinder than those who were in the "world"?

I became even more confused when it came down to matters concerning my father. I felt severe pain whenever I heard someone say something bad about my father. I became very bitter toward these people, mainly because I would hear these comments behind my father's back, yet see them smile to his face. I wondered how these Christians could be so cruel. Wasn't my father a servant of God? Did he, as their leader, deserve this treatment? I remember overhearing one particular woman challenge my father's judgment. I was hurt, for I truly believed that my father would not intentionally do anything that was wrong; however, I realized that my father was still human. I knew that he was not God and was only a messenger. Let me say that I never have been close to my father, probably because deep down I wish that he was perfect and all that the church members think he ought to be. For most of my life I have seen Dad in two lights, the one whom I knew through his thoughts in his sermons, and then as the man I could never open up to about my feelings. I love my father, but I have always wished that we had been able to communicate more as I was growing up and to know each other more personally. Instead, I became quite close with my mother, since she had stayed home to raise me.

There came a time when I could not merely rely on my family's opinions or views of God. I began a search to find out who God was for myself. My freshman winter in college was the first time that I learned to depend truly on God. This was because I found myself walking around in disbelief at actions going on about me. There was an incident in which a black professor was harassed, insulted, and tape-recorded without consent. I remember seeing a terrifying picture of the professor on the front page of an ultra-right-wing newspaper on campus. The photo, taken in the heat of fury and chaos, angered me just to look at it. I thought the newspaper staff had gone too far this time. It was not the first time that this professor had been harassed. Because of the newspaper's history of articles negatively portraying blacks and other minority groups, I suspected that racism was involved. However, it was not purely a white-versus-black issue; it was also about threatening one's dignity and reputation as a type of sophomoric blood sport. I was sick and tired of seeing articles in that newspaper that tried to make blacks seem inferior. I was tired of these pompous guys acting as if only they knew how things should be. With some self-proclaimed authority they figured that they could say or do anything they wanted and get away with it, hiding their racism behind the smoke screen of freedom of the press. What was so scary and almost intimidating was the paper's persuasive style; many people could read it and say, "Yeah, that's a good point." A little serious thought and consideration of undertones would reveal that something was wrong. Unfortunately, the newspaper's writing style swayed quite a few people into believing that its presentations were accurate and true.

This and much similar outrageous racism on the part of the newspaper turned my resentment into a force which propelled me to protest. I began to participate in rallies, to picket stores advertising in the paper, and to express views and concerns in ways that were unthinkable for me before coming to college. The people to whom I felt closest during that time were those engaged in these activities with me. I felt a common bond with them because we were working for the same cause. While walking on campus, I was always on guard, just waiting to hear someone talking about the incident with that professor, or to see someone stare at me or the ribbon symbolizing black liberation pinned to my jacket. The air was filled with bad vibes.

Living next door to one of the newspaper's editors made those days much more trying. One day as I was studying at my desk, I heard a loud conversation going on just outside my door about the "reactionary blacks blowing things out of proportion." This comment presumably was made in response to student protests and TV and newspaper reporters flooding the campus. I was struck motionless at my desk. I felt trapped within the confines of my room. I was tense and angry and full of pain and frustration. I badly wanted to go out there and give an argument that would put all those men into a state of awe and speechlessness. It angered me even more when they spoke of the Afro-American Society and its predominantly black dorm.

They put everything down yet admitted that they had never stepped foot inside the building. I doubt if any of them even had a black friend. I wondered how such otherwise intelligent people could have such closed minds and be so ignorant about others. Every time I heard the pip-squeak voice of one young man who was talking in the hallway when the comments were made, I became extremely annoyed and angry. I was frustrated because, although I was angry at the students for being so uninformed and insensitive, I also was disappointed with myself for being so bothered by their actions. I longed to be stronger.

Dorm events didn't end there. Every day as I passed my editor-neighbor's door there were mean and degrading statements written about minority groups and feminists on his memo board. It would include things like: "No radicals, feminist witches, black racists, or gays wanted." With each glance, I wanted to rip the board down, or just scribble on it. I wanted to kick that stupid door—do something that showed that someone was not afraid of him or his malicious words. Something, however, always restrained me. No matter how great my resentment, I told myself I could not stoop to the level of that hateful young man who lived in the room next door. I prayed that I might maintain my dignity and self-control. Each day my roommate (who was black) and I talked late into the night about everything that was happening and our growing concerns. I always felt like a captive in the dorm, for even these private conversations were whispered so that none of our white neighbors would hear what we said. We were not really afraid of what might happen if others heard us, but we didn't want to run the risk of having our comments misinterpreted or purposely distorted.

It was during the days of protest that I began to understand the pressures upon people in the civil rights struggles of the sixties. More than 20 years later, efforts to correct situations of injustice continued. My uncle told me before I went to college, "Always remember where you've come from, where you're going, and who and what has helped you to get where you are and hope to be." There is no way that I can ever forget or ignore my past or the problems that still exist today.

During those days, I spent my mornings in class and my afternoons and nights protesting. I studied during any free moment I had. It was hard to do, but I had put protesting high up on my list of priorities. This was in spite of the fact that I knew other freshmen who had been asked to take a 1-year leave to reevaluate their goals after a poor performance first term. I had to do what seemed right at the time. I worked hard to do the best I could in my classes—I had tutors and went to see my professors regularly. I was glad they all were understanding and knew the position I felt obligated to take. My Chinese language professor asked me to see him after class one day. He said he knew that I was involved in the protests and wanted to know how I was doing. We talked for quite a while and both of us had teary eyes. I could tell that he cared and that what was happening was affecting him too. He was willing to work with me to make my classwork more manageable during this period. I knew that he and other professors understood the situation, and many were actively involved in the protests. For example, I met an English professor while we were both out picketing. He chatted with me then and whenever I saw him throughout the rest of the term.

I really valued the friendships that developed during the days of protesting. It seemed rare to find people who would *really listen* to what you had to say: not just hear your words but not your meaning. This was because we discussed, in addition to the incident with the black professor, many issues about student life which came to the surface. For example, many whites wondered why blacks seemed to separate themselves at dinner. Blacks wanted to know why we so often had to take time away from studying to protest things which shouldn't be happening in the first place.

In the midst of all the confusion, I learned to pray continuously. My time in prayer seemed to be the only time when I was at peace and the only thing that gave me strength to make it through the day. At the end of the term, in a class where I was the only black, we had a discussion about all the things that had happened. After hearing the comments about the "typical black" (which I didn't know existed) as well as some other radical and conservative views from my classmates, I felt obligated to say something. Before I did, however, I prayed briefly that I would be understood and not just heard. After stating my opinion and feelings, I thanked God for making me stronger that term than I ever had been in my life. From that day onward, I valued my college more than before because it had, however unintentionally, taught me to communicate with people from a wide variety of backgrounds and outlooks. It is only too bad that it took a crisis for people to start expressing their true feelings and concerns.

As I started to develop new friendships in college, I tended to share only parts of me, almost like a puzzle. Each piece would fit well with certain individuals, and not so well with others. I learned how best to mix and match those pieces so as to get along with different types of people. No matter how great the differences are between people, there has to be a common ground somewhere. It is unfortunate that a person's skin color, religious beliefs, nationality, or difference of views can sometimes distract us from other traits he or she might possess which could bring us closer. My friends who are Jewish, gay, foreign, and Caucasian have helped me to recognize the basic good in everyone.

Though I value the relationships I have with others outside my race, just as I do those within it, my four closest friends are black. They have seen me both at times when I was bubbling with energy and stressing out over something. There are few other people I feel are trustworthy enough for me to open up to. I can't imagine what my life at college would be like without them, because they have not only been friends since I arrived on campus but also family. Combined, I can say they know almost as much about me as I do. It was really strange when I went abroad one term and did not have them to lean on. However, I did get to know God as a friend who would be wherever I went.

In the summer after freshman year, I was able to go abroad for the first time in my life. Looking back, it seems evident that in Taiwan I learned more about myself than I ever thought possible. This knowledge helped me to gain increased confidence and direction. Most importantly, I became close to God in a way that I had never known. By taking classes and having Chinese roommates, I was able to learn a great deal about the language, lifestyles, and traditions of the people. I felt so at peace at this Christian university because religion seemed to be a part of many people's lives. I was able to respect those who were of different faiths because they were not ashamed to express their beliefs in any setting. All these things made me eager to develop my own spiritual life.

On my nineteenth birthday I was awakened by an alarming announcement recounted here from my journal:

I heard something or a voice say "You are going to die young." What a scary thought to wake up to on your birthday. I don't know if it was my conscious self, the end of a dream, or God. All I know is that I won't forget these words ever. I must take each second seriously, and value it, because the next moment is not promised.

New doors will open up to me, and I must be sure to live as a Christian and take advantage of those gifts. I don't want to separate myself, I just want to be me—a goal-oriented, religious, and successful person. It's not ambition, for sometimes that's bad. It is determination to do the very best I can. As long as I follow God's word, there is nothing that I can't do. No matter how short a life I live, I must be first and foremost thankful to God who gave it to me. I hope that I make the right decisions and can in some way be a positive influence on someone else. I love the Lord and pray that he will always be with my family and me.

Praying continuously, I came to know God as my personal savior. I did whatever the Holy Spirit led me to do and reaped many blessings because of it. I was unafraid to go into any church on the island and sit down. I jumped on buses and trusted that whoever I met would help me reach my destination. Listening to the English translations of the sermons at the chapel made me believe in the power of God that was touching my life halfway around the world. I never felt alone or afraid because I knew the Lord was watching over me. I continuously thanked God for the blessings that he had bestowed on me each day.

As my faith grew, I also looked to God for direction with my future. By taking the time to be still and listen for an answer, it was revealed to me that I would spend my life going to different countries and helping people with their health problems. Afterward, I would spread the word about the goodness of God and His ability to make all things possible. Having been given this awareness of my destiny I felt fulfilled and content. I knew where I was headed and felt happy about the enormous possibilities for growth in my work in serving the Lord. Soon, I began to meet missionaries who were doctors and other health care workers. After talking with them, I couldn't wait to get home and share the news with others about my future career.

When I returned to college in my sophomore year, I was on a spiritual high. I worked with the chaplain and for the first time realized what a wonderful calling my father had. I couldn't think of anything more satisfying than dedicating one's life to God. As I continued to think about my future in health care, I became obsessed with the idea of doing everything I could to make God proud of me. Gradually I spent more time thinking about the future and less time in my daily devotions without fully realizing that I was doing so.

As the year progressed, I started to feel empty and unsatisfied with my academics. I initially thought it was because of the difficulty of college; it never occurred to me that God was trying to tell me something. I was reminded of the picture that my high school guidance counselor tried to paint for me of what life at a highly competitive college would be like. She told me to imagine the smartest person in my most difficult class who seemed to get As without really working hard for them. I should then think of a school where almost everyone was that type of student. She said that she knew that I got where I was (at the top of my class) by working extremely hard and by putting in extra time and that was an accomplishment in itself. She warned me, however, that it might become unfulfilling or burdensome later. I found it difficult to accept that what I had always taken pride in (working hard) was now something that might not lead to success in the future. Once again in my life, someone was trying to discourage me from getting ahead. By reading extra books, doing additional problems, and asking about the practical applications of the course in class, I felt I was preparing for my future as a physician. That was my motivation, so although I was competing with people who caught onto some principles quicker than me, my concern was not with them, but with my goals.

As a college student I am beginning to see that perhaps Mrs. Riley was right in warning me about what I was going to be up against. I know that I have potential to succeed, so I have worked extremely hard in my classes and met with professors, obtained advice from grad students, had a tutor every term, and frequently met with my premed advisor and the academic skills director. Regardless of my efforts, my academic standing is not high. I have become disgusted with the grading system at my college. First of all, the science courses are graded on a curve. I hate to always have to compare myself to the mean, or actually all the other students in the class. I despise that, since learning is something that I feel is very personal. If my grade falls below the mean, my attitude toward the class changes. No longer is my emphasis on doing the best I can on an exam, but instead it is on getting at least the mean. I realize now that I was lowering my standards and settling for doing about the same as everyone else.

For the first time in my life, I have become accustomed to Cs and being a satisfactory student. I have had professors say to me "Cs are not bad. You'll still get into med school." By being on a campus where my right (or any other minority's) to be there is continuously being questioned, I have come to realize that it is necessary to excel and get As and Bs. Otherwise, people will doubt my credibility and, even worse, my ability.

It has been difficult for me to accept doors being closed due to the GPA. I remember that when invitations were sent out to students in my class to discuss the honors program as well as internship opportunities, I wasn't invited. Many people asked me why I wasn't there. Since I always walked about with a positive attitude, was involved in a professional society, and knew many important people on campus, they assumed I was somewhere near the top of my class. I couldn't really answer them because the pain I felt was unimaginable; I knew that I should have been there and I felt left out. As a result, I had to make a special appointment to discuss these programs. It hurt to realize that I had learned about them not because the college thought that I should know about them, but because of my own efforts. My mom always told me that sometimes you have to make things happen for yourself. I had to work very hard to get into higher levels of English and math years ago, so I naturally continue to seek out people and opportunities now that I am in college. I try to overcome any obstacles in my path, for my success has always come about because I have refused to settle for anything—regardless of the situation.

It was at a national youth leadership meeting in high school that I realized the true leader in me. Since that time I have been coming up with ideas of things I'd like to do. A while ago I developed a project that would try to encourage middle school students to become interested in science through role models. This project meant a lot to me, for I knew from personal experience that when you talk to people who are where you want to be, you begin to believe that you really can get there too. During breaks, I had always called physicians, med students, or anyone else in health care who could tell me about the field and steps to get into it. In turn, I often spoke to students at different churches to try to get them interested in continuing their education. I believed these things could keep dreams alive for someone.

After spending a couple of months meeting with different people who could give me ideas about how to get my project started, I was just about ready to get it off the ground. I had a meeting with my former professor and friend, whom I always go to when there's something on my mind or a new thing I'm interested in doing. After he agreed to help me carry out the project, I said to him, "I know that there still might be some trouble getting funding to do this, since my grades could be stronger." When I told him my standing, the expression on his face was that of shock and disappointment. He suggested that perhaps I should try to constrain my ideas until I was in a position in my life to make the greatest contribution. He went on to say that he knew that I was going to make great changes one day, but all good leaders need a solid background. It was his wish to see me concentrate my energies on improving my grades, so I could get into the best medical school in the country. Though I did not doubt his sincerity, I felt all alone and stripped of the very thing that had made me feel so fulfilled for so long—a project that would spark energy and enthusiasm in kids who, like me, may have to overcome many academic obstacles. What would I do now? I left that office and tried to come to grips with the fact that things don't always work out as planned.

In the next term, I tried to concentrate more on my studies. After laying my project aside for a while, I became confused about where my life was headed. Some mornings I would lie in bed wondering why I should get up. Why should I put myself through so much pain for so little gratification? Why couldn't I stop school, get a job, and do whatever I wanted? Even though these thoughts kept running through my mind, I knew that they wouldn't make me happy. I always felt a great sense of accomplishment and joy when I worked in the lab all night, completed a paper or problem set, or developed ideas for the future. These things made me see that academics were a necessary part of my life.

At the term's closing, I felt drained of all energy. I had hit a burnout point. It was during these days of physical and emotional strain that I realized I had been leading a life that was not dependent on God. For many months I had been taking my life into my own hands. Because I wanted to take advantage of anything associated with being a doctor, I rushed through the first half of college. There were many warning signs and people telling me to slow down, but I overlooked them or simply regarded them as more barriers that I had to overcome. It never occurred to me during that stressful time that perhaps God was trying to tell me that great things can be accomplished only through His will. Attainment of my goals will not come through my efforts alone; only He possesses the master plan for my life. I had to take some time off from school in order to understand at last that if I was to *succeed,* I needed to turn over my life to God and let Him choose my path.

Presently, my attention is focused on increasing my happiness, flexibility, and spirituality. I no longer take for granted the relationships I've had or lessons learned. After breaking up with my college boyfriend, I realized that too often I have let my goals draw me away from those whom I love the most. I can become so involved with what I am doing that I don't give others the time to show me how they feel about my actions. I need to take time out to listen to others. I realize that my friends have always been there for me when I needed them. Therefore, I have no real reason to believe that they will disappear if I allow them to see my innermost fears of not being able to obtain the very high goals I set for myself. Often they have been the ones who have given me happiness and support that I couldn't find elsewhere.

It has been this type of support that has helped me to see my potential and to go after my goals with an almost uncontrollable desire. It is only after reading the biographies of those who have inspired me in the past that I now realize they achieved success by hard work *and* strong spiritual beliefs. They were all happy people, who had endured pressures, by trusting that God would lead them through those times. Even though I have overcome barriers in the past, I have always carried a bit of resentment toward those things or persons who I felt caused them. I should have actually been thankful for them, since God had control over my future and knew what was best.

My first response to any advice conflicting with my goals has been to first regard it as a barrier and then to try to see what *I* can do to prevent it from having a negative effect. I need to spend more time praying to God to see how *He* wants me to deal with the situation. I know He is able to do this because while I was abroad it was from His word that I received direction in all parts of my life. I long to have this type of relationship with God again.

While growing up I used to wonder how God would influence my life. I have heard some older folks say that He is a "heart fixer, a way maker, and a mind regulator." God is able to be all these things for me. My life is in God's hands, and it is through His guidance that tomorrow's joy, treasures, and perhaps even a medical degree, shall be mine. I am so glad God forgives those who, like me, make the mistake of vainly trying to completely control their own lives. I truly believe the message in the words of the gospel song I have paraphrased in the first person to fit my own story:

> *I know somehow, and I know some way,*
> *I'm gonna make it!*
> *No matter what the test, whatever comes my way,*
> *I'm gonna make it!*
> *With Jesus on my side, things will work out fine!*

15

Reflections on My Survival

MALIK

The following autobiography is the tale of an incredible journey—from being the young son of an abusive and neglectful crack-addicted mother to graduating as valedictorian of his high school class and acceptance to a top college. Our author describes his mother's decline into addiction and her failed attempts at rehabilitation. All the while, he learned to cope by learning to depend only on himself and by seeing his mother "as a dead woman" and thereby not able to hurt him. An attempted suicide by his older sister brought his father back into the picture and led to his living with his father's new family just as he entered high school. While he referred to his father as his "savior" he also attributed his success to the belief in himself he got from the early love and nurturance of his mother.

Writing as a college sophomore, Malik explores both the healthy aspects of his character as well as the residual damage of his earlier life. He ends by pondering what role he might reasonably play to help his sister and her children from continuing in the cycle in which they both grew up and in which she is still trapped.

Today, the principal asked that I report to the library after my last period algebra class. I thought to myself, "What have I done this time? I haven't done anything wrong in a while. Well, at least there is nothing that I think they know about." The principal even sent a student to "make sure Malik goes directly to the library." So, I reported to the library as told. As I entered, I noticed a couple of unfamiliar faces. First they told me, "We would like to talk to you about your mother." I knew now that these were social workers from the bureau of child welfare. The social workers asked me, "Does your mother use drugs? Does your mother abuse you? Does your mother abuse your sister? Have you ever been molested? When was the last time you ate a meal at home?" After being overwhelmed by the questions thrown at me, I began to cry as a sign of submission. Originally, I tried to lie, but as the questions came I could only cry.

What follows is a personal account of my life—13 years of suffering in a hostile environment. My life has been preoccupied with the struggle for survival. I cannot begin to explain what it is to be the son of a "crack addict" raised in a single-parent home. However, I hope to provide a glimpse of the reality that I emerged from.

Everything I am and everything I will be I owe to my friend who opened my eyes to the potential hidden within me. The friend I speak of is my father. Somewhere between fate and consequence I struck pure fortune; the chance to regain the life I lost. The following is how I can best describe that survival and revival into my being—Malik Jones.

Sandra Jones gave birth to the baby boy she later named Malik Jones. As my mother gave birth to me, my father rushed to the hospital so that he could at least witness the birth of his only son. However, as soon as he entered the maternity ward, the hospital staff tried to deny him from seeing the mother or his child. The attendants stated, "We have strict orders from the mother not to allow you to see her or the baby." My father claimed he had a right to see the child, and after a damn near physical confrontation, he was allowed to see his son. A nurse was sent into a room full of newborns to show him which child was Malik. To the nurse's surprise, when she picked me up, I instantly attained my first erection, looked up, smiled, and giggled. My father laughed and said, "God damn, that's my boy."

Before I was born, my mother and father were divorced. My mother told me, "As a couple, your father and I were unable to settle our differences and he walked out on us." My mother never mentioned anything more about my father or their relationship. Years later, I learned the history of that relationship.

My mother and father were a young couple married at the ages of 19 and 21. Under the stress of trying to make a decent living, my parents grew apart from each other. In addition, my mother began to break down into the violent fits that she was known for. The violent acts included setting fire to her own house and trying to shoot my father. These acts led to separation, then divorce. My mother constantly violated my father's visitation rights and demanded that "he never come around again." So, my father kept his distance in hopes that one day, he would visit or gain custody of his children. My mother never mentioned any of these facts to me. Therefore, during childhood I thought of my father as dead and grew up with Mommie as my sole source of parenting.

Mommie is the term I am most comfortable using when referring to my mother, because Mommie represents the intimate bond that I remember sharing with my mother. Mommie attended college during the day and our household was supported by the job she held as a bartender at a local nightclub. Between day care and baby-sitting, the only quality time spent with Mommie occurred during holidays and weekends. Our quality time consisted of educational games we played together and occasionally a trip to the zoo. Even though I understood that Mommie had to work and go to school, I could never understand why she was always so busy. Then one day, I began to see where her time was being spent. Besides spending hours writing in her room and working, my mother had a social life that came in the form of my soon-to-be stepfather.

I remember stumbling upon the realization of another man in the house. Saturday morning, I climbed out of bed, walked to the kitchen, and began to fix a bowl of Captain Crunch cereal. Next, I strolled into the living room to watch some cartoons. As I sat down on the living room couch, I noticed a pair of underwear on the floor that had tiger stripes on them. I picked up the underwear, ran to my room, and flung them at my older sister, Niya.

"Ugh! Whose are these?" asked Niya.

"I don't know," I replied.

Finally, my mother came out of her room and asked, "What y'all making so much noise for?"

We both said, "Nothing, Mommie."

"Who was out in the living room?" she asked. Hesitantly, I responded that it was me.

Then she said, "I guess I should introduce y'all to someone."

"Who?" I asked.

"Richard."

Immediately, everything began to make sense. I thought, "Richard must own the underwear I was playing with, and now Mommie won't have time for me any more." Instead of walking back to the living room and cordially introducing myself to Richard, I grabbed my 5 lb. weight, walked in the living room, and dropped it on his foot. Mommie slapped me senseless and promised to "whip my ass good." However, Richard calmed her down and told her, "It's only natural for a boy to defend his mom." Although I got out of a beating, I sensed that I would soon experience an abrupt change.

Up until this point, life had been all that a boy in the 2nd grade could ask for. I started school early because Mommie taught me at home everything that kindergarten, 1st, and 2nd grade covered. In addition, during holidays I always received more gifts than my sister Niya. I was obviously "Mommie's favorite." There were three reasons why I was Mommie's favorite. First of all, I was my mother's only son in a family comprised predominantly of women. Second, I am the youngest child in the family. Finally, I was born with "light skin."

Being "light skinned" and Mommie's baby boy had its advantages and disadvantages. Since I had "light skin," family members referred to me as yellow, golden, piss-colored, and puss-colored. The different names reflected the attitudes that some people carried toward me solely for bearing "light skin." My grandmother would openly refer to me as her favorite "light-skinned" grandson. Furthermore, she felt it necessary to give me a nickname—"Humpty." Mommie told me she called me that because I was egg-shaped as a baby. Humpty could do no wrong around my grandmother. So, life was pleasant being a favorite. However, when Richard entered my life, I knew that my status as favorite would change.

My mother made plans to marry Richard but I had to ask two questions before I would allow this to occur: "Do I have to call Richard 'Daddy'?", and "Do you love Richard more than you love me?" My mother's response was, "Richard is your father now and I do expect you to call him 'Daddy' sooner or later. And Malik, you just don't understand something. Richard can do some things for me that you could never do." As a child, this statement only added to my bewilderment and frustration. So I accepted what she said and tried to deal with Richard.

Richard genuinely loved my Mommie. Nevertheless, Richard was an alcoholic who made a bad habit of spending his paycheck on liquor. Richard received his paycheck every other Thursday. Paycheck nights became the established horror every 2 weeks. There would be the usual Richard and Sandra routine as soon as my sister and I entered the house from school. Richard would be staggering around the house, pounding on his chest demanding his respect. Mommie would ask him how much of his paycheck he spent. It never did matter to him. The usual response was, "It's my money and I does what I want with it." The moment Richard fell asleep, Mommie would call his friends and ask if someone held his money for him. Later on, Richard would wake up and realize that he urinated in the bed. He would then begin to cry and promise, "This shit ain't gonna happen no more, baby." This story occurred every other Thursday without fail or deviation. Occasionally, there would be a new aspect involved, such as drug use. However, Mommie would never complain about his use of cocaine because she smoked marijuana joints as if they were tobacco cigarettes.

The turbulence of the "Thursday night routine" caused Mommie's temper to flare up. I remember often being the victim of her displaced aggravation. One Thursday night, after diligently studying for a spelling quiz, I walked into the kitchen to show my Mommie how well I studied. Unfortunately, I forgot to take into account that today was paycheck night. I walked into the kitchen totally unsuspecting of my mother's turbulent state of emotions. So I innocently asked, "Mommie, you wanna test me on my spelling words?" She turned around and broke a coffee cup over my head by slapping me with it and then shouted a resounding, "NO!" I walked out of the kitchen half dazed and heard Mommie crying. Later on she came into my room and apologized for hitting me and told me, "You need to be aware of when you should be seen and not heard. Next time, stay clear of me if you think I'm in a bad mood." She then promised that somehow she would do what's right for Niya and me.

Mommie figured that more money in the household would solve our problems. Consequently, she began to make money by selling drugs out of our apartment. During this time, I noticed significant behavioral changes in her. She began to spend hours in her room with the door closed. When she did open the door, it was only because Mike from downstairs came by to pick up something. After he left, Mommie would continue to stay in her room with the door closed.

One time, Mike came upstairs and asked to see my mother but she told me, "Tell Mike I'm busy." He then gave me an envelope and told me, "Give this to your mom. Wait a minute. Let me show you something." Mike opened the envelope and pulled out a plastic tube about an inch long with a white substance in it that looked like wet toilet tissue. Then Mike said, "You see this shit. Tell your mom that the rocks are too small." On the streets, any successful drug dealer will tell you that the key to his success is one simple rule—"You can't get high off your own supply." Mommie must have cut the rocks so that she was getting a little high off of each piece she made. By this time, both Mommie and Richard had an addiction of equal potency.

The violence that I witnessed and experienced intensified as a result of Mommie's new crack addiction. When Mommie was under the influence of crack, she became hyper and determined to find ways to get more of the high that just entered her lungs. Then paranoia struck and she became edgy, at which point everything that Niya and I did was wrong. I might get punched in the mouth if I simply asked about dinner.

Mommie would harshly discipline me for my misbehavior in school and mediocre academic achievement. Academics played an important part of the social structure at home. If you were doing well in school, you won the attention and praise of family members. However, poor achievement would lead to nasty incidents. One time, I walked into the house knowing that I was going to get beat up. It was report card day, and I received a D in music. Naturally, my mother just could not understand that my voice was cracking at this age and that I could not sing well. The rest of my grades were As and Bs, but the one D was too many failures for her. At first I tried to avoid the issue of report cards, but my sister did well this term and boasted of her grades as soon as we entered the house. Mommie asked to see my grades, so I gave her my report card. "Motherfucka, I'm gonna kick your ass." Those were the last words I heard before I was mauled. The next day, I went to school with a swollen lip and a blackened eye. My 3rd-grade teacher pulled me to the side after class and asked me, "Who did this to you?" Of course, I gave a stupid excuse that only kid-logic can create. I said, "I fell and hit my eye on a door knob." My teacher just looked at me and said, "I know your mother did it." All I could do was cry at the truth in her statement.

At first, there was only the Thursday paycheck routine. Then we started to have "feature Fridays" as well. I remember coming home from school on Fridays to a madwoman. My mother had been caged up in her room getting high all day. As soon as my sister and I got in, she would send us outside to play. She would say, "Here is some money for pizza and ice cream. Y'all go outside and have fun. Oh, and don't worry about curfew, just come home when you're ready." Most kids would have been filled with feelings of euphoria at hearing these words. However, my sister and I knew what this really meant—we better not be in the house because we might see something we were not supposed to see. I couldn't stand being kicked out the house. I had no friends and nowhere to go. As a result, arcades and poolrooms became my hang outs.

By the end of the year, my mother's condition was so bad that Richard, by this time my stepfather, had to clean up his act in the house because my mother's condition was worse than his. She was not the woman he married, nor was he the man that she married. Consequently, they both decided to enter rehabilitation programs. Richard entered an Alcoholic's Anonymous group and my mother went through a detoxification and rehabilitation program in midtown Manhattan. During the summer, I stayed with my grandmother since both of my parents were in rehabilitation.

Staying at my grandmother's house all summer taught me all there is to know about being a lazy welfare mother. Every morning, I woke up to the sound of telephone gossip. My grandmother would be on the phone with another relative talking about the condition of my parents. After my grandmother realized that I was up, she would make me some breakfast and demand that I watch the game show "The Price is Right" with her. When I was through with breakfast, I would wake up my sister and my cousin, Katina, who lived with my grandmother because her mother had died of an overdose of "dope." As soon as everyone was up and dressed we went outside to play. Next, my grandmother would prepare our food for whenever we were ready to eat.

There was one thing I noticed about my grandmother that summer: She never turned off her television. In addition, every discussion she held was centered around either television or gossip. Only rarely would my grandmother leave the house, and then only to get food. I wondered how she made money to pay for her apartment and food. After learning about what welfare entailed, I understood that this situation was a classic abuse of the welfare that people complain about paying taxes to uphold.

When both Richard and my mother were out of rehabilitation, they decided to move to another neighborhood. During that summer, both my parents remained clean, and I can say it was one of the more enjoyable parts of my life. They both worked, and my mother was well known in our community as one of the most active parents. That summer, we spent some of the quality time together that we had missed in the past. On July 4th, Mommie, Richard, Niya, and I went to the playground with a picnic basket. To my surprise, when Richard opened the picnic basket, there were fireworks in the basket instead of food. My mother and Richard promised that they would light the fireworks for us as soon as it got dark. I was not allowed to touch fireworks but I stood in awe of the display that Richard had set up that night for Niya and me.

The beauty of those fireworks symbolized the energy that my family had—riding the waves of hope only to be dashed onto the rocks of reality. Of course, the good times were to last just that one summer.

As soon as Mommie started "hitting the pipe" again, I considered her dead. Mommie did not die a physical death. Instead, her death was more symbolic, for the woman whom I knew as Mommie was no longer Mommie. She was a living, breathing, walking corpse. Once the smoke of crack filled her lungs she would disintegrate into an amoral being. My mother even began to display physical signs of change. She was no longer beautiful because of the various side effects of drug usage. First there was a noticeable amount of weight loss from about 140 lb. down to 115 lb. Next, her young, tight skin began to sag and darken around the eyes and other places where her skin seemed to just bunch up. My mother's once dainty hands became calloused around her fingertips from holding the pipe. Her fingertips began to swell and blister to where I remember thinking she had the hands of a monster. The long nails that my mother had acquired during this time reminded me of a claw-bearing monster. These transformations were manifestations of the drug "crack."

Inside of my soul, I found the strength and weakness of my heart. I began to realize that by considering my mother as a dead woman, she could no longer hurt me. But I also felt that I had grown cold on the inside. My heart began to freeze until it would crack and only ice could flow through my veins. A frozen heart remains damaged even when thawed. Can I still feel the love I once felt toward my mother for any other? If I do learn to care, will my emotions be like a ball of glass, ready to shatter at any moment? All I do know is that I have to somehow survive.

At this point in my life, it really did not matter how bad things were. At 12, I was determined to get myself out of this situation by any means necessary. I figured that if I did the opposite of whatever my mother told me to do, I would be able to achieve more than everyone expected. I have a cousin named Darnell, Katina's older brother. Instead of being released into my grandmother's custody, Darnell was placed in a shelter for boys. Rather than being deterred by his situation, Darnell graduated from high school a valedictorian and proceeded to attend college. Due to an unexpected pregnancy, Darnell left college with an associates degree and made a career out of the military. He was the one person whom I could look up to in my family. So, I decided I would be just like Darnell.

Meanwhile, my sister was going through a difficult time in her life. I remember waking up suddenly, out of breath. I heard the shouts of a screaming woman. "My baby jumped out the window!" My mother came into my room and shouted, "Malik, Niya jumped out of the window and killed herself!" I thought, "Yeah, OK mom. Sure, Niya jumped out of the window and killed herself. Can I go back to sleep now?" My mother just walked out of the room. I looked out of my window just to humor her and I gasped at what I saw. My sister lay there, seven stories below me, face down on the ground. I ran downstairs to call an ambulance. When I reached the spot where she lay, I found Niya crying. She kept saying, "I want my Mommie." One of my friends told me, "I saw Niya walking down the side of the building. She tried to get downstairs by tying bed sheets together to form a rope, like in the movies." Unfortunately, her attempt at an escape was unsuccessful. My mother told me, "The reason why Niya tried to run away is because she is 4-months pregnant and I was going to force her to get an abortion. Niya just wanted to keep her baby. Looks like she will probably lose it anyway."

While in the hospital, Niya confided in a nurse and told her all about her situation at home. I can only guess that this nurse reported Niya's situation to the proper authorities. I went to visit my sister only to find that the fall only caused a compound fracture in her leg. So, she and her baby would live to be just fine after all. During one of my visits, I found a man standing over her bed who looked extremely similar to myself. My family did not kid around when they said, "You look just like your father."

My initial feelings toward my father were of mixed emotions. As soon as he saw me he said, "Damn, you growing up to look like the twin brother I never had. Malik, I know something is wrong with your mother and I am going to do something to correct your situation. I have been waiting for this chance all my life, to do what's right for you and your sister. Finally, I think it is going to happen." My father went to court and gained custody of my sister and me. All I could think of at the time was, "Whatever I'm in for, it can't be any worse than what I have been through." The bureau of child welfare came to my elementary school and took me away to live with my father in the Bronx.

The neighborhood where my father lived was composed of middle-class working men and women, and the living conditions were much better than the city-owned housing complex of my old home. I entered his apartment and, to my surprise, it was furnished so well that I thought he was rich. Later, I would come to realize that my father was not rich. Rather, the living conditions that I existed in before were so bad that what is normal, I considered to be wealthy.

A healthy relationship between my father and me developed spontaneously. He introduced himself to me as a friend, rather than a father. In essence, my father acknowledged that he was not around to father me. He could, however, provide proper guidance for me. Therefore, all decisions that affected me were solely my own decisions, tempered with his advice. My father used patience in dealing with me. He made me aware of my faults and taught me responsibility. His words were, "Son, any old excuse will do. I don't care what happened! Don't give me excuses. If there is a problem, you solve it. Never pout over something that was done wrong, just find a way to solve the problem. Whenever you find yourself in a bad situation, just ask yourself, 'Well, what do I do about it?' Consequences are the past working on the future."

One day, I came home from work late. I was assigned to do the dishes that night but I worked too late to do them. The next day I tried to explain to my father that it was not my fault that the dishes were not done. I had to work. His response was, "Any old excuse will do. You have to take responsibility for your action. So don't give me excuses, just do something about the dishes." As a result, I paid my brother to do dishes on the nights that I came in late from work. That way, everyone was happy. This is an example of how my father taught me to think whenever I get into a bind.

As soon as I moved in with him, my father introduced me to my stepmother, my two stepsisters, and my half brother. After my introduction to my new family, my father told me that my chores were to clean both bathrooms twice a week and to take out the garbage on alternate weeks with my brother. "Easy enough," I thought, "I have no problems doing a little housework." My sister Niya decided to move in with her boyfriend. She objected to living with my father because he was never around during her childhood; she found his efforts now to be hypocritical. Niya made a choice of her own not to follow our father's guidance even though his experience and wisdom were what she and I had been missing. I simply followed the advice of my father while she complied with the pressures of her peers and the influence of her boyfriend and his family.

In addition to the transition to my father's home, I also was moving at this time from elementary to high school. During elementary school I was a truant. Girls considered me to be ugly, and I never had clean clothes or new shoes. Now, at this point of transition, I had a chance to change all of this. All of my life, I attended Catholic school because my mother was firm in her Catholicism. During my final year of elementary school I received a scholarship to attend a Catholic school located in Harlem, which was located about 45 minutes away from my new home in the Bronx. One of the most dangerous and fabulous spots of New York City is Harlem's 125th Street. Harlem had a wonderful and exciting reputation, and since Catholic school would be free for me, I decided to attend.

One of my father's wisest decisions was that I would wear a suit to the first day of class. Then, when I asked my father to get me a book bag, he bought me a briefcase that matched the suit I wore. The suit I wore and my being there on a scholarship helped create the impression that I should be put into the more challenging classes. I believe that moment of appearing as an academically focused student helped steer me in the direction of pursuing academia. My father wanted me to further my education past the one that he had received, thereby fulfilling his own dreams. To that end, he encouraged my endeavors in education. The faculty saw me as a serious student from the day I walked in, and I lived up to the standards that they expected of me.

During my sophomore year in high school, I decided to quit the track team and play basketball. I had practiced all summer long because the year before I was cut from the team during tryouts. I did not express any feelings of hurt at the time. I rationalized that, "I'm just going to run track because I get to be the star." So, after a summer of practice, I came back to high school 3 inches taller, 15 pounds heavier, stronger, and faster. Not only did I make the team that year, I was the starting point guard and led the team as captain.

Basketball opened a whole new world for me—I was cool now. There was no more free time when I just sat around and created art work. Now I had practice that ran for about 3 hours a day. My high school has one of the premiere basketball teams in the country. It was so difficult to make the team that simply playing for them made me popular. After games, girls would talk to me and give me their phone numbers. In addition, I began to attend the school parties and my social life was improving due to my consistent performance on the court.

In high school, I had a friend, Parker, who showed me how to be cool and charismatic. When I first met Parker, my life wasn't running so smoothly. He gave me some advice: "Hey kid, if you ever want to get a girl you need to get rid of your glasses, get a real haircut, get rid of the braces and get some confidence. My name is Anthony, but call me Parker. By the way, I cut hair for a small fee. Come see me if you need some help, kid. Peace."

I took Parker's advice and after attending parties, getting rid of my glasses, braces, suits, and receiving a haircut from him, I came to find out that girls thought I was very attractive. My reputation as one of the best defensive players in the city and my newfound social life only meant that I was living up to my father's expectations. My father was a great player in high school in terms of both the game of basketball and women. Once again, it seemed that history had a habit of repeating itself.

My life outside of school, as a stepchild, was all too frustrating. According to my stepmother, I "couldn't do anything right." She seemed obsessed with finding fault in me because she constantly compared my stepbrother Jason and me. "Malik can play basketball, but Jason is good at basketball, baseball, and football. Jason has natural talent whereas Malik has to work and practice at the one game he can play." As a result of talk like this, Jason and I would compete ferociously on the basketball court against each other, as if we had something to prove to the other. As I got older and wiser, I realized that we did not compete against each other; we competed against the argument that my stepmother perpetuated. My father and my stepmother argued over who the children should listen to, and by demonstrating that I was a better student and Jason a better athlete, they thought that we would somehow prove each other's points. Jason and I grew up to play together as an unbeatable force on the basketball court. Jason is very charismatic and has a type of personality that is very hard to dislike. We got along well because we had similar interests. We both played basketball, listened to rap music, and liked to draw. To prevent further competition, Jason and I went to separate schools.

Even though I lived with my father, there was still a limited interaction between my mother and me. If I heard anything about my mother, I knew it was going to be bad news. My family always kept quiet when I made any reference to my mother because her existence was not mentioned. Knowledge of my mother's existence was made available only during a situation of extreme crisis involving either life or death. That is exactly the way it was one Friday after I arrived home from school.

"I heard from your grandmother that your mother is in the hospital again. This time it's pretty serious. She was involved in a car accident and has broken a couple of her ribs and she needs surgery," my father told me.

"Is that all? Seems like my mother can survive about anything," I responded.

"Would you like to go to the hospital and see her? I'm going, you should come along. Don't worry, we won't be there too long," he replied.

When I visited my mother, I hated every minute of it. The same old questions and comments time after time. She would say, "Boy, you look more and more like your father every time I see you. Are you dating yet? I hope you ain't no fag. Seemed to me like you didn't like girls." Usually, I would hesitate to answer her questions. However, this time I decided to answer her bluntly. I just told her, "I feel as if I have outgrown answering your immature questions. And, commenting on my sexuality only shows insecurities that you have with your own sexuality. So, please let's just keep this conversation as short as possible." My candid answers gave me a sense of power because I no longer feared the repercussions of my actions toward her. In addition, I felt as if I had mentally outgrown her because of a strong formal educational background. As I look back now, I know I acted like a pompous fool. I should have tried to at least empathize or sympathize with my mother. Instead, I acted as if I were somehow better than her. I did not respect the experience and effort my mother has under her belt. I doubt that she meant to bother me with her questions. Those questions could be a sign of her affection. I could at least have made her feel better by being polite. I did not have to appease her, but I did not have to disrespect her either. I guess that is a part of the rebellion that fires the heart of an adolescent. If I had the opportunity to relive that episode, I think I would be a little more sensitive toward her condition.

The last encounter I had with my mother occurred when I found out that she was HIV positive. Again, I was asked to go visit my mother. According to my grandmother, my mother was on her death bed. I still had mixed feelings about going to see her. I thought that I should remember my mother in her most positive light. Thoughts of Mommie gently caressing my face saying, "All right, Baby" still remain the most beautiful memory in my realm of thought. I remember some nights when my mother would allow me to sleep with her in her bed. When I would sleep with her at night, she would always wear a satin pajama set. As I slept, I would rub against the satin and I knew I was close to Mommie. This feeling made me feel so secure that even until this very day, I can relax or fall asleep by feeling satin between my fingers. So, when I think of the mother that I love, I don't try to remember the bad. I still remember that her discipline, desire, and determination helped make me all that I am and will be. Therefore, I don't think I would have felt the hurt as much if I did not visit her at the hospital and see her like that. But my father pointed out to me that you may only have one chance to say good-bye to a person. I went to the hospital against my will and I behaved well by not saying much.

After my mother left the hospital, she was arrested for using and distributing drugs. During her stay in prison, my father always sent money and clothing. Whenever she called, I would tell her that my father was not home because she only called to demand money, and I knew that the money was being used for drugs. I tried explaining this to my father, but he has a bigger heart for people in need. I didn't understand why my father always helped at the chance of her rehabilitation. His belief was that any effort for rehabilitation, no matter how late, is definitely worth pursuing.

My father always told me, "Give everything your best. If you fail, you can't complain because you've done only what you could do—your best." I gave my mother my best hopes for rehabilitation and each time she failed me. As a result, I no longer have any sympathy or empathy left to give. I did my best and I guess my best was not good enough. Sometimes, I wish my mother would just die. Death has to be better than the life she lives. She is trapped by the "crack" monster, and it seems that there is no chance for escape or rehabilitation. So why not death?

As I went through high school I tried not to think of my mother. If I did, it would only distract me from my studies. So, I went about life as if everything was normal. The only thing that changed for me was finding a passion toward helping others. As a part of the curriculum in my high school, all seniors were required to do at least 100 hours of community service in order to graduate. To fulfill my service requirement, I began teaching art at an after-school program for children ages 5 to 10.

In addition to teaching, during Christmas my friends and I had a toy drive for underprivileged children in the area. I recall one Christmas Eve, my friends and I got the toys together, and with the money we collected, we bought more toys. We set up all the toys on a church stage and told all of the kids in the after-school program to come over because Santa Claus would be there. I knew many of the children in the audience personally and I knew that they would be very disappointed if Santa did not show up. As my luck would have it, the Santa we hired could not come out to our church for the show. However, there was a Santa outfit in the closet and since I was the "light-skinned" member of our group, everyone decided that I should play Santa. I thought to myself, "As soon as I leave this room, all those kids out there will know that I'm not Santa and start crying."

To my surprise, when I walked out on stage in my Santa outfit, all of the children swore I was Santa. Each child came up on stage and sat on my lap and picked out the toy that they wanted. The toys were covered behind me and as soon as I walked on stage the sheets were lifted above the toys. So, not only did I look like Santa to these children, they thought that I possessed some type of magic. Many of the little girls were so happy they kissed me on the cheek and cried tears of joy. Some of the children approached me and asked for things that I could not give them, like a new home or a Daddy. Even now, as I reminisce about that Christmas, I cannot say that there is any feeling of giving that compares to what I gave to those children that day.

I was able to overcome the same conditions that those children face growing up in the inner city. I graduated as valedictorian with many honors. However, it is hard to believe that many black males, like myself, have so many obstacles to overcome just to merely graduate from high school. An education is only what I am entitled to as an American. So I wonder, can I really get an equal education? My freshman class in high school began with 140 African American males. Only 60 of the 140 made it to graduation. My transition from my mother's home to my father's home helped me become a part of the 60 students who graduated. I can't help but wonder, "Did the 80 students who failed have the same opportunity I had?" I know that the conditions in their homes were similar, if not worse. Why do I know? Because a close friend of mine was one of the 80 that did not make it. I always knew he was much brighter than me. So, what happened?

I chose to attend college but I felt very little support in my efforts. My father did not advise me to attend the college of my choice. He thought I should attend a school that offered me the best financial package. The school with the better financial package was oriented toward the sciences. When I visited this university for 2 days, I became homesick. I am never homesick unless I have significant reason to be unhappy. So, I chose to attend the school I fell in love with at first sight and I have solely supported myself through college. I pay both the student and parental contribution. Working in the summer helped pay most of the cost of college. However, I still work odd jobs to take care of the bills that I did not expect. Working and making the transition into college is hard but times have been harder.

Sometimes, reflecting on my survival, I look back and recall looking in the refrigerator to see nothing but the powdered milk, peanut butter, and jelly that was given out along with free cheese. My mother would trade all the food stamps she received for crack. In order to feed myself, I would attend school early at 7 o'clock and eat school breakfast. My school would also provide the free government lunches that I learned to love. Later on, for dinner, I would eat at the community center or look for a free dinner at one of the local churches. It was a great plan for feeding myself, but on weekends the school and the community center closed. I would collect enough bottles to purchase a 99-cent bag of potato chips. When I ate a whole bag of potato chips and drank a lot of water I felt full, though I was not full. The next morning I would wake up so hungry that I would have to gather up strength to get out of bed. Waking up hungry is one of the worst feelings I have experienced. Whenever my sister would get some money for both of us to eat on the weekends, she would cheat me. She would give me five dollars and say that she was "looking out for me." But behind my back, she would hold the other five of the ten dollars that I was supposed to receive. Sometimes, none of the money made it to me.

Whenever I think back to times like those, I feel a great sense of accomplishment. I know that my life has changed drastically and definitely for the better. However, it's very disturbing to go home and see my baby nephews. When I visit my sister, I see that she barely has enough to feed her children. I receive a meal plan at college that could probably cover me and my nephews. Now I go home to my family, look them in the eye, try to smile, and make idle conversation. What is there to talk about? Most of my family lives near or below the poverty level. My dormitory room is bigger than the apartment that my sister, her boyfriend, and their children share. Should I go home and talk about my experience at college, or how I can help? I love my nephews and I will take care of them when I can. So, what do I do now?

My sister has the potential to turn into what our mother has become. She does her best to make the right decisions for her children, but in the small amount of time that I spend home, I see my nephews as Niya and me all over again. I know that Niya uses the same discipline techniques that my mother used with us. Sometimes I question whether or not she is continuing a sick cycle of abusive behavior toward her children. The faults of child abuse and substance abuse need to stop here. My sister will never see me as more than her little brother. I wish she would listen to me sometimes. Whether she likes it or not, she needs to realize that I may have the ability to make good decisions.

When I reflect back on my family and my past, I know that I must remain strong because I struggle for a cause greater than myself. I want to prevent what happened to me by educating my nephews and people like my sister, but I am reminded of the saying: "You can never be a prophet in your own hometown." At home, I am never taken seriously, unless there is money involved. In contrast, when I am away from home, people do listen. If I can touch just one life in my process of making things right, I can grow to be a stronger man regardless of how much money I have. I think that by giving financial support, I am just putting a band-aid on the open wound that is my family. If I can help explain and prevent some things, maybe I can do more to help heal the wound in my family.

I have the ability to learn from other people's experience. By watching carefully the mistakes of my family and friends, I know what pressures to avoid. My favorite saying is: "I would rather lead a group of two that included myself than follow a society that I knew was wrong." Such convictions are products of my strong will, determination, and self-confidence. These attributes were fostered by my family when they favored me over my peers and deemed me "special." I received a larger vision of myself when my father said to me, "You must be destined for greatness because there were so many reasons that you should not have survived."

My reflection on the intimacy shared between Mommie and me comes from the perspective of a sophomore in college. I do not know if I clearly convey my emotion. However, I am what my girlfriend considers a sensitive man. I suppose I feel some anger toward Mommie when I write. How could she become the person I loved to hate? She was the one person I sought to love. I did love Mommie. I invested more love in her than any other individual. Our love was betrayed by the destruction of her true personality. Bad decisions made my mother the person I still feel animosity toward. Moreover, I cannot fail to recognize that my mother made me what I am. I don't think she would be at all surprised at my many accomplishments. Mommie expected great things of me. Knowing that I had her love gave me the confidence to become a self-made man. The discipline and respect for authority she instilled in me has served as the backbone for the work ethic which inspires my determination. Furthermore, the isolation I experienced as a child built an emotional strength and dependence on only myself. This continues to protect me from hurt and anguish. Despite my emotional defense mechanism, I have discovered that I do have the ability to love another woman.

My father is my savior. I cannot pretend that environmental influence did not play a major role in my character development—it sure did. The under-standing and patience my father exhibited in dealing with me was exemplary and, to say the least, incredible. He tolerated my attitude and ignorance to show me what a strong will could accomplish. My father says, "Son, all I did was point you in the right direction. You took the ball and ran with it." I owe my father for the direction he gave me. Mommie instilled value and father gave me a path. The path I chose to follow is lighted by my father's wisdom. I know whatever I do is supported by him. If no one else believes in me, even if I don't believe in myself, my father does. Faith is what makes every religion real for that individual. My father's faith in me makes every idea I have an achievable and realistic goal.

At this point, the major motivation in my life has come from my step-mother, Charlene. Every time she said I "did not do it good enough," I did everything better. There were many things she said that I could not achieve on my own. I now ask her to look in awe on those achievements deemed "impossi-ble." Even as Charlene motivated me, it took someone else to really inspire me. My cousin Darnell and the example he set forth always provided me with a glimpse of hope when the odds were so heavily stacked against me. He truly accomplished the impossible, and I can only emulate his success.

The paradox of the relationship between my mother, family, and extended family is that I am what they created. For all the negative I encountered, some-how, it became positive. I see that I hold the light of hope for my young nephews. My goal in attaining education is to do my best to see that what hap-pened to me does not happen again. My sister may not break the cycle of vio-lence she has experienced, but I have. Hopefully, I can help resist the negative influence that destroyed my mother.

Presently, I maintain a healthy relationship with my girlfriend. I find it easy to talk to women since most of my siblings were girls. By witnessing their likes and dislikes regarding men, I managed to sculpt myself into the character of a good man. Thus, I have had successful relationships with women and now have a significant other. One problem I have with intimacy is trust. I do seem to leave a little room between myself and women because I can't allow myself to be hurt to the point where I might break down. So I remain a little distant, but not to the point that I am not warm. I feel that enough time with one woman will alleviate that distance that I set.

One last note. The last news I had of my mother was last week. She was hospitalized for treatment of gangrene on three of her fingers. Apparently, while prostituting herself, she got into an altercation with someone who cut her hands with a dirty knife. All of this in pursuit of the drug crack. I ask you, in all hon-esty, do you think this is Mommie? And, is my life normal yet?

16

Quest for Peace

DENISE

Denise's story explores the dark, lonely world of suppressed emotion. Following the death of her mentally ill father at the hands of brutal and careless police officers, Denise lost faith in her country and in the institutions designed to help and protect its citizens. Consistent with her family's pattern of silence, she suppressed all anger and frustration. Although she excelled in school and found some reprieve in writing poetry, Denise's success became a source of ridicule among her siblings, who tried to deny her black identity because of her intelligence. As difficulty after difficulty stacked up: living through the daily trials of poverty, multiple deaths of close friends and teachers, being molested by a stranger, struggling to acknowledge her emerging sexual attraction toward women, and the final straw—the Rodney King beating and acquittal—Denise's façade of the "smiling" perfect girl began to crumble, and she begins the slow, painful process of coming to terms with emotions and thoughts long suppressed. This essay was written in her senior year.

My father was murdered while I was in my Houston school. I was sitting quietly at my desk working on a class assignment when my teacher called out my name. She informed me that I needed to go home immediately. As I walked the three short blocks to my house, I thought about how good it felt to be outside instead of in that 3rd-grade classroom. I was about halfway home when a weird feeling came over me. Why did I have to go home? Who had sent for me? What was so important that I had to miss school? My parents always said that unless we were dying, we had to go to school. Education was everything. So why was I sent home? Had something happened? I started to worry.

When I walked through the front door of my house, a wave of sickness coursed through my 9-year-old body. Something was not right. Something bad had happened. I could feel it in the air. Although I knew they were there, I didn't really see my brothers and sisters standing in the living room.

My eyes focused immediately on my mother, who was standing in the kitchen. She was the only person I could see. I watched as her skin drained of its natural color, and her beautiful face took on a look of utter despair and terror. Her body trembled as she doubled over, fell to her knees, and cried out, "He's dead, He's dead!" over and over again. I knew who she was talking about at once. I don't know how I knew, but I did. The "he" whom she was crying about, the "he" who was dead, was my father.

My mother lay on the kitchen floor for what seemed like 10 minutes with tears streaming down her face and her voice trembling, now barely above a whisper, "They shot him, they shot him. He's dead, he's dead."

At that moment I could not grasp exactly what she meant. My whole body was overwhelmed with sadness, fear, and disbelief. There were so many questions. What happened to Daddy? Where was he? Who shot him? Why him? Why? I didn't cry. I didn't scream. I didn't say a word. I was in absolute shock. Nothing was real.

I went to my mother and put my arms around her. She wouldn't stop crying. She couldn't pick herself up from the kitchen floor. She had no strength, no power. What was going on? I was confused. I had never seen her like this before. What did it mean that daddy was dead? I had never known anyone who had died before. What did it mean?

If you wanna get to heav'n lemme tell you how, juss keep yo' han' on de gospel plow. Keep yo' han' on de plow. Hold on, hold on.

—"Hold On," an African American Spiritual

A few months before my father was killed, his doctor told him that he no longer needed his medication or shock treatments. My father believed his doctor, whom he had been seeing for years. "Besides," he told my mother, "I have been taking this medication for half of my life to treat my schizophrenia. Now, I am finally able to be normal." But soon after he stopped taking his medicine his behavior became strange. He was no longer the calm and gentle person I've been told he had once been. My sole memory of him is how strange he was acting. He paced back and forth and repeatedly checked all of the windows and doors of the house. Later, he talked to himself and heard voices. His behavior frightened me. What was happening to him? Why was he so fidgety and nervous?

My brothers and sisters and I didn't know that he was sick. We noticed that he was changing, but we couldn't understand why. We were not told that daddy had an illness. My mother pleaded with him for months to take his medicine again. He refused. She pleaded with the doctor to reexamine him and to make him take his medication again. The doctor refused. He thought that the shock treatments and the medication were no longer necessary. Why not? Didn't he believe that my mother was telling him the truth about the pacing, the nervousness, and the voices? Although she knew that it could have been prevented, she had no other choice but to begin seeking both a restraining order for our safety and the institutionalization of my father for his own safety.

My stepfather is the man whom I refer to as my "dad," as he is the only father I've ever known. (My biological father and mother divorced when I was a baby.) I can't remember the last time I ever saw my dad alive. In fact, I don't remember anything about him. I have no recollection of his face, his voice, or his touch. I refused to remember all that I had shared with him—including his love. My mother recently told me about how I interacted with him because I have blocked all but one memory. My father, who was a self-employed watch repairman, was a gentle man who used to bathe me and my siblings when we were young and volunteered for our little league teams, but he didn't talk much. As a child, I used to sit on his lap and play with him, and he'd ask me questions about how I was doing and how I was feeling.

On that morning, January 3, 1979, while people were still saying "Happy New Year" to anyone who would listen, my dad got his gun and drove to his mother's house. The newspapers wrote that neighbors called the police about a man shooting into the air and at parked cars. When the police arrived, no one was outside. My father, the man who had been shooting, was already inside the house. His mother was not home. My father was there alone. The first two officers on the scene tried to get him to open the front door or talk to them. He refused to respond. They called for backup. Carloads of police came and surrounded the house.

They tried coaxing him out using a bullhorn, but he wouldn't budge. They threw tear gas through a couple of windows, and the house caught on fire. My father came running out of the burning house and right into the hands of a great number of policemen. As he ran out, unarmed, they shot him repeatedly, even after he was lying on the ground, unmoving. Witnesses' accounts in the newspaper described his limp body dancing on the ground from the impact of the bullets that ripped through him. Their accounts stated that it was "like watching an assassination." The police shot dozens of bullets into my father, an unarmed, mentally ill, black man.

I was not directly told any of this in great detail. I caught snatches of it here and there, mainly through the TV news, newspapers, grown-ups' whispers, and the interviews my mother gave on our living room couch to hungry reporters night after night.

They would not leave us alone because two officers had been wounded; one died a few days later. There were conflicting accounts about what happened. The official police report stated that they had no choice but to open fire because my father was armed and shooting at them as he ran out of the house. Witnesses to the shooting declared that he was unarmed as he ran out of the burning house. This clear discrepancy was just cause for a year-long FBI investigation which revealed that the police report was a cover-up for the officers' mistake of getting trigger happy on a defenseless black man. The firefighters' official report showed evidence that the gun that supposedly killed the officer was found, charred, on the coffee table in the living room of the burned-down house. My father could not have shot anyone, much less killed someone. As it turned out, one officer had mistakenly shot and killed another officer while trying to shoot my father. The surviving officer injured himself when his gun backfired.

That was the year that I learned what "expendable" meant and to whom the term applied. I could no longer live in a world that saw me, and people who looked like me, as expendable. I could no longer say the Pledge of Allegiance at the beginning of each school day. How could I allow the words "liberty and justice for all" to cross my lips, knowing that they were untrue? Knowing that my dad did not get liberty or justice? Would the white police officers have paid more attention to what was or was not in his hands if my father had been white and not black? I would simply stand there with my hand over my heart and say nothing. I performed my own silent protest. My country had betrayed me.

I felt very alone and frightened. Which one of us would be killed next? Who would protect the rest of us from doctors who did not care to give us an accurate diagnosis? Who would protect the rest of us from brutes with badges and guns? Who? No one could protect us. It was horrifying to think that no one would come to our rescue, no one would get punished, and no one would care. In fact, the first question would be, "What did you do this time to bring it on yourself?"

My mind searched for a way out of this reality. My self-defense mechanism must have kicked in at that point because somehow I began to distance myself from my emotions. I struggled daily to keep my thoughts and emotions under control. In my all-out effort to protect myself from painful emotions, I had to suppress *all* emotions. I paid a price, however, for this protective measure stripped me of my passions as well as my anguish.

Throughout my schooling, my teachers never noticed that I wasn't saying the pledge to the flag. This oversight, I believe, was because I always did what was expected of me. I never got out of line. I was a "teacher's pet," a class clown, and an athlete. On the first day of school each year, my teachers were usually pleased to know that I was a Johnson kid because we all did well. I strove to be accepted by my classmates and had a smile for everyone all of the time. My father's murder did not phase me. I simply blocked it out of my mind. I never thought about him.

It wasn't too difficult not to think about him or how he died because my family never talked about him. After his funeral, his murder was a taboo subject. In the midst of our denial, however, the police department would call to frighten my mother into not pressing charges against them. They knew that they were wrong and they did not want to be taken to court. The FBI investigation showed clear evidence of police brutality with malicious intent. My mother, a newly widowed black woman with eight children and only a high school diploma, was scared to death for our safety. She did not want to risk losing anyone else. Her white lawyer convinced her that if she settled out of court she would get monetary retribution, but if she didn't settle, she would get nothing because "blacks did not win cases against the city" in Texas. So, she settled out of court. A couple of officers were fired, and we received a few thousand dollars. The settlement was able to pay for most of the funeral expenses and all of the lawyer's fees. To me, no amount of money could replace a human life, especially the life of my father.

I didn't witness any anger in my mother, and because she didn't display any anger, I didn't either. I followed her lead because I didn't know how I was supposed to react to this whole thing, other than to try my best to forget that it had ever happened. She said, "Being who we are and where we are has its consequences. That's how things are right now. We have to accept that and go on." Our extended family was nearby, also in Houston. Furthermore, we didn't have the funds to move anywhere else and we needed the support of our friends and family.

We restructured our lives after my father's murder. It took 2 years to reach a settlement, during which time my mother was preoccupied with finding a way to feed us. She had eight mouths to feed, in addition to her own, and she didn't have a job that could support us all. Mom was a very religious young woman who believed that "God would make a way somehow" and that "if you lived right, talked right, and prayed right, then heaven belonged to you." For a while we had food and clothes, and most of our bills were being paid. The bank miraculously allowed a 1-year grace period for the house notes, which kept a roof over our heads. But we had less and less food, and funds were always low or even nonexistent. We could no longer afford to take piano lessons, or play on little league teams. We could no longer take ballet lessons or drama classes. All of these things stopped abruptly. We understood that we had no money, so we didn't complain.

However, we couldn't understand why we didn't have food to eat. At one time or another, we each complained to our frustrated and overwhelmed mother that we were hungry. I'm sure that she hated to see us go to bed hungry, to wake up hungry, and to send us to school hungry. How could we learn when our minds were drawn to our stomachs and our hunger pangs? We were also constantly growing, but we couldn't afford to buy clothes. My relatives and people from the church and community gave us their old clothes to wear. We had to take the public bus everywhere or walk because our car had burned along with our grandmother's house. My mother eventually had to go on public assistance until she could acquire enough skills to get a job that paid well enough to feed us and put clothes on our backs. I hated the stigma of food stamps and school lunch cards. Being poor is "sinful" in this society, and I learned to be ashamed of our poverty, although I knew that what had happened to us was not our fault. Our senses of humor sharpened; we had to laugh to keep from crying, because our existence was so dismal.

I started constantly misplacing things and forgetting what I was saying in the middle of sentences because I had difficulty dealing with the present. I lost the ability or the will to concentrate. I was always so spaced out that I acquired the new nickname "the absent-minded professor" at home. Upon my father's death, my books, my writing, and my mother became my world. It was difficult being black and female and having a creative relationship with words while growing up in Houston. My verbal expression was indicative of my different way of thinking, and it set me apart from my siblings. I am the sixth child out of eight. I have four older brothers, one older sister, and a younger sister and brother. I felt misunderstood by them because of their teasing. My use of language caused me to stick out. Like most Texans I used words and phrases like "y'all" and "fixin' to," but I didn't have the drawl or the dialect of most Southern black people. Being an avid reader gave me a different vocabulary, and it also sharpened my thought processes. The combined effect of people, culture, and the shaping of language fascinated me. I read books about how people in various cultures lived and I took notice of how language shaped their interaction with their environment and each other. I became fascinated with possibilities of what could be, which helped to ameliorate my pain.

Something spiritual stirred inside of me when I expressed myself on paper. I used writing to take me away from everything. This desire to write down what was on my mind was an inexplicable, yet exceedingly powerful force. In sports I could only express myself within the boundaries of the game. Usually that was enough, as I could release a lot of frustration in a non-self-destructive way. But writing was an experience without restrictions. I wrote poetry about race relations, the oppression of females, religion, violence, and longings. I felt free of these things when I wrote about them, lessening the power of their hold on me. I felt like a healer and a creator. I felt important without feeling judged or alienated. I felt complete, lacking nothing. I spent as much time writing and reading as I possibly could. Only on rare occasions did I share my poetry. I learned very early in my life to fear sharing such deep emotions and thoughts with anyone.

I never thought to assign value to my way of thinking because it came naturally to me. Other people, however, valued my thinking process. They never let me forget that I was different. "You don't talk like us," they would say. "You soun' like a white girl." I wanted to forget that I was different because it made other people uncomfortable, which made interactions between us difficult. This made me uncomfortable with myself.

Like most people, my siblings often mistook my different way of thinking for me wanting to be something or someone other than who and what I was. "Why she talk propa' like white people? She muss wanna be white," they agreed among themselves, unable to understand or make sense of my unique behavior. This was not a compliment. They believed, as did I, that white people were greedy and violent. Nevertheless, because I would not conceal my intelligence, they would exclaim, "You're an Oreo!" with great conviction.

Ever since I could speak, my brothers and sisters insulted me, and this continued throughout high school. I could not understand how the way I spoke indicated to them what I "muss wanna be." Still, my self-expression became unacceptable to me because it was unacceptable to others. I began to believe that I could not accept myself until other black people accepted me. New doubts augmented the loss of self-worth I had experienced upon my father's murder.

In my effort to be accepted, I found myself making constant readjustments so that I would not stand out. I didn't want to be considered different. My siblings taught me that to be singled out intellectually among other black people meant automatic rejection. If I were rejected by my black sisters and brothers, then I had nowhere left to turn for comfort or protection. Their negative reactions taught me to be silent or to suffer consequences. By the time I reached adolescence, I had become silent, reactionary, defensive, and eager to be accepted. When I met other black people, I would wait for them to speak before I opened my mouth. This allowed me to judge the way that they expressed themselves so that I could have some idea of how they would regard me after hearing me speak.

The only person who constantly supported me through life and didn't think me a "freak" was my mother. A teacher's aide, she took an active interest in the education of all her children. Beaming, she would introduce me to people as "the smart one," which, although it saddened me somewhat, always made me feel that she was on my side. It seemed to make her happy to tell people that I was smart, so I dealt with the consequences.

One consequence of being introduced as "the smart one" was that it made me very aware that I was different from my siblings. Throughout my childhood, strangers would exclaim, "This one here is going to college." I felt like a curiosity, somehow alienated, as if I were more desirable, yet less understood than my siblings. My mother's acknowledgment of my intellect seemed to give them permission to tease me, to dislike me, and to question my "blackness." They had bought into white stereotypes of black people—that we must all be alike and that we could not excel intellectually, only athletically. They had other gifts such as visual artistry, athletics, and technical knowledge, but I was the first one to go to a 4-year college. I felt all the pressure was on me to succeed on behalf of my family.

My relationship with my sister Cynthia was particularly damaged. She was 2 years my senior, and I adored her and always wanted to be around her. She would say hurtful things to me and she seemed not to want me around. When I would complain to our mother about how Cynthia treated me, mom would say, "Oh, she's just jealous of you. Don't pay her no mind." Cynthia's rejection of me was hurtful and confusing. Why should she be jealous of me? She always knew what she wanted and went for it, whereas I had a lot of self-doubt, constantly second-guessing myself. I thought that I was lucky to have such a determined person for an older sister. Unfortunately, she was determined to make my days and nights hell.

Soon after my father's murder, I was sleeping next to Cynthia in the queen-sized bed that I shared with her and our younger sister. Suddenly, I was awakened by the pillow being yanked from beneath my head and Cynthia screaming, "Uh uh. Uh uh. Get offah my pillah. You need to find yo own pillah." I was wide awake at this point with my eyes bugging out and my mouth hanging open. I tried to explain to her that I wasn't trying to invade her space, but that I simply rolled over in my sleep. She wouldn't listen. I refused to sleep in the same room with her again. The only other place available was with my mother in her king-sized bed. I shared a bed with my mother from grade school until I left for college.

That shift in sleeping arrangements shaped the dynamics of my relationship with my 2 sisters until high school. Pam, who is two years younger than I, became very close to Cynthia. They shared laughter, clothing, and secrets. They made fun of me while I looked on, feeling left out, lonely, and betrayed. They were friends. It was them against me. I escaped into my books and writing even more. It wasn't until Pam and I attended the same high school that we became friends.

The new sleeping arrangements also influenced my relationship with my mother. After mom became a widow, I tried, in my little kid kind of way, to make sure that she was ok. At night I'd occasionally hear her crying herself to sleep and I would ask her why she was crying. She really missed dad. I didn't have tears of my own to shed. I was not an orphan because I still had mom. She, on the other hand, had lost everything that our society said gave her worth—her husband. At that point I swore to never allow myself to become dependent on anyone or anything other than myself.

Though I continued to do well in school, I was struggling to hide my anxiety. I lived with the fear that someone else in my family was going to be killed. I didn't feel safe anywhere but I didn't show this fear. I put on smiles for everyone. Through the years, my mom and I became each other's confidant, but I couldn't share these thoughts with her. I knew better than to break the family taboo of talking about our father's murder.

At the end of 3rd grade, I was informed that the next year I would be bussed to a vanguard class at a different school where kids like me, who were "gifted," could learn together. When I switched schools, I still stood out. At recess, two little blond girls followed me around. They'd wait for my shoelaces to come loose then proceed to fight over who would get to tie them. This blew my mind. I wanted them to stop following me. When I asked them why they did this, they shrugged their shoulders, but they had huge smiles on their freckled faces. The look of admiration in their eyes revealed to me what they could not express in words: They had crushes on me. I just ignored their following me like lost puppies until they finally stopped. I think that that was the first time I realized that girls could have crushes on other girls. It made me uncomfortable.

Each year after that, I was bussed to one school or another to be with kids who were "smart." I was in special programs for "gifted" students such as vanguard, honors, and magnet programs, where most students were white, a handful were Mexican American, and only a few were African American or Asian American. I had become very conscious of race and of people noticing me. I spent a lot of time with Constance, whom I met when I first switched schools in 4th grade. She mostly kept to herself at school, but after school Constance hung out at the YWCA located directly across the street from her house. It didn't cost anything to attend, so I went with her. The two of us became inseparable. We shared secrets, and I slept over at her house sometimes. She loved to read as much as I did, so we exchanged library books. We remained best friends throughout junior high school, where we were placed in the same honors classes.

The summer before I started high school, when I was 14 years old, I was molested by a stranger in my home. The only thing that my mother had to say about sex was that it was to be saved for marriage, and I thought that it would upset my mom too much to tell her that I was molested. I didn't want to make her feel bad. I tried to protect her and I felt as if I were to blame. The reaction to my father's murder taught me that denial and silence were how to handle traumatic events in my life. I was becoming accustomed to suffering alone in silence. Constance was the only person that I felt I could tell.

The house was being renovated that summer. One day the plumber and I were the only people in the house. He asked me to go back to the unfinished bathroom with him to show me what kind of pipe I needed to tell my mother to get. I had no reason not to believe him, yet as soon as we got to the bathroom I felt uneasy. The bathroom was very small, and he was standing much too close to me. Even more disturbing was the fact that he was standing between me and the door. He shut it behind him. When I turned around to ask what he was talking about he pounced on me. He pushed me up against the wall and began groping me. I tried to fight him off but he was so big. His hands were all over me. My heart was beating fast. I had to get out of there. I tried talking him into letting me go. He wasn't listening. I tried to hit him, but he just grabbed my hands, pinned me hard against the wall and made me touch him. I panicked even more. Sweat was pouring down his white face and his hot breath was all over me. I almost got sick. Finally, after much struggling, groping, screaming, and fast talking, he let me go. I ran into my sisters' bedroom. There was no lock on the door, so I put furniture up against it. I curled up on the bed in a fetal position and tried to block out what had just happened.

The next day I biked over to Constance's house and told her what had transpired. I was very upset and crying and I wanted to forget. But I could not forget. Instead, I stuck the memory in that section of my brain where I put things I couldn't handle. I was getting better at denying traumatic events. While my house was being completed, I spent time at Constance's; I didn't feel safe in my own home anymore.

Apparently, molestation was becoming an important issue in this country at that time. I read articles and books and watched a TV movie called *Something About Amelia* about a girl who was sexually abused by her father. I learned that it wasn't my fault. My body belonged to me. Still, I couldn't help but feel responsible in some way. I told myself I shouldn't have been there, but then reminded myself that I was in my own home and I had every right to be there. I was supposed to be safe at home. After the incident, I wanted to be invisible.

My grandmother died about a month later. I wasn't sure how much more I could take. I wanted to scream NO at the top of my lungs to let out the pain that I was feeling. I didn't want males looking at me. I started wearing really oversized t-shirts and baggy jeans and shorts. I kept to myself. I felt trapped in a body that no longer belonged to me. I felt trapped in a life that I didn't want.

When school started I dove into my schoolwork and tried to keep my chin up. It was difficult having guys close to me, and I became very suspicious of them. I didn't want to be touched by anyone, but at the same time I needed to be comforted. I couldn't bring myself to tell my mother about what had happened, but I needed her reassurance that everything was going to be okay. I would sit on her lap and hug her. She would call me her "big baby" and roll her eyes, but I didn't care as long as she held me. I forced myself to smile and pretend that everything was okay. I tried to project outward the security I craved inside. I longed to feel calm, but my stomach was always in knots and I never felt the same as before I was molested. I always felt on edge but tried hard not to show it.

My days were filled with church activities, school, reading books that I borrowed from the library, and hanging out with Constance at the YWCA. I listened to my brothers' and sisters' conflicts with mom, but I told myself that I didn't have any. I denied the fact that I was sexually assaulted. I was the perfect daughter who never gave mom any trouble nor had any problems. I did what I thought she expected of me. I did well in school, did not show any interest in boys, and put God first. I convinced myself that I also wanted these things for myself.

Constance, though, was getting out of control. Her grandparents, who had raised her and her younger sister, both died within 6 months of each other and a few months before we started high school. Her mother moved into the house with Constance and her sister. Constance and her mom fought a lot. She needed things that I was incapable of giving her because I too was struggling. On weekends spent with her cousin, she was introduced to drugs. Before long she was skipping school and shooting up. I kept asking her why she was doing this to herself, but she didn't know why. I stopped asking her why, but I warned her about HIV transmission through sharing needles. We grew apart.

> *Sister, you've been on my mind. Oh sister, we're two of a kind.*
> *So sister, I'm keepin' my eyes on you.*
> —"Miss Celie's Blues," *The Color Purple*

At the same time that Constance and I were growing apart, Trisha and I were growing closer. Trisha intimidated me, but she was so appealing that I could not resist trying to know her and spend time with her. She had a radiant energy about her that was captivating. She and I both ranked first in our class the first semester of our freshman year. We were recommended by our math and science teachers for a special program for minority students. She didn't want to go, but I did.

The program at a New England boarding school lasted for 6 weeks each summer in high school. It opened up a whole new world for me. For the first time in my life, I was interacting with black students who were smart like me. It amazed me that they were not afraid to show their intelligence. For the first time in my life, I felt ok about being young, gifted, and black.

The classes at the boarding school were surprisingly challenging. In the public schools back home I was usually bored, but there I constantly learned new things. I didn't feel compelled to stifle my enthusiasm for learning. I was, however, disturbed by the great discrepancy between my public school education and my private school education. My private school education was so much better than what I got in public school. It upset me that I had to get a full scholarship to attend a school far away from home to get a challenging education. Most inner-city kids could not afford to wait on such "thoughtfulness" because most times it did not come.

Back in public school my sophomore year, I decided that I was wasting my time at the Medical Professions High School. I wanted to own a bookstore and sell books by and about black people. I also couldn't stand to watch Constance slowly killing herself and not be able to do anything about it. I also knew that I didn't want to be a doctor. After my father's misdiagnosis, I grew to mistrust doctors. So, I transferred to the Finance Professions High School, also known as FPH$. Before I left, I explained to Constance that I was not abandoning her. My mother asked why I wasn't spending as much time with Constance, so I told her she was doing drugs. There was nothing left to say. We were both familiar with how drugs were invading and devastating our own community and even our own home. Two of my older brothers' drug of choice was alcohol. In a drunken rage one night, one of them put his head through a wall, yelling that he wished he were dead. I thought to myself that he wasn't the only one who wished to be dead.

The magnet program at the new school had dedicated teachers. My favorite teacher, Jim Trails, took time out of classes when he saw that something was bothering us. I felt comfortable talking to him. However, the atmosphere there was so depressing. The feeling of poverty and hopelessness hung in the air. Many teenage mothers attended the regular, nonmagnet high school because free child care was provided for the students' children. I felt other people's pain like it was my own.

I missed Trisha a lot also. We kept in touch by phone, but I wanted to see her. I called her two nights before Christmas, when she said that she would be home, but strangely, no one answered the telephone. The next morning someone called very early, but I didn't answer the phone. A couple of minutes later Cynthia came in and woke me up with shocking news: Trisha had been killed in a car accident the night before. She was driving her parents' car home from her church's youth group meeting when she lost control. Her brother was seriously injured, but he had survived. I went numb.

That Christmas break, I felt ready to die. My heart felt so heavy. I marveled at the peace that I would surely have if I were dead. That's all I thought about for months. I didn't know how much more I could take without breaking down.

Fortunately, Panu, who would become my good friend, transferred to FPH$ the next semester, so I didn't feel so alone. In fact, because I was a counselor's assistant, it was my duty to show her around the campus. When I walked into the counselor's office, our eyes met and smiles lit up our faces that whispered, "Where have you been?"

My attraction to females began to surface a little because of Panu, but I still wasn't ready to acknowledge my attraction. She shared her poetry with me. She was first-generation American, and her parents were strict. Half an hour on the phone in the evenings was her limit, so we wrote letters to each other almost daily and exchanged them at school the next day. Panu invited me to her home often for dinner and to spend the night. We slept together in her full size bed, but we made sure not to touch each other at all. Her parents got to know me very well through our in-depth conversations about India's culture and languages. Her father and I had many debates about the value placed on male and female children in Pakistani culture. Occasionally Panu's parents would lend her the car to go to a movie or to the mall on the weekend, but only if I were going because they trusted me.

I think that there was a mutual attraction between us. She and another friend would praise my body parts when the three of us were alone. Panu would feel my behind as we walked down the hall or up the stairwell. I was definitely attracted to her, but I couldn't bring myself to return her touch. We never talked about what her "love pats" were about.

By the time I was 16 or 17 years old, I disagreed with church teachings which were prejudiced against people who were different. The minister, whom I looked up to, said that homosexuality was wrong and that women should submit to men. I wanted no part of that, but I went to church anyway because it was expected of me. I really didn't want to disappoint my mom. I also had become dependent on gospel music as a source of strength. I learned to take what was good from the sermons and leave the rest at the church.

Like my older brothers, I worked after school. In high school I worked at a burger joint in a nearby mall. My mom worked upstairs in an elite beauty salon. I was worried about her though, because she was one of two black people there. One of her coworkers pulled a knife on her once. Between shifts at my other job I would go upstairs and help out. During the week, mom went straight from work to a junior college to take evening courses. She left early every morning and didn't get back until after midnight. She was always on the run, but she somehow managed to smile and be there for us when we needed her. She was always so strong, supportive, and caring.

The summer before my senior year, I went to the last session of summer boarding school. It was great to return and see my old friends again. I had become good friends with a girl from New York City named Lisa and that summer we were roommates. One day, I got surprising news from one of my public high school friends. She sent a newspaper clipping that said people with HIV shouldn't be allowed to teach, and there was a feature story on Jim Trails. My favorite teacher had died. Once again I suppressed my feelings and threw myself into my work.

That summer, our class visited colleges in New England. Lisa and I both decided that we wanted to go to the same New England college. I liked the campus and the students and the administrators that I met on our visit, but mostly I liked the foreign study and language programs. I agonized over how I'd be received in this predominantly white college environment. I decided to apply because it was my right to go wherever I was accepted.

> *They said I wouldn't make it. They said I wouldn't be here today. They said I'd never amount to anything. But I'm glad to say that I'm on my way, and I'm growing more and more each day. Though I've been talked about and I've been criticized I've had to wipe so many tears from my eyes. But I'm still holding on to His hand.*
>
> —"I'm Still Holding On," a gospel song,

Lisa and I were both accepted to the same New England college and we were roommates as freshmen. Our friendship didn't last the year. Lisa spent a lot of time in the room with her boyfriend. I studied best in my room and had problems concentrating because she and her boyfriend were so loud. She would try to be more considerate, but it never lasted. Her boyfriend, Chris, had moved in by the middle of fall term. Lisa got upset with me for locking our personal bathroom door while I showered. Between clenched teeth she said, "Denise, you need to keep the bathroom door unlocked. Chris had to go down four flights of stairs to use the public bathroom." I couldn't make her understand my need to feel safe. She didn't know about my molestation, my fear. By the end of freshman year we weren't even speaking.

In addition to attending classes, I joined the school's gospel choir, worked, and did some community service. Although I didn't attend church services regularly, gospel music and other African American music helped me to make it through many days. Music reminded me that my ancestors, who suffered through the Middle Passage and were enslaved, had paved the way for me to be where I was and to make the choices I made. In meditation, I drew upon their strength.

I also became close to Eddie, a guy from my home city. We clicked immediately. We felt incredibly comfortable with each other. We spent a lot of time together and became best friends. He was having a hard time at college. He was gay, black, and, like me, had little or no financial support from home. When he confided in me about his sexuality, we became even closer. Part of me felt that I could open up to him even more because his gay identity made me feel safe with him. I didn't think that he would want to get close to me sexually. I grew up believing in society's assumption of heterosexuality; I naturally assumed that I was heterosexual although I hadn't even dated yet.

Freshman winter, Eddie decided that he had to leave college. I panicked. I felt as if I was going to die if he left me. After a while and after much analyzing, I told him that my dad had died when I was younger and that I never got to say good-bye. I told him about projecting my unresolved feelings for my dad onto him. He understood, but he had to leave anyway. After Eddie left, I had no support whatsoever. I tried to explain to my mom why I wasn't happy, but she couldn't understand. She pushed me into staying. "Oh, you're tough, you can stick it out," she said. So I stuck it out.

This particular college was not good for my self-esteem. I stopped writing poetry my freshman year. Most other African Americans acted as if they were from higher economic classes than me and they mainly seemed to be concerned with which elite black Greek house to join. Whites could not relate to what I felt at all. They couldn't seem to grasp that two or more drastically different realities could exist simultaneously. They were resistant to and doubtful of the validity of my thoughts, feelings, and reality. I believe their mistrust was due mainly to ignorance and fear, rather than hate.

There were times when their disbelief was almost laughable, but at other times I could not afford to laugh. When an anthropology professor pointed out in class that every other race descended from Africans, who were the first people on the planet, gasps echoed throughout the classroom. The one or two other black students in the class and I looked across the room at one another and shook our heads. It took a white, male professor to validate what I and others had tried to communicate to our classmates before.

I worked for a self-proclaimed, liberal white woman, whom I later found had difficulty keeping students of color working for her. When she said something that I perceived as racist, I asked her for clarification. She got defensive. I explained to her why I asked for clarification, and she was offended. After the incident, I spoke to a Korean American student and an African American student who had worked for her in the past. I explained the incident and asked about their interactions with her. They both hesitated, but then told me that they quit working for her because of her racist comments. I, on the other hand, finished the term with her and was not asked back to work there the following term.

College, for the most part, was a debilitating experience to endure rather than an empowering experience to embrace. Gradually, my spirit broke. I could not force myself to smile any longer. Many of my classmates' spirits seemed broken too. That is why Eddie left. What does this college do to us that breaks our spirit? For my part, I felt stifled, suffocated, and lacking a support system.

Although Eddie left, he and I remained close. I saw him during breaks from school. By sophomore year, I found myself falling in love with him, but I was confused because I thought that I was attracted to women. I just wasn't sure of anything. Eddie was sure, though, and he said that he must be bisexual because he had fallen in love with me. I told him that I liked him a lot but that I thought that I was attracted to women. He quickly yelled, "NO, you can't be!" He was the first person I told. It took me 2 years before I could voice that again. I dated only men throughout the rest of college. In fact, while I was on exchange at a university in California, I got engaged to Dan, a guy I loved dearly, but I was not "in love" with him.

> *We who believe in freedom cannot rest. When will the killing of black men, black mothers' sons be as important as the killing of white men, white mothers' sons? We who believe in freedom cannot rest until it comes.*
> —"Ella's Song," Sweet Honey in the Rock

Up until the first week of May of my senior year in college, I never talked about my father to anyone except Eddie. It was much easier to push this loss out of my mind and to concentrate on achieving. I was pleasing my mother and preparing myself for independence.

When the video of the Rodney King beating came out, I was not surprised. I was horrified, but not surprised. I wasn't that naive. Police brutality was nothing new to me. Still, I did not know how to react to it. Occasionally, I'd think that maybe this time would be different. Maybe, just maybe, our lives would be valued and something would be done. The video was proof to the rest of America what we've always known in the black community—that black people are second-class citizens, not protected under the law, nor by the law's enforcers. In my gut, I knew that the people responsible for King's beating would get around the law somehow. They always did, and I had to acknowledge that fact.

Although the television stations played the King videotape as if it were going out of style, it wasn't until the verdict was announced that I was able to feel any emotion and begin to mourn the loss of my father. My fiancé, Dan, called and told me the news. My heart sank. Although I expected the acquittal, I really didn't want to accept it. My mind groped for any hope at all that I had for humanity.

I hung up in total shock. I just went to bed and tried to think about something else. I awoke the next morning, and the reality of the previous night's telephone conversation hit me. The acquittal of the LAPD officers represented yet another bullet through the heart of my father, to whom justice had also been denied. All hope for humanity left me.

I tried to get out of bed, but my legs could not hold me up. I fell onto the floor next to my bed and tears came streaming out. I had no control over myself. My whole body was in convulsions. I think that I passed out at that point, but I don't recall. I remember raising my head from the floor and thinking that daddy was dead and that we were getting beaten and killed in the name of the law. Daddy was dead, and I didn't get to tell him that I loved him. I didn't get a chance to say good-bye. A knot formed in my throat, in my chest, and in my stomach. I was terrified. I felt like a helpless little kid who was confused and couldn't find her way. I didn't know what to do with my anger, but I knew that I had a right to it. I had a right to express that anger too.

I was afraid of my emotions, but most of all, I was afraid of my anger. Expression of anger is unacceptable even when it is legitimate. This perception is especially true for women. Our society has no acceptable way of expressing anger. Therefore, black people's anger in this country has been left invalidated, which causes it to accumulate, to create a climate of hostility. I knew that most white people would not understand this concept. That would be acknowledging too much. They refuse to accept this concept because they continue to flourish financially from social conditions like the legacy of slavery and the "good ole boy" network.

My mother's comfort and happiness has always been a priority over my own. How could I express my anger without alienating myself from her and other people? I was determined not to be a part of the disappointment or chaos following the King verdict. This determination came at a great emotional and psychological price to me. It may have also had a physical price. My senior fall I found a hard lump in my right breast while performing my monthly breast self-examination. Upon discovering this intruder, I wondered where my rage had gone. If the rage didn't leave my body, then where did it go?

I went to class that morning, but I couldn't understand what people were saying. The professor mentioned the King verdict at the beginning of class, and afterward I went up to her and asked if she could make any sense of it. She could not. I found myself blurting out that my father had been unjustly murdered by police officers when I was 9 years old. She and the other students who were standing nearby didn't know what to say. How is someone supposed to react to something like that? I felt so alone and confused as I went back to my room and tried to make sense of my existence. I couldn't think straight at all. I was in a daze.

All alone in my room, I cried for the loss of my father. All that I could do was cry. I cried for my inability to change the state of the world. I felt helpless and hopeless, and for the first time in my life I was able to admit those things to myself. I felt that whatever I could possibly do was never going to be enough. Why was I in college if I couldn't change things? I tried to get involved in the rallies and other things that were going on, but I was not really there. I had no strength.

On Monday morning, I called a counselor that I had been seeing over at the student infirmary about my sexuality and about why the time I spent with my fiancé was harder than the time we spent apart. I told her that I couldn't recall the last time that I had eaten or had a good night's rest. She strongly recommended that I stay in the infirmary so that I could rest and start eating again. I was there for a week and was medicated for my depression. I phoned my fiancé and told him where I was. After much debate, I phoned my mom and told her where I was and why I was there. I could hear her disappointment. She couldn't quite understand why I was allowing myself to think about my father. She wanted to protect me from this pain, but I told her that it was already too late. I finally found enough courage to allow myself to think about him and how he died. I asked her to send me some of the newspaper articles about his murder that she kept in the file cabinet in her bedroom closet. She refused.

I got angry at her, but I didn't tell her so. She answered a few questions that I had about the murder, but she urged me not to let my mind get caught up in that pain but to keep on going. I should be concerned with my studies and forget about this mess because "God will take care of it," she said. I told her that God has given us the ability to take care of it ourselves. She was trying to protect herself from her own doubt, fear, pain, and loss. I didn't tell any of my friends where I was. I felt that no one knew exactly what I was going through and so they couldn't possibly help me, other than by giving me time and space to get through this.

Upon the suggestion of my counselor, I began to write poetry again. I felt so much better while I wrote poetry. I allowed myself to connect with the pain and sorrow that comes with grief and mourning. I didn't fight it any more. I let it all out. I wrote a letter to my dad. I wrote a letter to the Houston Police Department. But mostly I wrote poetry. One poem in particular, entitled "Discomforting Thoughts," helped me to get all of my feelings out in a coherent way.

When daddy was murdered
my universe was no longer together.
I was no longer together.
There was only chaos, fear
and loneliness within me,
and in the world around me.

I constructed a high wall around me
to shield myself from everyone.
Everyone who had expectations of me
and from others who did not
yet know my name.
I could not let anyone know
that I knew that the world was not
*   perfect. That I was not perfect.*

"Everything's fine,"
said the nine-year-old smile
that I politely pasted onto my face.
I had to put on an innocent smile for
*   everyone.*
Only rarely could I smile for myself.
Others needed the reassurance
more than I.
Besides, what was there to smile
*   about?*
How could I let them down
without letting myself down?
Either way I was dying.
A part of me is dying every day.
Who could I talk to about

my fears, my frustrations, my fail-
    ures?
Oh, and I do fear, I get frustrated, and
    I do fail.

Why does it seem as if I am not
    allowed to fail? I am human, right?
Why do I have such different thoughts
    from my peers?
We do not speak the same language.
Not inherently, for I always speak
in terms for others to understand.
In the process, I lost a part of me.
I lost the meaning of my words,
and what I really meant.

Why am I so different,
and feel things so differently?
I appreciate my differences
—my uniqueness makes me special.
But it also makes me lonely.
It places unfair burdens on me.
On the outside I put on a front that
    I've learned to hide behind.
It's called being polite, being a clown,
and being the intellect.
Doing the expected thing.
Always answering "fine" and "okay"
when I am not fine, and when I am not
    okay.

I hide the tears behind the laughter.
But how can I honestly cry
for having lost someone that I refuse
to remember ever having? Daddy.
The word seems so alien to me,
even coming from my own lips.
That's a word that the other kids used.
They were so certain that they'd get a
    response from their calls to their
    daddies.

What is it like to have a father, a
    daddy?
Why don't I know what it's like to be
    protected from hate and igno-
    rance?

Why can't I let others know that I
    hurt?
Why can't I admit to myself that I
    have pain?
Why is everyone else's comfort
such a priority over my own?

I don't want to let momma down.
She works hard to make sure that I'm
    okay.
She loves me and supports me,
so how can I tell her that there are
    things
that I need that she can't possibly
    offer?
Things that she does not understand?

Mom, I'm separate from you.
We are two different people.
You can't always speak for me.
I have to do that for myself now.
I know that I have to be strong.
That's one of the many things
that you've taught me.
But do I have to be strong all of the
    time?
When do I get to be me?
A person with vulnerabilities and
    dreams.
Maybe I'm not as strong or sure as I
    let on.
I'm not yours or anyone else's Super-
    woman.
In fact, I despise the term!
I am tired.

Although writing poetry helped me to gather my thoughts, it was not enough. I still felt so much rage. Still, I was able to sleep and eat more and was released from the infirmary.

I happened to be taking a self-defense class for women at that time, and a couple of male volunteers came in to simulate physical attacks. They wore protective gear, so when it was my turn I went off on them. While I was fighting them off, I thought of them as police officers like the ones who killed my dad, the ones who beat my brothers, and the ones who beat Rodney King. I also thought of them as the plumber. I had so much rage inside that I vented onto them. While I was beating them, the other women in the class cheered me on, and afterward they applauded me. I simply did everything that we were taught to do, but I felt bad getting praised for beating people up. I have felt so beaten down that I had trouble beating others, even defending my own life. Who had taught me that my life was less valuable than my attackers' lives were? Why did I believe that bullshit? After I finished with the men, they took off their face masks and sat out for a while. One of them had a bruised eye. I felt that I should apologize for hurting them, but I couldn't. I had to protect myself. They knew what they were getting into when they took on the job. I did ask them if they were okay. I told them that I felt bad, but they had these cheesy grins on their faces and said, "No, no, you were great!" If I was so great, then why did I feel so bad?

Reality was beginning to set in again. I was getting concerned about my classes. My professors knew that I would be in the infirmary for a few days, but I had to catch up on my work if I expected to graduate the next month as planned. I had three midterm exams to make up, in addition to papers. I had been doing very well in my classes until I went into the infirmary, but when I took my exams I couldn't concentrate. A week or two after I completed my exams, I finally felt like myself again. I resorted to blocking out my feelings and concentrated on my schoolwork. My key motivation was the fact that upon completion of my course work, I could get out of there. I could leave this college and its discontents behind me and begin to nurture my broken spirit in a healthy environment of my choice. The sooner done, the better. I finished with grades ranging from B+ to A-.

I am still struggling with my anger, but I've come to realize that emotions can be controlled. At least I know that I won't hurt anyone by allowing myself to be angry. I feel as if I can finally be myself and not have to live up to other people's expectations. I'm living for me now, not for my mom or anyone else. I've learned that I cannot be held accountable for other people's feelings, especially my mother's. I am going to have a talk with her face-to-face and tell her how I feel. It's ok to be angry, even at those people we love the most. It's ok to remember someone who is dead. I feel as if I can finally say good-bye to my father.

References

Anderson, E. (1990). *Streetwise: Race, class and change in an urban community*. Chicago: University of Chicago Press.

Arce, C. (1981). A reconsideration of Chicano culture and identity. *Daedalus, 110,* 177–192.

Becerra, R. M. (1988). The Mexican American family. In C. H. Minderl, R. W. Habenstein, & R. Wright, Jr. (Eds.), *Ethnic families in America: Patterns and variations* (3rd ed.) (pp. 141–159). New York: Elsevier.

Billingsley, A. (1968). *Black families in white America*. Englewood Cliffs, N.J.: Prentice Hall.

Bourdieu, P. , & Passerson, C. (1977). *Reproduction in education, society, and culture*. Beverly Hills, CA: Sage.

Bowles, S., & Gintis, H. (1976). *Schooling in capitalist America*. New York: Basic Books.

Bowman, P. J., & Howard, C. (1985). Race-related socialization, motivation and academic achievement: A study of black youth in three-generation families. *Journal of the American Academy of Child Psychiatry, 24,* 134–141.

Boykin, W., & Toms, F. D. (1985). Black child socialization: A conceptual framework. In H. McAdoo & J. McAdoo (Eds.), *Black children: Social, educational and parental environments* (pp. 33–51). Beverly Hills, CA: Sage.

Bronfenbrenner, U. (1986). Alienation and the four worlds of childhood. *Phi Delta Kappan, 67(6),* 430–436.

Brookins, C. B. & Robinson, T. L. (1995). Rites of passage as resistance to oppression. *The Western Journal of Black Studies, 19,* 172–180.

Burton, L., Obeidallah, D., & Allison, K. (1996). Ethnographic insights on social context and adolescent development among inner-city African American teens. In R. Jessor, A. Colby, & R. Shweder (Eds.), *Ethnography and human development: Context and meaning in social inquiry*. Chicago: University of Chicago Press.

Cass, V.C. (1979). Homosexual identity formation: A theoretical model. *Journal of Homosexuality, 4,* 219–235.

Children's Defense Fund. (1994). *Progress and peril: Black children in America*. Washington, D.C.

Clark, K. B. & Clark, M. (1940). Skin color as a factor in racial identification of Negro pre-school children. *Journal of Social Psychology, 2,* 154–167.

Clark, R. (1983). *Family life and school achievement: Why poor children succeed or fail*. Chicago: University of Chicago Press.

Comer, J. P. (1995). Racism and African American adolescent development. In C. Willie, P. Rieker, B. Kramer, & C. Brown (Eds.), *Mental health, racism and sexism* (pp. 151–170). Pittsburgh: University of Pittsburgh Press.

Cose, E. (1993). *The rage of a privileged class*. New York: Harper Collins.

Cross, W. E. (1971). Negro-to-black conversion experience. *Black World, 20,* 13–27.

Cross, W. E, (1978). The Thomas and Cross models of psychological nigrescence: A literature review. *Journal of Black Psychology, 4,* 13–31.

Cross, W. E. (1991). *Shades of black: Diversity in African American identity*. Philadelphia: Temple.

Dana, R. H. (1993). *Multicultural assessment perspectives for professional psychology*. Boston: Allyn and Bacon.

Darder, A. (1992). *Culture and power in the classroom: A critical foundation for bicultural education*. New York: Bergin and Garvey Press.

Debold, E. (1995). *Body politic: Transforming adolescent girls' health*. A report of the 1994 proceeding of the Healthy Girls/Healthy Women Research Roundtable. New York: Ms. Foundation for Women.

Dryfoos, J. G. (1990). *Adolescents at risk*. New York: Oxford University Press.

DuBois, W. E. B. (1920). *The souls of black folk*. Chicago: A. C. McClurg & Co. (Original published 1903.)

Dugan, T. F., & Coles, R. (Eds.) (1989). *The child in our times: Studies in the development of resiliency*. New York: Brunner/Mazel.

Entwisle, D. R. (1990). Schools and the adolescent. In S. Feldman & G. Elliott (Eds.), *At the threshold: The developing adolescent*. Cambridge: Harvard University Press.

Erikson, E. H. (1950). *Childhood and society*. New York: W. W. Norton.

Erikson, E. H. (1956). The problem of ego identity. *Journal of the American Psychoanalytic Association, 4,* 56–57.

Erikson, E. H. (1968). *Identity, youth and crisis*. New York: W. W. Norton.

Feldman, S., & Elliott, G. (1990). *At the threshold: The developing adolescent*. Cambridge: Harvard University Press.

Fordham, S., & Ogbu, J. (1986). Black students' school success: Coping with the "burden of acting white." *Urban Review, 18(3),* 176–206.

Fordham, S. (1988). Racelessness as a factor in black students' success: Pragmatic strategy or pyrrhic victory. *Harvard Educational Review, 58(1),* 54–84.

Freeman, R., & Holzer, N. (1985). Young blacks and jobs: What we now know. *Public Interest, 78,* 18–31.

Garcia-Coll, C., Lamberty, G., Jenkins, R., Pipes McAdoo, H., Crnic, K., Wasik, H., & Vasquez Garcia, H. (1996). An integrative model for the study of developmental competencies in minority children. *Child Development, 67,* 1891–1914.

Garrod, A., Smulyan, L., Powers, S., & Kilkenny, R. (1995). *Adolescent portraits: Identity, relationships and challenges* (2nd ed.). Boston: Allyn and Bacon.

Gibbs, J. T. (1987). Identity and marginality: Issues in the treatment of biracial adolescents. *American Journal of Orthopsychiatry, 57,* 265–278.

Gibbs, J. T. (1988). *Young, black and male in America: An endangered species.* Dover, MA: Auburn House.

Gibbs, J. T. (1989a). Black American adolescents. In J. Gibbs, A. Huang, & Associates (Eds.), *Children of color: Psychological interventions with minority youth* (pp. 179–223). San Francisco: Jossey-Bass.

Gibbs, J. T. (1989b). Black adolescents and youth: An update on endangered species. In Reginald L. Jones (Ed.) *Black adolescents.* Berkeley, CA: Cobbs & Henry.

Gibbs, J. T. (1993). British black and blue. *Focus*, April 3–8. Washington, D.C.: Joint Center for Political and Economic Studies.

Gibbs, J. T. (1997). Triple marginality: The case of young Afro-Caribbean women in London and Toronto. *Canadian Social Work Review, 13*, 143–156.

Gibbs, J. T. (1998). *The California crucible: Toward a new paradigm of race and ethnic relations.* San Francisco: Study Center Press.

Gibbs, J. T., & Hines, A. M. (1989). Factors related to sex differences in behavior among black youth: Implications for intervention and research. *Journal of Adolescent Research, 4*, 152–172.

Gibbs, J. T., & Hines, A. M. (1992). Negotiating ethnic identity: Issues for black-white biracial adolescents. In M. P. P. Root (Ed.), *Racially mixed people in America* (pp. 223–238). Newbury Park, CA: Sage Publications.

Gibbs, J. T., and Huang, L. N. (1998). *Children of color: Psychological interventions with culturally diverse youth.* San Francisco: Jossey-Bass.

Gibbs, J. T., & Moskowitz-Sweet, G. (1991). Clinical and cultural issues in the treatment of biracial and bicultural adolescents. *Families in Society, 72(10)*, 579–592.

Gilligan, C. (1982). *In a different voice.* Cambridge: Harvard University Press.

Giordano, P. C., Cernkovich, S. A., & DeMaris, A. (1993). The family and peer relations in black adolescents. *Journal of Marriage and The Family, 55*, 277–287.

Goethals, G. W., & Klos, D. S. (1976). *Experiencing youth: First-person accounts.* Boston: Little, Brown.

Gramezy, N. (1984). Stress-resistant children: The search for protective factors. In J. E. Stevenson (Ed.), *Recent research in developmental psychopathology* (pp. 213–233). (Book Supplement No. 4). Oxford, England: Pergamon Press.

Hacker, A. (1992). *Two nations: Black and white, separate, hostile, unequal.* New York: Charles Scribner's Sons.

Haizlip, S.T. (1994). *The sweeter the juice: A family memoir in black and white.* New York: Simon and Schuster.

Hardiman, R. (1982). *White identity development: A process-oriented model for describing the racial consciousness of white Americans.* Unpublished doctoral dissertation, University of Massachusetts, Amherst.

Harris, K. (1982). *Teachers and classes: A Marxist analysis.* Boston: Routledge and

Kagan Paul.

Hauser, S. T., & Bowlds, M. K. (1990). Stress, coping and adaptation. In S. Feldman & G. Elliot (Eds.), *At the threshold: The developing adolescent* (pp. 388–413). Cambridge: Harvard University Press.

Helms, J. E. (Ed.) (1990). *Black and white racial identity: Theory, research, and practice*. New York: Greenwood Press.

Helms, J. E., & Parham, T. A. (1984). *Racial identity attitude scale*. Unpublished manuscript.

Helms, J. E., & Piper, R. E. (1994). Implications of racial identity theory for vocational psychology. *Journal of Vocational Behavior, 44(2)*, 124–138.

Hill, R. (1972). *Strengths of the black family*. New York: National Urban League.

Hilliard, A. G. (1996). Foreword in E. K. Addae (Erriel D. Roberson) (Ed.), *To heal a people: Afrikan scholars defining a new reality* (pp. xxiii–xxvii). Columbia, MD: Kujichagulia Press.

Hollinger, D. A. (1995). *Postethnic America*. New York: Basic Books.

Holmes, B. J. (1983). Black students' performance in the national assessment of science and mathematics. *Journal of Negro Education, 51(4)*, 392–405.

hooks, b. (1994). *Teaching to transgress: Education as the practice of freedom*. New York: Routledge Press.

Huang, L. N. (1994). An integrative view of identity formation: A model for Asian Americans. In E. P. Sakett & D. R. Koslow (Eds.), *Race, ethnicity and self: Identity in multicultural perspective*. Washington, D.C.: National Multicultural Institute.

Jacobs, W. R. (1985). *Dispossessing the American Indians* (2nd ed.). Norman: University of Oklahoma Press.

Jaynes, G. D., & Williams, R. M., Jr. (Eds.). (1989). *A common destiny: Blacks and American society*. Washington, D.C.: National Academy Press.

Kich, G. K. (1982). *Eurasians: Ethnic/racial identity development of biracial Japanese/white adults*. Unpublished doctoral dissertation, Wright Institute of Professional Psychology, Berkeley, CA.

Kich, G. K. (1992). The developmental process of asserting a biracial, bicultural identity. In M. P. P. Root (Ed.), *Racially mixed people in America* (pp.304–317). Newbury Park, CA: Sage.

Kobasa, S. (1985). Stressful life events, personality and health: An inquiry into hardiness. In A. Monat & R. Lazaru (Eds.), *Stress and coping* (2nd ed.) (pp. 174–188). New York: Columbia University Press.

Kohlberg, L. (1984). *The psychology of moral development*. San Francisco: Harper & Row.

Kohlberg, L., & Gilligan, C. (1972). The adolescent as philosopher: The discovery of the self in a postconventional world. In Kagan & Coles (Eds.), *Twelve to sixteen: Early adolescence*. New York: W. W. Norton.

Lerman, R. I. (1997). Meritocracy without rising inequality? Wage rate differences are widening by education and narrowing by gender and race. *Urban Institute,* *(2),* 1–5.

Loevinger, J. (1976). *Ego development.* San Francisco: Jossey-Bass.

Lorde, A. (1988). Age, race, class and sex: Women redefining difference. In P. S. Rothenberg (Ed.), *Racism and sexism: An integrated study* (pp. 352–358). New York: St. Martin's Press.

Marcia, J. (1980). Ego Identity Development. In J. Adelson (Ed.), *The handbook of adolescent psychology.* New York: Wiley.

Masten, A. S. (1994). Resilience in individual development: Successful adaptation despite risk and adversity. In M. Wang & E. Gordon (Eds.), *Educational resilience in inner-city America: Challenges and prospects* (pp. 3–25). Hillsdale, NJ: Lawrence Erlbaum.

McIntosh, P. (1988). *White privilege and male privilege: A personal account of coming to see correspondences through work in women's studies.* (Working Paper No. 189). Wellesley, MA: Wellesley College Center for Research on Women.

McLaughlin, M. (1993). Embedded identities: Enabling balance in urban contexts. In S. B. Heath & M. W. McLaughlin (Eds.), *Identity & inner-city youth: Beyond ethnicity and gender* (pp. 36–38). New York: Teachers College Press.

McLeod, J. (1985). *Ain't no making it: Aspirations and attainment in a low-income neighborhood.* Boulder, CO: Westview Press.

McLeod, R. H. (1974). *Issues in social ecology: Human milieus.* Palo Alto, CA: National Press Books.

McLoyd, V. (1990). The impact of economic hardship on black families and children: Psychological distress, parenting and socioemotional development. *Child Development, 61,* 311–346.

Millett, R. (1998). West Indian families in the United States. In R. Taylor, *Minority families in the United States: A multicultural perspective.* Upper Saddle River, NJ: Prentice Hall.

Monk, G., Winslade, J., Crocket, K., & Eptson, D. (1997). *Narrative therapy in practice: The archaeology of hope.* San Francisco: Jossey-Bass.

Moynihan, D. P. (1965). *The negro family: The case for national action.* Washington, D.C.: U.S. Government Printing Office.

Murray, C. B., Smith, S. N., & West, E. H. (1989). Comparative personality development in adolescence: A critique. In R. Jones (Ed.), *Black adolescents.* Berkeley: Cobbs and Henry.

Myers, H. F. (1989). Urban stress and mental health in black youth: An epidemiologic and conceptual update. In R. Jones (Ed.), *Black adolescents.* Berkeley: Cobbs and Henry.

Nakashima, C. L. (1992). An invisible monster: The creation and denial of mixed race people in America. In M. P. P. Root (Ed.), *Racially mixed people in America* (pp. 162–178). Newbury Park, CA: Sage Publications.

National Center for Health Statistics (1994).

Njeri, I. (1997). *The last plantation: Color, conflict and identity*. New York: Houghton Mifflin.

Nobles, W. (1980). Extended self: Rethinking the so-called negro self concept. In R. Jones (Ed.), *Black adolescents*. Berkeley: Cobbs and Henry.

Ogbu, J. (1986). The consequences of the American caste system. In U. Neisser (Ed.), *The school achievement of minority children: New perspectives* (pp. 45–66). Hillsdale, NJ: Lawrence Erlbaum.

Ogbu, J. (1988). Black education: A cultural ecological perspective. In H. P. McAdoo (Ed.), *Black families* (pp. 139–154). Newbury Park, CA: Sage.

Oliver, W. (1989). Black males and social problems: Prevention through Afrocentric socialization. *Journal of Black Studies, 20 (1),* 15–39.

Ossana, S. M., Helms, J. E., & Leonard, M. M. (1992). Do "womanist" attitudes influence college womens' self-esteem and perceptions of environmental bias? *Journal of Counseling and Development, 70,* 402–408.

Parham, T. A., & Helms, J. E. (1985). Relation of racial identity attitudes to self-actualization and affective states of black students. *Journal of Counseling Psychology, (32)* pp. 431–440.

Peters, M. F. (1985). Racial socialization in young black children. In H. P. McAdoo & J. McAdoo (Eds.), *Black children* (pp. 159–173). Beverly Hills, CA: Sage Publications.

Phinney, J. (1989). Biracial identity—Asset or handicap? In H. W. Harris, H. C. Blue, & E. E. Griffith (Eds.), *Racial and ethnic identity: Psychological development and creative expression*. New York: Routledge.

Phinney, J. (1989). Stages of ethnic identity in minority group adolescents. *Journal of Early Adolescence, 9,* 34–49.

Phinney, J. S., & Chavira, V. (1995). Parent ethnic socialization and adolescent coping with problems related to ethnicity. *Journal of Research on Adolescence, 5(1),* 31–53.

Piaget, J. (1972). Intellectual evolution from adolescence to adulthood. *Human Development, 15,* 1–12.

Pierce, C. M. (1995). Stress Analogs of Racism and Sexism. In C. Willie, P. Rieker, B. Kramer, & C. Brown (Eds.), *Mental health, racism and sexism* (pp. 277–293). Pittsburgh: University of Pittsburgh Press.

Pinderhughes, E. (1989). *Understanding race, ethnicity, and power*. New York: Free Press.

Pinderhughes, E. (1995). Biracial identity—Asset or handicap? In H. W. Harris, H. C. Blue, and E. E. H. Griffith (Eds.), *Racial and ethnic identity: Psychological development and creative expression*. New York: Routledge, 1995.

Ponterotto, J. G. (1988). Racial consciousness development among white counselor trainees: A stage model. *Journal of Multicultural Counseling and Development, 16,* 146–156.

References ■ 287

Pope-Davis, D. B., & Ottavi, T. M. (1994). The relationship between racism and racial identity among white Americans: A replication and extension. *Journal of Counseling and Development, 72*, 293–297.

Poston, W. S. C. (1990). The biracial identity development model: A needed addition. *Journal of Counseling and Development, 69*, 152–155.

Randolph, S. (1995). African American children in single-mother families. In B. Dickerson (Ed.), *African American single mothers: Understanding their lives and families*. Thousand Oaks, CA: Sage Publications.

Reynolds, A. L., & Pope, R. L. (1991). The complexities of diversity: Exploring multiple oppressions. *Journal of Counseling and Development, 70*, 174–180.

Robinson, T. L. (1998). The intersections of dominant discourses across race, gender, and other identities. *Journal of Counseling and Development*, winter.

Robinson, T. L., & Howard-Hamilton, M. (1994). An Afrocentric paradigm: Foundation for a healthy self-image and healthy interpersonal relationships. *Journal of Mental Health Counseling, 16*, 327–339.

Robinson, T. L., and Ward, J. V. (1991). "A belief in self far greater than anyone's disbelief": Cultivating healthy resistance among African American female adolescents. In C. Gilligan, A. G. Rogers, & D. Tolman, *Women, girls and psychotherapy: Reframing resistance* (pp. 87–103). Binghamton, NY: Harrington Park Press.

Robinson, T. L., & Ward, J. V. (1995). African American adolescents and skin color. *Journal of Black psychology, 21*, 256–274.

Root, M. P. P. (Ed.) (1992). *Racially mixed people in America*. Newbury Park, CA: Sage Publications.

Root, M. P. P. (Ed.) (1996). *The multiracial experience: Racial borders as the new frontier*. Thousand Oaks, CA: Sage Publications.

Root, M. P. P. (in press). Experiences and processes affecting racial identity development: Preliminary results from the biracial sibling project. In *Cultural diversity and ethnic minority psychology*.

Rutter, M. (1985). Resilience in the face of adversity. *British Journal of Psychiatry, 147*, 598–611.

Rutter, M. (1987). Psychosocial resilience and protective mechanisms. *American Journal of Orthopsychiatry, 57(3)*, 316–331.

Rutter, M. (1990). Psychosocial resilience and protective mechanisms. In J. Rolf, A. S. Masten, D. Cicchetti, K. H. Neuchterlein, & S. Weintraub (Eds.), *Risk and protective factors in the development of psychopathology* (pp. 181–214). New York: Cambridge University Press.

Sabnani, H. B., Ponterotto, J. G., & Borodovsky, L. G. (1991). White racial identity development and cross-cultural counselor training: A stage model. *The Counseling Psychologist, 19*, 76–102.

Scanzoni, J. H. (1971). *The Black family in modern society*. Boston: Allyn and Bacon.

Scott-Jones, D., & Whites, A. B. (1990). Correlates of sexual activity in early adolescence. *Journal of Early Adolescence, 10,* 221–238.

Scheinfeld, D. R. (1983). Family relationships and school achievement among boys in lower-income urban Black families. *American Journal of Orthopsychiatry, 53,* 127–143.

Shorris, Earl (1992). *Latinos: a biography of the people.* New York: W. W. Norton & Co.

Smith, J. A. (Ed.) (1976). *Outstanding black sermons.* New York: Edwin Mellon.

Spencer, M. B. (1987). Black children's ethnic identity formation: Risk and resilience of castelike minorities. In J. S. Phinney & M. J. Rotherdam (Eds.), *Children's ethnic socialization: Pluralism and development.* Newbury Park, CA: Sage Publications.

Spencer, M. B., Dornbusch, S. M., & Mont-Reynaud, R. (1990). Challenges in studying minority youth. In S. Feldman & G. Elliott (Eds.), *At the threshold: The developing adolescent* (pp. 123–146). Cambridge: Harvard University Press.

Sudarkasa, N. (1988). Interpreting the African heritage in Afro-American family organization. In H. McAdoo (Ed.), *Black families.* Newbury Park, CA: Sage Publications.

Sue, D. W., &, Sue, D. (1990). *Counseling the culturally different: Theory and practice.* New York: Wiley.

Takaki, Ronald T. (1989). *Strangers from a different shore.* Boston: Little, Brown.

Tatum, B. D. (1987). *Assimilation Blues: Black feminism and white community.* New York: Greenwood.

Tatum, B. D. (1997). *Why are all the Black kids sitting together in the cafeteria?: And other conversations about race.* New York: Basic Books.

Taylor, J. M., Gilligan, L., & Sullivan, A. M. (1995). *Between voice and silence: Women and girls, race and relationship.* Cambridge: Harvard University Press.

Taylor, R. (1991). Childrearing in African American families. In J. Everett, S. Chipungu, & B. Leashore (Eds.), *Child welfare: An Africentric perspective.* Princeton, NJ: Rutgers University Press.

Taylor, R. (1995). African American youth in the 1990s. *Humboldt Journal of Social Relations, 21(2),* 165–190.

Taylor, R. (Ed.) (1998). *Minority families in the United States* (2nd ed.). Hillsdale, NJ: Prentice Hall.

Taylor, R. D. (1994). Risk and resilience: Contextual influences on the development of African American adolescents. In M. Wang & E. Gordon (Eds.), *Educational resilience in inner-city America: Challenges and prospects,* (pp. 119–130). Hillsdale, NJ: Lawrence Erlbaum.

The Consortium for Research on Black Adolescents. (1990). *Black adolescence: Current issues and annotated bibliography.* Boston: G. K. Hall and Co.

U.S. Bureau of the Census. (1994). *Statistical abstract of the United States.* Washington, D.C.: U.S. Government Printing Office.

U.S. Department of Education (1997). National Center for Education statistics. The condition of education 1997. NCE597–388, Washington, D.C.: U.S. Government Printing Office.

Walsh, F. (1996). The concept of family resilience: Crisis and challenge. *Family Process, 35,* 261–282.

Wang, M. C., Haertel, G. D., & Walberg, H. J. (1994). Educational resilience in inner-cities. In M. Wang, and E. Gordon (Eds.), *Educational resilience in inner-city America: Challenges and prospects* (pp. 45–72). Hillsdale, NJ: Lawrence Erlbaum.

Wang, M., & Gordon, E. (Eds.) (1994). *Educational resilience in inner-city America: Challenges and prospects.* Hillsdale, NJ: Lawrence Erlbaum.

Ward, J. V. (1991). "Eyes in the back of your head": Moral themes in African American narratives of racial conflict. *Journal of Moral Education, 20,* 267–281.

Ward, J. V. (1995). Raising resisters: The role of truth telling in the psychological development of African American girls. In B. Leadbeater, & N. Way, *Urban girls: Resisting stereotypes, creating identities* (pp. 85–99). New York: New York University Press.

Ward, J. V. (forthcoming). *Raising resisters* (tentative title). New York: Free Press.

Werner, E. (1989). Children of the garden island. *Scientific American* 107–111.

Werner, E., & Smith, R. (1982). *Vulnerable but invincible: A longitudinal study of resilient children and youth.* New York: Adams, Bannister, and Cox.

Werner, E., & Smith, R. (1992). *Overcoming the odds: High-risk children from birth to adulthood.* Ithaca: Cornell Universiy Press.

Willie, C. V. (Ed.) (1985). *Black and white families: A study in complementarity.* New York: Greenwood Press.

Wilson, W. J. (1978). *The declining significance of race.* Chicago: University of Chicago Press.

Wilson, W. J. (1987). *The truly disadvantaged: The inner city, the underclass, and public policy.* Chicago: University of Chicago Press.

Witherell, C., & Noddings, N. (1991). *Stories lives tell: Narrative and dialogue in education.* New York: Teachers College Press.

X, Malcom. (1965). *The autobiography of Malcom X.* New York: Grove Press.

About the Editors, Contributors, and Foreword Writer

James P. Comer, M.D. is Maurice Falk Professor of Child Psychiatry at the Yale University Child Study Center. He has been a researcher, consultant, and advisor to programs serving children and adolescents nationwide and internationally. He is the author of *Maggie's American Dream* and co-author of *Raising Black Children*. He has won numerous awards, most recently the prestigious 1996 Heinz Award for Service to Humanity.

Andrew Garrod is Associate Professor of Education and Chair of the Department of Education at Dartmouth College, Hanover, New Hampshire, where he teaches courses in adolescence, moral development, and educational psychology. His recent publications include, *Preparing for Citizenship: Teaching Youth to Live Democratically* (written with Ralph Mosher and Robert Kenny), a co-edited volume, *First Persons, First Peoples: Native American College Graduates Tell Their Life Stories* (with Colleen Larimore), and the coedited book, *Crossing Customs: International Students Write on U.S. College Life and Culture* to be published in 1999 (with Jay Davis). In 1991 he was awarded Dartmouth College's Distinguished Teaching Award.

Jewelle Taylor Gibbs is the Zellerbach Family Fund Professor of Social Policy, Community Change and Practice at the School of Social Welfare, University of California, Berkeley, California. She is the author of *Race and Justice: Rodney King and O. J. Simpson in a House Divided*, and editor of *Young, Black and Male in America: An Endangered Species*. She is a Fellow of the American Psychological Association, a founding member of the Advisory Council of the National Center for Children in Poverty and has served as a consultant to the Carnegie Foundation and the Ford Foundation. She has received numerous awards for her research and advocacy on behalf of African American youth from national, state, and local groups.

Robert Kilkenny is instructor in Psychology, Department of Psychiatry, at Harvard Medical School and Research Child Psychologist at McLean Hospital. He has published an article in the Life Span Development Series with Gil Noam, Sally Powers, and Jeff Beedy on adolescent relationships in a life-span perspective and is co-editor of *Adolescent Portraits: Identity, Relationships, and Challenges* (with Andrew Garrod, Lisa Smulyan, and Sally Powers). He is Executive Director of the Alliance for Inclusion and Prevention, Inc., a public-private partnership providing mental health and special educational services to at-risk students in the Boston public schools.

Peter C. Murrell Jr. is Associate Professor in the Departments of Education and Psychology at Northeastern University, where he is also the Director of the Master of Arts in Teaching Program in the Center for Innovation in Urban Education. He teaches courses in cognitive psychology, learning and cognition, cognitive development, and the social contexts of urban teaching. His current area of focus is the development of urban schools through Professional Development Schools initiatives and community mobilization, for which he works closely with several elementary, middle, and high schools in urban Boston and Cambridge.

Tracy L. Robinson is Associate Professor in the Department of Counselor Education at North Carolina State University, Raleigh, North Carolina, where she teaches courses in counseling issues and psychosocial identity development. She is co-author of *The Convergence of Race, Ethnicity, and Culture: Multiple Identities in Counseling*, to be published in 1999 (with Mary Howard-Hamilton). Her research interests include the convergence of race, gender, and culture in psychosocial identity development. In the spring of 1998 she was invited to spend her sabbatical in the Department of Education Studies at the University of Waikato in Hamilton, New Zealand.

Janie Victoria Ward is Associate Professor in the Department of Education and Human Services and in the African American Studies Department at Simmons College, Boston, Massachusetts, where she lectures frequently on racial identity formation in adolescence and on educational and psychological issues in the psychosocial development of African American women and girls. She is co-editor of *Mapping the Moral Domain: A Contribution of Woman's Thinking to Psychological Theory and Education* (with Carol Gilligan and Jill Taylor) and is the author of several articles and book chapters. She is a past recipient of a Rockefeller Foundation Postdoctoral Research Fellowship.

Index